The Comeback Chronicles

365 Days of Recovery and Reinvention

By

Daniel E. Sims

Title: **The Comeback Chronicles: 365 Days of Recovery and Reinvention**

Printed in the United States of America

For permission requests, write to the publisher at the address below:

dan@corieosity.com

First Edition: October 2023

ISBN: 979-8863434162

Preface

Gentlemen,

If you've found yourself holding this workbook, it's clear you're at a pivotal moment in your life. The aftermath of a divorce is an experience filled with a whirlwind of emotions, confusion, and, sometimes, despair. But, what if I told you that within these pages lies a path to healing, self-discovery, and transformation?

Every day for the next 365 days, this workbook will be your trusted companion. Here's what you can expect:

1. **Daily Lesson**: Start each day with an invaluable lesson. Think of it as a daily dose of insight, wisdom, and perspective tailored for your journey. These are crafted not just to soothe, but also to empower.
2. **Challenge**: Following the lesson is a challenge, a call to action. Because real change doesn't just come from understanding—it comes from *doing*. These challenges will push you, maybe even test your limits, but they will also propel you forward.
3. **Reflection Space**: End your day with introspection. The space provided is for you to spill your thoughts, process your emotions, and track your progress. It's in these moments of reflection that true growth occurs.

I urge you to make this workbook a daily habit. Much like a morning cup of coffee or a nightly ritual, let it be the anchor you return to. Your commitment to this process can make all the difference. Remember, it's not just about surviving the storm but emerging from it stronger, wiser, and more resilient.

By the time you turn the last page of this guide, one year from now, you won't just be another man who went through a divorce. You'll be a man who rose from its ashes, redefined himself, and took control of his narrative. A better man.

So, are you ready to embrace this journey? Your future self is counting on you.

To a better you, one day at a time.

Time to Man Up

Your Legal Battle Starts Now

Master Your Feelings

Kids and Assets

Self-Care Isn't for Sissies

Cut Off the Dead Weight

Identity Reboot

Money Talks

The Dating Game

Forgive to Live Free

New Normal

You Survived, Now Thrive

Essential Resources for Men Navigating Divorce

YouTube:

1. **Alpha M.-** Alpha M. offers real-world help and advice regarding image, style, and grooming. Their goal is to help you look and feel your best every day of your life.
2. **Coach Corey Wayne** Coach Corey Wayne is a life and peak performance coach who teaches self-reliance. His content covers a wide range of topics, including pick-up, dating, relationships, business, health, leadership, goal setting, and more.
3. **Tripp Advice** Tripp Advice is a dating coach for shy guys. Learn where to meet women, create attraction, get a date, and find a fit, friendly, and feminine girlfriend. Tripp's strategies help even those with social anxiety become confident with women.
4. **Kevin Samuels** Description: (Please provide more information about the content and focus of Kevin Samuels' YouTube channel to include here.)
5. **Better Bachelor** Better Bachelor is a channel for open-minded men to discuss current events, news, opinions, humor, and self-improvement. While primarily focusing on single men's issues, their content may be applicable to a wider audience, providing multiple perspectives on various topics.

Reddit

1. **r/DivorcedDads:** A community focused on supporting divorced dads and addressing questions related to parenting, family growth, and shared experiences.
2. **r/Divorce_Men:** This subreddit is dedicated to discussing the legal, financial, and social challenges that men face during divorce. It emphasizes the importance of consulting with an attorney.

Facebook

1. **Divorce Support For Men:** A welcoming community for men who are newly divorced, in the midst of the divorce process, or divorced for some time. It offers support, suggestions, advice, and inspirational quotes to help men stay positive and focus on personal growth as fathers and individuals.

WebSites

1. **DivorceCare.org** - DivorceCare is a divorce recovery support group where you can find help and healing for the hurt of separation and divorce.
2. **DivorceHelpForDads.com-** This website offers hundreds of free advice articles to empower fathers going through divorce. It provides tools and resources for success during this challenging time.

Time to Man Up

In the turbulent aftermath of divorce, these 30 days are a rollercoaster of emotions, challenges, and pivotal moments. From the heart-wrenching silence of an empty house to the complexities of legalities and the battles within, this journey is a raw and unfiltered exploration of what it means to start anew. With each passing day, you'll confront the unthinkable, find moments of solace, and begin to rebuild amidst the chaos. Join us on this transformative path from ground zero to a hopeful glimpse of what lies ahead.

Day 1: Reality Check- Your Life Just Exploded

Listen up, man. Your life just got turned upside down, inside out, and every which way but loose. Your marriage? Over. And guess what? You can't hit the rewind button. You can't un-explode a bomb, and that's what's happened here. Your life? Kaboom. It's exploded. But the shockwave? That's where we're at.

Do you get it? This is no time for denial, no time to dwell on "what ifs." Forget what you see in movies; this isn't a rom-com where you win her back with a grand gesture. This is the raw, unfiltered reality, my friend. Face it head-on.

And you know what? It's OK. It's OK that your life just got rattled to its core. Because from chaos comes clarity. From the rubble comes a foundation for something new, something better—only if you're willing to put in the work. So, you have two choices. Choice one: you curl up, play the victim, let the world happen to you. Choice two: you stand up, dust yourself off, and take control. What's it gonna be?

Your emotions? They're gonna be a rollercoaster. Accept it. But you're in the driver's seat of this insane ride. Don't let your feelings dictate your actions. You've got legal battles ahead, assets to protect, maybe even kids to think about. Can't do that well if you're a mess, can you?

You're at a crossroads, and it's time to decide who you're gonna be. The guy who got defeated by divorce? Or the guy who rose from its ashes? Stop dwelling on what went wrong and start focusing on how you're gonna make things right—starting with yourself. Don't sleepwalk through this. Wake up. Get real. Because this is as real as it gets. You've got 364 more days in this transformation journey. Day 1 starts now. What are you gonna do about it?

Daily Challenge: Take a deep breath, look in the mirror, and tell yourself, "I acknowledge the pain, but today, I choose to move forward." Commit to one positive action today, no matter how small."

Daily Reflection:

What resonated with you from today's lesson? How can you apply this truth in your life?

_____

_____

_____

_____

Day 2: Stop Whining- Time to Take Control

Y ou're here, on Day 2. That's good; it means you didn't run off or stick your head in the sand. But let's get one thing straight: if you're spending your time whining, complaining, or moping around, you need to cut that crap out. Right. Now.

Look, it's human to feel sorry for yourself, but what's that gonna solve? Spoiler alert: absolutely nothing. If you're wallowing in self-pity, you're losing valuable time, energy, and focus that you could be using to get your life back on track. Time's ticking, my friend, and nobody's gonna flip that hourglass back over for you.

Whining about how unfair life is? How she did you wrong? Save it. The reality is, life is unfair, relationships end, and people do messed-up things. It's not what happens to you; it's how you react that defines you. So, how are you gonna react? Here's a radical idea: take control. Take control of your actions, your mindset, your freaking destiny. You want to come out of this divorce stronger, smarter, better? Then own it. Own your choices, your failures, your successes—every single part of your life that you have control over, seize it.

Legal stuff ahead? Get the best lawyer you can afford. Kids in the mix? Be the dad they deserve. Your finances? Lock them down like Fort Knox. This isn't a spectator sport; it's your life, and you're the star player. Either you step up to bat, or you strike out.

Stop outsourcing blame. Stop waiting for a miracle. Stop whining. The universe doesn't owe you jack. If you want something, go out and get it. If you want to change, make it happen. The ball's in your court. So what's it gonna be? You gonna whine, or you gonna win?

Daily Challenge: For the next 24 hours, every time you catch yourself complaining or whining, pause, take a deep breath, and replace that negative thought with a proactive step you can take to improve the situation. Commit to action, not lamentation.

Daily Reflection:

What resonated with you from today's lesson? How can you apply this truth in your life?

_____

_____

_____

_____

Day 3: Emotional Rollercoaster

Hey, welcome back. You've made it to Day 3, and by now, you probably realize you're strapped into an emotional rollercoaster that's got more ups and downs than the stock market. You might feel on top of the world one minute and then plunge into despair the next. And you know what? That's totally normal. But here's the kicker: normal doesn't mean you have to let it wreck you.

This rollercoaster? It's not going away anytime soon. So what can you do? Simple: Keep your hands inside the ride. Hold on tight. Understand that these emotional peaks and valleys are part of the process, but they don't get to dictate your actions.

Feeling angry? Sure, you're allowed. But throwing a temper tantrum, sending that raging text, or smashing stuff? Not gonna help you. Not one bit. Anger can be fuel, but only if you channel it the right way. Let it propel you to take positive actions, like focusing on your fitness or diving into a new project.

How about sadness? Yeah, it's gonna hit you, and it's gonna hit hard. But drowning in it? Nuh-uh. Use that sadness to reflect, to understand what went wrong in your marriage, and what you can do better next time. Remember, introspection is a tool, not a prison. Anxiety? Listen, if you're not a little anxious, you're not paying attention. But don't let it paralyze you. Use that heightened awareness to strategize, to get ahead of potential problems, and to arm yourself for the challenges ahead.

Bottom line: your emotions are going to be all over the place. Accept it. But don't let them take the wheel. You're the driver here. Keep your hands inside the ride, hold on tight, and steer this thing where you want it to go. You in control yet? Good. Because this ride's far from over.

Daily Challenge: Today, when an intense emotion surges, take three deep breaths before reacting; then choose one constructive action to channel that feeling. Remember, you're in control.

Daily Reflection:

What resonated with you from today's lesson? How can you apply this truth in your life?

_____

_____

_____

_____

Day 4: Delete, Block, Move On

Welcome to Day 4, and let's get right to it. You know that device in your pocket? Yeah, your smartphone. It's either your best friend or your worst enemy right now. Why? Because social media can be an absolute minefield during a divorce. One wrong step, one ill-advised post, and boom—you've just made life way more complicated for yourself.

Here's my advice: Delete, Block, Move On. Sounds harsh? Well, sometimes life calls for harsh measures.

First off, delete those pictures, those posts, the lovey-dovey stuff that's gonna make you feel like crap every time you see it. Archive it if you must, but get it off your main feed. And while you're at it, remove her from your immediate social media sphere. That means unfollow on Instagram, unfriend on Facebook, the whole nine yards.

Second, block if necessary. Listen, I'm not saying she's gonna go all psycho on you, but why even allow room for drama? Block her, her close friends, maybe even some family members. Right now, your focus needs to be on you, not on whatever narrative they're pushing on social media.

Last but not least, move on. Once you've cleaned up your social media act, don't dwell on it. Don't go snooping. Don't go looking for emotional scraps to feed on. Social media is a highlight reel, not a documentary. You're not getting the full story, so why torture yourself?

Use your social media to build up your own life. Share your wins, no matter how small. Reconnect with old friends. Dive into new interests. Use this tool to craft the life and image you want, not to sulk in the past. Delete, block, move on. It's a mantra for this stage of your life. Get on it.

Daily Challenge: Today, cleanse your digital world. Unfollow, delete, or archive anything that holds you back, and commit to only engaging in uplifting and positive social media activity for the next 24 hours.

Daily Reflection:

What resonated with you from today's lesson? How can you apply this truth in your life?

_____

_____

_____

_____

Day 5: Self-Pity is Poison

Welcome to Day 5. Let's cut to the chase: self-pity is poison. Period. You let it in, it'll eat you alive. So, how about we kill it right now?

Listen, you're going through a divorce. It sucks, no question about it. But the moment you start feeling sorry for yourself is the moment you give up control. You're handing over your power to external circumstances, to other people, and to the past. And guess what? None of those things care about you.

Feeling like the victim might give you a temporary emotional high. You get to be the center of your own sob story, collecting sympathy and 'poor you' comments. But what does it actually accomplish? Zilch. Nada. Zero. It's a dead-end street that leads nowhere good.

Instead, how about you flip the script? You're not a victim; you're the protagonist of your own life. The hero of your own movie. And what does the hero do? He faces challenges head-on, learns from them, and comes out stronger on the other side. That's your job now.

So, the next time you catch yourself wallowing in self-pity, stop. Just stop. Acknowledge it, understand it's a natural feeling, but then kick it to the curb. Replace it with action, with steps that move you forward, not backward. Whether it's hitting the gym, diving into work, spending quality time with your kids—do something that adds value to your life.

Self-pity is a poison, and you've got the antidote. It's called taking control, taking action, and taking no crap from yourself. Kill the self-pity early, and let's keep moving forward. You in?

Daily Challenge: Today, every time you catch a hint of self-pity, pause and name three actions you can take to better your situation or mood. Commit to doing at least one of them immediately.

Daily Reflection:

What resonated with you from today's lesson? How can you apply this truth in your life?

_____

_____

_____

_____

Day 6: You're Not a Victim- Scrap That Mindset

Alright, you've hit Day 6. Time to tackle a mindset that could cripple your progress: the victim mentality. Trust me, you don't want to go down that road.

You might feel like life has tossed you into a tornado, spinning you around without any control. It's easy to start seeing yourself as a victim when you're caught in that whirlwind. But here's the truth: letting yourself believe you're a victim is like tying your own hands behind your back. It's self-defeating and counterproductive.

Why? Because a victim mindset puts you in a defensive, reactive mode. It's a mindset that says, "Stuff is happening to me, and I can't do anything about it." And that, my friend, is a one-way ticket to stagnation and misery.

You might not have control over what's happening around you—the divorce, the legal battles, the emotional chaos—but you absolutely control how you respond to it. You make choices every day—how you act, how you speak, what you focus on. Those choices can either drag you down into a pit of despair or elevate you to a better place.

What's more, when you take charge of your own narrative, you become the director of your life story, not just a character in someone else's drama. You decide the tone, the plot twists, and, most importantly, the ending. So, what kind of story will you write for yourself?

Remember, the mindset you adopt right now sets the stage for everything that follows. So ask yourself: Do you want to be the guy who let life happen to him, or the guy who shaped his own destiny? The clock's ticking. Time to scrap that victim mindset and seize the reins of your story.

Daily Challenge: Today, catch yourself anytime you slip into a victim mentality. Whenever you notice it, stop, take a deep breath, and remind yourself: "I am the director of my life story." Choose one positive action in response.

Daily Reflection:

What resonated with you from today's lesson? How can you apply this truth in your life?

_____

_____

_____

_____

Day 7: Lawyer Up - Don't Skimp, This Matters

Welcome to Day 7. A full week into this journey, and if you haven't already, it's high time to talk about lawyering up. And listen, don't even think about skimping here; your choice of legal representation is not where you want to cut corners.

Here's the cold, hard truth: divorce is a legal battle. It's not just an emotional rift or a lifestyle change; it's a full-blown, paperwork-laden, courtroom-centered battle. And like any battle, you need the best soldier by your side—someone who knows the terrain, the tactics, and the rules of engagement. That soldier is your lawyer.

You might be tempted to go cheap, to pick a friend-of-a-friend who passed the bar but specializes in something entirely different. Bad move. Divorce law is a specialized field, with its own set of complexities and pitfalls. A generalist isn't going to cut it. You need a specialist, a seasoned pro who's navigated the divorce minefield time and time again.

Why does this matter so much? Because the stakes are sky-high. We're talking about your assets, your kids, your future earnings, maybe even your reputation. One misstep, one overlooked detail, and you could find yourself on the losing end for years to come. I get it, lawyers are expensive. But think of it as an investment, not a cost. An investment in your future, in your peace of mind, and, let's be real, in your fight for what's rightfully yours.

So, if you haven't already, start researching. Ask for recommendations, read reviews, schedule consultations. And when you find the right fit, lock it in. You're setting the stage for everything that follows in this legal process. Make sure you're setting it with the best possible team on your side. So, are you ready to lawyer up like your life depends on it? Because, in a way, it does.

Daily Challenge: Today, dedicate 30 minutes to researching local divorce attorneys, reading reviews, and making a list of top three to schedule consultations with; your future self will thank you.

Daily Reflection:

What resonated with you from today's lesson? How can you apply this truth in your life?

_____

_____

_____

_____

Day 8: Keep Friends Close, Enemies Closer

I t's time to get real about your social circle. You've heard the saying, "Keep your friends close and your enemies closer"? Never has that been more relevant than right now.

First off, your friends. These are your allies, your support system. They'll offer a shoulder to lean on, advice, maybe even a couch to crash on. But listen, not all friends are created equal. Some are gonna be there for you no matter what, while others might pick sides, fade away, or even turn against you. Identify who's genuinely got your back and keep them close.

Now, about those enemies. I'm not just talking about your ex, though that's a given. I'm talking about anyone who might align against you in this situation—could be some of her friends, some of yours, even family members. Keep tabs on them. Not to play dirty, but to stay one step ahead. Information is power, and knowing what your 'enemies' are thinking or planning can be invaluable.

And here's a pro tip: social media is a gold mine for this. People love to share, sometimes overshare. Keep your eyes open; you never know what tidbits might come in handy.

So why is your network so crucial? Because divorce isn't just a legal and emotional battle; it's a social one too. Your reputation is on the line, your relationships are in flux, and the balance of power is constantly shifting. Your network can either be your secret weapon or your Achilles' heel.

Start evaluating your circle. Strengthen ties with the loyal ones, and keep a watchful eye on potential foes. This is chess, not checkers, and every move counts.

Ready to leverage your network like a pro? Time to make your next move.

Daily Challenge: Today, reach out to two friends who have been supportive, expressing gratitude for their presence. Then, spend 10 minutes observing social media without engaging, noting any valuable information. Remember, awareness is your ally.

Daily Reflection:

What resonated with you from today's lesson? How can you apply this truth in your life?

_____

_____

_____

_____

Day 9: Stop Blaming Her

Welcome to Day 9. Today, we're tackling a tough pill to swallow: accountability. It's super easy to blame her for everything that went wrong, but that's a dead-end road. Time to shift focus onto your own mistakes.

Look, she might have her fair share of faults—maybe she lied, cheated, or whatever. But you're not in control of her actions; you're in control of yours. And let's be brutally honest: nobody's perfect. You screwed up somewhere, somehow. Own it.

Why does this matter? Because blaming her keeps you stuck in the past, focused on a narrative you can't change. Focusing on your own mistakes gives you a roadmap for the future. It shows you what not to do, what to improve, and how to be a better man moving forward.

This isn't about self-flagellation or wallowing in guilt. Nope. This is about constructive criticism, the kind that builds you up by breaking down your flaws so you can fix them.

So, take a hard look in the mirror. What could you have done better? Were you inattentive, uncommunicative, stubborn? Did you let your ego run the show? Whatever it is, identify it. Acknowledge it. And then make a game plan to improve it.

Turn those mistakes into lessons, those lessons into actions, and those actions into a new and improved you. By focusing on your own shortcomings, you empower yourself to fix them—and that's a win, not just in divorce but in life. So, are you ready to stop the blame game and start the gain game? Your better self is waiting, but you've got to make the first move.

Daily Challenge: Today, set aside 10 minutes for reflection. Write down one mistake you made in your relationship, how it affected both of you, and one concrete step you'll take to ensure you don't repeat it in the future.

Daily Reflection:

What resonated with you from today's lesson? How can you apply this truth in your life?

_____

_____

_____

_____

Day 10: She's Not Coming Back, And It's OK

Day 10, double digits. You're making progress, but there's a hard truth we need to face: she's not coming back. And you know what? That's not just OK; it's an opportunity.

Look, clinging to the hope that she'll walk back through that door is like clinging to a sinking ship. It's not going to float again, and the longer you hang on, the deeper you'll go. Time to let go and swim to the surface.

Why is this acceptance so crucial? Because it frees you, man. It frees you from the 'what-ifs,' the 'maybes,' and the endless cycle of hope and disappointment. It lets you focus on the one thing you can actually change: yourself.

You might think that her leaving is the worst thing that could happen to you. But ask yourself, was everything really sunshine and roses before? Chances are, if the marriage ended, it wasn't a utopia. So, why yearn for something that was fundamentally broken?

Now's the time to embrace the possibilities ahead of you. No, seriously, the world's your oyster. Want to travel? Do it. Dive into a new hobby? Go for it. Focus on your career, your friends, your kids? The time is now.

Letting go isn't about admitting defeat; it's about seizing victory from the jaws of a different outcome than you expected. Your life isn't over; a new chapter is just beginning. And guess who's holding the pen? You are.

So, are you ready to accept that she's not coming back—and that it opens the door to a world of opportunities? Your next chapter starts now, but only if you're ready to turn the page.

Daily Challenge: Reflect on one opportunity or dream you held back from pursuing; today, take one step towards making it a reality, embracing the new chapter ahead of you.

Daily Reflection:

What resonated with you from today's lesson? How can you apply this truth in your life?

_____

_____

_____

Day 11: Your Finances - Time to Lock Down

Day 11, and we've got to talk money. It's not sexy, it's not fun, but it's important. Your finances? Time to lock them down, and lock them down tight. Look, divorce isn't just an emotional war; it's a financial one too. And whether you like it or not, money matters. It's the fuel for your future, and you can't afford to let it spill away in the chaos of a breakup.

First things first: separate your accounts. If you've got joint accounts, either freeze them or split the assets fairly. I can't stress this enough—do it now. The last thing you want is for emotions to flare up and money to start disappearing. Trust me, it happens.

Next, get a clear picture of your assets and debts. Make a spreadsheet, consult a financial advisor, do whatever it takes to know exactly where you stand. Because if you don't know what you've got, how can you protect it? And don't forget about alimony, child support, and property division. These are legal issues that'll be settled in court, and you want to be prepared. The more you know about your financial standing, the better you can negotiate. Remember, this is about securing your future, not just surviving the present.

Let's not forget credit. You've built a credit history, and you don't want it tarnished because of late payments or other financial messes stemming from your divorce. Keep an eye on your credit report and make sure everything's in order.

This is not the time for financial laxity; it's the time for financial vigilance. Lock down your accounts, know your assets, and stay on top of your obligations. Money might not buy happiness, but it sure buys options—and right now, you want as many options as possible. So, are you ready to lock down your finances like Fort Knox? Your future self will thank you.

Daily Challenge: Today, set aside 20 minutes to review your bank accounts and credit report. Ensure there are no discrepancies and make a list of action items to secure your financial future.

Daily Reflection:

What resonated with you from today's lesson? How can you apply this truth in your life?

_____

_____

_____

_____

Day 12: Exit Strategy - Prepare, Don't Despair

Listen, if you're getting a divorce, you need an exit strategy. No, this isn't admitting defeat; it's about being prepared. Think of it as your game plan, your playbook, your roadmap. Call it whatever you want, but you need one. Prepare, don't despair—got it?

First off, where are you going to live? If you're moving out, get that sorted ASAP. And if you're staying, figure out how to make that space yours again. Time to redecorate, renovate, rejuvenate—whatever it takes to make it a place where you can thrive.

Next, your stuff. You've got assets, and they're not all just money and property. Think about your sentimental items, your personal belongings. Make a list, check it twice, and secure them. Divorces get messy, and the last thing you want is to lose something irreplaceable in the chaos.

Now, the kids—if you've got them, you need a parenting plan. Don't wing it, don't make verbal agreements. Put it in writing, make it official. Your relationship with your kids is too important to leave to chance.

And let's talk contingencies. Stuff's gonna go sideways; it always does. Have a Plan B, a Plan C, even a Plan D. The more prepared you are for the unexpected, the less it'll knock you off course.

Look, nobody plans for a divorce, but once it's happening, you better have a plan to navigate it. Your exit strategy is your blueprint for the future. So sit down, map it out, and then execute like a boss. Ready to stop despairing and start preparing? Your future's waiting, but only you can build the path to it.

Daily Challenge: Take 15 minutes today to jot down the first three steps of your exit strategy, focusing on immediate needs like living arrangements and safeguarding personal items. Remember, preparation is empowerment.

Daily Reflection:

What resonated with you from today's lesson? How can you apply this truth in your life?

_____

_____

_____

_____

Day 13: Manhood Test

Listen up, because we're diving into something that's gonna make some of you uncomfortable: the whole Alpha vs. Beta debate. Whether you like it or not, going through a divorce is a litmus test for your manhood. Hold up, I know what some of you are thinking: "Labels? Really?" But here's the deal—this isn't about labels; it's about mindset. It's about taking control or letting life steamroll you. You get to choose.

Now, let's break it down. Being Alpha in this context isn't about being a macho, arrogant jerk. Nah, it's about taking charge of your own destiny, owning your mistakes, and standing up for what you believe in. It's about leadership—leading your own life.

On the flip side, going Beta here means letting circumstances dictate your actions. It means bending to the whims of your ex, the lawyers, or anyone else who's not you. It's reactive, not proactive. And let's be real, that's not where you want to be.

So how do you flip that Alpha switch? First, own your emotions. Feel sad, angry, betrayed? Fine, feel it, but don't let it rule you. Take those emotions and channel them into something productive. Second, set boundaries. This is non-negotiable. You've got to know what you'll tolerate and what you won't. No boundaries equals no respect—simple as that.

Lastly, vision. Where do you see yourself post-divorce? What kind of life do you want? Alphas have vision; they have goals. Betas? They let life happen to them. So, ask yourself: are you gonna step up, take control, and be the Alpha of your own life story? Or are you gonna sit back, let things unfold, and play the Beta? The clock's ticking, and the choice is yours. Make it a good one.

Daily Challenge: Today, take a moment to reflect on one area of your life where you've been reactive instead of proactive. Identify one actionable step you can take to regain control and lead with intention in that area. Commit to it

Daily Reflection:

What resonated with you from today's lesson? How can you apply this truth in your life?

_____

_____

_____

_____

Day 14: Machiavelli Was Right

Boom, Day 14! Listen up, because today we're gonna talk about why you need to be cunning and calculated. Yeah, you heard me. Machiavelli had it right—sometimes you gotta play the game to win. Let's get one thing straight: I'm not telling you to be deceptive or manipulative in a way that's unethical. Nah, this is about being smart, knowing the rules, and then bending them to work in your favor. You think divorce is just paperwork and lawyers? No! It's 4D chess, and you better be thinking five moves ahead.

Why? Because everyone else is. Your ex, her lawyer, maybe even your own friends and family—they're all making moves, some visible, some not. If you're just reacting, you're not in control. But if you're calculated, if you're cunning, you set the pace. So, how do you do it? Start by understanding the motivations of everyone involved. What does your ex want? What's her lawyer gunning for? The more you know about what drives them, the better you can predict their moves. And the better you can predict, the better you can prepare.

Next, think long-term. Short-term wins feel great, but this is about the long game. Your future post-divorce life is what's really at stake here. Assets, custody, your frickin' happiness—they're all long-term plays. So make your moves with that endgame in sight.

Here's the kicker: being calculated doesn't make you cold or heartless. It makes you effective. It makes you someone who gets stuff done, who takes control of their destiny instead of leaving it up to chance. So, are you ready to be that person? Are you ready to be cunning, calculated, and take control of this chaotic mess? Time to decide, because the game's already started, whether you like it or not.

Daily Challenge: Today, jot down the motivations and goals of everyone involved in your divorce. Predict their next moves, and strategize your own in response. Remember, play the long game.

Daily Reflection:

What resonated with you from today's lesson? How can you apply this truth in your life?

_____

_____

_____

_____

Day 15: Your Assets - Protect What's Yours

Listen, you've busted your butt for what you have, and just because you're going through a divorce doesn't mean you should lose it all. Let's get one thing straight: your assets aren't just numbers on a paper; they're a reflection of your sweat, tears, and hustle. So, protect what's yours. Period.

You think this is just about money? Nah, this is about your life's work, your legacy! We're talking real estate, investments, even your freakin' baseball card collection. Anything of value—lock it down! Step one: separate accounts. If you haven't done it yet, what are you waiting for? An invitation? This is your wake-up call!

Step two: inventory your assets. Know what you've got so you can know what you're protecting. No shortcuts, no estimates—get precise figures. This isn't the time for rounding errors; this is real life!

Step three: get a financial advisor on board. Don't go cheap; this is about your future. Skimping now could cost you big later. You need someone who knows the game inside and out, who can guide you through the financial jungle and help you come out the other side like a champ.

Listen to me. This is a pivotal moment. You can either be the guy who lets it all slip through his fingers or the guy who stands his ground and protects what he's built. So, ask yourself: which guy are you gonna be? Time's ticking, my friend. Time to take action, time to secure your future. Let's get it!

Daily Challenge: Today, take 15 minutes to list out your most valued assets, tangible and intangible. Reflect on their significance in your life and make a commitment to safeguarding them during this transition. Don't procrastinate; start the protection process now.

Daily Reflection:

What resonated with you from today's lesson? How can you apply this truth in your life?

_____

_____

_____

_____

Day 16: Don't Seek Validation

Day 16, listen up! Stop scrolling, stop whatever you're doing, and focus. Today's lesson is crucial: Stop seeking validation, especially not from her. You hear me? Stop it.

You're going through a divorce, not a popularity contest. Who cares what she thinks of you now? Who cares what anyone thinks? The only opinion that should matter right now is yours. You got that? Yours.

Look, validation is a drug. Once you start craving it, you're screwed. You'll make stupid choices, sacrifice your own needs, and for what? A nod of approval? A 'like'? Forget that noise.

Here's the raw truth: You're enough, with or without her approval. You're enough, with or without anyone's approval. Start getting comfortable with that. Start living it.

Are you worried what she might say about you to friends, family, or—God forbid—your kids? Stop worrying. Actions speak louder than words. Be a great dad, be a great person, and let your life do the talking.

And social media? Don't even think about posting for sympathy or subtle jabs. You're not a teenager; you're a grown man. Act like one.

Remember, you're not defined by this divorce or by her perception of you. You define you. So, are you going to waste more time worrying about what she thinks, or are you going to start living for yourself? The clock's ticking, my man. Make your choice.

Daily Challenge: For the next 24 hours, avoid any urge to check or post on social media and instead, write down three things you genuinely love about yourself. Celebrate them without needing anyone else's approval.

Daily Reflection:

What resonated with you from today's lesson? How can you apply this truth in your life?

_____

_____

_____

_____

Day 17: Don't Play Mind Games

Day 17, let's get into it! Today, we're talking about mind games. You know what I'm talking about—the emotional chess, the mental gymnastics, the manipulative tactics. Listen closely: if you're gonna play mind games, you better play to win. Otherwise, don't play at all. Got it?

Here's the thing: divorce is a battlefield, and on any battlefield, there are mind games. Maybe she's trying to get in your head, make you second-guess yourself. Maybe you're doing the same. But remember, mind games aren't just petty; they're dangerous. They can mess with your emotions, your decisions, even your legal standing.

So, first rule: be aware. Know when mind games are happening. Is she suddenly being super nice? Is she making promises she never did before? Red flags, my man, red flags. Don't take the bait. Second rule: check your own behavior. Are you playing games too? Are you trying to get a rise out of her, push her buttons? If you are, you better have a very good reason and a clear strategy. Impulse plays are for rookies, not for winners.

Third rule: keep your eyes on the prize. What's your endgame? A fair settlement? Custody of the kids? Protecting your assets? Keep that goal in your sights, and don't let mind games distract you.

Look, life is a game where the stakes are high and the rules are always changing. If you choose to play mind games in this already complicated situation, you better play with purpose, with strategy, and with the will to win. So, you in or out? Time to decide how you're gonna play this game. Just remember, if you're not playing to win, you're setting yourself up to lose.

Daily Challenge: Commit today to be a strategic player in the game of divorce, focusing on your ultimate goals and refusing to be swayed by mind games, because in this battle, playing to win means securing your future.

Daily Reflection:

What resonated with you from today's lesson? How can you apply this truth in your life?

_____

_____

_____

_____

Day 18: Get Comfortable Being Alone

Alright, Day 18! Buckle up, because we're diving into something everyone faces but no one wants to talk about: loneliness. Yeah, I said it. You're gonna feel alone, but guess what? You've gotta get comfortable with it. I'm serious; this is non-negotiable.

Why? Because loneliness isn't just a feeling; it's a state of mind. And if you let that state of mind dictate your actions, you're going to make crappy decisions. I'm talking rebound relationships, poor financial choices, and a whole lot of self-pity. You want that? Didn't think so.

So, how do you get comfortable being alone? First, reframe the narrative. You're not "alone"; you're in the company of the one person who will never leave you: yourself. Start enjoying your own company, man! Dive into hobbies you've neglected, hit the gym, read, cook—whatever!

Second, reconnect with your tribe. You've got friends, family, maybe even colleagues who genuinely care about you. Spend time, not just late-night texts or beers at the bar. Really engage.

Third, professional help. Yeah, I'm talking therapists, counselors, life coaches. These people are trained to help you navigate emotional minefields. Don't see it as a sign of weakness; see it as leveling up your mental game.

Look, loneliness is like a gym for your emotional muscles. It's where you train yourself to be independent, self-reliant, and mentally tough. And let me tell you, once you're comfortable being alone, you become unstoppable in every other area of your life. So, ready to tackle the new loneliness like it's just another opponent you're destined to beat? Your future self is waiting, but only you can make the first move.

Daily Challenge: Embrace solitude as an opportunity for personal growth and self-discovery, reconnect with your support network, and consider seeking professional help to strengthen your emotional strength during this challenging time.

Daily Reflection:

What resonated with you from today's lesson? How can you apply this truth in your life?

_____

_____

_____

_____

Day 19: No More Mr. Nice Guy

Boom, Day 19, and if you're still playing Mr. Nice Guy, it's time for a reality check. Listen to me: the doormat days? They're over. Done. Finished. You're not a pushover, you're a powerhouse, and it's high time you start acting like one.

Why's this so important? Because playing Mr. Nice Guy doesn't just hurt you; it devalues you. It says, "My needs, my desires, my goals—they don't matter." And that's straight-up bull. You matter. Your life matters. So, stop letting people walk all over you.

First step: boundaries. Yeah, you've heard the term, now it's time to implement it. You've got lines that shouldn't be crossed. Define them. Make them clear. And if someone does cross them? You hold your ground. No exceptions.

Step two: assertiveness. I'm not talking about being a jerk; I'm talking about standing up for what you believe in, what you want, and what you deserve. Someone tries to push you into a decision you're not cool with? You push back. It's your life, and you call the shots.

Step three: value yourself. You bring something to the table—skills, personality, experience, whatever. Recognize your worth, and don't settle for anything less. Whether it's in your relationships, your job, or your divorce settlement, you don't take scraps; you go for the full meal.

Here's the deal: life's not gonna hand you respect; you've got to earn it. And the first person you've got to earn it from is yourself. So, no more Mr. Nice Guy, got it? From now on, you're Mr. Get-It-Done, Mr. Take-No-Crap, Mr. I-Know-My-Worth. Ready to ditch the doormat and step up as the powerhouse you are? Let's go. Your new life's waiting, but it's not gonna wait forever.

Daily Challenge: Define your boundaries, stand up for what you believe in, and recognize your worth as you embrace the transformation from Mr. Nice Guy to Mr. I-Know-My-Worth.

Daily Reflection:

What resonated with you from today's lesson? How can you apply this truth in your life?

_____

_____

_____

_____

Day 20: What Will Your Future Self Thank You For?

Day 20, here we are! Today is all about your future self. I want you to think about that guy—the man you're becoming. What's he like? What's he achieved? What's he grateful for? And most importantly, what are you doing right now to make his life better?

Listen, life is a marathon, not a sprint. The decisions you make today echo into your future. So, are you making choices that set you up for success or failure? Are you investing in yourself or are you wasting time on stuff that doesn't matter?

First off, your health. Are you taking care of yourself? Eating right, exercising, sleeping well? Because let me tell you, your future self doesn't want to deal with health problems you could've avoided. Next, your relationships. Are you nurturing connections that enrich you, or are you clinging to toxic ties that drag you down? Time to clean house. Keep the winners, ditch the losers.

And let's talk money. Are you managing your finances like a pro, or are you treating your bank account like a dumpster fire? Your future self wants financial freedom, not debt and stress. Make it happen. Finally, personal growth. Are you learning, evolving, pushing your boundaries? Or are you stuck in a rut, repeating the same mistakes? Your future self wants wisdom, experience, and a great story to tell. So, make it worth telling.

The point is, every choice you make is a brick in the foundation of your future. Build a shack, and that's all you'll have. Build a fortress, and you become unshakeable. So, what's it gonna be? What will your future self thank you for? The clock's ticking, and your next move could be a game-changer.

Daily Challenge: Envision your future self and take a concrete step today that aligns with the man you're becoming, whether it's a healthy choice, a positive relationship action, a financial move, or a step toward personal growth.

Daily Reflection:

What resonated with you from today's lesson? How can you apply this truth in your life?

_____

_____

_____

_____

Day 21: Fitness is Not Optional

Day 21, three weeks in, and if you're still lounging around feeling sorry for yourself, it's time for a reality check. Fitness is not optional. Nope, not a luxury, not a 'when I feel like it' thing. It's a must. Get off the couch! Why? Because your body is your vehicle in this game called life, and right now, you need it running at peak performance. You're dealing with stress, emotional upheaval, maybe even legal battles. Do you really think you can handle all that if you're out of shape, sluggish, and stuck in a rut?

First point: cardio. I don't care if it's running, cycling, swimming, or even dancing in your living room—get that heart pumping. Cardiovascular health isn't just about your heart; it's about your mental clarity, your stress levels, your freaking life expectancy. Next up: strength training. You think lifting weights is just for bodybuilders or gym rats? Think again. Building muscle boosts your metabolism, improves your posture, and yes, it ups your confidence. Walk into a room knowing you're strong, and it shows.

Don't forget flexibility. Yoga, stretching, Pilates—whatever floats your boat. A flexible body is a resilient body, one that can take hits and bounce back. And given what you're going through, resilience is your new best friend. And here's the kicker: the benefits aren't just physical. Exercise releases endorphins, the feel-good hormones. It clears your mind, sharpens your focus, and elevates your mood. It's like a natural antidepressant, no prescription needed.

Bottom line: Fitness is your new non-negotiable. It's the cornerstone of not just surviving this period, but thriving through it. So, are you gonna make excuses, or are you gonna make progress? Your choice, your future. But the couch isn't gonna get you there. So get up, gear up, and show up—for yourself.

Daily Challenge: Today, commit to at least 30 minutes of heart-pumping cardio exercise to boost your physical and mental toughness, proving to yourself that you're ready to take charge of your future.

Daily Reflection:

What resonated with you from today's lesson? How can you apply this truth in your life?

_____

_____

_____

_____

Day 22: Dread Game - Why You Should Know It

Day 22, and we're diving into some heavy stuff: Dread Game. We're decoding this tactic so you don't become the sucker, the pawn in someone else's messed-up game. Dread Game, for those not in the loop, is when someone deliberately creates a sense of insecurity or fear in their partner to gain control. Twisted, right? But it's real, and you need to recognize it when it's happening to you.

First off, emotional rollercoasters. If she's hot one minute and cold the next, making you question your standing, that's a red flag. Emotional unpredictability can be a tactic to keep you off balance.

Second, pulling away. This is classic Dread Game—suddenly becoming distant, unavailable, leaving you wondering what you did wrong and how to fix it. Listen, if someone wants to be with you, they'll make the effort. Period.

Third, jealousy plays. If she's suddenly flaunting friendships or connections that she knows will make you jealous, it's not just to make her life more colorful. It's to make you anxious, to make you compete for her attention.

Knowledge is power, my man. If you can spot these tactics, you can call them out. You can choose not to engage, not to be manipulated. You don't have to play the game if you know the moves.

So, are you ready to decode the Dread Game? Are you ready to take control of your emotional destiny and not be someone's puppet? It starts now, and it starts with awareness.

Daily Challenge: Stay vigilant and recognize the signs of Dread Game in your interactions, refusing to be manipulated and taking control of your emotional well-being.

Daily Reflection:

What resonated with you from today's lesson? How can you apply this truth in your life?

_____

_____

_____

_____

Day 23: Books You Need to Read

Day 23, and if you think you can navigate this new chapter in your life without arming yourself with knowledge, think again.

First on the list: "The Rational Male" by Rollo Tomassi. Look, if you're going through a divorce, this is your bible. It delves into intersexual dynamics and helps you understand the 'why' behind the 'what.' Read it. Digest it. Live it.

Next up, "No More Mr. Nice Guy" by Dr. Robert Glover. If you've been the doormat, the people-pleaser, this book is your wake-up call. It teaches you how to reclaim your life and stop seeking validation from others. Trust me, it's a game-changer.

Don't sleep on "12 Rules for Life" by Jordan Peterson. Forget the politics; focus on the advice. It's about taking responsibility, facing chaos, and carving out order in your life. You want a roadmap to stability? This is it.

Now, let's talk "The 3% Man" by Corey Wayne. This isn't just dating advice; it's a masterclass in understanding relationships and, more importantly, understanding yourself. Corey Wayne teaches you how to be the kind of man who understands his worth and how to translate that into a fulfilling love life.

There's more out there, but these are your cornerstones. Books that don't just tell you how to survive, but how to thrive. How to transform this period of upheaval into a launching pad for a stronger, wiser, more empowered you. So, what are you waiting for? Your new life's not gonna build itself. Start reading, start absorbing, start applying. The knowledge is out there; all you've got to do is grab it.

Daily Challenge: Stay vigilant and recognize the signs of Dread Game in your interactions, refusing to be manipulated and taking control of your emotional well-being.

Daily Reflection:

What resonated with you from today's lesson? How can you apply this truth in your life?

_____

_____

_____

_____

Day 24: Time for a Wardrobe Overhaul

Boom, Day 24, and it's time to get real about something you've probably been neglecting: your style. Listen, you might think fashion is fluff, but it's not. Your style isn't just fabric; it's a statement. It's your brand, and right now, your brand needs a revamp.

First things first: Ditch the old stuff. Those baggy jeans, outdated shirts, and worn-out sneakers? Trash 'em. You're not in college anymore, and you're definitely not the guy you were in your marriage. You're someone new, so look the part. Next up: Invest in the essentials. I'm talking fitted jeans, crisp white shirts, versatile jackets, and shoes that aren't falling apart. You don't have to break the bank, but you do have to care.

Accessorize, but don't overdo it. A watch, a leather belt, maybe a bracelet if that's your vibe. Accessories are the exclamation points of your style, but remember, nobody likes a run-on sentence. And here's the kicker: Tailoring. You ever see a guy in a suit that fits like a glove and think, "He's got it together"? That could be you. Tailoring isn't a luxury; it's a necessity. Off-the-rack is for amateurs; you're going pro.

But remember, style isn't just what you wear; it's how you wear it. It's walking into a room and owning it, not because you're the best-dressed guy, but because you're the most confident guy. Your clothes aren't wearing you; you're wearing them.

So, what's the plan? Are you gonna keep rocking that 'I-gave-up' look, or are you gonna step up and show the world the new, improved, ready-for-anything version of you? Your closet's waiting, and so is your future. Make the choice, make the change, and make it happen.

Daily Challenge: Embrace the transformation - declutter your wardrobe, invest in essential pieces, add subtle accessories, and get your clothes tailored, but above all, wear them with confidence as a statement of your renewed self.

Daily Reflection:

What resonated with you from today's lesson? How can you apply this truth in your life?

_____

_____

_____

_____

Day 25: Know Where You Stand

Day 25, and we're cracking open a topic that most people tiptoe around: power dynamics. Yeah, you heard me. We're pulling back the curtain on who holds the power, why, and how you can tip the scales in your favor.

First, let's talk about your relationships. Whether it's with your ex, your kids, or even your friends, someone's got the upper hand. Recognize it. You think you're on equal footing? Wake up. Even the most balanced relationships have a subtle power dynamic.

Now, the workplace. You might think it's just the boss who holds the cards, but that's surface-level thinking. Office politics, alliances, even the office gossip—all of it plays into the power structure. Knowing where you fit in that ecosystem is strategic intelligence, my friend.

And let's not skip over social circles. Who's the alpha in your group of friends? Who sets the tone, picks the hangout spots, calls the shots? Understanding this dynamic lets you navigate social situations like a pro, not like a sheep following the herd. So how do you shift these dynamics in your favor? First, knowledge. You can't play the game if you don't know the rules. Second, leverage. Find out what you bring to the table and use it. And third, timing. Power dynamics ebb and flow; knowing when to make your move is half the battle.

Look, life's not a democracy; it's a power play. The sooner you understand that, the sooner you stop being a pawn and start being a player. You're not just here to participate; you're here to dominate. So, are you ready to dissect these power dynamics and take control? The game's always on; the question is, are you playing or getting played?

Daily Challenge: Identify the power dynamics in your relationships, workplace, and social circles, and begin strategizing how to leverage your strengths to shift them in your favor.

Daily Reflection:

What resonated with you from today's lesson? How can you apply this truth in your life?

_____

_____

_____

Day 26: Master Time Management

Day 26, and here's the deal: If you don't control your time, someone else will. End of story. You think time management is for nerds with planners and color-coded schedules? Think again. It's for anyone who wants to grab life by the horns and not get bucked off.

First up: Prioritize. I'm not talking about making a to-do list; I'm talking about making a 'what-matters-most' list. What's gonna move the needle for you? What's gonna get you closer to where you want to be? That's where your time goes. Period.

Next: Eliminate distractions. Your phone, social media, that TV show you binge when you should be hustling—cut 'em out. They're not just wasting your time; they're stealing your potential. Let's talk deadlines. Not the kind your boss gives you, the kind you give yourself. Set them, meet them, beat them. Make it a game, make it a challenge, but make it happen.

Now, here's a pro tip: Time-block. Break your day into chunks and dedicate those chunks to specific tasks. You think you can multitask? Science says you're wrong. Focus is the name of the game. And don't forget to allocate time for yourself. Exercise, meditation, reading—whatever fuels your fire. Self-care isn't selfish; it's strategic.

Look, time management isn't just about being productive; it's about being empowered. When you control your time, you control your life. No more reacting to what comes at you; you're proactive, you're in charge, you're the CEO of your existence. So, are you gonna let life happen to you, or are you gonna happen to life? Your time's ticking, either way. Master it, and you master your destiny.

Daily Challenge: Take control of your time by prioritizing what truly matters, eliminating distractions, setting and meeting deadlines, time-blocking your day, and dedicating moments to self-care, because mastering your time means mastering your destiny.

Daily Reflection:

What resonated with you from today's lesson? How can you apply this truth in your life?

_____

_____

_____

_____

Day 27: Where Do You Rank?

Day 27, and we're diving into the deep end of social dynamics. Social Market Value—ever heard of it? It's not about being superficial or treating life like some kind of popularity contest. It's about understanding where you stand in social settings, and guess what? That knowledge is power.

First off: Self-awareness. You need to know what you bring to the table. Are you the life of the party, the listener, the advisor? Each role has its value, but you've got to know yours to play it right. Next: Presentation. Yeah, we talked about style, but this goes beyond clothes. It's how you speak, how you carry yourself, even how you react in different situations. All of this feeds into your Social Market Value.

Now, let's hit on Skills and Talents. Can you play guitar like a rockstar? Are you a whiz in the kitchen? Skills like these don't just make you interesting; they make you valuable. And don't overlook your Network. The people you surround yourself with can elevate you or drag you down. You've heard it before: You're the average of the five people you spend the most time with. So, choose wisely. Lastly: Adaptability. Life throws curveballs, social scenes change, and you've got to be ready to adapt. The more versatile you are, the higher your Social Market Value. Simple as that.

Listen, you're not just floating through social settings like a leaf in the wind. You're there to make an impact, to elevate yourself and, by extension, those around you. Understanding your Social Market Value isn't narcissistic; it's strategic. So, where do you stand? More importantly, where do you want to stand? Time to assess, adjust, and ascend. You're not just part of the social fabric; you're a thread that makes it stronger.

Daily Challenge: Take a moment to reflect on your unique strengths and the role you play in social settings, then set a goal to enhance one aspect of your Social Market Value today, whether it's improving your communication skills, nurturing your talents, or expanding your network.

Daily Reflection:

What resonated with you from today's lesson? How can you apply this truth in your life?

_____

_____

_____

_____

Day 28: How to Tell the Family and Friends

It's day 28, and listen, there's no sugarcoating it—today is about those conversations you'd rather not have but must. Telling your kids, your family, your circle about the divorce. It's awkward, it's painful, but dodging it is a disservice to you and them. So let's get real on how to do it right.

First up: Kids. Look, they're smarter than you think; they probably already sense something's up. So be honest but age-appropriate. No blaming, no badmouthing the other parent. Just the facts and a whole lot of reassurance that your love for them hasn't changed. Now, Family. You think they'll judge you? Maybe. But this is your life, not a family court. Be straightforward, be honest, and most importantly, be ready for a mixed bag of reactions. It's not about pleasing them; it's about informing them.

And let's talk Friends. You might lose some, and that's okay. The real ones will stick around. When you break the news, be direct. No drama, no gossip, just the reality of what's happening. And watch who steps up; that'll tell you a lot about your circle. Here's the kicker: Timing. Don't drop this bomb in the middle of someone's birthday party or right before a big event. Choose your moment, because once you say it, there's no taking it back.

Remember, these conversations aren't just for them; they're for you, too. The sooner you have them, the sooner you rip off that Band-Aid and start the real healing process. It's not just about ending a chapter; it's about clearing the slate for the new one you're about to write. So, are you ready for the hard talks? They're not a roadblock; they're a gateway. Step through, own your truth, and let the chips fall where they may. Your new life is waiting, and it starts with being honest—first with yourself, and then with the world.

Daily Challenge: Today, face the uncomfortable conversations head-on - be honest with your kids, family, and friends about your divorce, focusing on truth, reassurance, and readiness for their reactions.

Daily Reflection:

What resonated with you from today's lesson? How can you apply this truth in your life?

_____

_____

_____

_____

Day 29: Anger Management

Day 29, and it's time to tackle the big, ugly elephant in the room: Anger. Look, it's normal to be pissed off right now. You're human. But here's the deal: Anger's a terrible fuel. It burns hot and fast and leaves nothing but ashes.

First things first: Identify the triggers. What sets you off? Is it a text from your ex? Is it seeing happy couples? Know the triggers, so you're not blindsided.

Next: Redirect that energy. Instead of fuming, how about hitting the gym? Writing? Whatever it takes to convert that negative energy into something useful, do it. Let's talk coping mechanisms. Deep breathing, counting to ten, stepping away—sounds cliché, but it works. It gives you that pause to prevent you from doing something you'll regret.

And don't underestimate the power of a solid support network. Friends, family, therapists—people who can serve as your emotional sounding board. Vent to them, not at the problem. Now, here's the big one: Forgiveness. Yeah, I said it. It's not about them; it's about you. Carrying that anger is like drinking poison and expecting the other person to die. Let it go, not for their sake, but for yours.

Look, you can use anger as a crutch, or you can use this period to grow, to evolve, to become the kind of man who can handle life's curveballs without losing his cool. The choice is yours.

So, what's it gonna be? Will you let anger rule you, or will you take control and channel it into something productive, something that elevates you? Your life's not dictated by your emotions, but by how you handle them. Time to step up.

Daily Challenge: Transform your anger into a source of strength and growth by identifying triggers, redirecting energy, utilizing coping mechanisms, seeking support, and embracing forgiveness as a path to personal empowerment.

Daily Reflection:

What resonated with you from today's lesson? How can you apply this truth in your life?

_____

_____

_____

_____

Day 30: The First Milestone

Day 30, and give yourself some credit—you've made it a month into this grind. You're a different man than you were 30 days ago, whether you feel it or not. So let's hit pause for a second. Not to rest, but to reassess.

First up: Self-evaluation. What have you learned? What's changed? This isn't some fluffy, feel-good exercise; it's crucial data collection. You can't know where you're going if you don't know where you've been. Now, Goals. You set some a month ago, right? Time to check in. Did you meet them? Miss them? Either way, what did you learn? Goals aren't set in stone; they're stepping stones. Adjust as needed.

Let's talk Progress. Small wins, big wins, they all count. Celebrate them. Why? Because progress fuels momentum, and momentum is what's gonna carry you through the next 30 days and beyond. And don't forget Challenges. You've faced them, maybe you're still facing them. Good. Challenges aren't setbacks; they're setups for comebacks. Identify them, tackle them, and turn them into your next wins.

Here's the kicker: The Next 30 Days. You've got a foundation now. Time to build on it. What are the next steps? What's the plan? If you're not moving forward, you're sliding back, and that's not an option. Look, this isn't just a milestone; it's a launching pad. You've got the tools, the insights, and the will to keep going. So, are you ready for the next leg of this journey? Strap in, because it's gonna be one amazing ride.

Daily Challenge: Take a moment to reflect on your journey, evaluate your progress, adjust your goals as needed, and embrace challenges as opportunities for comebacks as you prepare to launch into the next 30 days of your transformation.

Daily Reflection:

What resonated with you from today's lesson? How can you apply this truth in your life?

_____

_____

_____

_____

Your Legal Battle Starts Now

In the second chapter of your divorce journey, we delve deep into the legal intricacies that will define your path ahead. From the critical hunt for the right attorney to mastering the art of documentation, we leave no stone unturned. Understand your legal rights, financial obligations, and the emotional toll of battles wisely chosen. The financial reckoning will demand your attention, and we'll guide you through the complexities of spousal support and child custody. As you prepare to face the courtroom, we provide invaluable insights into decorum, witness preparation, and the judge's verdict. But it doesn't end there. This chapter also explores the financial realities post-divorce, from alimony to child support. Get ready to emerge from this legal crucible with a clearer picture of your financial future and the legal preparations necessary to turn the page.

Day 31: The Legal Gauntlet

Alright, you've reached a pivotal point: the legalities. I won't sugarcoat it; this part can get ugly. You're not just dividing assets; sometimes, it feels like you're tearing apart a life. But here's the deal: You can either be a passive participant or an active player. Choose the latter.

First up: Find a Lawyer. Not just any lawyer, but someone who specializes in divorce and knows the ins and outs like they know their morning coffee. This is your gladiator; pick wisely. Documents, Documents, Documents. Start collecting all the paperwork you'll need—bank statements, property deeds, whatever. The more organized you are, the smoother this process will be. Know Your Rights. Yeah, it sounds basic, but you'd be surprised how many guys go into this blind. Get acquainted with divorce laws in your state, understand alimony, child support, all of it.

Negotiation is Key. Listen, not everything has to be a battle. Know what you absolutely can't budge on and where there's room for compromise. Sometimes a strategic retreat can lead to a bigger win down the line. And for the love of everything, keep emotions in check. The courtroom is not the place for emotional outbursts or revenge plots. Keep your eyes on the prize: a fair settlement and your freedom.

Here's the bottom line: The legal process is a gauntlet, a test of your flexibility and wits. But guess what? You're more than capable of coming out the other side not just intact, but stronger and more empowered. So, ready to face the Thunderdome? Equip yourself, prepare for battle, and walk in there like the warrior you are. Your future's on the line, so fight for it

Daily Challenge: Embrace the Legal Thunderdome - Seek out the right attorney, gather your documents, know your rights, and master the art of negotiation, because you're not just a passive participant; you're a warrior in the battle for your future.

Daily Reflection:

What resonated with you from today's lesson? How can you apply this truth in your life?

_____

_____

_____

_____

Day 32: Lawyer Up- Choose Your Gladiator Wisely

You're about to enter a battlefield, and who you bring with you can make or break the outcome. Your lawyer isn't just a hired hand; they're your gladiator, your advocate, your strategist. So how do you pick the right one? Listen up. Experience Matters. This isn't the time for charity or giving a newbie a shot. You want someone seasoned, someone who's been in the trenches and knows how to navigate the legal maze.

Specialization is Key. Divorce law is its own beast, filled with nuances and complications. Your cousin who just passed the bar and specializes in traffic tickets? Not the guy for this job. Get References. Word of mouth is gold in this game. Know someone who's been through a divorce and came out alright? Ask who they used. Dive into reviews, but take them with a grain of salt.

Chemistry Counts. You're gonna be sharing intimate details of your life with this person. If you can't stand them, or worse, don't trust them, it's not gonna work. Meet face-to-face, get a feel for their vibe, and trust your gut.

Talk Money. Legal battles aren't cheap, but this isn't the place to skimp. Know their rates, understand the billing, and make sure it's all transparent. Last thing you need is a financial blindside on top of everything else.

Here's the real talk: Your lawyer is your partner in this journey. A bad choice can cost you, not just in dollars, but in stress, time, and potentially even your assets and rights. A good choice can be the difference between getting dragged through the mud and walking away clean. So, are you ready to choose your gladiator? Time to lawyer up and enter the arena armed and ready. Your future's waiting, and it's worth fighting for.

Daily Challenge: Today, take action to find and interview at least one experienced divorce lawyer who specializes in family law, and make sure you feel a strong rapport and trust with them before making your decision.

Daily Reflection:

What resonated with you from today's lesson? How can you apply this truth in your life?

_____

_____

_____

_____

Day 33: Document Everything

You might be tempted to wing it, to go off memory and goodwill. Bad idea. In divorce, documentation is your best friend, your shield, your undeniable proof. So what should you be hoarding like a squirrel before winter? Here we go.

Financial Records: Bank statements, tax returns, pay stubs—you name it, you keep it. Money matters in divorce, and you want every cent accounted for. Communication: Texts, emails, voicemails between you and your ex? Save them. You never know when you'll need to prove what was said—or what wasn't.

Child Interactions: If kids are in the picture, keep a log of your interactions. Pickup and drop-off times, nights spent, even notable conversations. Trust me, it can make a difference in custody discussions. Property Inventory: Make a comprehensive list of your assets—houses, cars, valuables. Take pictures, note conditions. The more detailed, the better.

Legal Documents: Court filings, lawyer correspondence, any official paperwork related to your divorce—keep it organized and accessible. Here's why this matters: Your memory is flawed; documents are not. When disputes arise—and they will—the first question will be, "Can you prove it?" With solid documentation, yes, you can.

This isn't about being paranoid; it's about being prepared. Every document you collect is another piece of armor, another layer of protection in this legal battle you're waging. So, ready to make documentation your new obsession? In the world of divorce, it's not the one with the best memory who wins; it's the one with the best records. Time to start collecting.

Daily Challenge: Become the Documentarian - Today, commit to meticulously collecting and organizing all the essential records and documents related to your divorce, because in this battle, your paperwork is your power.

Daily Reflection:

What resonated with you from today's lesson? How can you apply this truth in your life?

_____

_____

_____

_____

Day 34: Custody Wars - Fight for Your Kids

This is the frontline, the part of the divorce battlefield that's not just about you—it's about your kids. Make no mistake, this is a war zone, and you need to come in armed to the teeth, but not just with legal arguments. You're fighting for hearts and minds—your kids' and the court's. Know the Law, Inside and Out. You think you can wing this? Think again. You need to understand every nuance of custody laws in your state, from "best interests of the child" to what "joint custody" really means. And if you don't, make sure your lawyer does.

Your Track Record is Your Best Weapon. You've been there for soccer games, school plays, and bedtime stories? Good. Now prove it. Emails, texts, photos—anything that shows you're an involved, caring parent. Don't Mud-Sling. Tempting as it may be to drag your ex through the mud, courts don't take kindly to character assassination. Stick to the facts and let your own record speak for itself.

Get Back-Up. Friends, family, teachers—anyone who's seen you in action as a dad needs to be ready to vouch for you. Your word's good, but corroboration is better. Keep Your Cool, Always. The moment you lose your temper, you lose the high ground. It's tough, especially when your kids are being used as pawns. But you need to keep your emotions locked down, in and out of court.

Listen, this is a fight you never wanted but now you've got no choice but to win. It's not about beating your ex; it's about ensuring your kids have the parent they deserve—you—in their lives. You ready for this? Strap in and armor up. Your kids are counting on you, and that's the only motivation you should need to fight.

Daily Challenge: Today, commit to becoming a master of composure and self-control, both in and out of court, as you navigate the turbulent waters of divorce for the sake of your children's well-being.

Daily Reflection:

What resonated with you from today's lesson? How can you apply this truth in your life?

_____

_____

_____

Day 35: Alimony- Don't Let It Break You

Alright, listen up. You're staring down the barrel of alimony, and it's easy to feel like you're getting screwed. But hang on a second. This isn't a life sentence; it's a business negotiation. And in business, the prepared win. So what's your prep look like?

Get to know alimony laws like you know your car's engine. Different states, different rules. Don't get caught off guard. Your lawyer should be your co-pilot here, not a passenger. This person's your advocate, your playbook, your lifeline. Pick someone who's gonna fight tooth and nail for you.

Your financials? They better be crystal clear. Every asset, every liability, every paycheck—get it documented. You walk into that negotiation with your financial life laid bare. No surprises, no weak spots.

And here's a pro tip: Think outside the monthly payment box. There are options—lump sum payments, property transfers, you name it. Get creative, but keep it realistic. Your lawyer will help you game it out.

You're not a victim in this; you're a player. And players have strategies, moves, counter-moves. So what's yours gonna be? Time to ditch the defeatist mindset. You're negotiating your future here, so step up and own it. No one's gonna hand you a fair deal; you've got to fight for it.

You ready to go to war over this? Because that's what it takes—a warrior's mindset. Strap in, gear up, and let's do this.

Daily Challenge: Today, become a financial warrior by dedicating time to research and understand the alimony laws in your state, work closely with your lawyer to strategize, and ensure your financial documents are in tip-top shape for the upcoming negotiations.

Daily Reflection:

What resonated with you from today's lesson? How can you apply this truth in your life?

_____

_____

_____

_____

Day 36: Community Property

Alright, here's the deal: Community property isn't just about who gets the house or the car. No, my friend, it's the entire financial empire you've built, however big or small. So let's get straight on what's at stake.

First off, know the laws. Not every state is a community property state. In some places, it's about "equitable distribution," which is a fancy way of saying it's not always a 50/50 split. Got it? Good. Now, get your lawyer in the loop if they're not already. This is complex stuff.

Second, inventory your assets. I'm talking everything—real estate, bank accounts, investments, even debts. Yep, debts are shared too. Your lawyer can help you figure out what's in play, but you should already have a decent idea. No one knows your finances better than you do.

Third, negotiation is your best friend. You think you're gonna get everything you want by pounding your chest and playing tough? Get real. You need to know what you can give up to get what you really want. This is chess, not checkers.

Last point: Don't forget the tax implications. Assets aren't just assets; they're future liabilities if you're not careful. Consult a tax advisor along with your lawyer. Double the advice, double the wisdom.

This is a pivotal moment in your divorce journey. You're not just dividing assets; you're setting up your financial future. So take it seriously. Do your homework, have a strategy, and play to win. Your future self will thank you.

Daily Challenge: Today, take a proactive step towards understanding and managing your financial future by consulting with both your lawyer and a tax advisor to ensure you're making informed decisions during this pivotal moment in your divorce journey.

Daily Reflection:

What resonated with you from today's lesson? How can you apply this truth in your life?

_____

_____

_____

_____

Day 37: False Accusations

Alright, so you've got your lawyer, you're documenting everything, and you've mastered your emotions. Now what? Let's talk strategy, because when false accusations fly, it's war.

First, controlling the narrative isn't just legal; it's social. People talk, and you can't let rumors fester. Use your social capital wisely. A well-timed conversation with key people can help counteract gossip. But remember, always consult your lawyer before you talk to anyone about the case.

Second, let's talk about character witnesses. Your lawyer might suggest bringing in people who can vouch for your integrity. Choose these individuals carefully. You want unimpeachable character and credibility on your side.

Third, think defense, but also think counter-offense. False accusations can be a form of defamation. Discuss with your lawyer whether a counterclaim makes sense. Sometimes the best defense is a strong offense.

Lastly, keep an eye on the endgame. The goal isn't just to clear your name; it's to emerge from this ordeal stronger and wiser. What lessons can you draw? How can you protect yourself moving forward?

Being falsely accused can be a gut punch like no other, but it's also a test of your mettle. It's you against a world that might seem hostile right now, but remember: the truth is your ultimate ally. Gear up, stand tall, and never, ever back down.

Daily Challenge: Today, take control of the narrative by having a strategic conversation with a key person in your social circle to counteract any false rumors, but be sure to consult with your lawyer first to ensure it's the right move for your case.

Daily Reflection:

What resonated with you from today's lesson? How can you apply this truth in your life?

_____

_____

_____

_____

Day 38: Mediation

Hold up, let's talk mediation. Yeah, you heard me right. Mediation. Before you scoff and say it's for the faint of heart, listen up. This isn't surrender; this is strategy, and sometimes it's the smartest play in the book.

First things first: Mediation isn't admitting defeat. It's about taking control. In a courtroom, you're rolling the dice. With mediation, you've got a hand in shaping the outcome. You're at the table, making real-time decisions.

Point two: It's about saving resources. Court battles drain time, energy, and your bank account. Mediation is often faster and cheaper. Yeah, cheaper. Who doesn't like the sound of that?

Third: Information is king. In mediation, you get to hear the other side's priorities straight from the source. That's intel you can use, either in the mediation itself or in a subsequent court battle.

Four: Flexibility. Courts deal in legalities; mediators deal in possibilities. You can hash out creative solutions that a judge would never think of. That's freedom, my friend.

Last point: Mediation isn't for everyone. If your ex is hell-bent on scorched earth, then sure, gear up for battle. But if there's room to maneuver, mediation can be the stage where you take control, save resources, and potentially walk away with a better deal.

So, are you a chump for considering mediation? No. You're a strategic thinker who knows when to fight and when to sit at the negotiation table. Your move, champ.

Daily Challenge: Today, embrace mediation as a strategic opportunity, not a sign of weakness, and take the initiative to explore its potential benefits in your divorce proceedings.

Daily Reflection:

What resonated with you from today's lesson? How can you apply this truth in your life?

_____

_____

_____

_____

Day 39: The Best Defense Is a Good Offense

Listen, you're not in this just to weather the storm—you're here to steer the ship. Too many guys think defense when they should be thinking offense. Let's flip that script.

First thing: Know their playbook. Whether it's your ex or their lawyer, understand their tactics and motives. You can't counter an enemy you don't understand. Do your homework. What are they after? What's their next likely move? Anticipate it.

Second: Document like a historian. Every interaction, every expense, every minor incident—record it. A well-documented case is a strong case. Don't leave room for 'he said, she said.' Let the facts speak, and let them speak loudly.

Third: Be preemptive. If you see a potential issue down the line, address it now. Whether it's a custody arrangement or a financial dispute, don't wait for them to make the first move. Be strategic, consult your lawyer, and go on the offensive.

Fourth: Control the narrative. You've got a story to tell, so make sure it's heard. Work with your lawyer to frame your case in a way that puts you in the best light. You're not just responding to accusations; you're making your own case, loud and clear.

Last up: Keep your endgame in sight. Every move you make should serve your ultimate goals. Whether it's preserving assets, securing custody, or just getting the fairest shake possible, every tactical move should serve your strategic ends. You've got the tools, you've got the strategy. Now it's time to execute. So, are you ready to go on the offense? Because defense might save the game, but offense wins it.

Daily Challenge: Shift from Defense to Offense - Today, take the proactive step of identifying one aspect of your divorce where you can make the first move, whether it's clarifying your goals, gathering evidence, or strategically communicating your position.

Daily Reflection:

What resonated with you from today's lesson? How can you apply this truth in your life?

_____

_____

_____

_____

Day 40: Financial Forensics- Trace Every Dollar

Alright, listen up. Your financial situation isn't just what's in your wallet. It's a web, a puzzle, a maze. And if you're not tracing every dollar, you're leaving yourself open to some nasty surprises.

First off, bank accounts. Not just yours—joint accounts, hidden accounts, all of it. If you've got a name on it, you need to know what's going in and what's coming out. Get those statements and go through them line by line. And I mean every line.

Second, assets aren't just property and stocks. Think benefits, retirement accounts, even frequent flyer miles. Yeah, you heard me. Anything of value can be up for grabs. Know what you've got and know what it's worth.

Third, debts. Oh, you thought we were just talking about assets? Cute. Debts are shared too, so you better know what's looming. Credit cards, loans, even informal debts—they all count.

Fourth, hidden assets. If you've got any suspicion your ex is hiding something, dig. Tax returns, business records, even Venmo transactions. Anything can be a clue. If you're not comfortable doing this, hire a forensic accountant. This is no time for amateur hour.

Last point, it's not just about what you find; it's about what you do with it. Document everything and consult with your lawyer. Build a financial profile so ironclad that no one can poke holes in it. This isn't just about protecting what's yours; it's about laying the groundwork for your financial future. You want to come out of this divorce not just unscathed but ahead. That starts with knowing where every dollar is and where it's going.

Daily Challenge: Today, take a deep dive into your financial web – review all accounts, assets, debts, and even search for hidden assets if needed – because understanding your financial landscape is the first step to securing your financial future after divorce.

Daily Reflection:

What resonated with you from today's lesson? How can you apply this truth in your life?

_____

_____

_____

_____

Day 41: The Legal Pitfalls

Listen, we've talked strategy, finances, emotions, but let's get into the legal landmines that can blow your case sky-high if you're not careful. This is serious business.

First up, violating court orders. Seems obvious, right? But you'd be surprised how many guys think they can bend the rules. Spoiler: You can't. Whether it's asset freezes or custody arrangements, follow the letter of the law. No exceptions.

Second, don't play financial games. Trying to hide assets or fudge the numbers? Bad idea. Courts have zero tolerance for financial shenanigans, and it'll make you look shady. Transparency is your friend; deceit is your enemy.

Third, oversharing on social media. You might think that subtweet or Instagram story is harmless, but it can come back to haunt you. Anything you post is fair game in court. So think before you share. Better yet, go dark for a while.

Fourth, don't let your emotions dictate your actions. Angry texts, confrontations, badmouthing your ex to the kids—these are red flags that can be used against you. Keep your cool at all costs.

Last point, ignoring your lawyer. They're not just a hired gun; they're your strategic advisor. If you're not listening to them, you're shooting yourself in the foot. Take their advice, consult them before making moves, and for the love of God, keep them in the loop.

Legal pitfalls aren't just bumps in the road; they're cliffs you can fall off. Watch your step, follow the rules, and stay focused. This isn't a game; it's your life we're talking about.

Daily Challenge: Today, commit to being a legal eagle - respect court orders, maintain financial transparency, stay off social media, keep your emotions in check, and collaborate closely with your lawyer for a rock-solid case.

Daily Reflection:

What resonated with you from today's lesson? How can you apply this truth in your life?

_____

_____

_____

_____

Day 42: Temporary Orders- Navigate with Caution

Alright, listen up. You're in the middle of this legal maze, and boom—temporary orders come into play. These aren't just placeholders or minor inconveniences; they're indicators of where things could be headed. So let's get smart about this.

First off, these orders are binding. Yeah, they're "temporary," but violate them and you're in hot water. We're talking contempt of court, fines, and a bad look in front of the judge. Do. Not. Screw. This. Up.

Second, they set the stage. Temporary orders often cover child custody, spousal support, and asset division. How these orders go can give you a preview of your final divorce settlement. So if you don't like what you see, it's a red alert to step up your game.

Third, negotiation isn't off the table. These orders aren't handed down from on high; they're often hashed out between lawyers. If something's not sitting right, speak up. This is your life.

Fourth, stay vigilant. Complacency is your enemy. Just because these orders are temporary doesn't mean you can slack off. Keep documenting, keep communicating with your lawyer, and keep your eye on the prize.

Last point, temporary orders can be modified. If circumstances change, you're not stuck with these orders. But—and it's a big but—you better have a good reason and solid evidence to back it up. Temporary orders aren't a side quest; they're part of the main storyline. Navigate them with the caution, strategy, and focus they demand. Your future self will thank you.

Daily Challenge: Today, commit to thoroughly understanding your temporary orders, consult with your lawyer about any concerns, and start building a strategic plan for your divorce journey, keeping your long-term goals in sight.

Daily Reflection:

What resonated with you from today's lesson? How can you apply this truth in your life?

_____

_____

_____

_____

Day 43: The Strategy Session

Listen, when you sit down for that strategy session with your lawyer, you better be ready. This is where the rubber meets the road, where you map out your path through the legal jungle. Don't wing it; come prepared.

First thing: Know your objectives. What's your endgame? Custody? Keeping the house? A fair division of assets? Your lawyer isn't a mind reader; spell it out. The clearer your goals, the sharper your strategy.

Second, bring all the ammo. Documents, emails, financial statements—anything that can fortify your case. If it can be used, it should be on that table. Leave nothing to chance.

Third, ask the hard questions. What are your weak spots? Where can the other side hit you hardest? Identify these vulnerabilities so you can build defenses around them. Ignorance isn't bliss; it's a liability.

Fourth, set the timeline. Divorces can drag on, and you need milestones to measure progress. What should happen by when? Pin it down. Time can be an ally or an enemy; it's up to you.

Last point, be ready for blunt truths. A good lawyer won't sugarcoat. They'll give it to you straight—the good, the bad, and the ugly. Listen up, take notes, and adjust your expectations if needed. The strategy session isn't just a meeting; it's the foundation of your entire legal fight. Approach it with the gravity and preparation it deserves, and you won't just survive this divorce—you'll come out on top.

Daily Challenge: Today, commit to preparing for your strategy session with your lawyer by outlining your objectives, gathering all necessary documents, identifying your weaknesses, setting a clear timeline, and being open to candid advice – ensuring you're ready to navigate the legal journey ahead with confidence and determination.

Daily Reflection:

What resonated with you from today's lesson? How can you apply this truth in your life?

_____

_____

_____

_____

Day 44: Divorce Court Realities

Alright, you're heading to divorce court. Forget what you've seen on TV; this isn't a soap opera. There's no script, no dramatic music, just you, your ex, the lawyers, and the judge. Let's get real about what's going down.

First off, it's not personal; it's procedural. Judges have seen it all, and they're not there to pick sides. They're there to interpret and apply the law. So keep the emotional pleas in check; stick to the facts and the law.

Second, respect the formality. Dress appropriately, address the judge correctly, and for heaven's sake, turn off your phone. You want to show that you take this process seriously, and that starts with basic decorum.

Third, expect delays. Yeah, it sucks, but the legal system moves at its own pace. Court dates get postponed, paperwork gets delayed; it's frustrating but par for the course. Patience isn't just a virtue; it's a necessity.

Fourth, be prepared for curveballs. Witnesses might not show, evidence might get thrown out. The unexpected will happen, so stay adaptable. Your lawyer is there to navigate these bumps, so trust their expertise.

Last point, manage your expectations. You might not get everything you want, but that doesn't mean you've lost. A successful divorce isn't about winning or losing; it's about reaching a fair resolution so you can move on with your life. Divorce court isn't a stage; it's a forum for legal resolution. Know what to expect, stay focused, and remember: this is just one chapter in your life.

Daily Challenge: Approach divorce court with a calm and professional demeanor, focusing on the facts and respecting the process, understanding that it's a step towards a fair resolution and a new chapter in your life.

Daily Reflection:

What resonated with you from today's lesson? How can you apply this truth in your life?

_____

_____

_____

_____

Day 45: Your Legal Team

Listen up, your legal team isn't just a bunch of suits in a conference room. They're the experts you've brought in to navigate this legal maze. You wouldn't enter a boxing ring without a coach, so don't go into a divorce without a strong legal team.

First off, communication is key. You've got to be transparent with your lawyers, but it's a two-way street. They should be keeping you in the loop, updating you on progress, strategy shifts, and any roadblocks. If they're not, demand it.

Second, expertise matters. Family law? Check. Financial acumen? Check. Courtroom experience? Double-check. Make sure your team has a diverse skill set. Specialization is good, but a well-rounded team is better.

Third, availability. Your case isn't the only one they've got, but it should never feel that way. They need to be accessible, responsive, and proactive. If they're dropping the ball, it might be time to reassess.

Fourth, trust but verify. Listen to their advice, but don't follow it blindly. If something feels off or you're not comfortable with a strategy, speak up. It's your life, and you've got the final say.

Last point, it's a partnership. You're not just handing them a case file and walking away; you're actively involved. Ask questions, offer insights, be an active participant. The more engaged you are, the stronger your case will be. Your legal team is your asset, your resource, your weapon. Choose wisely, manage actively, and remember: you're the captain of this ship. Make sure your crew is up to the task.

Daily Challenge: Today, recognize that your legal team is your support system; communicate openly, ensure their expertise, demand availability, trust but verify their advice, and actively engage in your divorce proceedings to steer your ship toward victory.

Daily Reflection:

What resonated with you from today's lesson? How can you apply this truth in your life?

_____

_____

_____

Day 46: The Counter-Attack- When to Hit Back

Listen, divorce can feel like you're constantly on the defensive—dodging accusations, fighting for assets, juggling legalities. But sometimes, the best defense is a good offense. You've got to know when to counter-attack.

First off, don't act out of spite. This isn't about revenge; it's about strategy. You hit back when it serves your objectives, not your ego. Revenge might feel good, but it rarely serves you in the long run.

Second, choose your battles. Not every accusation demands a counter. Some fights aren't worth the time, money, or emotional energy. Consult with your legal team, weigh the pros and cons, and make a calculated decision.

Third, timing is everything. A well-timed counter can disrupt your opponent's strategy and swing momentum in your favor. But timing isn't just about speed; it's about choosing the right moment. Keep your eyes open and your finger on the pulse.

Fourth, be prepared for fallout. Counter-attacks can escalate conflicts and prolong proceedings. Know the risks and be prepared to manage them. Your legal team should help you anticipate potential consequences and plan accordingly.

Last point, always coordinate with your legal team. They'll help you gauge when to strike, how hard, and what to expect in return. Trust their expertise but keep your own strategy in mind. Counter-attacks aren't just about retaliation; they're strategic maneuvers designed to advance your interests. Approach them with caution, but when the time is right, don't hesitate to strike.

Daily Challenge: Today, focus on strategic responses rather than reactive emotions, and remember that the best counter-attacks are those that serve your long-term goals, not your immediate frustrations.

Daily Reflection:

What resonated with you from today's lesson? How can you apply this truth in your life?

_____

_____

_____

_____

Day 47: Protecting Assets

Look, you've worked hard for what you have, and a divorce shouldn't be a financial death sentence. But let's be clear: protecting your assets is a tactical move, not an emotional one. So how do you go about it?

First up, understand what's at stake. Marital assets, separate assets, joint accounts—know what falls under each category. If you're clueless about this, you're walking into a minefield blindfolded. Get educated.

Second, separate what you can, when you can. If there are assets that are unequivocally yours, make sure they're in your name only. The clearer the division, the less room there is for contention.

Third, documentation is your best friend. Receipts, bank statements, property deeds—the more evidence you have proving ownership, the stronger your case. You can't just claim something is yours; you have to prove it.

Fourth, consult financial experts. A divorce lawyer is essential, but they're not financial planners. You might also need an accountant or a financial advisor skilled in divorce cases. This is multi-dimensional warfare; arm yourself accordingly.

Last point, be transparent but firm. Hiding assets is illegal and can backfire spectacularly. But that doesn't mean you should give away the farm. Stand your ground, make your case, and let the law work in your favor. Protecting your assets isn't just about the here and now; it's about safeguarding your future. Approach it with the strategic depth it deserves, and you'll navigate this financial maze like a pro.

Daily Challenge: Today, commit to becoming a financial strategist by taking the first step to protect your assets - educate yourself on the categories of assets, and make a list of what's at stake in your divorce proceedings.

Daily Reflection:

What resonated with you from today's lesson? How can you apply this truth in your life?

_____

_____

_____

Day 48: The Deposition- Master the Interrogation

Listen, a deposition isn't a casual chat; it's a high-stakes conversation where every word you say can be used against you. You've got to walk in there ready, focused, and on-point. So how do you master this interrogation?

First off, know your facts. This isn't the time to get creative with your answers. Stick to the truth and keep it concise. The more you ramble, the more ammo you give the other side. Less is more.

Second, prep with your legal team. Go through potential questions, work on your responses, and get their take on your tone and demeanor. They've done this before; use their experience to your advantage.

Third, stay cool under pressure. You're going to get grilled; they'll try to catch you off guard, rattle you, make you slip up. Don't take the bait. Stay composed, stick to your story, and keep your emotions in check.

Fourth, listen carefully. Don't just hear the question; understand it. If you're unsure what they're asking, seek clarification. A wrong answer based on a misunderstood question is still a wrong answer.

Last point, don't volunteer information. Answer what's asked and nothing more. Offering unsolicited details can open up new lines of questioning that you're not prepared for. Stick to the script. Mastering your deposition is about more than surviving the ordeal; it's about controlling the narrative, guiding the conversation, and protecting your interests. Nail it, and you'll not only strengthen your case but also rattle the opposition.

Daily Challenge: Today, focus on mastering the art of precision in your communication; choose your words carefully and stick to the facts in all your conversations, ensuring you remain in control of the narrative.

Daily Reflection:

What resonated with you from today's lesson? How can you apply this truth in your life?

_____

_____

_____

_____

Day 49: The Settlement- When to Hold, When to Fold

Look, settlements are where most divorces ultimately land, but that doesn't mean you should jump at the first offer. It's a negotiation, not a fire sale. So how do you know when to hold your ground and when to fold?

First off, know your worth. You've got assets, custody considerations, future income—all of it's on the table. Have a clear sense of what each piece is worth to you. If you don't value your own stakes, no one else will.

Second, lean on your legal team. They've been down this road before; they know the strategies, the angles, the tricks. Listen to their advice, but remember, the final decision is yours.

Third, don't let emotions hijack the process. Sure, you're emotionally invested; it's your life we're talking about. But a settlement driven by anger or revenge is a bad settlement, period.

Fourth, consider the long game. Settlements aren't just about immediate gains or losses; they're about setting the stage for your post-divorce life. Think beyond the moment; envision your future.

Last point, be prepared to compromise. A settlement is a two-way street; you won't get everything you want. But focus on the essentials, the deal-breakers. Secure those, and you can flex on the rest.

Deciding when to settle is a blend of strategy, timing, and gut instinct. Get it right, and you walk away with a deal that serves not just present-you, but future-you as well. Get it wrong, and you're living with regret.

Daily Challenge: Today, evaluate your worth in every aspect of your life and be prepared to hold your ground when negotiating, whether it's in your divorce settlement, your career, or your personal relationships.

Daily Reflection:

What resonated with you from today's lesson? How can you apply this truth in your life?

_____

_____

_____

_____

Day 50: The Witness List- Choose Your Allies

Listen up, your witness list is more than just a formality; it's a strategic component of your case. You're assembling a team, but not just any team—a squad with credibility, reliability, and relevance. So how do you pick your all-stars?

First thing: relevance is king. Your best friend might want to help, but if they can't speak to the specifics of your case, they're a benchwarmer. Choose people who can testify on the key issues—custody, finances, character, whatever's crucial.

Second, credibility is a must. We're talking people who can stand up to cross-examination, who have no conflicts of interest, and who can present themselves well. You want your witness to add weight to your case, not sink it.

Third, prep them well. A witness who's caught off guard can do more harm than good. Brief them on potential questions, legal formalities, and the overall process. Make sure they know the game plan.

Fourth, gauge their willingness. Testifying can be nerve-wracking. You want people who are not only willing but eager to stand up for you. Reluctant witnesses can send the wrong message.

Last point, coordinate with your legal team. Your lawyer should have a say in who makes the list. They'll know who can offer the most legal impact and who might be a liability. Your witness list isn't just a list; it's a tactical asset. Choose poorly, and you weaken your case. Choose wisely, and you build a fortress of credibility around your story. The choice is yours, so make it count.

Daily Challenge: Today, identify at least one potential witness who meets the criteria of relevance, credibility, and willingness to support your case, and take the first step towards adding them to your strategic team.

Daily Reflection:

What resonated with you from today's lesson? How can you apply this truth in your life?

_____

_____

_____

_____

Day 51: Legal Loopholes

Hey, you. Yeah, you, staring down the barrel of a legal showdown. Listen up. There's a side door to this fortress, and it's called legal loopholes. No, this isn't cheating; it's playing smarter. It's like knowing a cheat code in a video game but completely legal. Got it? Good.

First, kick down the door of your own ignorance. Yeah, you've got a lawyer, but this is your life getting dissected in a courtroom. Don't just understand the law; dissect it. Make it your second language. Knowing the ins and outs puts you miles ahead, not just of your ex but of everyone else in that courtroom.

Now, about that status quo. Tear it up. If your lawyer says, "This is how it's usually done," ask them, "Why? Who made these rules?" Then break them. Not the laws, the norms. There are always exceptions, hidden clauses, and overlooked regulations that can work in your favor. Find them. Exploit them.

Details? They're not tedious; they're your best friends. One misplaced word, one unchecked box, and you could flip the whole script. So scrutinize every paper like you're deciphering the freaking Da Vinci Code.

Your legal team—don't just hire them and forget them. Engage. Be the annoying client who asks a million questions. Why? Because those questions lead to loopholes, and loopholes lead to wins.

Lastly, keep your hands clean. Loopholes are all about strategy, not deceit. Your win should elevate you, not drag you through the mud. You're not just trying to get out of this intact; you're setting the stage for the next act of your life. And trust me, it's gonna be a heck of a show.

Daily Challenge: Embrace the power of legal loopholes by becoming a strategic expert in your divorce proceedings, understanding the laws, questioning norms, paying attention to details, and working closely with your legal team, all while maintaining your integrity throughout the process.

Daily Reflection:

What resonated with you from today's lesson? How can you apply this truth in your life?

_____

_____

_____

_____

Day 52: Social Media Pitfalls- What Not to Post

Hey, we need to talk about your social media because, believe it or not, it's a warzone. You think it's just photos, status updates, and memes? Think again. Every post you make is a potential bullet—either for you or against you.

First, let's cut the crap. Stop venting about your ex or the legal process. Seriously, stop. Anything you post can and will be used against you. Your social media isn't your therapist; it's a broadcast station sending signals to lawyers, judges, and anyone else who's tuning in.

Now, your photos. That weekend getaway, the nights out with friends—sure, you're living your best life, but guess what? It's all evidence now. Evidence that can be twisted, manipulated, and thrown back at you. So be cautious. Filter your life, not just your photos.

And those DMs? Not as private as you think. Courts can subpoena your messages, and boom— your private chats are now public record. Keep it clean, keep it respectful. If you wouldn't say it in court, don't say it online.

Also, get familiar with your privacy settings. Lock down your profiles, but remember, it's not foolproof. The internet has a long memory and screen captures last forever.

Last up, don't ghost or delete your profiles. Why? Because that looks suspicious. It screams, "I have something to hide." Stay active, but be smart. Super smart. Every post is a chess move, so think five steps ahead.

Daily Challenge: Today, pledge to turn your social media into a fortress of strength and positivity, refraining from sharing any divorce-related frustrations or personal details, and ensuring every post reflects the composed and confident warrior you are becoming.

Daily Reflection:

What resonated with you from today's lesson? How can you apply this truth in your life?

_____

_____

_____

_____

Day 53: Surveillance and Evidence- The Spy Game

Listen up, man. This isn't just about divorce papers and lawyer fees. You're in the espionage ring now. Yeah, you heard right: espionage. You're being watched, documented, analyzed. And if you're not careful, you're screwed.

Firstly, you know that mini-computer you carry around? Your smartphone? It's a snitch. GPS, photos, even those 'harmless' social media rants—they're all ammo that can be used against you. Keep your phone, but make it a silent ally, not a loudmouth traitor.

Here's another thing: Your ex is on the offensive, gathering intel to use against you. So, what are you gonna do? Sit back? No. Turn the tables. Document everything—texts, emails, financial transactions. Build your arsenal, because you're going to need it.

Now, let's get into the dark arts—private investigators. They're real, and they're not your friends. Assume you're being followed and act accordingly. No slip-ups, no stupid moves. Give them nothing but dead ends.

Got a voice? Use it wisely. Record conversations, if the law allows. And remember, it's not just what you say, but how you say it. Tone, context, timing—it all matters. Your voice can be your greatest weapon or your biggest downfall.

Last but not least, your digital footprints. You think incognito mode is your friend? Think again. Your online searches can be your undoing. Be smart, be stealthy, and for God's sake, be aware.

Daily Challenge: Master the art of discretion by keeping your smartphone on your side, documenting everything meticulously, and staying one step ahead in this espionage game called divorce survival.

Daily Reflection:

What resonated with you from today's lesson? How can you apply this truth in your life?

_____

_____

_____

_____

Day 54: Paternity Issues- What You Need to Know

So, you thought this was just about splitting assets and deciding who gets the dog? Welcome to the next level—paternity. This is the unspoken battlefield that can change everything, from custody battles to your financial future. So listen closely; this is crucial.

First things first, uncertainty doesn't cut it. You have doubts about being the father? Get a paternity test. It's not about trust; it's about clarity. Doubts can cripple you, but facts arm you for the battle ahead.

Now, let's talk custody. If you're the biological father, you have rights. Know them. Own them. Don't let anyone tell you that you're just a secondary parent. You're not a visitor in your kid's life; you're a cornerstone. Act like it.

Financial obligations—yeah, they're real, and they're not going away. Child support is a long-term commitment, not a monthly nuisance. Plan for it, budget for it, and whatever you do, don't skip out on it. It's not just about money; it's about integrity.

And here's a curveball for you: What if you're not the biological father but have acted as one? It's called "psychological paternity," and it's a legal grey area. You might still have obligations, so get a lawyer who knows this terrain.

One more thing—communication. You and your ex need to be on the same page about the kids, especially if paternity's in question. No silent treatments, no passive-aggressive texts. Straight talk, even if it hurts.

Daily Challenge: Embrace uncertainty with courage today, taking the necessary steps to confirm or clarify paternity if it's a concern, because clarity empowers you to navigate the challenges ahead with confidence and integrity.

Daily Reflection:

What resonated with you from today's lesson? How can you apply this truth in your life?

_____

_____

_____

_____

Day 55: Trial vs. Mediation- Make the Right Call

You're at a crossroads: trial or mediation. This isn't just a choice; it's a tactical decision that'll shape your divorce outcome. No fluff, let's get into it. Trial? That's the courtroom drama. Every piece of evidence, every character flaw could be scrutinized in front of a judge. High-risk, high-reward. If you've got a strong case, you could come out on top, but if you lose, expect to be hit hard financially and emotionally. Also, a judge decides your fate, not you.

Mediation? That's negotiation in a closed room. No judges, no jury, just a mediator helping you and your ex hash out the details. It's confidential, less formal, and usually quicker. But here's the kicker: You both have to agree on the outcome, which means compromise is the name of the game.

Strategy is key. In a trial, your lawyer is your gladiator, fighting tooth and nail for your interests. In mediation, your lawyer is more like a strategist, advising you when to push and when to pull back.

Money. Trials can suck your finances dry with legal fees and court costs. Mediation is generally cheaper, but don't think it's a bargain bin. You're still paying for a mediator and potentially for a consulting attorney.

And here's something nobody tells you: public record. Trials are public; anyone can look up what happened. Mediation? Private, sealed, between you and your ex. Time for the gut check. What's your endgame? Do you want to fight it out and risk it all, or are you looking for a less volatile path? Your choice, your future.

Daily Challenge: Today, weigh the pros and cons of trial versus mediation, considering the potential risks and rewards, and take a step closer to making a strategic decision that aligns with your ultimate divorce goals.

Daily Reflection:

What resonated with you from today's lesson? How can you apply this truth in your life?

_____

_____

_____

_____

Day 56: Your Day in Court- Showtime Strategies

You've reached the big leagues now—your day in court. This isn't a rehearsal, it's showtime. Screw up here, and you're not getting a do-over. So, what's the plan?

First up, presentation. Yeah, it matters. Dress like you're going to the most important meeting of your life, because you are. This isn't the time for casual Friday. You're selling a narrative, and that narrative starts with how you look.

Now, the judge. This person holds your fate in their hands. Be respectful, be concise, and for heaven's sake, don't interrupt. They've seen a hundred people like you; don't be the one they remember for the wrong reasons.

Evidence—your lifeline. You've collected it, now use it. Chronological order, bullet points, whatever it takes. Make it easy for the judge to follow your story. Your goal is to be so organized that a child could understand your case. Your ex is there too, remember? They'll talk, they'll make accusations, they might even lie. Stay cool. Reacting emotionally won't win you points; it'll make you look unstable. Let your lawyer do the talking when it's high stakes.

Cross-examination isn't just for crime dramas. If you're on the stand, answer what's asked—nothing more, nothing less. Going off script is an amateur move that can backfire spectacularly.

Last but not least, your lawyer isn't just a legal aide; they're your director in this play. Trust their cues, follow their advice. You chose them for a reason. Now let them do their job.

Daily Challenge: Step onto that courtroom stage today with the confidence of a leading actor, presenting your case with unwavering professionalism, respecting the judge, and trusting your lawyer as your director.

Daily Reflection:

What resonated with you from today's lesson? How can you apply this truth in your life?

_____

_____

_____

Day 57: The Verdict- Brace for Impact

Here it is—the verdict. You've been in the trenches, done the hard work, and now Judgment Day has arrived. This is the culmination of everything you've been through, and man, it's heavy. So, how do you brace for impact?

Let's start by managing expectations. Look, you may have fought like a lion, but that doesn't guarantee a win. Courts are unpredictable. Be prepared for any outcome; hope for the best but plan for the worst.

Financial fallout—it's coming. Whether it's alimony, child support, or asset division, your bank account's going to feel it. If the verdict doesn't go your way, don't lose your cool. It's a setback, not a life sentence. Adjust and move forward.

Custody—this one's big. If you have kids, this verdict affects more than just you. Whatever the outcome, remember you're still a dad. Your relationship with your kids isn't defined by a court order. Make the time you have count.

Emotional toll—don't underestimate it. The verdict can feel like a weight lifted or an added burden. Either way, it's emotional. Give yourself permission to feel it, but don't wallow. Emotions are data, not directives.

What about your ex? Look, regardless of the verdict, she's still going to be a part of your life, especially if kids are involved. Keep it civil, keep it respectful. There's life after the verdict; don't make it harder than it has to be.

Daily Challenge: Embrace the Verdict with Resilience and Grace - Regardless of the outcome, maintain your composure, adapt to the financial changes, prioritize your role as a parent, and acknowledge your emotions, all while fostering a respectful relationship with your ex-partner for a brighter future ahead.

Daily Reflection:

What resonated with you from today's lesson? How can you apply this truth in your life?

_____

_____

_____

_____

Day 58: Post-Divorce Legalities

So, the gavel's dropped, the papers are signed, you're officially divorced. End of story? No. Post-divorce legalities are the skirmishes after the main battle. Don't let your guard down.

First up, alimony and child support. You think making the payments is the end? No way. Keep records of every single transaction. If she claims you missed a payment, you need ironclad proof to the contrary.

Let's talk custody agreements. You've got a schedule, stick to it. Late pickups and no-shows? They're not just bad form; they're grounds for revisiting custody arrangements. Don't give her ammo to use against you. And speaking of custody, what about modifications? Life changes— new jobs, relocations, remarriages. These are triggers for renegotiating terms. Always consult your lawyer before making big life shifts.

Property division isn't always clean-cut either. Shared assets like houses and cars don't get divided overnight. If your name's on something, you're still liable. Make sure to legally disentangle yourself from all joint liabilities.

Co-parenting. You're not together anymore, but you're forever linked by your kids. Keep communication channels open, but formal. Stick to email or co-parenting apps where everything's documented. Last but not least, periodic legal check-ins. Laws change, circumstances shift. A yearly consultation with your lawyer can save you headaches down the line. Stay updated, stay protected.

Daily Challenge: Today, commit to maintaining unwavering vigilance in post-divorce legal matters, ensuring meticulous record-keeping, strict adherence to custody agreements, proactive consideration of modifications, and annual legal check-ins to safeguard your future.

Daily Reflection:

What resonated with you from today's lesson? How can you apply this truth in your life?

_____

_____

_____

_____

Day 59: Legal Fees- Minimize the Damage

You thought going through a divorce was just an emotional drain? Well, it's a financial sinkhole too. Legal fees can be a silent killer that takes a machete to your savings if you're not smart. So let's cut through the fog and look at how to minimize the damage.

Let's start with the basics: your lawyer's rate. You think you're just paying for their time in court? Nah. Emails, phone calls, research—every minute gets billed. So when you communicate with your lawyer, be efficient. Bundle your questions, be concise, get to the point.

Next up: disbursements. These are the hidden costs—filing fees, court reporters, and even postage. Ask for an itemized bill and scrutinize every line. If something doesn't add up, question it.

Hiring experts? It's like adding a turbocharger to your legal fees. Forensic accountants, child custody evaluators, you name it. They offer valuable insights but at a steep price. Only go this route if it's absolutely necessary for your case.

And don't forget about retainer fees. That upfront cost is just the starting point. If your case drags on, you'll have to replenish it. Keep an eye on how fast it's depleting so you're not caught off guard.

Negotiate, negotiate, negotiate. Think your lawyer's fees are set in stone? Think again. Many are open to negotiation, especially if you can make a compelling case for why they should lower their rates. It never hurts to ask.

Daily Challenge: Today, be a financial guardian by implementing smart communication with your lawyer, scrutinizing every bill, and negotiating fees where possible to safeguard your finances during this divorce journey.

Daily Reflection:

What resonated with you from today's lesson? How can you apply this truth in your life?

_____

_____

_____

_____

Day 60: The Two-Month Checkpoint

So you've hit the 60-day mark. Congrats. This isn't just another day; it's a checkpoint, a pit stop. You've been running full throttle, but now it's time to assess and recalibrate. You with me? Good, let's get into it.

First off, your emotional state. Let's be real; you've been through the wringer. But being a wreck won't help you make sound decisions. Take a day, a week, whatever you need, to disconnect and recharge. Your mental health isn't a luxury; it's a necessity.

Legal battles—where are you at? If you're bleeding money, it's time to plug the holes. Check in with your lawyer, reassess your strategy. Are you getting the outcomes you need, or is it time for a new game plan? Be ruthless in your assessment.

Financially, do a deep dive. How are your accounts looking? Are you sticking to your budget or are you veering off course? Money's a tool in this battle; don't let it become another front you have to fight on.

Kids, if you have 'em. What's the situation? Are they adjusting or acting out? Their well-being is a crucial metric in assessing your own progress. If they're struggling, it's time to reevaluate your co-parenting tactics. Last but definitely not least, your future. You've been reacting, firefighting. It's time to switch from defense to offense. What are your goals for the next two months? The next six? Lay down some markers and start working toward them.

Daily Challenge: Today, be a financial guardian by implementing smart communication with your lawyer, scrutinizing every bill, and negotiating fees where possible to safeguard your finances during this divorce journey.

Daily Reflection:

What resonated with you from today's lesson? How can you apply this truth in your life?

_____

_____

_____

_____

Master Your Feelings

This section delves deep into post-divorce emotions. We explore riding the emotional rollercoaster, managing anger, sadness, and anxiety. Your emotional toolbox expands with venting, mindfulness, and stress management. Discover your emotional triggers, journal your path, and embrace vulnerability. Set boundaries, build resilience, and find freedom in self-forgiveness. Prepare emotionally for what's next.

Day 61: The Emotional Battlefield

You think this is just about legal battles and financial wreckage? Nah, man, the real front line is in your head. Your emotions are like a field littered with mines, and you better know the terrain if you want to make it through.

Anger? Sure, it's tempting to let it rip, but anger's a wildfire. It burns everything, including you. Use that energy, channel it into something productive. Go to the gym, immerse yourself in work, but don't let it consume you.

Then there's sadness, that heavy cloud that follows you around. Listen, it's okay to grieve; you're losing a part of your life. But don't get stuck in it. Remember, you're the captain of your ship. No one's coming to save you; you've got to do it yourself.

Anxiety, that gnawing in your gut? It's natural, especially with so much up in the air. But here's the deal: fear is a choice. You can let it paralyze you, or you can use it as fuel. Your call.

Don't underestimate loneliness. It's a silent killer, creeping in when you least expect it. But guess what? You're not alone. Reach out to your circle, your family, your bros. Isolation is a choice, and it's a bad one.

And here's the kicker—acceptance. You've got to come to terms with your new reality. No more what-ifs, no more could-haves. This is your life now. Own it.

Daily Challenge: Today, confront and defuse any explosive emotions by redirecting that energy into a positive and productive outlet, taking one step closer to mastering your emotional battlefield.

Daily Reflection:

What resonated with you from today's lesson? How can you apply this truth in your life?

_____

_____

_____

_____

Day 62: Anger- Harness the Fire

Anger. We all feel it, especially during a divorce. It's like a fire raging inside you, consuming everything. But here's the kicker: Anger isn't your enemy; it's a tool. It's all about how you wield it.

So you're pissed. Furious, even. Good. That fire in your belly? It's energy. Don't waste it on pointless revenge or self-destructive behavior. Channel it into rebuilding your empire—your life, your career, your body.

You feel like hitting something? Go to the gym. Turn that anger into physical power. Lift heavier, run faster, punch harder. Make that rage work for you, not against you.

Maybe the anger's more cerebral. You're stewing, plotting, planning. Fine, use that mental energy to strategize. You're in the middle of a legal battle, right? Well, use that anger to focus your mind, to scrutinize every document, every piece of evidence.

Here's a trap to avoid: Don't let that anger turn inward. That's a one-way ticket to self-pity and depression. You're better than that. You're not a victim; you're a warrior. Act like it.

Look, you can't avoid anger, but you can choose how it defines you. Will it be the fire that razes your life to the ground or the fuel that propels you to new heights? The choice is yours.

Daily Challenge: Transform your anger into a powerful force today, using it to fuel your physical and mental growth, rather than letting it consume you.

Daily Reflection:

What resonated with you from today's lesson? How can you apply this truth in your life?

_____

_____

_____

_____

Day 63: Sadness- Don't Drown, Learn to Swim

S o you're swimming in a sea of sadness. It's heavy, it's dark, and it's pulling you under. But guess what? You've got fins, my man, and it's high time you learned how to use them.

First up: Recognize the weight. Yeah, sadness is heavy, like an anchor. But acknowledging it gives you a starting point. It tells you, "Hey, I'm not okay," and that's the first step to getting better.

Now, action. Sadness loves inaction, feeds off it. So break the cycle. Whether it's hitting the gym to pump some iron or diving into a new project, put that sadness to work. Make it your fuel. Convert that heavy emotional energy into something tangible, something real.

Therapy—don't knock it till you try it. This isn't about lying on a couch talking about your feelings. It's about getting tools to navigate your emotional landscape. Think of it as your GPS in this sea of sadness.

Your circle—use it. You've got friends, family, people who care about you. Don't push them away. Open up, be vulnerable. You'd be amazed at how sharing lightens the load.

And lastly, focus outward. Sadness is incredibly self-centered. It wants all your attention. Flip the script. Volunteer, help a friend, do something, anything, that takes the focus off you.

Daily Challenge: Embrace the weight of sadness as a source of strength, taking the first step by recognizing it, and then actively channel it into positive action, seeking therapy, leaning on your support system, and finding purpose beyond yourself to navigate the sea of sadness.

Daily Reflection:

What resonated with you from today's lesson? How can you apply this truth in your life?

_____

_____

_____

_____

Day 64: Emotions Don't Rule You

Listen up. Emotions are powerful. They can inspire art, fuel revolutions, and yes, they can also tear you apart. But here's the game-changer: You're not a puppet on emotional strings; you're the puppet master.

Think about it. Anger, sadness, anxiety—they're all just data points, inputs. You're the processor; you're the one who decides what to do with that information. So stop treating your emotions like they're the CEO of your life. They're not even middle management; they're the interns.

When those emotions surge, take a step back. Take a deep breath, analyze the situation. Ask yourself, "What's this emotion trying to tell me?" Once you understand its message, you can choose your response. Reactivity is the enemy of rationality.

I get it, sometimes it feels like your emotions have gone rogue, acting without your consent. But that's all the more reason to regain control. Establish boundaries. Just like you wouldn't let an intern make major company decisions, don't let your emotions dictate your life's course.

One more thing: accountability. You're responsible for how you act on your emotions, not for feeling them. Feelings are natural; actions are choices. Make sure you're making the right ones.

Daily Challenge: Today, when you encounter a powerful emotion, pause, take a breath, and ask yourself, "What is this emotion trying to tell me?" Then, choose a response that aligns with your goals and values rather than letting your emotions control your actions.

Daily Reflection:

What resonated with you from today's lesson? How can you apply this truth in your life?

_____

_____

_____

_____

Day 65: Emotional Leverage- Use It or Lose It

Look, you're going through the grinder, no doubt. Divorce is emotional hell, but guess what? You've got this untapped superpower and it's called Emotional Leverage. You know what that is? It's taking those raw, gnarly feelings and turning them into jet fuel for your life. No joke.

Feeling like crap? Good. That's your fuel. Angry at the world? Even better. That's the high-octane stuff. I'm talking about harnessing those emotions and channeling them into something that benefits you. Take that anger and hit the gym. Transform that sadness into a business plan. Flip the script. Don't be a passenger in your own life, be the pilot.

You've got all these emotions swirling around, right? You can either let them sink you, or you can use them to soar. That's the choice. There's no in-between. You've got to be the alchemist of your own life, turning emotional lead into gold.

And here's a pro tip for you: document your feelings. Yeah, write them down. Keep a journal, record a voice memo, whatever. Capture how low you feel so you can remind yourself what you're fighting against—or even better, what you're fighting for.

Look, it's easy to play the victim, but it's rewarding to be the victor. Don't let your emotions go to waste. Leverage them. Turn your lows into highs, your pitfalls into launchpads.

Daily Challenge: Embrace your emotional superpower by channeling your feelings into productive action today—use your anger as motivation, your sadness as a catalyst, and document your emotions as a reminder of your strength and resilience.

Daily Reflection:

What resonated with you from today's lesson? How can you apply this truth in your life?

_____

_____

_____

Day 66: The Mindset Shift- From Victim to Victor

Listen, I get it. Life's served you a crap sandwich with a side of misery. But here's the deal: You can either choke on it or say, "No thanks," and make your own meal. You've been the victim long enough; it's high time to be the hero of this story. Your story. I'm not saying you've got to be Mr. Positivity 24/7. No. But you can't stay stuck in this "woe is me" loop. You know why? Because nobody cares. The universe doesn't care. Your ex certainly doesn't care. The only one who should care is you, about getting yourself out of this rut.

Start with your morning. The first hour sets the tone for your whole day. So what's it gonna be? Scrolling through old texts and feeling sorry for yourself? Or getting up and saying, "Today, I'm the one who decides how this goes"?

Next, action. Action beats emotion. You're sad? Do something. You're angry? Do something productive. Channel those emotions into fuel. Turn that fuel into fire. And let that fire light up the path ahead.

Your mindset shift isn't a one-and-done deal. It's a daily grind. It's choosing, every day, to be the victor, not the victim. To be the one who takes life's crap and turns it into gold. And let's talk about accountability. Stop looking for someone to blame. The divorce, the job loss, the failed investments—whatever it is, own it. Because when you own your problems, you own your solutions. Get this: Your mindset isn't just about you. It affects everyone around you—your kids, your family, your colleagues. You're setting an example, whether it's a good one or a bad one. So which will it be?

Daily Challenge: Today, choose to be the hero of your story by taking control of your morning, turning your emotions into fuel for action, and owning your problems as the first step toward a positive mindset shift that not only transforms your life but also sets a powerful example for those around you.

Daily Reflection:

What resonated with you from today's lesson? How can you apply this truth in your life?

_____

_____

_____

_____

Day 67: Anxiety- Face It, Don't Flee

Hey, listen up! Anxiety. We all face it, especially when your life's turning upside down. But let me tell you, running from it? Big mistake. Anxiety's like that schoolyard bully. The more you avoid it, the bigger and scarier it gets.

So what are we gonna do? We're gonna look that monster right in the eyes and say, "Not today." You get me? This is your fight, and it's one you can't afford to lose. You've got dreams, ambitions, goals, right? Well, anxiety is the roadblock standing between you and your best life. And it's time to bulldoze that sucker to the ground.

Let's get tactical. Breathing exercises. You heard me. It's not just some Zen BS. It's neuroscience. When you control your breath, you control your mind. And when you control your mind, you control your life. So start inhaling courage and exhaling fear.

Now, let's talk about the future—your future. Anxiety loves to project, to tell you all the ways things can go wrong. But guess what? You've got the pen. You're writing this story. You don't like the plot? Change it. Anxiety tells you you'll fail? Prove it wrong. And here's another thing. You've got people around you—family, friends. Don't let anxiety trick you into isolating yourself. Open up. Be real. You'd be amazed at how sharing can actually lighten your emotional load.

Remember, anxiety's just a feeling. It can't make decisions for you, can't take action for you, and sure can't live your life for you. It's a challenge, not a life sentence. You're in the driver's seat. So are you gonna pull over and let anxiety hijack your ride, or are you gonna hit the gas and say, "Buckle up, we're burning rubber and there's no looking back"?

Daily Challenge: Embrace your anxiety head-on today, practice breathing exercises, rewrite your future story, and reach out to a friend or loved one for support—show anxiety it won't hold you back from building your best life.

Daily Reflection:

What resonated with you from today's lesson? How can you apply this truth in your life?

_____

_____

_____

_____

Day 68: Emotional Triggers- Identify and Disarm

Alright, folks. Emotional triggers. You've got 'em. I've got 'em. We all do. They're those nasty little landmines planted in your psyche, just waiting for someone or something to step on 'em. And BOOM! Emotional explosion. But guess what? You can be the one who disarms them, not the one who detonates.

First thing's first. Identify those suckers. What is it that sends you off the rails? A text from your ex? Seeing someone else succeed? Whatever it is, you've got to pinpoint it. You can't fix what you don't know is broken. Identify, then scrutinize. Ask yourself, "Why does this get under my skin?" The answer's not always pretty, but it's necessary.

Now, strategy. You know what sets you off, so prepare for it. It's like going into a boxing ring. You wouldn't step in there without knowing your opponent's moves, would you? Same thing with your triggers. Know them so well that you can see them coming from a mile away.

Here's the kicker: reframe those triggers. Yeah, you heard me. Don't just dodge; redirect. Someone says something that usually ticks you off? Take that energy and channel it into your hustle, your grind, your mission. Let it fuel you, not rule you.

And let's cut the drama. No more overreacting. You're not a soap opera star. When you feel that trigger about to go off, pause. Take a breath. Ask yourself, "Is this worth the emotional energy I'm about to spend?" Nine times out of ten, the answer's gonna be a resounding "NO."

Look, you can't control what the world throws at you, but you can control how you react. So, are you gonna let these emotional triggers keep blowing up your life, or are you gonna be the bomb squad that defuses them? Your choice. Make it a good one.

Daily Challenge: Today, identify one of your emotional triggers, scrutinize why it affects you, and create a strategy to reframe and defuse it when it arises.

Daily Reflection:

What resonated with you from today's lesson? How can you apply this truth in your life?

_____

_____

_____

_____

Day 69: Emotional Blackmail- Recognize and Resist

We're diving into something ugly but crucial: Emotional blackmail. That's when someone, maybe your ex, maybe even a family member, tries to manipulate you with guilt, threats, or emotional rollercoasters. It's dirty, it's low, and you've got to be ready to tackle it head-on.

First up, awareness. You need to recognize when this toxic game is being played. Are you making choices because you want to, or because someone's making you feel like you have no other option? Dig deep. This is where self-awareness isn't a luxury; it's a necessity.

Now, boundaries. These are your emotional armor. Know what you stand for, what you won't tolerate, and make it crystal clear. And if someone tries to cross those lines? You've got to be ready to hold your ground, even if it's uncomfortable. Especially if it's uncomfortable. Let's not sugarcoat it; this is a power struggle. Someone's trying to take your autonomy, your decisions, your life, and make them their own. Well, guess what? You're not a doormat. You're not a pushover. You're a fortress, and it's time to raise those walls.

You're also not alone. Get your support network in the loop. People you trust can give you that third-party perspective you're too emotionally invested to see. Listen to them. Sometimes you need that outside voice to validate that yes, you're being manipulated, and no, you're not overreacting.

And here's the clincher: action. You've got your boundaries, you've got your support, now what are you going to do about it? Confrontation isn't fun, but sometimes it's the only way to break those puppet strings and reclaim your life. So, are you going to be someone's emotional pawn, or are you going to be the king of your own emotional chessboard? The move is yours. Make it count.

Daily Challenge: Today, commit to recognizing any instances of emotional blackmail in your life, and take one proactive step to assert your boundaries and regain control over your own emotions and decisions.

Daily Reflection:

What resonated with you from today's lesson? How can you apply this truth in your life?

_____

_____

_____

_____

Day 70: The Sunk Cost Fallacy

Listen up, you've got to grasp this: the Sunk Cost Fallacy. This is the delusion that just because you've poured time, money, or emotion into something, you've got to stick with it. Whether it's a failed marriage, a dead-end job, or a toxic friendship, you think you've got to stay committed. Why? Because you've already 'invested' so much. Well, I'm here to slap you with the truth: That's garbage thinking.

Stop romanticizing the past. What you spent is gone, vanished, sayonara! You're not getting it back, and clinging to it is dragging you down. You wouldn't hold onto a burning coal, would you? So why clutch onto past investments that are scorching your future?

Get this straight: The only thing that matters is where you're going, not where you've been. So shift your focus. You've got resources, whether it's time, money, or energy. Stop wasting them on lost causes and start investing in something that'll actually give you a return. You've got dreams, right? Goals? Ambitions? Well, they're not gonna achieve themselves. You've got to put in the work, the effort, the hustle. And you can't do that if you're shackled to yesterday's mistakes.

Here's your action plan: Make a list of all the things you're holding onto because of 'sunk costs.' Now, one by one, assess their future value. If they're not adding to your life, it's time to cut the cord. No regrets, no looking back.

So, what's it gonna be? You gonna let yesterday's losses dictate tomorrow's choices? Or are you gonna be the smart investor who knows when to fold and when to go all in? Your future's on the line. Make the call.

Daily Challenge: Identify and release the "sunk costs" in your life, whether it's a failed relationship, a dead-end job, or a toxic friendship, and refocus your investments on a brighter future.

Daily Reflection:

What resonated with you from today's lesson? How can you apply this truth in your life?

_____

_____

_____

_____

Day 71: The Emotional Poker Face

Hold on, let's get into it: The Emotional Poker Face. Life's a game, a high-stakes game, and you're at the table. You've got your cards—your feelings, your reactions, your vulnerabilities. How you play them? That's the art of the emotional poker face.

Think about it. When you're negotiating a business deal, or standing in a courtroom, or even navigating complicated relationships, you can't afford to wear your emotions on your sleeve. That's like showing your poker hand; you're giving away your power.

You've got to control your tells, those subtle giveaways that let people know what you're thinking and feeling. I'm talking about that nervous laugh, that eye twitch, even the way you fold your arms. People are watching, and the more they know about your emotional state, the more they can manipulate the game.

Don't get it twisted; I'm not saying become a robot. Emotions are what make us human, what drive us to succeed, to connect, to thrive. But there's a time and a place to show them. And when the stakes are high, when you're in the game, you've got to keep that poker face strong.

So how do you master this? Awareness and practice. Pay attention to your own reactions. The next time you're in a high-stakes situation, be conscious of your facial expressions, your body language, your tone of voice. Keep them neutral. Show no weakness.

Remember, every interaction has a winner and a loser. Do you want to be the sucker who spills his emotional guts on the table? Or do you want to be the poker champ, unreadable, unpredictable, unbeatable? Your life, your game, your call.

Daily Challenge: Today, practice maintaining your emotional poker face in a high-stress situation, and consciously work on minimizing subtle emotional tells to regain control and power in the game of life.

Daily Reflection:

What resonated with you from today's lesson? How can you apply this truth in your life?

_____

_____

_____

Day 72: Emotional Independence

Hold the phone, today we're talking emotional independence. Yeah, you heard that right. Forget financial independence for a second, because without emotional independence, you're just a loaded gun with no aim. You're the dude who thinks he needs someone else—be it a partner, a friend, or a family member—to validate his worth or dictate his mood. That's not just weak; it's handing over the keys to your kingdom.

Let's clarify something: Emotional independence doesn't mean emotional isolation. You don't have to be a lone wolf, but you do need to be the master of your own emotional domain. You should be the one steering the ship through the storm, not relying on someone else to bail out the water.

You want to talk about power? This is it. When you're emotionally independent, no one can push your buttons, because guess what? You've locked the control panel. You're the one deciding how you react to the highs and lows of life.

It's more than just control, though; it's about being complete within yourself. You don't need someone else's praise to feel good. You don't need someone else's criticism to feel bad. You've got your own internal compass, and it points the way, no matter what emotional weather you're facing.

How do you get there? Take stock. Understand what makes you tick, what sets you off, and start digging into why. Once you've got that self-awareness, work on it. Strengthen your emotional muscles like you would your biceps. The more you exercise them, the stronger they get.

Time to make a choice: Are you gonna keep using someone else as your emotional crutch, or are you ready to stand tall, all on your own? Your life, your rules. Make 'em count.

Daily Challenge: Today, practice emotional self-reliance by identifying one emotion-triggering situation and consciously choosing your response, independent of external validation or influence.

Daily Reflection:

What resonated with you from today's lesson? How can you apply this truth in your life?

_____

_____

_____

_____

Day 73: The Power of No- Set Boundaries

Listen, here's the reality check you didn't know you needed: 'No' is the most empowering word in your vocabulary. Seriously, if you're not saying 'No,' you're just handing out free passes to your time, your energy, and your sanity. Think about it. How often do you say 'Yes' when every fiber of your being screams 'No'? Stop that nonsense right now.

No is where you define your space, your boundaries. It's where you tell the world, "This is my turf, and you need a good reason to step onto it." Whether it's refusing to bend over backward for a demanding ex, or turning down a night out because you've got priorities, 'No' is your secret weapon to reclaim your life.

Don't underestimate the value of your time and energy. Every minute you waste doing things you don't want to do is a minute you're not grinding toward your goals. You've got ambitions, right? Well, saying 'No' clears the path. It eliminates the distractions and zeroes in on what truly matters.

And here's the kicker: people will respect you more. Yeah, you'll get pushback initially. You'll get those surprised looks, those raised eyebrows. But guess what? Once the dust settles, people will know not to mess with you. They'll know you're a person who respects himself, and that's a magnet for respect from others.

This is your life, not a dress rehearsal. Every choice you make, every boundary you set, shapes the person you're becoming. So what's it going to be? Are you going to be the doormat everyone wipes their feet on, or are you going to be the gatekeeper of your own destiny?

Daily Challenge: Embrace the power of 'No' today; practice saying it when necessary to establish and protect your boundaries, regain control of your time, and command respect from others.

Daily Reflection:

What resonated with you from today's lesson? How can you apply this truth in your life?

_____

_____

_____

_____

Day 74: Emotional Baggage- Lighten Your Load

You ever tried running with a backpack full of rocks? That's what you're doing if you're lugging around emotional baggage. You've got this collection of past hurts, disappointments, and failures, and you're letting them weigh you down. Let me be clear: that's a self-imposed prison, and it's time for a jailbreak.

Listen, we've all got history; we've all got scars. But if you're letting your past dictate your present, you're giving up control. You're letting yesterday's ghosts haunt today's dreams. What's up with that? You've got the key to free yourself, so why keep the cell locked?

You want to talk about liberation? It starts by examining what you're carrying. Dig into that emotional backpack and pull out those rocks one by one. Look at them, acknowledge them, but don't cling to them. Decide which ones you can toss away. Spoiler: most of them can go.

Now, don't get me wrong; some of these rocks have shaped you, made you stronger, given you wisdom. But they should be milestones, not millstones. You should be able to look back at them as lessons learned, not as burdens that keep you from moving forward.

It's not just about making your journey easier, it's about making it possible. You've got places to go, heights to soar to, and you can't do that if you're grounded by the weight of your past.

So, what's the plan? Are you going to keep dragging that baggage, making every step a struggle? Or are you ready to lighten the load and sprint toward your future? The choice is yours. Make it a good one.

Daily Challenge: Take a moment today to identify and release one emotional "rock" from your past that's been weighing you down, and envision yourself walking lighter towards your future.

Daily Reflection:

What resonated with you from today's lesson? How can you apply this truth in your life?

_____

_____

_____

_____

Day 75: Grief- The Five Stages, No Shortcuts

Alright, let's get real for a second: grief is the emotional tax you pay for the privilege of love, investment, or even just caring. When something meaningful ends—whether it's a relationship or a chapter in your life—you've got to go through it. And I'm talking about the five stages: denial, anger, bargaining, depression, and acceptance. No shortcuts, no cheat codes.

Here's the deal: you can't sidestep grief. You might think you're tough enough to skip a stage or two, but you're fooling yourself. These stages are like the levels in a game; you've got to clear each one to advance. You can't just jump from denial to acceptance and think you're good. It doesn't work like that.

Denial, it's that numbness, that shock. You've got to feel it, acknowledge it, and then punch through. Anger? Don't suppress it; channel it. Make it fuel for transformation. Bargaining is where you'll try to make deals with yourself, with fate, even with your ex. Spoiler alert: it's a waste of time. Move on. Depression isn't a sign of weakness; it's a sign of being human. Feel it, but don't let it consume you. And then, finally, you reach acceptance—the point where you can look back without being pulled back.

Let me tell you, each stage is a battle, and you've got to arm yourself with awareness, resilience, and a no-bull attitude. It's tough, it's brutal, but it's also necessary. You can't rebuild on a shaky foundation, and that means dealing with your grief, not sidestepping it.

So, what's it gonna be? Are you gonna let grief hold you hostage, or are you gonna go through it to get to the other side, where life is waiting? Your move, champ.

Daily Challenge: Embrace the discomfort, confront your grief head-on, and commit to navigating each of the five stages with courage and resilience, knowing that this emotional journey is a crucial step towards your healing and growth.

Daily Reflection:

What resonated with you from today's lesson? How can you apply this truth in your life?

_____

_____

_____

_____

Day 76: Regret and Guilt

Let's dive in, no holding back: Regret and guilt. Man, if these two emotions were commodities, we'd all be billionaires, right? But here's the raw truth—these feelings are the ultimate dead weight. They're like anchors that keep you stuck in the past, unable to sail into the future. Unless—big unless—you use them to learn and grow.

See, regret and guilt aren't just feelings; they're messages. They're your psyche's way of saying, "Hey, you messed up. Don't do it again." But here's where people trip up: They hear the message, but they don't take action. Instead, they wallow in these emotions like they're some kind of penance. Stop that. Now.

You messed up. Fine. Guess what? We all do. The question is, what are you going to do about it? Are you going to let regret and guilt define you? If that's your choice, congrats, you've just turned these emotions into a life sentence. But if you use them to change your actions, to become a better version of yourself, then you've just turned liabilities into assets.

This is more than just self-improvement; this is emotional alchemy. You're turning base emotions into gold, into life lessons that make you stronger, wiser, and more resilient. But to do that, you've got to be willing to listen, to reflect, and most importantly, to act. No half-measures, no excuses.

So, make the choice. Are you going to be weighed down by regret and guilt, or are you going to use them as stepping stones to a better you? This is your life. Don't let yesterday's mistakes rob you of tomorrow's opportunities.

Daily Challenge: Embrace the discomfort, confront your grief head-on, and commit to navigating each of the five stages with courage and resilience, knowing that this emotional journey is a crucial step towards your healing and growth.

Daily Reflection:

What resonated with you from today's lesson? How can you apply this truth in your life?

_____

_____

_____

_____

Day 77: Cognitive Biases- Don't Fool Yourself

Here's the lowdown: your brain is an incredible machine, but it's not infallible. It's susceptible to glitches, known as cognitive biases, that can seriously mess with your perception and decision-making. Ever wonder why you make some dumb choices even when you know better? Chances are, a cognitive bias is pulling your strings.

Let's talk confirmation bias, for starters. You hear what you want to hear and ignore the rest, cherry-picking information to validate your pre-existing beliefs. Dangerous game, my friend. You're essentially putting on blinders, and that's no way to navigate the complexities of life, especially post-divorce.

And how about that sunk cost fallacy? You know, when you continue down a crappy path just because you've invested time, money, or emotion into it? Cut your losses. Staying in a bad situation doesn't turn it into a good one; it just makes you a glutton for punishment.

Don't even get me started on the halo effect, where you give someone a pass on their flaws just because they excel in one area. Listen, just because she's stunning or captivating doesn't mean she's good for your life. Don't let one shining quality blind you to the rest of the picture.

Here's the antidote to cognitive biases: brutal self-awareness. You've got to catch yourself in the act of these mental shortcuts and challenge them. Question your thoughts, question your emotions, and for the love of everything, question your actions.

So, are you ready to stop letting these biases run your life? Are you willing to do the work, to call yourself out, to change the patterns? Because if you are, you've just leveled up in the game of life.

Daily Challenge: Embrace brutal self-awareness today; catch and challenge any cognitive biases that try to influence your perception and decisions and take control of your life's direction post-divorce.

Daily Reflection:

What resonated with you from today's lesson? How can you apply this truth in your life?

_____

_____

_____

_____

Day 78: Breaking the Lust Loop

Hey you, yeah, YOU! You ever felt that uncontrollable pull, that fire that takes over your mind, making you weak? That's called lust, and it's a game-killer. Today, I'm gonna give you the keys to break free from its grasp.

Recognize The Look Vs. Lust: We're human; we notice things. But there's a line between a quick glance and full-on obsession. Rule of thumb? 3 seconds. Look, appreciate, and then move on. Eyes Up, Champ: When talking to someone, keep your focus on their eyes. If you're gonna look away, go left or right – not down. It's respect, and it keeps you in check.

Stay Aware: Be real with yourself. Notice when those urges are creeping up. And when they do? Redirect that energy. Feel the lust? Instead, take a walk, belt out a song, or even hit the floor for some push-ups. Your mind and body will thank you. Spot Those Triggers: Know what lights up that lust-fire in you? Pinpoint it. Maybe it's social media, certain places, or people. Identify and break those patterns. Give your brain a break from that dopamine hit.

Stand Tall with Discipline: You want to be a force to be reckoned with? Be a man of integrity. Don't put yourself in questionable spots. Keep yourself accountable. It's on you to set the stage for success. Invest That Energy Right: Got someone special? Pour all that fiery energy into them. Amp up your date nights, shower them with genuine compliments. Rebuild and fortify the relationship. Elevate it, and elevate yourself. In short, stop letting lust run the show. Elevate your game, your respect, and your integrity. And remember, YOU got this..

Daily Challenge: Today, practice the three-second rule when you notice an attractive person, and remember to look, appreciate, and then move on to maintain control over your thoughts and actions.

Daily Reflection:

What resonated with you from today's lesson? How can you apply this truth in your life?

_____

_____

_____

_____

Day 79: The Emotional Audit

Alright, listen up. If you've ever run a business or managed your finances, you know the value of an audit. You scrutinize every asset, every liability, to understand exactly where you stand. Well, guess what? Your emotional life needs the same rigorous assessment. It's time for an emotional audit.

Let's kick it off with your emotional assets. These are your strengths, the positive influences in your life, the things that make you feel good and push you forward. Could be your resilience, your humor, your tight-knit circle of friends—whatever adds value to your life.

Now, on to the liabilities. These are the emotional debts dragging you down. Negative self-talk? That's a liability. Toxic relationships? Huge liability. Self-doubt, fear, procrastination? All liabilities. And just like in finance, the goal is to minimize these while maximizing your assets.

Here's where it gets real: the action plan. An audit's worthless if you don't act on the insights. So, take those emotional assets and leverage them. You're resilient? Fantastic, use that to face new challenges. You've got a supportive circle? Lean on them when you need to, and be there for them in return. As for the liabilities, start settling those debts. Cut off or limit toxic relationships. Challenge negative self-talk. Turn your liabilities into lessons that can transition into assets.

You want to talk about growth? This is where it starts. By understanding your emotional balance sheet, you can make targeted, effective changes. This isn't just maintenance; this is an overhaul, an upgrade, a transformation. So, are you ready to do the work? Because now's the time. Do the audit, make the plan, execute relentlessly. Your emotional wealth is waiting to be tapped.

Daily Challenge: Conduct an emotional audit today, taking stock of your emotional assets and liabilities, and commit to leveraging your strengths while actively addressing and minimizing your emotional debts to boost your emotional well-being.

Daily Reflection:

What resonated with you from today's lesson? How can you apply this truth in your life?

_____

_____

_____

_____

Day 80: The Blame Game- Quit Playing

Here's the straight talk: blame is the emotional junk food of life's hardships. It feels good for a moment, gives you that quick hit of self-righteousness, but long-term? It's a disaster for your emotional health. You keep blaming your ex, the lawyer, the system, even the weather, and what do you get? Zero progress.

Listen, I get it. Things went sideways, and it's easier to point fingers than to look inward. But every time you blame, you're handing over your power, your agency, to someone or something else. You're saying, "I'm not in control; they are." That's nonsense.

You want to reclaim your life? Then reclaim responsibility for it. No, that doesn't mean flagellating yourself over what went wrong. It means acknowledging your part in it—no more, no less—and learning from it. Look, you can spend your days gathering evidence for your blame case, stoking that fire of indignation. But while you're playing detective and judge, your life's ticking away, opportunities are passing you by, and guess what? You're still stuck in the same emotional rut.

This isn't a call to be a martyr or a saint. This is a call to be the CEO of your own life. A CEO doesn't waste time blaming the market or the competition. They adapt, they strategize, and they move forward. Blame has no place in that boardroom, and it shouldn't have any place in your life either. So, are you done playing a losing game? Are you ready to stop blaming and start owning your journey? The clock's ticking, and the only thing you stand to lose is wasted time and unrealized potential.

Daily Challenge: Today, commit to catching yourself every time you're about to blame someone or something, and instead, focus on one action you can take to move forward and regain control of your life.

Daily Reflection:

What resonated with you from today's lesson? How can you apply this truth in your life?

_____

_____

_____

_____

Day 81: Emotional Stamina- Build Your Resilience

Alright, we're diving deep today. You know physical stamina, right? You hit the gym, you run, you lift, all to make your body stronger, more resilient. Well, what are you doing for your emotional stamina? Yeah, you heard me. Emotional stamina is as real as physical, and buddy, it's time to hit that emotional gym.

First up, emotional weights. These are the challenges, the setbacks, the curveballs life throws at you. You can either let them crush you, or you can lift them, grow stronger. Divorce is a heavy weight, no doubt. But guess what? You can lift it, and when you do, you're going to be a powerhouse.

Now, emotional cardio. This is all about how you handle stress, anxiety, and pressure. It's mental pacing. When you're in the middle of a crisis, do you sprint emotionally, burn out, and crash? Or do you maintain a steady pace, managing your emotions as you navigate the hurdles? Don't forget flexibility—emotional flexibility. Life's not a straight line; it's a maze of twists and turns. Your ability to adapt, to bend without breaking, is key. Flexibility lets you face new situations without snapping. It's not about avoiding stress; it's about bending and bouncing back.

Nutrition? Yeah, there's emotional nutrition. Feed your mind and soul with positive experiences, with people who lift you up, with activities that bring you joy. Stop consuming the junk food of negative thoughts and toxic people. That's an emotional diet right there.

So, how do you build emotional stamina? By committing, by showing up at that emotional gym every single day. It's in the choices you make, the reactions you have, and the mindset you cultivate. No shortcuts, no cheat days. You in?

Daily Challenge: Today, consciously choose to lift and embrace a challenging emotion or setback, knowing that with each emotional weight you lift, you become emotionally stronger and more resilient in your divorce survival journey.

Daily Reflection:

What resonated with you from today's lesson? How can you apply this truth in your life?

_____

_____

_____

_____

Day 82: Emotional Outlets- Find Healthy Ones

You've got this pressure building up inside you, right? It's like you're this soda can that's been shaken too hard. Now, you can either let it explode and make a mess or you can release the pressure in a controlled, constructive way. That's what emotional outlets are for, and if you're not using them, you're setting yourself up for disaster.

Let's get into it. Sports, man. Whatever gets you moving, whether it's lifting weights, shooting hoops, or even yoga for the peace seekers among us. Physical activity is a miracle worker for stress. It's not just about getting fit; it's about getting your head right.

But maybe you're thinking, "I'm not the sporty type." Fine, how about picking up a guitar or scribbling your thoughts in a journal? Creative outlets let you channel those swirling emotions into something tangible, something that says, "I exist, and I matter." Don't discount the simple power of conversation either. And I'm not talking about the small talk BS; I mean real, soul-baring talks with people you trust. If you think you're an island, you're kidding yourself. Connection is part of the human experience. Embrace it.

Alright, hold up. Maybe you're thinking, "I don't have time for this." Listen, you don't have time NOT to have emotional outlets. They're your sanity, your balance, your ticket to getting through this storm without losing yourself. This is non-negotiable.

So, find those outlets. Experiment. Maybe it's a mix of pumping iron and painting landscapes, or maybe it's kickboxing and karaoke. Whatever it is, make it yours and make it regular. No excuses. You've got one life, and bottling up your emotions is not how you want to live it. Your outlets are your lifelines. Grab them.

Daily Challenge: Embrace your emotional outlet today, whether it's hitting the gym, picking up a musical instrument, journaling, or having a heart-to-heart conversation with a trusted friend— release the pressure constructively and prioritize your emotional well-being.

Daily Reflection:

What resonated with you from today's lesson? How can you apply this truth in your life?

_____

_____

_____

_____

Day 83: Self-Doubt- The Enemy Within

Alright, listen up, because we're diving into the murky waters of self-doubt today. It's that nagging voice in your head that loves to second-guess every move you make. "Am I doing this right? What if I fail? What if she was the best I could do?" Stop. Just stop. Self-doubt is not your friend; it's your internal saboteur, and it's time to kick it to the curb.

First, recognize that self-doubt is not humility or a reality check. It's a toxic mindset that cripples your potential. Every time you listen to it, you're putting shackles on your own progress. It's like stepping on your own foot while trying to sprint. Ridiculous, right?

Now, how do you combat this? With evidence. Your self-doubt says you'll fail? Prove it wrong. Take small steps, rack up small wins, and build your case against this inner critic. You got through a nasty divorce, didn't you? You're stronger than you give yourself credit for.

Next, let's talk about your circle. If you're surrounded by naysayers and critics, guess what? You're in an echo chamber for your self-doubt. You need people who believe in you, who challenge you, and yes, who call you out when you're genuinely wrong, not just when you think you are.

But here's the real kicker: self-doubt thrives on indecision. The more you waffle, the more it grows. You kill self-doubt by taking action, even if it's imperfect. Even a wrong move is better than standing still because you learn from it.

So, make today the day you start evicting that internal saboteur. Tear up its lease and throw it out of the apartment of your mind. This is your space, your life, and there's no room for self-doubt in it. Are you ready to declare war on this enemy within? Because the battleground is your mind, and the stakes are your dreams, your future, your very sense of self. Time to armor up.

Daily Challenge: Today, confront your self-doubt head-on by taking one concrete action that pushes you out of your comfort zone, proving to yourself that you are capable and resilient.

Daily Reflection:

What resonated with you from today's lesson? How can you apply this truth in your life?

_____

_____

_____

_____

Day 84: The Emotional Cleanse- Flush Out the Toxins

Y ou ever do a juice cleanse? You know, to flush out all the toxins and get your body back in gear? Well, guess what, your emotional system needs the same kind of detox. We're talking a full-on emotional cleanse, and trust me, it's way overdue.

First off, let's talk about those toxic thoughts you've been entertaining. Stop babysitting them like they're precious jewels. They're not. They're garbage. Thoughts like, "I'll never be good enough," or "I'm damaged goods," need to go. Today. Not tomorrow, not next week, now.

And what about those toxic people you've been hanging onto? You know exactly who I'm talking about. Friends who aren't really friends, family who bring you down more than they lift you up. Time to cut the cord. Emotional leeches have no place in your life.

Don't even get me started on grudges. You holding onto past slights and betrayals? What's that doing for you, except weighing you down? Dump them. They're just emotional clutter, and you need space for new, constructive emotions. Now, let's get practical. How about an emotional inventory? Sit down, write out what's bothering you, what's serving you, and what's just taking up space. Once it's on paper, it's easier to tackle. You see it for what it is, and you can start taking action.

So, are you ready for this cleanse or what? This is not a drill; it's an emotional overhaul. It's you, grabbing a metaphorical plunger and unclogging the emotional drains that have been slowing you down. You want to move forward? Then you've got to lighten the load, flush out the toxins, and make room for the good stuff. Get on it. Your emotional health isn't going to fix itself. You've got the tools; now do the work. No more procrastinating. Your future self will thank you.

Daily Challenge: Today, identify one toxic thought or belief that's been holding you back, and replace it with a positive affirmation that empowers you to move forward.

Daily Reflection:

What resonated with you from today's lesson? How can you apply this truth in your life?

_____

_____

_____

_____

Day 85: Loneliness- The Double-Edged Sword

Listen, loneliness is a double-edged sword. On one side, it's this soul-crushing void that can eat you alive if you let it. On the other, it's this incredible space where you can discover who you really are, unfiltered, unjudged. The key? You get to choose which edge you're on. Let's kick it off with the downside. Loneliness can make you desperate, make you settle for less than you deserve. It can lead you into the arms of the wrong people, into bad decisions, and, worst of all, into a mindset where you think this is all you're worth. Spoiler alert: You're worth more. A lot more.

But here's the flip side. Loneliness is also where you find your grit, your backbone, your authenticity. It's your personal lab for self-discovery. You get to experiment, screw up, and learn, all without an audience. You get to build yourself from the ground up. How do you make sure you're on the right edge of this sword? First, embrace the solitude. This is your chance to dig deep, to confront the real you without the noise and distractions. Read the books that challenge you, do the workouts that break you, take on the projects that scare you. This is your training ground.

Next, don't be scared to seek help. There's zero shame in it. Whether it's professional counseling, talking to trusted friends, or diving into communities of like-minded individuals, external perspectives can be game-changers. They give you a mirror to see yourself clearly.

Bottom line, you're going to face loneliness, especially in a journey like this. It's inevitable. But whether it becomes your prison or your playground, that's all on you. So, what's it going to be? Are you going to let loneliness define you, or are you going to define your loneliness? The clock's ticking, and only you can decide.

Daily Challenge: Embrace solitude today as your opportunity for self-discovery and growth, and seek at least one external perspective or support system to help you navigate the journey through loneliness.

Daily Reflection:

What resonated with you from today's lesson? How can you apply this truth in your life?

_____

_____

_____

_____

Day 86: Nostalgia- The Past Is a Trap

Alright, listen up, because we're tackling one of the most seductive emotional traps out there: nostalgia. You know what I'm talking about. It's that warm, fuzzy feeling you get when you start reminiscing about "the good old days," how things used to be, how you and your ex used to laugh and love. Hold on, pump the brakes. Nostalgia is a liar, a good one, and it's high time you called it out.

First, let's get one thing straight: the past wasn't perfect. Your brain has this sneaky way of filtering out the bad stuff and shining a spotlight on the good. It's like Instagram for your memories, all filters and no flaws. Don't buy into it. Remember, you're divorced for a reason, and it wasn't because things were fantastic.

Second, nostalgia can paralyze you. It can keep you stuck, staring in the rearview mirror while your life's passing by. You start comparing every new experience, every new person to this idealized past, and guess what? They'll never measure up because nostalgia set an impossible standard.

But here's the kicker: you can weaponize nostalgia. Use it as a benchmark, not for what was, but for what could be. If you were happy once, you can be happy again, probably even happier. But it's on you to create new moments, new memories that'll make the old ones look like rough drafts. So next time nostalgia comes knocking, don't let it in for a long visit. Acknowledge it, learn from it, but then show it the door.

Are you ready to stop letting your past hog the spotlight? Good, because your present is happening right now, and it's demanding your attention. Your future? It's still unwritten, and it's begging you to make it epic.

Daily Challenge: Today, when nostalgia comes knocking, remind yourself that your best days are still ahead, and take one concrete step toward creating new, memorable moments in your life.

Daily Reflection:

What resonated with you from today's lesson? How can you apply this truth in your life?

_____

_____

_____

_____

Day 87: Emotional Tactics in Legal Battles

Here's the thing: you're not just in a legal battle, you're in an emotional war zone. Trust me, it's easy to get swept up in the drama, especially when the stakes are high. But listen, if you let your emotions hijack your legal strategy, you're setting yourself up for failure. Judges, lawyers, they're trained to see through the smokescreen. They don't have time for emotional theatrics; they want facts, evidence, and a clear strategy.

Now, let's flip the coin. Brace yourself because you're not the only one with emotions in the game. Your ex is playing, too. And they might use every tactic in the book to get under your skin. It could be guilt-tripping, manipulation, or even flat-out lies. See it coming. Don't engage. Let them show their cards while you keep yours close to your chest. Your secret weapon? Emotional intelligence. You've got to be the chess player, not the pawn. Understand what makes the judge tick, decode your lawyer's strategy, and for goodness sake, don't let your ex push your buttons.

You also need a fortress, emotionally speaking. Outside that courtroom, you need a rock-solid support system that keeps you grounded. Could be your friends, your family, or even a mental health pro. Don't underestimate the power of a good support system. It's like having a pit crew in a grueling race. They help you recalibrate, refuel, and get back out there to win this thing.

So here's your takeaway: Master your emotions, and you'll master the courtroom. You'll not only come out of this battle wiser but also stronger, emotionally and mentally. Now, are you ready to step up your game? Because this isn't a scrimmage; it's the playoffs, and it's your life that's on the scoreboard.

Daily Challenge: Stay emotionally resilient today by focusing on facts, evidence, and a clear legal strategy, while maintaining your emotional intelligence, and leaning on your support system when needed to keep your cool in the midst of the emotional war zone.

Daily Reflection:

What resonated with you from today's lesson? How can you apply this truth in your life?

_____

_____

_____

_____

Day 88: Emotional Milestone- Measure Your Growth

Listen, you're at a pivotal point—Day 88. Let's not glaze over this. Eighty-eight days of emotional rollercoasters, legal battles, and a relentless fight for your future. But today isn't about survival; it's about measuring how far you've come. Because if you're not tracking your growth, how do you know you're not running in circles?

Here's the deal: pain, struggle, heartbreak—they're your teachers, not your jailers. You've been schooled in the hardest life lessons, and it's time to take your emotional inventory. Are you still the same person who started this journey You should be smarter, stronger, and more resilient. And if you're not, it's time for a gut check. Ask yourself, 'Why not? What's holding me back?'

Don't fall into the trap of using your past as a crutch or an excuse. Your past is a launching pad, not a life sentence. So how do you measure your growth? Start by looking at your reactions. Are you still fuming over the same issues, or have you learned to pick your battles? Are you still wallowing in self-pity, or have you built emotional resilience?

Next, your relationships. Have you surrounded yourself with people who elevate you, or are you still clinging to emotional vampires because you're afraid of loneliness? Quality over quantity—always. You want a circle that lifts you up, not one that sinks you further.

And let's talk about your goals. Not just financial or legal goals, but emotional goals. Have you set them? Are you tracking them? Because if you're not, you're like a ship without a compass, aimlessly floating. So, today is your milestone, your checkpoint. Are you ready to level up? Because the world doesn't wait, and neither should you.

Daily Challenge: Take a moment to reflect on how far you've come in your divorce journey, and identify one concrete step you can take today to continue your personal growth and progress towards a brighter future.

Daily Reflection:

What resonated with you from today's lesson? How can you apply this truth in your life?

_____

_____

_____

_____

Day 89: Emotional Future-proofing

Look, you've made it to Day 89. You're not here to play small ball. You're here to build a freakin' empire, emotionally speaking. You've got to be the Elon Musk of your emotional world, constantly innovating, always five steps ahead. You think you've been through the wringer? Good. That's your training ground. Now, what's next? Emotional future-proofing isn't about waiting for the next disaster; it's about being so rock solid that when disaster strikes, it bounces off you like you're made of Teflon.

We're talking emotional agility, my friend. Life's gonna zig, you've got to zag. When the unexpected happens—new job, new relationship, heck, even a global pandemic—you need to maneuver like an F1 driver. No crash and burn, only sharp turns and acceleration.

But hold on, this isn't just about defense; it's about offense. You've got to have goals so audacious they make your old self look like a sloth. And I'm not talking just career and money; I mean emotional milestones. How do you want to feel next week, next month, next year? Paint that picture, then reverse engineer the crap out of it.

Don't get complacent. You know what complacency is? It's the quicksand of progress. It'll suck you in and leave you stuck in mediocrity. Keep pushing the envelope. New challenges, new adventures, new emotional highs and lows. Keep yourself in a state of emotional evolution.

You're the architect of your life, and blueprints are ongoing drafts; they're never final. So, keep drawing, keep planning, keep building. If you're not growing, you're dying. And you're not here to die; you're here to dominate. Are you ready to future-proof your emotional state? 'Cause if you're not, you might as well go home. But if you are, then buckle up. We're just getting started.

Daily Challenge: Today, set audacious emotional goals that challenge your old self, and take one concrete step toward making them a reality, because you're not here to play small ball; you're here to build an emotional empire.

Daily Reflection:

What resonated with you from today's lesson? How can you apply this truth in your life?

_____

_____

_____

Day 90: The Quarter-Year Mark

Ninety days in, and if you're not feeling the heat, you're not in the kitchen. This is the quarter-year mark, folks. You've had three months to sit in your feelings, get mad, get sad, get whatever. But now? Now it's time to level up. No more kiddie pool; we're diving into the deep end.

Here's the hard truth: life's not stopping for your sob story. You're either moving forward, or you're getting left behind. You want to be the guy who got divorced and never recovered? Didn't think so. You're here to be the comeback king, the guy who took life's hardest punches and came back swinging.

So let's talk strategy. You've had three months to figure out your emotions, to get a handle on the legal stuff. Now, what are you doing to make the next three months count? Are you leveling up your skills? Are you expanding your network? Are you crushing it at work? If not, why not?

This is the moment to set new targets. And I don't mean weak goals like "get by" or "feel better." Nah, you're aiming for the stars. You want that promotion? Go get it. You want to date again? Make yourself irresistible. You want peace of mind? Build your emotional fortress.

You need to be so good, so on top of your game, that your ex looks at you and thinks, "What did I give up on?" But don't do it for them, do it for you. This is your life, your journey, your story to write. And trust me, nobody's going to write it for you.

So, get out of your comfort zone. Stretch your limits. Challenge your beliefs. The next 90 days should make the last 90 look like a warm-up. You've got the playbook, you've got the strategies. Now, what are you gonna do about it?

Daily Challenge: Embrace discomfort as your pathway to growth, setting audacious goals and pushing your boundaries to make the next 90 days your most transformative chapter yet.

Daily Reflection:

What resonated with you from today's lesson? How can you apply this truth in your life?

_____

_____

_____

_____

Kids and Assets

Explore the world of co-parenting with this comprehensive guide. From the first conversation with your kids to shared custody, property, and possessions, we've got you covered. Discover the true meaning of child support, navigate school meetings solo, and tackle extended family and shared friends.

Learn how to set ground rules, prioritize your child's well-being, and handle relocations. We address blended families, changes in your child's behavior, and co-parenting apps. Find tips for holiday seasons, managing conflicts, and introducing new partners to your kids.

We'll discuss shared debt, your child's records, revisiting legal documents, and dealing with your ex's new partner. Plus, maintain boundaries with in-laws and decide what stays in the family portrait.

Day 91: Co-Parenting 101- It's Not About You

Alright, listen up! Co-parenting 101: The first thing you've gotta grasp, it's not about you anymore. Nope. It's about the little humans you're responsible for. That ego of yours? Time to check it at the door. You may despise your ex, and guess what? That's fine, but when it comes to your kids, you've gotta get your act together. You think they don't notice the tension? The hostility? Kids are like emotional sponges, soaking up the atmosphere. And you don't want to poison their minds and future relationships with your unresolved issues.

Let's talk strategy. Communication: Keep it open, keep it clean. You don't have to like each other, but you've got to communicate for the sake of your kids. Get a shared calendar, plan out holidays, medical appointments, and activities. No surprises, no excuses.

Boundaries, man. Set 'em and respect 'em. Your ex's time with the kids is theirs, not a window for you to interfere or spy. It's also not your platform to play the 'Cool Parent' and undermine your ex. Your kids need structure, not parents competing in a popularity contest.

Flexibility. Things change. Jobs, schools, even the weather. Be prepared to adapt and adjust your co-parenting plans. Rigidity is your enemy here; you've got to be fluid without losing sight of what's best for your kids.

Accountability. You screw up? Own it. Apologize and move on. No blame games, no excuses. You're teaching your kids accountability through your actions. Make it count.

Final words: Co-parenting isn't a sprint; it's a lifelong marathon. So gear up, because the road is long, and it's not about you anymore. It's about equipping your kids to navigate this messy, beautiful thing called life.

Daily Challenge: Today, practice letting go of your ego and focusing solely on what's best for your children in your co-parenting journey, even when it's challenging.

Daily Reflection:

What resonated with you from today's lesson? How can you apply this truth in your life?

_____

_____

_____

_____

Day 92: Asset Division- Don't Get Played

Alright, listen closely. Asset division—this is the arena where fortunes are made or shattered, and I'm not just talking about cash. So, put on your game face, 'cause we're about to get real.

First off, know your assets like the back of your hand. This isn't just about your house or your car. It's about stocks, businesses, even intellectual property. If you don't know what you've got, how can you protect it? Get yourself a financial advisor, and fast.

Rule number two: Legal representation. Don't even think about going in without a sharp lawyer. This isn't a do-it-yourself situation. Your future's on the line, so invest in someone who knows how to navigate the complexities of asset division.

Now, let's talk strategy. It's easy to get sentimental—wanting to hold onto the house because of memories or whatever. Stop it. This is chess, not a Nicholas Sparks novel. Every move counts, so think long-term value, not short-term emotion.

Negotiation is your best friend and worst enemy. You've got to know when to push and when to back off. But remember, never show your full hand. Keep your priorities secret until it's time to lay down your cards. Documentation, my friend. If it's not on paper, it doesn't exist. Keep records of everything—every transaction, every agreement, every single paper that could tip the scale in your favor. Don't slack off on this; it's your armor.

Last point: tax implications. Yeah, you might get the house, but what about the property taxes? You may win the battle but lose the war if you're saddled with heavy financial burdens later. Keep the long game in mind.

Daily Challenge: Take charge of your financial future by familiarizing yourself with your assets, seeking professional advice, and making strategic decisions during the divorce process.

Daily Reflection:

What resonated with you from today's lesson? How can you apply this truth in your life?

_____

_____

_____

_____

Day 93: The Kids Are Watching- Be a Role Model

Alright, time for some tough love. Today, we're talking about the little eyes that are watching you go through this whole mess: your kids. They're absorbing everything, like sponges, even when you think they're not paying attention. So listen up, because this is where you've got to step up and be the role model they need.

First things first, your emotions are your own. Don't let them spill out and flood your kids' world. You're angry, resentful, frustrated? Fine, but don't make that their problem. You're the adult, so act like one. They need stability, not a soap opera. If you think you can bad-mouth their mom and win them over, you're wrong. Kids aren't pawns in your emotional chess game. They love both of you, and you're only hurting them when you pit them against the other parent. Play it smart, play it fair, and keep their best interests at heart.

Let's talk about presence. And I don't mean FaceTime or occasional texts. I mean real, quality time with your kids. Don't let your battles in the courtroom take away from your responsibilities at home. You're fighting for custody? Then act like someone who deserves it.

Regardless of how you feel about alimony or child support, your kids should not bear the brunt of financial instability. This is where you show your true character. Step up and don't make excuses.

Lastly, let's get into mindset. Your kids will mirror your attitude toward this whole situation. If you're constantly playing the victim, don't be surprised when they start adopting a 'woe is me' outlook on life. Show resilience, show strength, and teach them how to bounce back from adversity. Your kids are watching, and what they see will shape who they become. So make sure they're seeing someone worth emulating.

Daily Challenge: Be the unwavering role model your children need by controlling your emotions, co-parenting with respect, spending quality time, providing financial support, and fostering a resilient mindset to guide them through this challenging journey.

Daily Reflection:

What resonated with you from today's lesson? How can you apply this truth in your life?

_____

_____

_____

_____

Day 94: Shared Debt- Handle With Care

Alright, let's tackle something that's about as fun as a root canal: shared debt. I get it; you're divorced, and the last thing you want to think about is money. But ignoring shared debt is like letting a ticking time bomb sit in your living room.

First, clarity is your lifeline. Sit down and dig through every financial record you've got. I'm talking credit card bills, loans, mortgages, the works. Make a list. Know exactly what you're dealing with. Ignorance is not bliss in this game.

Now, don't go rogue. Get legal advice. You might think you're a financial wizard, but divorce law is a beast of its own. An attorney who specializes in this stuff is worth every penny. They can help you navigate the murky waters of splitting debt.

Negotiate like a pro. Debt can be a bargaining chip. You might agree to take on some debt if it means getting a bigger slice of assets. But and this is crucial, don't let emotions dictate your decisions. This is a business transaction, not a therapy session.

Protect your credit score. Remember, shared debts impact both of your credit scores. If your ex isn't holding up her end of the deal, it could tank your credit. Make sure you've got a system in place to track payments and hold her accountable if she drops the ball.

Finally, the aftermath. Once the divorce is final, clean up your financial act. Refinance mortgages, transfer credit card balances, do whatever it takes to sever those financial ties.Shared debt is a beast, but it's one you can tame with strategy and a level head. Don't stick your head in the sand. Face it head-on, and you'll come out of this mess in a much better financial position.

Daily Challenge: Take control of your financial future by creating a comprehensive list of shared debts, seeking legal guidance, negotiating with a business mindset, safeguarding your credit score, and proactively untangling your financial ties after divorce

Daily Reflection:

What resonated with you from today's lesson? How can you apply this truth in your life?

_____

_____

_____

Day 95: The Ex-Spouse Dynamic- Navigate Wisely

Alright, let's talk about a dynamic that's stickier than super glue: the relationship with your ex-spouse. You might be divorced, but you're not done dealing with each other, especially if you've got kids. Here's how to navigate this tricky terrain.

First off, communication is key. I know, talking to your ex can feel like rubbing sandpaper on a sunburn, but it's a must. Keep it civil, keep it focused on the kids or any shared responsibilities, and for the love of sanity, keep the emotions in check. Emotional outbursts won't get you anywhere.

Boundaries, my friend, set clear boundaries. Decide what's off-limits in your interactions. Are you comfortable with late-night calls? Discuss that. Do you want to keep personal lives separate? Make it known. Boundaries prevent misunderstandings and drama. Respect is a two-way street. Treat your ex-spouse with respect, and expect the same in return. Name-calling and finger-pointing are a waste of your precious energy. Rise above the drama; it's not worth your time.

Now, co-parenting. If you've got kids, this is your new normal. Coordinate schedules, share information about the kids, and make decisions together. Remember, it's about what's best for them, not what's convenient for you.

And lastly, don't rush into new relationships. It might be tempting to fill the void with a new partner, but take your time. Make sure you're emotionally ready and that your kids are comfortable with the idea. Navigating the ex-spouse dynamic is like walking through a field of landmines. One wrong step, and boom. But with communication, boundaries, respect, and patience, you can make it through without blowing up your life.

Daily Challenge: Today, commit to practicing patience in your interactions with your ex-spouse, knowing that maintaining a calm and composed demeanor will ultimately benefit both you and your children in the long run.

Daily Reflection:

What resonated with you from today's lesson? How can you apply this truth in your life?

_____

_____

_____

_____

Day 96: Joint Accounts- Unlink and Secure

Today, we're diving into the financial jungle of joint accounts. You might think they're a convenient way to handle bills and expenses, but after a divorce, they're more like a ticking time bomb.

First things first, unlink those accounts ASAP. The last thing you need is your ex-spouse having access to your money or vice versa. Get in touch with your bank and sever those financial ties. Now, the money shuffle. Once you've untangled those accounts, figure out how to divide any joint assets and debts. It's not fun, but it's necessary. You might need to close some joint credit cards, refinance loans, or sell shared property. Be prepared to make tough decisions.

Change your passwords and PINs. This isn't just about financial security; it's about personal privacy. You don't want your ex snooping around your emails or social media, do you?

Update your beneficiaries. If your ex-spouse was listed as a beneficiary on your accounts or insurance policies, change that pronto. You don't want them cashing in on your hard-earned money if something happens to you. Now, consider seeking financial advice. A professional can help you make sense of your new financial situation and plan for the future. It's an investment in your financial well-being.

Lastly, keep an eye on your credit. Monitor your credit reports regularly to make sure no joint accounts are haunting you or damaging your credit score. Joint accounts might have made sense when you were together, but post-divorce, they're more trouble than they're worth. Unlink, secure your assets, and take control of your financial future.

Daily Challenge: Take decisive action to regain control of your financial future by immediately unlinking joint accounts, dividing assets and debts, securing your online privacy, updating beneficiaries, considering financial advice, and monitoring your credit regularly to ensure a brighter financial path ahead.

Daily Reflection:

What resonated with you from today's lesson? How can you apply this truth in your life?

_____

_____

_____

Day 97: Home Sweet Home?- The House Debate

L et's dive into the home sweet home debate, a battleground for many divorcing couples. It's where memories were made, where your kids grew up, but now it's a hot potato, and you need to decide who gets it.

First, be practical. Emotions run high when it comes to the family home, but think with your head, not just your heart. Can you afford to keep it? Consider mortgage payments, taxes, and maintenance costs. It might be sentimental, but if it breaks the bank, it's not worth it. Negotiate like a pro. If you both want the house, see if you can work out a deal. Maybe one of you buys out the other's share or agrees to a fair division of other assets. Be open to creative solutions.

Think about the kids. If you have children, their stability is crucial. Consider what's best for them, even if it means letting go of the house. It's about their well-being, not your attachment. Plan your exit. If you're the one leaving the family home, make sure you have a place to go. Don't end up couch-surfing or in a tiny apartment. Be practical about your living situation post-divorce.

Embrace change. Moving out of the family home can be emotionally tough, but it's also a fresh start. Decorate your new place the way you like, create new memories, and focus on building a new chapter.

The home sweet home debate is no walk in the park, but it's a crucial decision in your divorce journey. Be practical, negotiate wisely, prioritize your kids, plan your exit, and embrace the change. Your future self will thank you.

Daily Challenge: Today, take a practical step towards resolving the home sweet home debate by researching the financial aspects of keeping the family home or finding a suitable alternative, and remember to prioritize the well-being of your children in your decision-making process.

Daily Reflection:

What resonated with you from today's lesson? How can you apply this truth in your life?

_____

_____

_____

_____

Day 98: Family Traditions- Rewrite or Retain?

Day 98 brings us to a crossroads: family traditions. After a divorce, you might be wondering if it's time to hit the reset button on those cherished rituals or keep them alive in a new form.

First, evaluate what traditions truly matter to you and your children. Some may hold sentimental value, while others might have lost their meaning. Be willing to adapt and create new traditions that suit your current circumstances.

Communicate openly with your ex-spouse. If there are traditions that both of you value and want to maintain, discuss how you can do so without causing tension or confusion for your children. It's all about cooperation and compromise.

Consider creating unique traditions for your new family dynamics. Embrace the opportunity to start fresh and build rituals that reflect your new life. It can be exciting and empowering to establish your own traditions.

Be mindful of your children's emotions. Going through a divorce is challenging for them, and changes in family traditions can add to their stress. Listen to their feelings and involve them in the decision-making process when possible.

Remember, it's not about erasing the past but finding a balance between honoring the old and embracing the new. Family traditions are a part of your history, but they don't have to dictate your future. Use this as a chance to reinvent, rewrite, or retain them in a way that brings positivity and joy to your family's life.

Daily Challenge: Today, take a reflective journey through your family traditions, and make a commitment to preserve, adapt, or create them with love and consideration for your new family dynamics.

Daily Reflection:

What resonated with you from today's lesson? How can you apply this truth in your life?

_____

_____

_____

_____

Day 99: Real Talk- How to Discuss Divorce with Kids

Alright, let's dive into one of the toughest conversations you'll ever have as a parent: talking to your kids about divorce. This ain't gonna be a cakewalk, but it's necessary. First off, choose the right time and place. Find a cozy, safe spot where you won't be interrupted. Make it a comfortable space for your kids to open up.

Now, be honest, but keep it age-appropriate. Break it down in a way they can understand. No need for complicated legal jargon. And please, don't play the blame game. It's not their fault, and they shouldn't feel like it is.

Reassure them like there's no tomorrow. Let them know that your love for them is unwavering. Kids can have crazy ideas when divorce comes up, like thinking you won't love them anymore. Shoot that down pronto.

Here's a biggie: Listen. And I mean really listen. Encourage your kids to talk about their feelings, even if it's a mess of anger and tears. Don't judge, just be there for them.

Keep the drama to a minimum. Don't badmouth your ex-spouse, no matter how tempting it might be. Your kids need a healthy relationship with both of you. Try to keep things consistent. Routine is your best friend right now. Kids thrive on it, and it helps give them a sense of stability.

But hey, if things get tough, don't be afraid to bring in a pro. A therapist or counselor can work wonders when your kids are struggling to cope. This conversation isn't a one-and-done deal. Be prepared for follow-up questions and feelings that might resurface. It's a journey, and you're the guide.

Daily Challenge: Create a safe and comfortable space to have an open and honest conversation with your kids about divorce, reassuring them of your unwavering love and encouraging them to share their feelings.

Daily Reflection:

What resonated with you from today's lesson? How can you apply this truth in your life?

_____

_____

_____

_____

Day 100: Emotional Baggage & Shared Spaces

Day 100, my friend. We're diving into the heavyweight topic of emotional baggage and shared spaces. Time for a detox, both mentally and physically.

First off, your shared space is no longer just a place; it's a battleground of memories and emotions. It's where you laughed, loved, and fought. Now, it's time to declutter. Start by physically purging what you no longer need. Get rid of those reminders of the past that weigh you down. Don't cling to possessions out of guilt or nostalgia. Let 'em go.

But the real detox is mental. Those emotional bags you've been lugging around? They're heavy, man. Resentment, anger, sadness – it's time to unpack. Face those feelings head-on. Forgive, not for their sake, but for yours. Holding onto grudges is like drinking poison and expecting the other person to die. It only hurts you.

Set boundaries. Your shared space may still involve your ex-spouse. Define the rules, respect each other's space, and avoid unnecessary conflicts. It's about creating a peaceful environment. Focus on the future, not the past. Your shared space should be a place of growth, not a museum of regrets. Set goals, make plans, and build a new chapter. And finally, self-care is non-negotiable. This emotional detox is draining. Exercise, meditate, talk to a therapist – do whatever it takes to keep your mental and emotional health in check.

Day 100 is a milestone. It's about shedding the old and embracing the new. Your shared space should be a reflection of your fresh start, not a reminder of what's gone. Detox, my friend, and create a space for the next chapter of your life.

Daily Challenge: Begin the emotional and physical detox by decluttering your shared space, letting go of possessions tied to the past, forgiving for your own well-being, setting clear boundaries, focusing on the future, and prioritizing self-care to pave the way for a fresh start in your life's next chapter.

Daily Reflection:

What resonated with you from today's lesson? How can you apply this truth in your life?

_____

_____

_____

_____

Day 101: The Ex-In-Laws- Maintain or Cut Off?

L ook, I get it. Divorce ain't just about you and your ex. It's a tidal wave that hits every relationship connected to you. And those ex-in-laws? They're right in the heart of that storm. So, what's the play? Keep 'em close? Or cut ties?

First off, no BS here - it's your life. Stop letting anyone, and I mean ANYONE, dictate your narrative. The past is done; it's about the NOW. Are these relationships adding value to your life? Are they lifting you up, or dragging you back into old dramas? Be brutally honest.

Family ties? Blood? Forget that noise. Just because you were once connected by marriage doesn't mean you owe anyone anything. Loyalty is earned, not gifted by association. But here's the thing: if those in-laws were your rock, your support system, don't ditch 'em just because of a title change. Remember, life's about relationships, and real ones are hard to find.

On the flip side, if they're toxic, if every convo feels like a trip down regret lane, then cut. it. off. Time is the ONE thing you can't get back. Don't waste it on relationships that don't serve your growth.

Bottom line? Do what's right for YOU. Not out of spite, not out of obligation. Pure, unfiltered, what's-best-for-YOU decision making. That's the game. Play it right.

Daily Challenge: Evaluate your relationships with your ex-in-laws and decide whether they contribute positively to your life and growth, making decisions based on what's best for your own well-being, not out of obligation or spite.

Daily Reflection:

What resonated with you from today's lesson? How can you apply this truth in your life?

_____

_____

_____

_____

Day 102: Child Support- Your Responsibilities

Listen up, everyone! Day 102, and we're diving deep into the realm of child support. Let's cut through the fluff and get straight to the heart of it.

Child support isn't just a legal obligation; it's a MORAL one. You brought a life into this world, and guess what? That means you've got a responsibility to ensure it thrives. It's not about you and your ex-partner anymore. It's about that child's future, their well-being, their dreams.

Stop making excuses. "Oh, my ex is using the money for themselves." "I barely see my kid." Enough of that victim mentality. The system might be flawed, but your child isn't. Don't punish them for adult complications. Every dollar you invest in child support is a statement that you value their future.

Think it's tough on you? Remember who's watching. Your kids are sponges. They absorb everything, from your actions to your attitude. Do you want them growing up thinking it's okay to shirk responsibilities? That commitments are mere suggestions? No!

Life's full of choices. You've got the power in every moment to decide who you are. Are you the parent who hides, dodges, and makes excuses? Or are you the one who steps up, even when it's hard, even when it hurts, because you know your child is worth it?

Put your ego aside. This isn't about winning or losing post-divorce battles. It's about ensuring the next generation has every shot at success. So, step up, pay what you owe, and prove to your child that they can always count on you. Period.

Daily Challenge: Today, commit to viewing child support not as a burden, but as an opportunity to invest in your child's future, reminding yourself that your actions shape their values and beliefs.

Daily Reflection:

What resonated with you from today's lesson? How can you apply this truth in your life?

_____

_____

_____

_____

Day 103: Alimony Revisited - How It Affects You

Listen up! Day 103, and we're diving headfirst into the world of alimony. Let's cut the crap and get straight to it. Alimony isn't about winning or losing; it's about understanding and adapting. Yeah, you heard me right. Whether you're the one cutting the check or the one cashing it, this is about more than just money. This is about your future, your mindset, and how you perceive value.

First, let's debunk a myth: Alimony isn't a punishment. Stop viewing it as a penalty for past mistakes. It's a system, flawed as it may be, meant to level the playing field post-divorce. It's not about evening scores; it's about ensuring both parties have a fighting chance in the next chapter of their lives.

But here's the hard truth: alimony is also a mirror reflecting your past financial decisions and commitments. And if you don't like what you see, then it's on YOU to change, grow, and adapt. Complaining about it? Not gonna change a thing.

For those paying: Don't let resentment build. This isn't charity; it's responsibility. It's an acknowledgment of a past where two people built something together. For those receiving: Don't get complacent. This isn't a free pass. It's a temporary boost, not a crutch.

At the end of the day, money's just a tool. It's your ATTITUDE that defines you. Alimony's just a phase, not your forever. Face it, learn from it, and then hustle your way to the next chapter. Because every setback, every payment, every challenge is an opportunity to rebuild and come back ten times stronger.

Daily Challenge: Embrace alimony as an opportunity for personal growth and financial responsibility, recognizing it as a steppingstone towards building a stronger future, no matter whether you're paying or receiving it.

Daily Reflection:

What resonated with you from today's lesson? How can you apply this truth in your life?

_____

_____

_____

_____

Day 104: New Partners- Introducing Them to Your Kids

Listen up! Day 104: Introducing a new partner to your kids? Here's the straight-up truth: It's NOT about you anymore; it's about them. Your ego, your excitement, your fear? Put it on the back burner. Your kids, their feelings, their stability? That's your North Star now.

You think they won't notice if you rush it? Think again. Kids are the ultimate BS detectors. They feel the energy, the vibes, and the intentions. If you're introducing someone new just because you're lonely or trying to get back at your ex, your kids will feel it. And trust me, that's a recipe for disaster.

This isn't a game. You can't just throw someone into their lives and expect them to accept it. Kids need stability, trust, and consistency. Your new partner might be the bee's knees to you, but to your kids? They're a stranger walking into their sacred space.

So, what do you do? You communicate. Talk to your kids, be honest with them. Understand their feelings and fears. And for the love of everything, take it slow! You're building a foundation here, not a house of cards. Lay the groundwork, be patient, and let relationships develop organically.

Remember, your kids' well-being is the priority. New partners come and go, but the bond with your kids? That's forever. Respect it, nurture it, and protect it at all costs. That's the truth. No sugarcoating. No bull. Just raw, honest reality. Own it.

Daily Challenge: Prioritize your children's well-being above all else today by communicating openly, taking it slow, and ensuring their feelings and stability are at the forefront when introducing a new partner into their lives.

Daily Reflection:

What resonated with you from today's lesson? How can you apply this truth in your life?

_____

_____

_____

_____

Day 105: Shared Custody- Do's and Don'ts

Shared custody? Let's drop the filters and get real. This isn't about you and your ex anymore. It's about the future, the potential, the dreams of those kids you both brought into the world. And trust me, they feel everything—every glance, every whispered word, every tense exchange.

You think the pain and confusion is intense for you? Multiply that by a thousand for them. They're looking to you, searching for stability in a world that just got turned upside down.

Every interaction with your ex? It's a chance. A chance to rise, to show maturity, to be the bigger person. It's not about rehashing old arguments or fighting those ancient battles. That war's over. Now, it's about peace, and creating a harmonious environment for those little souls to grow.

Look, I get it. The wounds are fresh. The hurt runs deep. But every day is an opportunity. An opportunity to heal, to show love, to teach resilience. You want your kids to be strong, compassionate, understanding? Then BE that. Model that.

And on those tough days, when the past pulls at you, threatening to drag you back into bitterness and anger, pause. Take a deep breath. Reflect. Remember why you're doing this. It's not about proving a point or getting back at your ex. It's about a legacy. A legacy of love, of growth, of understanding.

So, gear up. Every day in this shared custody journey is a step. A step towards healing, towards understanding, towards love. Embrace it. Own it. Live it. Because this is your story. Make it count for those kids.

Daily Challenge: Today, consciously choose kindness and cooperation in your interactions with your ex, setting a positive example for your children's future and focusing on their well-being above all else.

Daily Reflection:

What resonated with you from today's lesson? How can you apply this truth in your life?

_____

_____

_____

Day 106: Relocation Woes

Listen up, gentlemen. We're diving deep into the nitty-gritty of post-divorce life, and there's one word I need you to understand: relocation. Now, I won't sugarcoat it; relocation sucks. But guess what? Life isn't about being comfortable. It's about growth, adaptation, and relentless hustle.

After a divorce, your home might not feel like "home" anymore. Familiar walls become reminders of past arguments, shared dreams, and broken promises. The urge to bolt and start fresh somewhere new is real. And sometimes, it's necessary. But don't be fooled into thinking that packing up your belongings and heading for a new zip code will magically erase the pain. Physical distance doesn't always equate to emotional healing.

Relocating is like ripping off a band-aid. It's quick, it's painful, and sometimes, it's downright bloody. You'll have to re-establish yourself in a new community, make new friends, and potentially even tackle a new job. It's not for the faint-hearted. But neither is life after a divorce.

So here's the deal: If you're relocating, do it with purpose. Don't run from your past; run towards your future. Find a place that aligns with your passions, ambitions, and the new life you're carving out for yourself. And remember, a fresh start isn't about forgetting; it's about reshaping, redefining, and relentlessly pursuing a better version of yourself.

Be smart about it. Know your why. Is it for a job? A fresh scene? Closer to family? Whatever it is, own it. Dive in headfirst and don't look back. Life post-divorce is about seizing control and driving your narrative forward. So, gear up, face those relocation woes head-on, and remember: every new beginning comes from some other beginning's end.

Daily Challenge: Today, take a step toward your relocation goal by researching potential destinations and making a list of the opportunities and connections you can pursue there to shape your new beginning with purpose and determination.

Daily Reflection:

What resonated with you from today's lesson? How can you apply this truth in your life?

_____

_____

_____

Day 107: Presence Over Presents

Listen up, fellas. In the post-divorce chaos, it's easy to get sucked into the mindset that showering your kids with gifts will bridge the gap, heal the wounds. But guess what? That brand-new PlayStation or those expensive sneakers? They're just temporary band-aids on a wound that needs a lot more than materialistic salve.

You want the raw truth? Your TIME is the most precious currency you've got. Not dollars, not gifts. Your presence. The moments you sit down, look your kid in the eye, and LISTEN. That's the gold. That's where the magic happens.

I get it. The guilt, the urge to compensate for the family breakdown with lavish gifts. But here's the kicker: kids aren't looking for your wallet. They're looking for YOU. Your attention. Your love. Your genuine, undivided focus.

Every soccer game you attend, every bedtime story you read, every tear you wipe away — that's the stuff they'll remember. Not the toy that broke in a week or the gadget that's outdated in a year. YOU. Your laughter, your advice, your shoulder to lean on.

Wake up! Stop trying to buy love or forgiveness. It's not up for sale. Instead, invest. Invest your time, your emotions, your moments. Dive deep into their lives. Be curious about their day, their dreams, their fears. BE THERE, genuinely and wholeheartedly.

In a world of fleeting materialism, be the constant. Be the rock. Be the dad who's there, not the one who sends stuff. Time over toys. Moments over money. Presence over presents. Always. Period.

Daily Challenge: Today, set aside dedicated quality time with your child, engage in an activity they love, and truly listen to what they have to say without distractions or interruptions.

Daily Reflection:

What resonated with you from today's lesson? How can you apply this truth in your life?

_____

_____

_____

_____

Day 108: Communicate Openly

Alright, gents, pull up a chair. We're diving deep. You think you're the only one feeling the aftershocks of this divorce? Think again. Those little humans in your life, the ones looking up to you with those big eyes? They're absorbing every tremor, every silent moment, and every hidden tear. And trust me, they're not just "sensing" it; they're living it.

Here's a raw truth: Kids are like emotional sponges. They pick up on the vibes, the unsaid words, the tension. You think you're shielding them with those closed-door conversations and hushed arguments? Newsflash: they're piecing it all together in their minds, sometimes painting a picture far worse than reality.

So, what's the game plan? Communication. And I'm not talking about the "because I said so" kind. I mean real, heart-to-heart, genuine conversations. Dive into their world. Ask about their fears. Listen to their concerns. Because guess what? They're concocting stories in their heads, and some of those stories might have them as the villains in their own narrative.

You want to be the hero in their story? Make sure they know the divorce isn't on them. Not now, not ever. It's easy to say, "It's not your fault," but it's another thing to make them believe it. Be transparent about the situation, at a level they can understand. Reassure, reinforce, and repeat.

You've got one shot at this, one chance to anchor their trust. So, man up, step up, and speak up. They're not just your kids; they're your responsibility. Handle with care. And for heaven's sake, communicate.

Daily Challenge: Today, make it a priority to have an open and honest conversation with your children about the divorce, reassuring them that it's not their fault and that you're there for them every step of the way.

Daily Reflection:

What resonated with you from today's lesson? How can you apply this truth in your life?

_____

_____

_____

_____

Day 109: Consistency is Key?

Alright, men, let's cut through the bull and get straight to it. Divorce? It's messy. Your emotions? All over the place. But your kids? They don't need that chaos. They need stability, they need routine, and they need YOU to provide it. So, let's roll up those sleeves and dive deep.

You remember those bedtime stories? Those weekend trips to the park? Those might seem like small things in the grand scheme of the storm you're weathering, but to your kids? They're the anchor. They're what keep their world from spinning out of control.

Consistency isn't just about keeping a routine; it's about sending a message. It's telling your kids, "Hey, a lot's changing, but Dad's still here, and he's not going anywhere." It's about laying down a foundation in shifting sands. In this whirlwind of lawyers, paperwork, and emotional upheaval, be the one thing they can count on.

Listen, I get it. Some days you'll want to shut down, skip that story, or cancel that trip. But here's the truth: This isn't about you. It's about them. Every time you show up, every time you stick to the routine, you're building trust. You're proving that no matter what's going down in your world, you're putting them first.

Don't underestimate the power of consistency. It's not just about schedules; it's about security. It's about love. It's about commitment. So, man up, be there, and be unwavering. Your kids are counting on it. And trust me, when they look back, they won't remember the chaos of the divorce, they'll remember that Dad always showed up. Period.

Daily Challenge: Today, commit to a consistent routine for your kids, no matter how chaotic life feels; show up for bedtime stories, weekend trips, and quality time, because your unwavering presence is their anchor in the storm.

Daily Reflection:

What resonated with you from today's lesson? How can you apply this truth in your life?

_____

_____

_____

_____

Day 110: Co-Parenting, Not Combat:

You're divorced, sure, but guess what hasn't changed? Your role as a dad. Your kids? They're watching. Every argument, every passive-aggressive text, every cold shoulder—it all impacts them. You want to win? Put the gloves down and step out of the ring.

It's called CO-parenting for a reason. "CO," as in together, as in teamwork. Remember that team you played on where you didn't like everyone, but you still passed the ball? That's you and your ex right now. You might not be in love, but you're forever linked by the most crucial project of your life: raising incredible humans.

Now, I get it. Emotions are high. But here's a newsflash: it's not about you OR your ex anymore. It's about those little eyes looking up at you, wanting stability, love, and a sense of normalcy.

Swallow that pride. Heck, choke on it if you have to, but don't let it get in the way of working as a unit. Every decision, every conversation—ask yourself, "Is this best for my child?" If it's not, pivot.

Here's the hard truth: kids don't care about your emotional baggage. They care about being loved, feeling safe, and having both parents in their lives. So, you're hurt? Get a therapist. Angry? Hit the gym. But when it comes to your kids, you show up as a united front with your ex.

In the end, it's not about the battles you win against your ex; it's about the wars you prevent in your kid's heart. Get your priorities straight. Co-parent like a pro. For them.

Daily Challenge: Today, commit to setting aside your personal differences and strive to communicate openly and respectfully with your ex-partner for the sake of your children's emotional well-being and stability.

Daily Reflection:

What resonated with you from today's lesson? How can you apply this truth in your life?

_____

_____

_____

_____

Day 111: Be Their Unshakeable Rock

Hey, bro, pull up a chair and let's cut through the noise. You know that life after divorce is like being thrown in the deep end without a life jacket. But guess what? Your kids? They're in the same water, flailing, scared, and looking for something solid to hold onto. That solid thing? It's gotta be you.

You think you're the only one with a storm inside? Think again. Your children are navigating their own hurricane of feelings, and it's wilder than anything you've experienced. They didn't sign up for any of this. They're collateral in a war they didn't start.

Now, you might think that keeping your feelings bottled up makes you strong. Bull. Real strength? It's showing vulnerability. It's letting your kids see that it's okay to feel, to cry, to get angry, and then teaching them how to channel those emotions. Be the role model they need. Talk. Share. Connect.

Look, they don't need another superhero. They don't need Spiderman or Batman. They need you: a dad who's there, who listens, who understands, who guides. A dad who might not have all the answers, but it, he's there trying.

You want to be their rock? Then dig deep. Plant your feet firmly and weather the storm with them. Hold them tight when the waves crash. Laugh with them when the sun shines. And remind them, every single day, that even in the midst of chaos, they've got a dad who's got their back, no matter what. Wake up, man! Be the anchor in their storm. Because when everything else is uncertain, you're the one constant they need. Step up. Be that rock.

Daily Challenge: Today, open up and have an honest conversation with your children about your own feelings and emotions, setting an example of vulnerability and showing them that it's okay to express their own.

Daily Reflection:

What resonated with you from today's lesson? How can you apply this truth in your life?

_____

_____

_____

_____

Day 112: Educate Yourself: For Your Kids' Sake

Alright, guys, let's cut the crap and get straight to it. You're going through a divorce, and it's not just you riding this tsunami—it's your kids too. You might be getting hit left and right with legalities, but your kids? They're grappling with an emotional whirlwind, and it's on you to guide them through it.

Look, I get it. It's easy to drown in your own emotions, your own "what ifs" and "should haves." But here's the raw truth: Your kids didn't sign up for this rollercoaster. They're on it because of choices you and your ex made. That's a hard pill to swallow but swallow it you must.

So, what do you do? You **educate** yourself. Dive deep into understanding how kids process divorce. You think you're hurting? Imagine being a kid watching their whole world split in two. Their reactions, fears, guilt—it's all a complex web, and it's not one-size-fits-all. Each kid is unique. Some might act out, some might retreat, and some might seem eerily okay (spoiler: they're probably not).

You've got the internet at your fingertips, a library around the corner, professionals ready to spill the tea. There's zero excuse for ignorance. Read the studies, watch the videos, attend the seminars. If you're feeling it, start a support group.

Be proactive. Anticipate their reactions. When they lash out or break down, you need to be the rock, the safe space, not the added storm. And if you think you can wing it without understanding what's going on in their heads, you're in for a rude awakening. Step up, man. For them. This isn't about ego; it's about empathy. They need a dad who gets it, who's there, and who's fighting for them every step of the way. Don't just be present—be prepared. It's game time.

Daily Challenge: Today, commit to learning something new about how children process divorce and take one proactive step to better understand and support your kids through this emotional journey.

Daily Reflection:

What resonated with you from today's lesson? How can you apply this truth in your life?

_____

_____

_____

_____

Day 113: Lean on Community

You might think you're some lone wolf, some stoic hero who can shoulder the world's weight alone. But let me hit you with a truth bomb: that's BS, and deep down, you know it. You're human, and humans are wired for connection.

Going through a divorce? That's like being thrown into the boxing ring blindfolded. You think you can dodge those emotional jabs and uppercuts solo? Think again. You need a team in your corner, cheering you on, handing you the water bottle, and patching you up.

Now, I'm not saying spill your heart out to every Tom, Dick, and Harry. But find your tribe. Those guys who've been through the wringer and come out the other side? They've got wisdom to share. Those therapists who've trained for years to help navigate this mental minefield? They're your strategists. And those friends who've been with you through thick and thin? They're your rock.

It's not weak to seek help. In fact, it's the opposite. It takes a real man, a smart man, to recognize when he's out of his depth and needs a lifeline. And remember this: if you're a dad, it's not just about you. It's about those kids looking up to you, learning from your actions. Show them that strength isn't just physical; it's emotional, it's mental, and it's communal.

So, get off that island of isolation. Dive into the community waters. Swim with those who've been there, done that, and can guide you to safer shores. Because, brother, it does take a village. Not just to raise a child, but to raise a man back up when he's down. Don't sleep on that.

Daily Challenge: Reach out to at least one trusted friend or support group member today, share a bit of your journey, and let them be a part of your support team as you navigate the challenges of divorce.

Daily Reflection:

What resonated with you from today's lesson? How can you apply this truth in your life?

_____

_____

_____

_____

Day 114: Rebuild Trust: Actions Over Words

Alright, gents, let's cut to the chase. Trust. It's that elusive, intangible thing, isn't it? Once shattered, picking up the pieces can feel like trying to assemble a jigsaw puzzle in a hurricane. But here's the raw truth: if you're aiming to rebuild trust, especially after a divorce, words are about as useful as a chocolate teapot. It's all about ACTION.

Think about it. You can spout promises till you're blue in the face, but if your actions don't align, you're just blowing hot air. And let me tell you, no one has time for that, especially not your kids. They're watching, always watching. They're the little radars picking up on every broken promise, every unmet commitment.

Want to re-establish trust? Stop talking. Start doing. Show up when you say you will. Be consistent. If you promise a weekend outing, make it happen, rain or shine. Missed a soccer game? Don't just apologize; ensure you're front and center for the next one.

And look, nobody's saying it's easy. But this isn't about easy. It's about integrity. It's about showing the world, and more importantly, showing YOURSELF, that you're a man of your word. Every action, every commitment met, every promise kept, lays down another brick on the road to rebuilding trust.

Divorce might've thrown you off course, but here's your chance to steer the ship right. And it starts with consistent, genuine action. Let your deeds scream what words never could. Time to step up, and more importantly, SHOW UP. Trust is built in drops and lost in buckets. So, start filling that bucket, one drop, one action, at a time. Let's get to work.

Daily Challenge: Today, commit to taking at least one concrete action that demonstrates your trustworthiness and reliability to someone important in your life, whether it's keeping a promise to your child, showing up for a friend, or following through on a commitment to yourself.

Daily Reflection:

What resonated with you from today's lesson? How can you apply this truth in your life?

_____

_____

_____

_____

Day 115: Celebrate Small Moments

Alright, men, let's break this down. We live in a world obsessed with the grandiose. Big wins, huge milestones, grand gestures - that's the noise everyone's chasing. But here's the secret sauce, the real truth: It's the tiny, often overlooked moments that make life worth living, especially post-divorce.

Remember that quick smile your kid flashed when you made them breakfast? That unexpected chuckle you shared with them over a silly joke? That brief, warm hug before bedtime? Those aren't just random occurrences; those are the lifeblood of healing and connection.

Post-divorce, it's easy to get consumed by the big picture - the legal battles, the emotional turmoil, the shifting dynamics. But while you're navigating this maze, don't lose sight of the daily magic. Every single day, there are moments of pure, raw, unfiltered joy. They're subtle, they're fleeting, but man, they're powerful.

Here's the deal: Those moments? They're your anchor. They ground you, they remind you of the love and bond you share with your kids, and they give you the fuel to push through the toughest times. And trust me, you're going to need that fuel.

So, start valuing the small. Look for it. Cherish it. Celebrate it. Because when the dust settles and you look back, it won't be the courtroom battles or the heated arguments that'll stay with you. It'll be those quiet moments, the shared laughs, the warmth, the connection. That's your legacy. That's your triumph. Embrace it with everything you've got.

Today's challenge: Embrace the power of the small moments by actively seeking and cherishing at least one meaningful, heartwarming interaction with your children or loved ones, no matter how brief or subtle it may be.

Daily Reflection:

What resonated with you from today's lesson? How can you apply this truth in your life?

_____

_____

_____

_____

Day 116: Plan for the Future

Listen up, gentlemen! If there's one thing I need you to get laser-focused on post-divorce, it's this: securing your kids' future. I get it, emotions are high, and you're navigating a sea of challenges. But here's the raw truth: your responsibilities as a dad aren't taking a backseat. The game has changed, and you need to level up.

First off, those legal documents? They're not just paperwork; they're the blueprint for your child's future. If they're outdated, they're worthless. Update them. Now. Every asset, every penny, every detail - make sure it's squared away.

Think about trusts. You're not just storing money; you're creating a fortress of financial security. A safety net. Something that says, "Even if I'm not here, I've got your back." It's your legacy, your mark of commitment. Don't let it be an afterthought.

And let's get one thing straight: this isn't about winning against your ex. This is about ensuring that your child is cared for, come what may. So, collaborate if you must, debate if you need to, but get it done. Leave no stone unturned. Your child's future isn't a part of the negotiation; it's non-negotiable.

Look, life's throwing curveballs, and while you're dodging and ducking, remember to play the long game. It's not just about the present moment; it's about laying down tracks for the future. It's about making sure that, no matter the storm, your child's ship sails smoothly.

Gear up, take charge, and make it happen. Your child's future is in your hands. Let's ensure it shines bright.

Daily Challenge: Today, take concrete steps to review and update your legal documents and financial arrangements to secure your child's future, because being a responsible father means planning ahead and leaving no room for uncertainty.

Daily Reflection:

What resonated with you from today's lesson? How can you apply this truth in your life?

_____

_____

_____

_____

Day 117: Communication Lines

Alright, fellas, let's get right to it. Communication – it's the lifeblood of any relationship, and just because you're navigating a divorce doesn't mean you can let it slide. In fact, now? It's even more crucial.

You think you can ghost your way out of confrontations or bury your head in the sand? Think again. Avoidance might seem like the easy route, but it's a ticking time bomb. What you don't face today will come back tenfold tomorrow. So, you've got to step up, man up, and speak up.

The name of the game? Clarity. Be crystal clear about your intentions, needs, and boundaries. No one's a mind reader here. If you've got something on your chest, let it out. But – and this is key – do it respectfully. You can be assertive without being aggressive. Remember, it's not about winning an argument; it's about understanding and being understood. And hey, listen! And I mean really listen. Don't just wait for your turn to speak. Absorb, process, respond. That's how meaningful dialogues are built. That's how bridges, instead of walls, are constructed.

Tough conversations? You bet there'll be plenty. Whether it's about assets, kids, or future plans – face them head-on. Equip yourself with facts, keep emotions in check, and always aim for resolution, not retaliation. Lastly, invest in yourself. Read up, attend workshops, or even seek counseling. Elevate your communication game. It's a tool, a weapon, and a lifeline, all rolled into one. Nurture it.

Bottom line? Talk it out. Whether it's with your ex, your kids, or even yourself. Keep those communication lines open and clean. It's your path forward. Don't let it get cluttered.

Daily Challenge: Embrace the power of communication today by initiating an open and respectful conversation with someone important in your divorce journey, sharing your intentions, needs, or boundaries, and actively listening to their perspective.

Daily Reflection:

What resonated with you from today's lesson? How can you apply this truth in your life?

_____

_____

_____

_____

Day 118: The Cost of Co-Parenting

You're on a new playing field now, and guess what? It's not just about emotions and who gets what; it's about the cold, hard numbers.

First off, if you're thinking this is just about splitting school fees and weekend outings, think again. This is about your child's life, their experiences, and their future. You're not just budgeting for now; you're forecasting for the next decade or more.

Start by putting your ego aside. This isn't the time to play the blame game or prove a point. Every dollar, every decision, impacts your child. Remember that. Now, get organized. Map out the basics: education, healthcare, daily expenses. But don't stop there. Think extracurriculars, hobbies, birthdays. And don't forget those unplanned expenses. Trust me, they'll pop up.

Communication is key. You and your ex need to be on the same financial page. Set a monthly budget meeting. Stay transparent, stay proactive. Because reactive co-parenting? It's a financial sinkhole. Here's the golden nugget: invest in tools and resources. Financial planners, apps, books—whatever it takes to stay ahead of the curve. And if you think you can wing it, you're setting yourself up for a world of financial hurt.

Look, gentlemen, co-parenting is not a sprint; it's a marathon. Every dollar, every cent, it counts. But more than that, it's about ensuring your child thrives, no matter the circumstances. So, gear up, get your finances in order, and remember: co-parenting is teamwork. And in this game, the real winners are the kids. Let's make sure they come out on top.

Daily Challenge: Today, commit to setting aside your ego and engage in open, proactive communication with your ex about your child's financial needs and future, because in this new playing field, teamwork is essential for your child's success.

Daily Reflection:

What resonated with you from today's lesson? How can you apply this truth in your life?

_____

_____

_____

Day 119: The Extended Family

Divorce doesn't just hit you; it ricochets through the entire family tree. Suddenly, those Sunday family dinners and holiday gatherings? They're a minefield. That aunt or uncle who was your go-to? They might now be singing a different tune. It's tough, but here's the real talk: extended families can get messy, especially post-divorce.

You're going to feel it. The sideways glances, the hushed conversations. It's not in your head. But here's the thing: you can't control their narratives, but you can control your reaction. Loyalty might waver; relationships you thought were rock solid might tremble. It's time to recalibrate, re-evaluate, and most importantly, respond with maturity.

Remember, everyone has their version of the story, colored by their biases, past experiences, and loyalties. But this isn't about picking sides in a schoolyard fight. It's about maintaining dignity in a situation that's inherently fraught with emotion.

If there are kids in the picture, it's even more vital. They shouldn't become collateral damage in family politics. Their relationships with grandparents, uncles, aunts, and cousins? Those should remain untainted, unbiased, and most importantly, supportive.

This isn't about winning people over. It's about understanding the new normal. Some relationships might strengthen, some might drift, and some might break. But through it all, your peace, dignity, and well-being should remain non-negotiable. Life post-divorce with extended family is like navigating uncharted waters. Keep your compass of self-respect handy, stay the course, and remember: rough seas make skilled sailors. Dive in, navigate, and sail on.

Daily Challenge: Today, choose grace over confrontation when faced with challenging interactions within your extended family, reminding yourself that your peace and dignity are your top priorities as you navigate the post-divorce dynamics.

Daily Reflection:

What resonated with you from today's lesson? How can you apply this truth in your life?

_____

_____

_____

_____

Day 120: Home Front Milestone

Alright, guys, pause and take a moment. Day 120. You've reached a significant marker on this wild journey. But let's get this straight: today isn't just about reflecting on the past four months; it's about gearing up for what's next. This is your life, and your kids are looking to you.

Look, you might be dealing with a whirlwind of emotions, but your home – that sacred space – is where your heart, especially your role as a father, truly resides. The home isn't just walls and a roof; it's memories, emotions, and connections.

So, what's the game plan? Step one: Reclaim your space. Make that home a sanctuary for you and your kids. Whether it's rearranging the furniture or hanging up new art, it's time to refresh and re-energize. Your environment plays a massive role in your mindset. Make it count.

Next, let's talk connection. Your kids? They need stability. They need YOU. Double down on those fatherhood moments. Whether it's movie nights, cooking together, or just having heart-to-hearts, show up for them. Every. Single. Time.

And don't forget about self-reflection. Four months in, what have you learned? What can you do better? This isn't just about moving on; it's about leveling up. It's about understanding your worth, owning your role, and facing forward with confidence and purpose.

You're setting the stage for the next phase, and trust me, the best is yet to come. You've got this in the bag. Keep that momentum, stay focused, and remember: you're building a legacy, brick by brick. Make Day 120 count. Let's get it!

Daily Challenge: Take intentional steps today to refresh and re-energize your home environment, strengthen your connection with your kids through quality time, and engage in self-reflection to continue leveling up as a father and building a lasting legacy.

Daily Reflection:

What resonated with you from today's lesson? How can you apply this truth in your life?

_____

_____

_____

_____

Self-Care Isn't for Sissies

Begin your journey to personal renewal with our guide to self-care essentials. Dive into exercise, nutrition, sleep, mindfulness, and more. Rediscover your passions, build a strong support network, and express your creativity.

Set achievable goals, explore new interests, and prioritize mental wellness. Celebrate your successes, break free from unhealthy habits, and embrace the joy of giving back. Reconnect socially, anticipate future romance, and reflect on your growth.

Experience the power of music on your mood, stay accountable, and apply emotional first aid when needed. Track your self-care progress with a pivotal milestone.

Day 121: Physical Health- The Foundation of Recovery

L isten up, gentlemen. Let's get real. Divorce is a gauntlet, and while your mind is racing with a thousand thoughts, there's one thing you can't afford to push to the back burner: your physical health. If you think you're going to navigate this storm while running on empty, you're playing yourself.

Your body? It's your fortress. And right now, it's the very foundation holding everything together. You think you can be the rock for your kids or show up in life when you're surviving on junk food and two hours of sleep? Wrong move. Your body needs more respect than that, especially now.

Fuel yourself right. That means making choices about what you eat that give you energy, not just fill a hole. And while we're on the topic, get moving. I'm not talking marathons. Just move. Every day. Whether it's a walk, a gym session, or some push-ups during a TV commercial break, make it non-negotiable.

Sleep? It's not just for the weak. It's your body's way of recharging, and trust me, you need all the energy you can muster right now. And those vices you think are helping you cope? Cut them out. They're just Band-Aids on a wound that needs real healing.

In this crucial phase, taking care of your body is your secret weapon. It's not vanity; it's survival. Every time you make a choice that's good for your health, you're investing in yourself and everyone counting on you. So, lace up those sneakers, make a healthy meal, get that sleep, and face this head-on. You've got this. Let's roll.

Daily Challenge: Today, prioritize your physical health by making a conscious choice to eat nourishing foods, engage in some form of physical activity, ensure a restful night's sleep, and let go of any unhealthy coping mechanisms – because taking care of your body is your key to survival during this challenging time.

Daily Reflection:

What resonated with you from today's lesson? How can you apply this truth in your life?

_____

_____

_____

_____

Day 122: Mental Fitness- Sharpen Your Mind

Listen up, fellas. Divorce is a marathon, not a sprint. And just like you'd train your body for a physical marathon, you've got to prep your mind for this emotional and mental one. Mental fitness? It's not a luxury; it's a necessity.

Here's the truth: Mental fog, confusion, and emotional turmoil? They're your biggest adversaries right now. But guess what? You've got the power to transform that brain of yours into a high-performance machine.

First, start with the basics. Mindfulness and meditation? They aren't just buzzwords. They're tools. Tools that successful, high-functioning men use daily. They ground you, keep you centered, and give you clarity amidst the chaos. Dive into them. Make them non-negotiables.

Next, feed your brain. Dive into books, podcasts, seminars - whatever gets your neurons firing. Learn something new. Redirect that mental energy from ruminating over the past to building your future. And your inner circle? It matters. Surround yourself with go-getters, thinkers, doers. Let their energy rub off on you. Ditch the naysayers; you've got no time for that noise.

Also, challenge yourself. Set goals. Then crush them. Small wins build confidence. And right now, you need that confidence to rebuild, reframe, and reenergize. Lastly, remember this - you're the captain of your ship. Storms will hit. Waves will crash. But with a sharp mind, you'll navigate through, stronger and smarter.

Mental fitness isn't just about being smart. It's about resilience, clarity, and determination. So, gear up. Train that mind. Make it your strongest asset. Because with a fit mind, you're unstoppable.

Daily Challenge: Embrace the power of mindfulness and meditation today; spend at least 10 minutes grounding yourself and finding clarity amidst the emotional turbulence.

Daily Reflection:

What resonated with you from today's lesson? How can you apply this truth in your life?

_____

_____

_____

_____

Day 123: Diet Overhaul- Fueling a New You

Look, gentlemen, life just threw you a curveball. Divorce? It's a game-changer, no doubt. But here's the raw truth: while you're navigating this emotional maze, your body is taking the brunt. Stress eating, skipping meals, downing junk? That's not the way forward. Let's flip the script.

It's time for a diet overhaul. And I'm not talking about hopping on some fad diet train. I'm talking about fueling up for the new chapter in your life. Your body is your vessel, and what you feed it determines how you navigate, how you think, and how you feel.

Now's the time to level up. Ditch the sugar-laden sodas and processed junk. You think they're comfort foods? Wrong. They're holding you back. Every unhealthy bite is a step away from the best version of yourself. You want to come out of this stronger, sharper, and more focused? Then treat your body like the temple it is.

Load up on the greens, the lean proteins, the good fats. Hydrate like it's your job. Every meal is an opportunity to invest in yourself, to rebuild and rejuvenate. It's not just about looking good (though, hey, that's a bonus), it's about feeling unstoppable.

And, guess what? This isn't just about your physical well-being. A proper diet impacts your mental game. Clearer thoughts, better mood, sharper focus – that's the ROI on eating right.

You've got this, man. Remember, every time you're about to make a food choice, you're making a decision about your future. Choose wisely. Fuel the new you. It's game time.

Daily Challenge: Today, commit to making one healthy food choice that fuels your body and contributes to your journey of becoming the best version of yourself post-divorce.

Daily Reflection:

What resonated with you from today's lesson? How can you apply this truth in your life?

_____

_____

_____

_____

Day 124: The Power of Sleep

Alright, gentlemen, let's cut the fluff and dive straight in. Sleep. You might think it's just that thing you do when you're not hustling, grinding, or nursing emotional wounds. But here's the raw truth: sleep isn't a luxury; it's your secret weapon, especially when navigating the turmoil of divorce.

You're in the midst of one of life's most challenging battles. You think pushing through on 4 hours of sleep is a badge of honor? Think again. That's like trying to win a marathon with a sprained ankle. You're setting yourself up for failure, burnout, and a ton of avoidable mistakes.

Listen, sleep is your body's built-in reset button. It's when the brain processes emotions, heals wounds, and gets you ready to face another day. Shortchange sleep, and you're robbing yourself of clarity, focus, and emotional resilience. Ever tried negotiating with your ex or making vital decisions on a foggy brain? It's a disaster waiting to happen.

Now, don't get me wrong. I'm not saying dive under the covers and hide from the world. But prioritize sleep like you do your workouts, your work, and your responsibilities to your kids. It's the foundation. Everything else you do, every decision you make, is built on that.

In this game of life, especially in challenging times like divorce, you need every advantage you can get. Don't let pride or stubbornness rob you of this essential edge. Hit the sheets, get those solid 7-9 hours, and wake up ready to conquer. Because, gentlemen, sleep isn't just rest; it's your strategy for resilience. Embrace it. Own it. It's game time. Sleep to win.

Daily Challenge: Prioritize your sleep tonight, aiming for a solid 7-9 hours, and wake up ready to conquer the challenges of the day with a well-rested mind and body.

Daily Reflection:

What resonated with you from today's lesson? How can you apply this truth in your life?

_____

_____

_____

_____

Day 125: Emotional Resilience- Build Your Armor

Emotional resilience isn't some fluffy, feel-good buzzword. It's the armor you need when life throws its hardest punches. And let's be real – divorce? It's a heavyweight champ of a challenge. But here's the kicker: you're tougher than you think.

You're not a robot, and you shouldn't act like one. Feeling pain, confusion, anger? That's human. But how you respond to those emotions, how you bounce back, that's where emotional resilience comes into play.

Ever seen a boxer in the ring? It's not about how hard they hit, but how they take a hit and keep moving forward. That's resilience. And just like any skill, you can develop it. But it starts with a mindset shift. Stop playing the victim. Stop asking "why me?" and start asking "what's next?"

Acknowledge your emotions, but don't be enslaved by them. Dive deep, understand them, and then use them. They're fuel. Use the anger to push yourself in the gym. Channel the sadness into creative outlets. Redirect the confusion into learning and growth.

Connect. Surround yourself with people who lift you up, not those who drag you down. And when you're feeling low, remember, it's okay to lean on others. That's strength, not weakness.

Most importantly, invest in yourself. Read, learn, meditate, exercise. Strengthen your mind and body. This isn't about masking the pain; it's about growing through it. Every setback, every challenge, every tear is an opportunity to become a stronger version of yourself. Divorce might have knocked you down, but it's not keeping you there. Build that emotional resilience. Wear it like armor. And march forward, unstoppable. Because you've got this.

Daily Challenge: Today, when faced with a challenging emotion, embrace it as an opportunity for growth, channel it into a positive action, and seek support from those who uplift you on your journey to emotional resilience.

Daily Reflection:

What resonated with you from today's lesson? How can you apply this truth in your life?

_____

_____

_____

_____

Day 126: Redefining Your Now

Listen up, you! Ever wonder why you're stuck bad-mouthing your past? Here's a hard truth: you're probably doing it because things aren't going right in the present. Yep, staying cozy in what's familiar is easier than stepping into the unknown. But remember this - every time you blame your past for your present, you're handing over the power. You're letting yesterday control today. Crazy, right?

We've all been through some stuff. Traumas, betrayals, you name it. When something big and emotional happens, your brain takes a snapshot. And then? You might end up trapped in that memory's emotional loop. Wake up thinking about past problems? Your brain's back in time. Feel those old emotions? Now your whole body's back there with it. And if you're letting those feelings run the show, guess what? You're just recreating the past, over and over.

People might ask why you haven't changed. If you're pointing fingers at someone else or some past event, you're playing the victim card. But you're in control. It's time to break that cycle! Look, the truth is when things are good, you won't be re-living those memories. I've been there, faced betrayals and traumas. But they don't define me. And they shouldn't define you either.

Want to break free? Here's a game plan. Jot down those negative thoughts, habits, and emotions. Review them daily. Recognize them. Move past them. List out the thoughts you WANT in your head. Spend time daily wiring those into your brain. Every day, picture the behaviors you want to showcase. Visualize your best self. Get your brain primed for the future. Meditate, but focus on your future emotions. Don't end it until you truly feel them. Most importantly? Commit. Do the work. Make it about your future, not that past that's holding you back. Stick with it, and before you know it, you'll be living in the present with gratitude for the past that shaped you.

Daily Challenge: Replace negative thoughts and habits from the past with positive ones that align with your desired future.

Daily Reflection:

What resonated with you from today's lesson? How can you apply this truth in your life?

_____

_____

_____

_____

Day 127: Fitness Goals- Beyond the Dad Bod

Listen, fellas, I get it. Divorce hits hard, and maybe you've let yourself slide a bit. Maybe you've embraced that dad bod thinking it's the new "in" thing. But let me hit you with some truth: self-care isn't just about emotional healing. Your body's the vehicle driving you through this journey called life, and right now, it needs a tune-up.

You've been through the wringer, mentally and emotionally. But guess what? Every time you sweat it out, every rep you push, every mile you run, you're reclaiming a piece of yourself. Fitness isn't just about looking good; it's about feeling powerful, centered, and in control when everything else seems chaotic.

Don't use the divorce as an excuse to let go. Use it as fuel. Every drop of sweat is a testament to your resilience, your fight, your commitment to coming out of this stronger than ever. And hey, it's not just for you. Think about your kids, your family, the people who still look up to you. Show them that setbacks can be setups for comebacks.

Think the dad bod is your destiny? Think again. You've got the power to redefine, reshape, and reclaim your health. This isn't about revenge body or trying to outdo your ex. It's about investing in yourself. Remember, the mind and body are interconnected. A healthier body leads to a sharper mind, better decision-making, and a surge in confidence.

So, get off that couch. Stop drowning your sorrows in junk food. Hit the gym, the road, the track, wherever. Set those goals. Crush them. Rise above. Transform. Because you're worth it, and it's time you believe it. Fitness is more than just muscles; it's a mindset. Own it.

Daily Challenge: Today, commit to a physical self-care routine that includes exercise, whether it's hitting the gym, going for a run, or doing a home workout—reclaim your physical strength and use it as a symbol of your resilience and commitment to your own well-being.

Daily Reflection:

What resonated with you from today's lesson? How can you apply this truth in your life?

_____

_____

_____

_____

Day 128: Journaling- Unlock Your Inner Thoughts

You're going through a divorce, and let me hit you with a truth bomb: holding in your thoughts and emotions isn't doing you any favors. It's time to put pen to paper and let it all out. Why? Because journaling isn't just for teenagers or poets; it's a tool, a weapon, for guys like you who need clarity in chaos.

Think about it. Your brain's a mess right now. Thoughts, regrets, what-ifs, they're all swirling around. How do you make sense of it? By getting it out. Dump it all on paper. It doesn't have to be Shakespeare; it just has to be real. The act of writing forces you to confront what you're feeling, to organize the chaos in your head. It's raw, it's therapeutic, and it's necessary.

But don't just vent. Reflect. Dive deep. Ask yourself the hard questions. What went wrong? What role did you play? What can you learn? This isn't about blame, but about growth. It's about understanding yourself better, so you don't end up in the same spot again.

Here's another kicker: journaling boosts your mental health. It's like a gym session but for your mind. The more you do it, the stronger you become. You'll find patterns, triggers, and more importantly, solutions.

So, grab a notebook, find a quiet spot, and just write. Daily, weekly, whenever it hits you. It's not about the frequency; it's about the honesty. This isn't just self-care, it's self-discovery. Through words, you'll unlock parts of yourself you didn't even know existed. Dive in, confront, grow, and most importantly, heal.

Daily Challenge: Today, take 15 minutes to sit down with a journal and write down your thoughts, emotions, and reflections about your divorce journey, allowing yourself to release the weight and find clarity amidst the chaos.

Daily Reflection:

What resonated with you from today's lesson? How can you apply this truth in your life?

_____

_____

_____

Day 129: Cut the Vices- No More Self-Sabotage

Y ou've been through the wringer, haven't you? Divorce isn't a stroll in the park. It's like being thrown into a boxing ring blindfolded. But here's the kicker: sometimes the biggest punches aren't from the outside; they're the ones you throw at yourself. Those vices? The drinks you're downing every night, the smoke breaks that are becoming more frequent, the junk food binges? That's you hitting yourself when you're already down. Self-sabotage at its finest.

You might think these vices are your escape, a way to numb the pain or fill the void. But let's not kid ourselves. Every bottle, every puff, every junk-filled cart is a crutch. And the more you lean on them, the weaker you become. Instead of building resilience, you're building dependencies. Instead of facing your pain, you're masking it. And let me tell you, it's not a good look.

But here's the good news: you have the power to change. You always have. It's time to cut the chains of those vices. Because if you don't, they'll drag you down deeper into that abyss, and trust me, climbing out of that is a whole other battle you don't want.

So, what's it going to be? Are you going to let these vices define your post-divorce life? Or are you going to stand tall, face the pain, and come out stronger on the other side? Remember, every vice you cut loose is a step towards reclaiming your life. It's a statement that you won't be defeated, not by divorce, not by anything. You've got this. So, start today. No more excuses. No more self-sabotage. Only forward.

Daily Challenge: Today, commit to identifying one of your self-sabotaging habits, and take a concrete step towards replacing it with a healthier coping mechanism or positive activity that contributes to your well-being and healing.

Daily Reflection:

What resonated with you from today's lesson? How can you apply this truth in your life?

_____

_____

_____

_____

Day 130: Financial Health- Build Your Nest Egg

Navigating the stormy waters of divorce isn't just about the emotional waves; it's about the financial ones too. Let's cut to the chase: your financial health is crucial. It's not about greed; it's about stability, security, and setting yourself up for future success.

Divorce might've shaken your financial foundation, but now's the time to rebuild, stronger and smarter. Remember, it's not about how much money you make; it's about how you manage it. Money isn't the end game; it's the tool that lets you craft the life you envision.

First step? Get a clear picture of where you stand. Ignorance isn't bliss. Know your debts, your assets, your monthly expenses. Knowledge is power, and in this case, it's the power to rebuild and thrive.

But it's not just about the now; it's about the future. Think nest egg. Think about where you want to be in 5, 10, 20 years. That dream isn't out of reach; it just takes planning. Start by setting aside a portion of your income, no matter how small. Consistency trumps amount. Over time, it'll add up. Invest wisely, seek advice when needed, and always keep an eye on the horizon.

And hey, don't get lured into the trap of emotional spending. It's easy to try to fill the void with material things, but that's a short-term fix for a long-term journey. Instead, focus on value over cost. Will that purchase serve your future, or is it just a fleeting distraction?

In the end, remember this: your financial health is a reflection of your commitment to yourself. It's about respecting yourself enough to ensure you're not just surviving, but thriving. So, dive deep, take charge, and build that nest egg. Your future self will thank you.

Daily Challenge: Today, take a step towards financial empowerment by setting a specific financial goal for your future, whether it's creating an emergency fund, starting a retirement savings plan, or paying off a debt, and commit to taking action to achieve it.

Daily Reflection:

What resonated with you from today's lesson? How can you apply this truth in your life?

_____

_____

_____

_____

Day 131: Creative Outlets- Paint, Write, Build

Listen, fellas, let's cut through the noise. Divorce? It's a beast, no doubt about it. Your emotions are all over the place, but here's the kicker: You can't let them fester. You've got to channel them somewhere, and what better way than through creative outlets?

Think about it. When was the last time you picked up a paintbrush, penned your thoughts, or built something with your bare hands? Now's the time. Dive deep into that reservoir of emotions and let it spill onto a canvas, paper, or project. Don't tell me you're not creative. That's just a cop-out. Everyone's got a spark; you've just got to find it.

Painting isn't just about pretty landscapes; it's a reflection of your soul. Writing? It's therapy without the hourly fees. Building? It's leaving a tangible mark on the world, proving you were here and you made a difference. Don't underestimate the power of creation. It's transformative. When words fail, let your hands and heart do the talking.

Look, you're navigating a storm right now, but channeling your emotions creatively can be your anchor. It's not about becoming the next Picasso or Hemingway. It's about discovery, expression, and healing. It's about taking those raw, unfiltered feelings and giving them a purpose. Every stroke, word, or nail is a step towards understanding and rebuilding yourself.

So, what are you waiting for? Dive into the world of creation. Embrace the mess, the chaos, the beauty of it all. Let it be your lifeline, your escape, your voice. Remember, it's not just about creating art; it's about crafting a new chapter for yourself. Don't sleep on this; your soul will thank you.

Daily Challenge: Today, channel your emotions into a creative outlet by starting a new artistic project, whether it's painting, writing, or building something, and let your heart speak through your chosen medium.

Daily Reflection:

What resonated with you from today's lesson? How can you apply this truth in your life?

_____

_____

_____

_____

Day 132: Spiritual Balance- Faith or Philosophy

Listen up. We're diving deep here. I'm not talking about a spa day or a massage, I'm talking about the core of who you are. In the midst of divorce, it's easy to lose yourself, to feel like you're spiraling. But guess what? That core, that spirit inside you? It's not gone. It just needs some recalibration.

Whether you're religious, spiritual, or an outright atheist, now's the time to tap into what gives your life meaning. Find that anchor. If it's faith, lean into it. Go to your place of worship, pray, meditate, do whatever it takes to reconnect. If it's philosophy, dive into those books that once gave you perspective. Rediscover those truths.

It's easy to play the blame game, to wallow in self-pity. But here's the thing: self-pity won't get you anywhere. Spiritual strength will. It's about understanding that this phase, as brutal as it is, is just that - a phase. And how you emerge from it, how you grow, that's entirely up to you.

Surround yourself with positivity. If there are toxic influences, people who pull you down, cut them out. You need clarity. You need to be surrounded by voices that uplift, not ones that drag you deeper into the mire.

Take time daily to reflect. Five minutes, ten minutes, an hour – whatever you can spare. Use that time to center yourself, to find balance, to remind yourself of who you are and where you're headed.

Life's thrown a curveball, sure. But within you is the power, the spirit, the essence to hit back twice as hard. Tap into that. Find your spiritual balance. Because once you do, you'll be unstoppable.

Daily Challenge: Today, take at least 15 minutes to reconnect with what gives your life meaning, whether it's through prayer, meditation, reading, or reflection, and reaffirm your inner strength and purpose in the midst of divorce.

Daily Reflection:

What resonated with you from today's lesson? How can you apply this truth in your life?

_____

_____

_____

_____

Day 133: Therapy Isn't a Dirty Word

Therapy? Yeah, some of you might be rolling your eyes. Thinking it's just for the "broken" or "weak." But let's get one thing straight. Therapy isn't a dirty word. It's a tool, a resource. And just like hitting the gym to sculpt those muscles, therapy is the gym for your mind.

You've been through the wringer with divorce. It's messy, it's painful. Pretending you've got it all together? That's just ego talking. But guess what? Ego won't help you heal. Denying pain? It's like slapping a Band-Aid on a gaping wound and expecting it to heal. It won't.

So, why therapy? Because it's about gaining perspective. It's about understanding patterns, breaking cycles. It's about equipping yourself with strategies to handle stress, anger, resentment. You wouldn't walk around with a broken leg without seeking help. Why do the same with emotional wounds?

It's easy to drown sorrows in a bottle or to mask pain with distractions. But that's temporary. Real men face their challenges head-on. They seek to understand, to grow. So, if you think therapy is just a couch and some guy with a notepad judging you, think again. It's a mirror. It's a roadmap to navigate the complexities of your emotions, to rebuild a stronger, resilient you.

Look, no one's saying you've got to have weekly sessions for life. But giving it a shot? Understanding yourself a little better? There's nothing to lose. Invest in yourself. Your mental well-being, your peace, your future relationships - they're worth it. You're worth it. Remember, seeking help isn't a sign of weakness. Dive deep, face those demons, and come out stronger. That's what real self-care is all about. Ever heard of DivorceCare? Do yourself a favor and search the web for a DivorceCare group near you. It's a lifeline.

Daily Challenge: Embrace the strength within you and take the courageous step of exploring therapy as a valuable tool for healing and personal growth during this challenging time.

Daily Reflection:

What resonated with you from today's lesson? How can you apply this truth in your life?

_____

_____

_____

_____

Day 134: Yoga- Flexibility in Body and Mind

You think yoga's just for the ladies or those dudes who wear tie-dye shirts and chant in the park? Think again. Yoga isn't about fitting a stereotype; it's about breaking them. So, you've been through the ringer with this divorce, right? Your mind's all over the place, your stress level's through the roof, and let's not even talk about that lower back pain from all those nights on the couch. Enter yoga.

Look, I get it. Maybe you're the guy who's all about lifting weights, hitting the gym, or shooting hoops. But let me drop some truth here: flexibility isn't just about touching your toes or nailing a downward dog. It's about adapting, evolving, and rolling with the punches. Life threw a curveball with this divorce, and yoga? It's going to teach you how to catch that ball and throw it right back.

Every time you step onto that mat, you're not just stretching your body; you're stretching your mind. Those poses, that breath work, the meditation – it's all training. Training for resilience, for endurance, for mental clarity. It's a game changer. And in this game of post-divorce life, you need every advantage you can get.

And hey, don't get it twisted. This isn't about becoming some zen master or spiritual guru. This is about self-care. It's about recognizing that if you're going to navigate this new chapter, you've got to be in top form, both mentally and physically. And yoga, my man, is the tool to get you there.

So, put aside the ego, the preconceptions, and the skepticism. Grab a mat, find a class or an online tutorial, and get moving. Because in this post-divorce hustle, flexibility isn't just a nice-to-have; it's a must-have. Adapt, evolve, and show life that you're not just ready for what's next; you're eager for it. Yoga's your ticket in. Don't sleep on it.

Daily Challenge: Embrace the unexpected and step onto your yoga mat today to cultivate both physical and mental flexibility, proving that you're ready to adapt, evolve, and thrive in this post-divorce journey.

Daily Reflection:

What resonated with you from today's lesson? How can you apply this truth in your life?

_____

_____

_____

Day 135: Social Health- Friends Aren't Optional

Listen, gentlemen, I'm going to hit you with some cold, hard truth. You're not an island. You might think that going through a divorce means you've got to put on this tough guy facade, shoulder the burden solo, and push everyone away. But that's where you're dead wrong.

Social health? It's not just some fancy term. It's the lifeline you didn't know you needed. Friends? They aren't optional; they're essential. You know that saying about 'show me your friends, and I'll show you your future'? There's a reason it's stuck around. Your tribe determines your vibe, especially during the rough patches.

You might feel like leaning away, hiding out, and keeping your struggles to yourself. But that's the exact opposite of what you should be doing. Lean in. Your buddies, your mates, your pals - they've got your back. And if they don't? Time to find some new friends who will.

Now, I get it. Ego. Pride. Not wanting to appear vulnerable. But vulnerability isn't weakness; it's strength. It's authenticity. It's real. And right now, more than ever, you need to get real with yourself and with those around you. Share your struggles, let them in on your journey, and I guarantee you, they'll help lighten the load.

Divorce isn't just a legal ending; it's an emotional rollercoaster. And who better to ride that rollercoaster with than your crew? Don't shut them out. Open up, reconnect, and build those bonds stronger than ever. Because in the end, when the dust settles, it's the relationships we nurture that truly define our strength. So, prioritize your social health. Friends aren't just an option; they're the game-changer you didn't know you needed.

Daily Challenge: Today, reach out to a friend or loved one, share a part of your divorce journey with them, and let them in on your struggles - remember, vulnerability is a source of strength, and your support network is there to help you through this.

Daily Reflection:

What resonated with you from today's lesson? How can you apply this truth in your life?

_____

_____

_____

_____

Day 136: Self-Compassion- Be Your Own Best Friend

Listen, man, I get it. Divorce hits like a freight train and suddenly you're questioning everything. Your worth, your choices, your identity. But let me lay it down for you straight: It's time to step up and be your own biggest advocate.

So you messed up, or maybe you didn't. It doesn't matter. What matters is what you do next. And step one is showing yourself some much-needed self-compassion. Why? Because if you're beating yourself up every day, who's going to have the energy to move forward? Not you.

You're your own best asset. Treat yourself like it. When you'd be understanding and forgiving to a friend, why not show yourself the same courtesy? Stop replaying the past. Stop with the "what ifs" and the "should haves." Divorce isn't a failure; it's a redirection. It's a chance to reassess and reinvent. But you can't do that if you're stuck in a cycle of self-blame.

Look in the mirror. That guy staring back? He's been through the ringer. He's hurting, sure, but he's also resilient, adaptable, and stronger than he gives himself credit for. So give him a break. Talk to him like he's a buddy going through a rough patch, because that's exactly what he is.

It's time to shift gears. Instead of being your own worst enemy, start being your own best friend. You're not in this alone. You've got yourself. And trust me, that's a lot. So, show some self-compassion. Give yourself the grace to heal, the space to grow, and the respect you deserve. Because at the end of the day, you're all you've got. Make it count.

Daily Challenge: Today, practice self-compassion by forgiving yourself for any perceived mistakes, letting go of self-blame, and treating yourself with the same kindness and understanding you would offer to a friend in need.

Daily Reflection:

What resonated with you from today's lesson? How can you apply this truth in your life?

_____

_____

_____

_____

Day 137: Laughter as Medicine- Lighten Up

You're in the thick of it, man. Divorce isn't a walk in the park. You're feeling the weight, the pressure, the emotional rollercoaster. It's rough, and no one's denying that. But here's the thing: laughter? It's not just something you do when you catch a funny movie or hear a joke. It's medicine. It's therapy. It's that powerful tool you're overlooking.

Let's break it down. You've heard "laughter is the best medicine" tossed around, right? It's not just a saying; it's the real deal. When you laugh, your brain releases endorphins. Those are the feel-good chemicals that combat stress and pain. So why aren't you laughing more? Why are you letting the weight of the world crush you when a good chuckle can lift you right up?

Now, I'm not saying ignore the pain. I'm not saying don't process your emotions. But in the midst of all this heavy, you need to find moments to lighten up. Whether it's revisiting that comedy series you love, hanging out with that friend who always cracks you up, or just finding humor in the absurdity of life – you've got to carve out moments to let loose and laugh.

You want resilience? You want to bounce back stronger? Laughter is your secret weapon. It's a reminder that amidst the chaos, there's joy. Amidst the pain, there's relief. And in the middle of this storm, there's a break in the clouds where you can see the sun shining.

So, take a moment. Take many moments. Laugh. Lighten up. Let it be the remedy that gets you through the darkest nights. Because trust me, when you look back, you'll realize those moments of laughter weren't just breaks from the pain; they were the stepping stones to your recovery.

Daily Challenge: Today, make a conscious effort to find humor in at least one situation, whether it's a funny video, a joke, or a light-hearted conversation, and let laughter be your medicine for the day.

Daily Reflection:

What resonated with you from today's lesson? How can you apply this truth in your life?

_____

_____

_____

_____

Day 138: Mindful Eating- More Than Just a Diet

Look, after a divorce, it's tempting to drown sorrows in junk food or skip meals altogether. But here's the truth: what you put in your body isn't just about the physical. It's about the mental, the emotional, the whole package. You can't expect to come out of this stronger if you're fueling yourself with garbage.

You've heard of mindful eating? It's not some trendy diet fad. It's a shift in perspective. It's about being present in the moment, understanding what you're consuming, and why. It's about respecting your body and giving it the nourishment it needs. Not because some magazine told you to, but because you recognize the value in treating yourself right.

Every bite you take? That's a choice. Every meal you have? Another decision. Start asking yourself: why am I eating this? Is it out of habit, boredom, or genuine hunger? Are you eating to fill a void left by the divorce, or are you genuinely nourishing your body?

And it's not about going extreme, cutting out entire food groups, or jumping on the latest diet bandwagon. It's about balance. It's about understanding that food isn't just fuel; it's medicine. It's therapy. It can be a source of joy, but it shouldn't be your only source of comfort.

So, as you navigate this new chapter, remember this: mindful eating isn't about restrictions. It's about empowerment. It's a commitment to yourself, a promise that even in the midst of chaos, you won't neglect the basics. Because when you take care of your body, you're also taking care of your mind and soul. It's all connected. And you? You deserve the best. So, make that choice. Choose mindful eating. Choose you.

Daily Challenge: Today, make a conscious effort to pause and reflect before every meal, asking yourself why you're eating and whether it's in alignment with nourishing your body and your well-being.

Daily Reflection:

What resonated with you from today's lesson? How can you apply this truth in your life?

_____

_____

_____

_____

Day 139: Gratitude- Count Your Wins, Not Losses

You're going through one of the toughest experiences in life, and it's easy to get lost in the sea of negativity, to dwell on what went wrong. But here's the truth, and it might sting a bit: dwelling on the losses won't change a thing. What you can change, however, is your perspective. It's time to practice gratitude. Count your wins, not your losses.

Gratitude isn't some fluffy, feel-good concept. It's a mindset shift, a weapon in your arsenal, a tool to pull you out of the rut. Think about it: every morning you wake up, you've got another shot, another day to make things right, to grow, to learn. That's a win right there.

Reflect on your life. Yeah, the marriage didn't work out, but what did you gain from it? Lessons learned, experiences shared, maybe kids who light up your world. Those are your wins. Every challenge you faced and overcame in the relationship, every time you picked yourself up, every ounce of love you gave – those are badges of honor, my friend. Wear them with pride.

Don't let the weight of the past pull you down. Instead, use gratitude as your anchor, grounding you to the present, to the positives. The more you focus on what you have, the less you'll mourn what you lost. And the more you'll realize that you're not just surviving; you're thriving.

It's all about perspective. You've got this. Start counting those wins. Embrace gratitude. It's not about denying the pain, but about recognizing the strength, resilience, and abundance in your life. Because when you do, you'll find that the world is still full of possibilities, just waiting for you to seize them.

Daily Challenge: Today, write down three things you're grateful for, no matter how small they may seem, and let them serve as a reminder of the positive aspects in your life during this challenging time.

Daily Reflection:

What resonated with you from today's lesson? How can you apply this truth in your life?

_____

_____

_____

_____

Day 140: Meditation- The Art of Doing Nothing

Meditation? Some of you might be rolling your eyes, thinking it's all woo-woo, or just for those "enlightened" folks. But let's cut through the noise. Meditation is the gym workout for your mind. And trust me, if there's ever a time your mind needs that workout, it's during a divorce.

Take a second. Think about all the chatter, the noise, the chaos going on up there. The "what ifs", the replayed arguments, the self-doubt. It's like a never-ending, chaotic traffic jam. Meditation? That's your traffic cop. It's about taking back control, hitting pause, and finding a brief moment of clarity in the storm.

Doing nothing? That's the biggest misconception. Meditation isn't about doing nothing; it's about understanding everything. It's about getting to the core of who you are, understanding your reactions, and giving yourself the space to breathe, reflect, and reset.

Look, I get it. Sitting still, focusing on your breath might sound simple, maybe even pointless. But think about how often you genuinely give yourself permission to just BE. No distractions, no judgments. Just you and your thoughts. It's harder than it sounds, but the rewards? Immense.

In this whirlwind of legal battles, emotional roller coasters, and reshuffling life, it's easy to lose yourself. Meditation is your anchor. A daily reminder that amidst the chaos, there's a calm, steady version of you, waiting to take the reins. So, stop dismissing it. Dive in. Give your mind the break it deserves, and watch how it transforms your reaction to everything around you. Remember, it's not about doing nothing. It's about understanding everything. Dive in.

Daily Challenge: Find 10 minutes today to sit in silence, focus on your breath, and meditate to regain control of your thoughts and bring clarity to your mind during this challenging time.

Daily Reflection:

What resonated with you from today's lesson? How can you apply this truth in your life?

_____

_____

_____

_____

Day 141: Nature Therapy- Get Outdoors

Look, the walls of your house? They're not just physical barriers. They're psychological ones too. After a divorce, they can close in on you, suffocate you. But here's the antidote: nature. You've probably heard about nature therapy, but let's cut through the fluff. Nature isn't just some trendy wellness buzzword; it's a tried and true reset button.

You're wired for connection, not just to people, but to the world around you. You think those hours you spend scrolling on your phone are helping? Think again. Every moment you're indoors, plastered to screens, you're missing out on the raw, unfiltered, no-bull clarity that nature brings.

Remember when you were a kid? Running wild, feeling the grass under your feet, the sun on your face? That wasn't just play; that was freedom. That's what you need right now. Those trees, mountains, rivers? They've seen centuries come and go. Your pain? It's real, but in the grand scheme, it's a blip. Nature has a way of putting things into perspective.

So, pull yourself off that couch. Lace up those shoes. Hit a trail, climb a mountain, or just sit by a river. Listen to the wind, the chirping birds, the rustling leaves. Breathe. Deeply. Let nature remind you of who you are, of your place in this vast universe.

It's not about escaping your problems, but facing them with a clearer mind. Nature doesn't judge; it heals. So, the next time the weight of the world is crushing you? Don't sulk. Don't dwell. Get outside. Let nature do its thing. It's therapy, the kind you can't get in any office.

Daily Challenge: Today, make a commitment to spend at least 30 minutes in nature, whether it's a park, a forest, or simply your backyard, and allow the natural world to provide you with the mental and emotional clarity you need to face your challenges head-on.

Daily Reflection:

What resonated with you from today's lesson? How can you apply this truth in your life?

_____

_____

_____

_____

Day 142: Volunteer- Give to Get Back

You're going through a divorce, and I get it, it feels like you've been hit by a ton of bricks. But here's a twist you might not have considered: Sometimes, when life feels like it's falling apart, the best move isn't to look inward, but outward. Yeah, you heard me right. Volunteer. Give back. It sounds counterintuitive, but trust me on this.

When you're knee-deep in paperwork, emotions, and the messy aftermath of a broken relationship, it's easy to get wrapped up in your own narrative. But there's a world out there that needs you, a world where you can make a difference.

When you give, you get back tenfold. Not in money or material things, but in perspective, purpose, and healing. Connecting with others, making a difference, realizing that there's a bigger picture out there—it's transformative. It shifts your focus from what you've lost to what you can give, and what you gain in the process is immeasurable.

You've got skills, talents, and experiences that can benefit others. Maybe it's mentoring a young guy going through a tough time, helping out at a local shelter, or using your professional skills for a cause you believe in. Whatever it is, dive in. Immerse yourself in the act of giving without expecting anything in return.

Because here's the truth: the act of giving not only helps heal the community, but it also heals you. It reminds you of your worth, your value, and your place in the world. In a time when everything feels uncertain, volunteering grounds you. It's a reminder that even in the midst of personal chaos, you can be a beacon of hope and positivity for others. So go on, step out and give. The return on investment is immeasurable.

Daily Challenge: Today, step out of your comfort zone and find a volunteer opportunity that resonates with you, because in giving to others, you'll discover the transformative power of healing and purpose during your divorce journey.

Daily Reflection:

What resonated with you from today's lesson? How can you apply this truth in your life?

_____

_____

_____

_____

Day 143: Music as Therapy

Listen up, gents. Divorce can throw you into a spiral, and the chaos around you can feel unbearable. But amidst this whirlwind, there's an anchor you might've overlooked: music. Yeah, that's right. Those beats, those rhythms, those melodies – they're not just for background noise. They're your lifeline.

Ever noticed how a single track can transport you back to a memory, a feeling, or even an entire era? That's the power of music. And right now, when you're wrestling with emotions, questioning decisions, and trying to find your footing, music can be that therapy you didn't know you needed.

Forget the clichés. This isn't about sappy breakup songs or rage-filled anthems. This is about harnessing music to navigate through the storm. Find those tracks that lift you, that inspire you, that make you want to get up and face another day. Dive deep into lyrics that resonate, beats that motivate, and harmonies that soothe the soul.

But don't just listen. Feel it. Let it wash over you. Let it challenge you. When words fail, music speaks. It's a universal language, one that connects us to our deepest emotions, our rawest vulnerabilities. It's a tool, a weapon even, to tackle the hardships head-on.

And if you're thinking, "Music? Really? How's that going to help?", then you're missing the point. It's not about the notes, the instruments, or the artists. It's about resonance. It's about finding something that connects with your soul, that gives voice to your pain, that helps you process, heal, and ultimately, move forward. So, the next time you feel lost in the maze of divorce, plug in those earphones, blast that stereo, or even pick up an instrument. Use music as your therapy. Tune in to those tracks, and tune out the noise. It's time to heal, one song at a time.

Daily Challenge: Today, seek out a song that resonates with your emotions and listen to it with intention, allowing its lyrics and melodies to guide you through a moment of self-reflection and healing.

Daily Reflection:

What resonated with you from today's lesson? How can you apply this truth in your life?

_____

_____

_____

_____

Day 144: Travel- Expand Your Horizons

Divorce is a reset button, whether you asked for it or not. It's a shakeup, a wake-up call, and while it's okay to mourn the past, there's a world out there waiting for you. You've been boxed in, maybe for years, and now? It's time to break out.

Travel. Yeah, I said it. Pack a bag, grab a ticket, and just go. See the world. Why? Because it's vast, diverse, and full of lessons you won't learn in your hometown. Every new place, every new culture is a chance to rediscover who you are outside of that relationship label. Man, there's nothing like standing on a mountain, diving deep into an ocean, or wandering through a city where no one knows your name. It's liberating. It's rejuvenating.

But it's not just about sightseeing. It's about expanding your mind, challenging your perspectives. It's about realizing that there's so much more to life than that bubble you've been living in. New experiences mold character, build resilience, and teach you adaptability. Maybe you've been defined by your relationship for so long that you've forgotten the other parts of you. Well, guess what? The world is a refresher course.

You want to move on? Really move on? Then move. Literally. Get out of your comfort zone. Meet new people, taste new foods, immerse yourself in a new language. Rediscover passions you forgot you had or find entirely new ones.

You're not running away; you're running towards something - a broader perspective, a deeper understanding, and a renewed sense of self. So, go. Dive into the unknown. There's a whole world out there, waiting to show you who you can really be. Don't miss out.

Daily Challenge: Today, take one concrete step towards breaking out of your comfort zone, whether it's planning a trip, signing up for a new class, or simply reaching out to someone new and striking up a conversation.

Daily Reflection:

What resonated with you from today's lesson? How can you apply this truth in your life?

_____

_____

_____

_____

Day 145: Massage and Bodywork- Physical Release

Y ou've been through the wringer. Your mind's a war zone, emotions are swinging left and right, but what about your body? You think it's not keeping score? Think again. Every sleepless night, every tension-filled argument, every moment of stress - it's all getting stored right in your muscles, your joints, everywhere.

Enter massage and bodywork. Don't brush it off as just a spa luxury or something reserved for a special occasion. This is about maintenance, man. Just as you wouldn't let your car run without an oil change, don't let your body go without some much-needed TLC.

Massage is more than just relaxation. It's a powerful tool for physical release. It digs deep, addressing those knots of tension, increasing circulation, and helping your body heal. All that pent-up stress? It's toxic. And massage is one way to flush some of it out, giving your body a chance to reset. But it's not just about the physical. There's a mental game here too. As your muscles relax, so does your mind. It's a break. A pause button in the midst of chaos. A chance to breathe and let go, even if just for an hour.

And don't just stop at traditional massage. Explore other bodywork modalities like acupuncture, chiropractic adjustments, or even more specialized treatments. Your body's been keeping the score, and it's time to settle the tab.

So, here's the deal. Prioritize it. Make it non-negotiable. Book that session. Your body's been through a marathon with this divorce, and it's screaming for a reprieve. Listen to it. Give it the release it craves. You owe it that much.

Daily Challenge: Schedule a massage or bodywork session today to provide your body with the much-needed release and reset it deserves after enduring the physical and emotional toll of your divorce journey.

Daily Reflection:

What resonated with you from today's lesson? How can you apply this truth in your life?

_____

_____

_____

_____

Day 146: Learning- Never Stop Growing

Listen, gents, I get it. Divorce can make you feel like you've been thrown into a tornado, everything spinning, nothing making sense. But here's the deal: when everything around you is chaos, the one thing you can control is your personal growth. You think this is the end? No way. It's a new beginning, a reset button. And the most powerful weapon you've got? Learning.

You see, when life knocks you down seven times, you get up eight. But each time you rise, you've got to be smarter, wiser, stronger. And that comes from constant learning. Don't let pain be your endpoint; make it your launchpad. Dive deep into books, podcasts, seminars, whatever fuels your mind. Knowledge isn't just power; it's resilience, it's growth, it's your ticket to a better tomorrow.

And here's the trick: don't just focus on stuff about relationships or healing. Broaden your horizon. Learn a new language, pick up a new skill, understand the world of finance, or explore the mysteries of the universe. Because when you expand your knowledge, you not only distract your mind from the hurt, but you also build a better version of yourself.

This isn't the time to stagnate. It's the time to hustle, to grind, to absorb everything you can. You owe it to yourself. So, when someone asks how you're dealing with the divorce, you can say, "I'm growing, I'm evolving, I'm learning." Turn this phase into a chapter where you come out not just healed, but elevated. Your future self will thank you. Remember, every setback is a setup for a comeback. And the key? Never stop learning. Never stop growing. Period.

Daily Challenge: Embrace the power of learning by dedicating at least 30 minutes today to acquire new knowledge or a skill that goes beyond your comfort zone, because your growth during this difficult time is your ultimate triumph.

Daily Reflection:

What resonated with you from today's lesson? How can you apply this truth in your life?

_____

_____

_____

_____

Day 147: Detox Your Social Circle

When you're going through a divorce, you've got enough on your plate. Emotions, legal battles, financial shifts; it's a whirlwind. But let's zero in on something a lot of guys overlook: the people you surround yourself with. Your social circle. Let me be straight with you: it's time for a detox.

You've outgrown certain friendships, and that's okay. It's life. We evolve, and so do our relationships. Some friends, as much as you've history with them, might be anchoring you to the past. Holding onto relationships that don't serve your growth? That's baggage. And right now, you can't afford extra weight.

Here's the deal. You need allies, not spectators. People who uplift you, challenge you, and genuinely want the best for you. Not those who feed off drama or see your situation as juicy gossip material. And trust me, it's easy to spot them if you're looking. They're the ones with unsolicited advice, the ones who are 'just checking in' a bit too often with a hint of schadenfreude.

Now is the perfect time to evaluate. Who's genuinely there for you? Who's just there for the show? You need a circle that pushes you forward, not one that drags you back into the mud. Surround yourself with positive influences, those who remind you of your worth and potential, and those who understand the journey you're on.

It's not about cutting people off with animosity. It's about recognizing what you need right now and giving yourself permission to seek it out. Your growth, your mental well-being, your future— it all starts with the company you keep. So, detox that circle. Prioritize yourself. You've got this.

Daily Challenge: Take a moment today to assess your social circle and identify at least one relationship that no longer serves your growth, then take a step toward distancing yourself from that negative influence and actively seek out positive allies who support your journey.

Daily Reflection:

What resonated with you from today's lesson? How can you apply this truth in your life?

_____

_____

_____

_____

Day 148: Make Time for Play

Listen up, guys. I get it. Divorce? It's a storm. But while you're navigating these rough waters, don't forget one thing: Life's not just about surviving the storm, it's about learning to dance in the rain. And that means making time for play.

Why play? Because you're not a robot programmed to just deal with legalities, assets, and heartbreak. You're a human being with needs, dreams, and a heartbeat that craves joy. Play isn't just some frivolous act; it's a lifeline. It's the oxygen when you're drowning in stress.

Now, I'm not just talking about video games or shooting hoops, although if that's your jam, go for it. Play is about finding joy in the little moments, getting out of your head, and into the game of life. It's about reconnecting with who you were before the world told you who you should be.

Remember those hobbies you shelved? The guitar gathering dust, the hiking boots in the back of the closet, the bike with flat tires? It's time to bring them back into your life. It's time to feel that adrenaline, that joy, that pure unadulterated fun. And here's the kicker: Play isn't just good for your soul; it's good for your health. It lowers stress, increases creativity, and boosts your mental well-being.

So, while you're figuring out the tough stuff, don't forget to schedule in some playtime. It's not being selfish; it's self-preservation. In this whirlwind of change, don't lose sight of yourself. Dive into play, embrace joy, and remember, life isn't waiting for the storm to pass; it's about learning to dance in the rain. Make time for it.

Daily Challenge: Today, rekindle a long-lost hobby or try something new that brings you joy, because amidst life's storms, finding time to play is essential for your well-being and resilience.

Daily Reflection:

What resonated with you from today's lesson? How can you apply this truth in your life?

_____

_____

_____

_____

Day 149: Coaches, Therapists, Advisors

Listen up, gentlemen. If you're still under the impression that reaching out for help makes you weak, it's time to ditch that outdated mindset. This isn't a game where you can press 'restart' when things go south. It's your life, and sometimes you need a playbook and a coach to guide you through it.

You think LeBron gets on the court without coaching? Think again. Coaches, therapists, advisors – they aren't just for athletes or people in movies. They're for every man who knows the value of a strategic play, especially when life throws a curveball like divorce.

Therapists? They aren't there to label or judge. They're your mental fitness trainers, helping you navigate the chaos, process the pain, and come out stronger on the other side. They give you tools, not just pep talks.

And advisors? Man, if you think you can navigate the financial maze of divorce on your own, you're setting yourself up. An advisor is that person ensuring you don't get blindsided, keeping you on track, and making sure you understand every play in the book.

It's easy to get lost in pride. But remember, every champ had a coach, every great mind had a mentor. You're going through one of the most challenging times in your life. Get that support, get that guidance. Swallow the pill of humility, and understand that seeking help isn't about weakness; it's about strategy. So, don't just stand there and take hit after hit. Get in the ring, but make sure you've got the best corner team backing you up.

Daily Challenge: Embrace the strength in seeking help and support; reach out to a therapist or advisor who can guide you through the challenges of divorce, because every champion had a coach, and every great mind had a mentor.

Daily Reflection:

What resonated with you from today's lesson? How can you apply this truth in your life?

_____

_____

_____

_____

Day 150: Self-Care Milestone

L isten up, gentlemen. Day 150. You've made it this far, but the journey's far from over. Now more than ever, it's crucial to check in with numero uno – yourself. You might be thinking, "Self-care? Isn't that just spa days and bubble baths?" Toss that mindset out the window. This is about rebuilding, recalibrating, and reclaiming your life.

You've been thrown into the storm, battered from all sides. But here's the truth - storms end, and what's left is up to you. So, are you going to come out of this stronger or stuck in the same rut? It's easy to drown in self-pity, replaying the what-ifs and might-have-beens. But you know what's hard? Taking a good, hard look in the mirror and deciding that you're worth the effort. Worth the growth. Worth the happiness.

Think of yourself as a prime investment. Would you let your best stock wither away without intervention? Heck no. So why do it to yourself? Hit the gym, not for her or anyone else, but for YOU. Read that book, learn that skill, take that trip. Fuel your body right. That junk food might give you a momentary high, but it's dragging you down in the long run.

You've been given a fresh slate, whether you asked for it or not. Now, how you fill it is in your hands. Don't waste it. Dive into hobbies, reconnect with old pals, discover new passions. Remember, healing isn't linear. Some days will be tougher than others. But every time you prioritize yourself, every time you choose growth over stagnation, you're making progress. Day 150 is just a milestone. Your journey? It's only just begun. Embrace it. Own it. You've got this.

Daily Challenge: Today, prioritize your well-being by taking a deliberate step towards personal growth, whether it's a small accomplishment or a big leap, because investing in yourself is the key to a brighter future.

Daily Reflection:

What resonated with you from today's lesson? How can you apply this truth in your life?

_____

_____

_____

_____

Cut Off the Dead Weight

Navigating the complexities of social dynamics post-separation can be challenging. This section explores the intricacies of facing public opinion, managing mutual friends, and maintaining professionalism at work. You'll also learn how to handle family gatherings without your ex, the nuances of social media connections, and the shift in your relationships with single friends. Rebuilding trust in friendships, addressing workplace rumors, and managing the dynamics of family and social events are all part of this journey. Discover new social norms, etiquette, and the art of redefining your social life.

Day 151: Old Friends- Keep or Cut?

After a divorce, your world is upside down, and guess what? Your circle of friends, they're part of that whirlwind too. You might be thinking, "These are my boys, they've got my back." And maybe some do, but others? They're dead weight. Now's the time to take a hard look at your roster.

Old friends? Yeah, there's nostalgia. Shared memories, inside jokes, history. But history isn't enough. Loyalty isn't about how many beers you've shared; it's about who shows up when your world is imploding. If they're whispering behind your back, if they're subtly siding with your ex or playing both sides, do you really need that kind of energy in your life?

Here's the truth: You're reshaping, rebuilding, redefining yourself. Every decision you make, every person you let in your circle, affects that process. You don't need anchors right now; you need rocket fuel.

So, ask yourself, does hanging out with that old buddy make you feel uplifted or drained? Supported or judged? Understood or alienated? It's not about cutting ties for the sake of it. It's about conscious choices. Quality over quantity, man. Would you rather have a tight circle of real allies or a crowded room of half-hearted acquaintances?

Bottom line: Keep the ride-or-dies, the ones who hold you up when you're down, who remind you of your worth and your strength. And the rest? Cut 'em loose. Your future self will thank you. Because as you grow, evolve, and rebuild, you need a tribe that's genuinely in your corner, not just spectators on the sideline. The choice is yours. Keep or cut? Choose wisely.

Daily Challenge: Evaluate your friendships today - assess whether they uplift, support, and understand you, and be willing to cut loose those who don't genuinely have your back as you reshape and rebuild your life post-divorce.

Daily Reflection:

What resonated with you from today's lesson? How can you apply this truth in your life?

_____

_____

_____

_____

Day 152: New Friends- Broaden Your Circle

You've come out of a storm, man. Your whole world flipped upside down, and suddenly you find yourself at crossroads with some of the folks you called friends. Here's a dose of raw truth for you: not everyone you shared beers with on Friday nights is worth carrying forward in this new chapter of your life. Harsh? Maybe. Necessary? Absolutely.

Your circle of friends – it's got to be a reflection of where you're headed, not just where you've been. So ask yourself, are these the folks who'll cheer you on as you rebuild, as you rise from the ashes? Or are they just there for the gossip, the old times, and the drama? You're not a soap opera; you're a man with ambition, goals, and dreams.

Here's the play: Step out of your comfort zone. Broaden your circle. There's a world full of people out there who share your passions, your interests, who've walked your path, or are walking it right now. You want to surround yourself with those who will challenge you, push you, elevate you. Seek them out. Join a club, attend workshops, network online. Dive deep into a hobby. Whatever it is, just get out there.

Nostalgia's a killer if you let it chain you down. The good ol' days? They were good for a reason, but they're in the past. Your focus? The present and the future. So, as you embark on this journey of rediscovery, ensure the company you keep is vibing with your future, not just reminiscing about your past. New friends, new energy, new momentum. Let's get it!

Daily Challenge: Take a bold step today to expand your social circle by reaching out to at least one new person who shares your interests and aspirations, and nurture a connection that aligns with the future you're striving to create.

Daily Reflection:

What resonated with you from today's lesson? How can you apply this truth in your life?

_____

_____

_____

_____

Day 153: Work Life- Divorce Doesn't Define You

Listen up, man. Just because you're going through a divorce doesn't mean you wear it like a neon sign flashing above your head at work. Your job? That's your turf, your domain. Your performance, your passion, your paycheck. Divorce? That's one chapter, not your entire narrative.

You think people at work care about your personal life? Maybe they do, for a hot second, when they're grabbing their morning coffee. But at the end of the day, it's about results, your drive, your hustle. You're not "John from accounting going through a divorce." You're "John, the guy who nails every project and smashes targets."

Divorce doesn't define you. You do. With every choice, every word, every action. If rumors start? Let 'em. You can't control the chatter, but you can control your reaction. Don't give them the satisfaction of seeing you sweat. Turn that pain into fuel, that frustration into focus. If someone tries to label you, prove them wrong. Show them you're bigger than your circumstances.

And yeah, it hurts. Nights can be long, and mornings can be brutal. But every time you step into that office, you have a choice: drown in pity or rise with purpose. So, what's it gonna be? You gonna let this define your entire identity, or are you gonna show the world – and more importantly, yourself – that you're made of tougher stuff?

Your legacy isn't written in ink; it's written in action. Your divorce is a speed bump, not a stop sign. Keep your foot on the gas, keep your eyes on the prize, and let the world see you for who you truly are a force to be reckoned with. Period.

Daily Challenge: Today, when you walk into the office, remind yourself that you are not defined by your divorce; you are defined by your determination, so focus on being the best version of yourself and let your actions speak louder than any labels or rumors.

Daily Reflection:

What resonated with you from today's lesson? How can you apply this truth in your life?

_____

_____

_____

_____

Day 154: Toxic Friends- Identify and Evict

Divorce is like a litmus test. It reveals the true colors of the people around you. Some friends? They're gold. They stand by you, rain or shine. Others? Well, they're like those freebie sunglasses you get at events - they look good for a moment, but they break when you need them most.

Now, post-divorce, there's no room for fair-weather friends. Those who whisper behind your back, the ones feeding off your downfall, or those just waiting to say, "I told you so"? It's eviction time. And I'm not talking about a gentle nudge. I'm talking a full-on kick to the curb. Your energy is premium real estate, and not everyone deserves a spot.

But here's the tricky part: identification. Toxicity doesn't always come screaming in your face. Sometimes it's subtle. It's the friend who subtly undermines your decisions. The buddy who always seems to bring up the past just when you're trying to move on. The one who makes light of your pain. Watch. Listen. Feel. Your gut knows.

This isn't high school. You're not here to win a popularity contest. Post-divorce life is about rebuilding stronger and better. And for that, you need a foundation that's rock solid. Not one that's crumbling with toxicity.

So, no more playing nice. It's time for some hard decisions. Who gets the VIP pass to your life, and who gets the boot? Remember, every person you allow into your space influences your mindset and your trajectory. So, be ruthless. Identify the dead weight and cut it off. Your future self will thank you for it. And trust me, that's the only validation you need.

Daily Challenge: Assess your circle of friends and acquaintances today and identify anyone who subtly undermines your well-being or progress; then, take the courageous step to distance yourself from toxic influences.

Daily Reflection:

What resonated with you from today's lesson? How can you apply this truth in your life?

_____

_____

_____

_____

Day 155: Mutual Friends- The Awkward Divide

Listen up. After the split, things get real with mutual friends. It's not child's play anymore. It's like the aftermath of a tornado. Everything's scattered, and you're trying to figure out where things stand. Some friends might side with her, and some might side with you. But here's the raw truth: It's not about sides.

Friends that make you pick? They're not friends. Period. If they're talking trash or feeding into the drama, cut them off. You don't need that noise in your life. It's a purification process, separating the wheat from the chaff. Remember, quality over quantity.

Now, I get it. There's history, memories, and shared moments. But if they're making it awkward, it's on them. You've got enough on your plate without dealing with petty loyalties. Loyalty shouldn't be circumstantial. Either they're with you, or they're not.

Navigating this awkward divide means being authentic. Stay true to yourself. Don't play games or try to win people over. It's not a competition. If someone's torn between you and your ex, let them figure it out. Your path? Forward momentum, with or without them. Mutual friends should be a source of support, not stress.

Look, it's a transition. And transitions? They're messy, uncomfortable, but necessary. Reframe it. It's not about losing friends; it's about gaining clarity. Recognize the ones who genuinely care. The ones who stick by you, not because it's easy, but because it's right.

Daily Challenge: Embrace the purification process of friendship and cut off those who make you choose sides or add unnecessary drama to your life, focusing on quality over quantity in your support network.

Daily Reflection:

What resonated with you from today's lesson? How can you apply this truth in your life?

_____

_____

_____

_____

Day 156: Keep Your Personal Life Personal

Listen up, because we're diving deep into some real talk. You just got out of a marriage, and I guarantee there's a whole bunch of noise buzzing around you. Friends asking questions, co-workers whispering, family tiptoeing. But here's the raw truth: Your personal life? It's called "personal" for a reason.

After a split, it's tempting to vent, to overshare, to rally troops to your side. But every time you spill your guts to the guy in the next cubicle or rant on social media, you're giving away a piece of your power. And man, after a divorce, you need all the power you can muster.

Why? Because it's a fresh start, a rebirth. But rebirths are messy, and you don't need the peanut gallery giving their two cents on your life choices. That unsolicited advice, the pitying glances, the "I told you so's"—they don't do jack to help you move forward.

You think Steve from accounting really cares about your well-being? Nah, he's just hunting for some office gossip. And Aunt Karen? She's got enough drama in her own life without adding yours to the mix. Your journey, your healing, your next steps—they're yours and yours alone. Guard them. Cherish them. Own them.

Here's the game plan: Keep it tight. Trust a select few. Those genuine buddies who've had your back since day one? Lean on them. Everyone else? Give them a nod, a smile, move on. Because at the end of the day, your personal life, your peace, your path forward—it's not up for public consumption. Stay focused, stay strong, and remember: Your story is yours to tell, on your terms. Keep it personal.

Daily Challenge: Today, practice the art of discretion by resisting the urge to share your personal struggles with the world; confide only in those genuine friends who have stood by you, and remember, your story is yours to tell, on your terms.

Daily Reflection:

What resonated with you from today's lesson? How can you apply this truth in your life?

_____

_____

_____

_____

Day 157: Family Matters- Your Rock or Your Anchor?

F amily. They can either be the rock that grounds you or the anchor that drags you down. After a divorce, it's a whirlwind. Everyone's got an opinion, a piece of unsolicited advice, or a "I told you so." But let's get one thing straight: This is YOUR journey. Yours. Not Uncle Bob's, not your in-laws, not even your parents. Yours.

You remember when you were a kid and you'd fall? Some family members would rush over, babying you, making it seem like the world ended. Others? They'd tell you to brush it off, stand up, and move. Both reactions came from a place of love, but one made you resilient, the other vulnerable. In the aftermath of a divorce, you're gonna face both these types again.

Listen, love and respect your family, but recognize the difference between support and smothering. Constructive advice and plain nosiness. Some family members will be your rock – pushing you, challenging you, supporting you. Others might unknowingly become anchors – constantly dragging up the past, feeding negativity, or just being overbearing.

It's on YOU to decide the role they play in your healing process. Set boundaries. Decide who you let in close and who you keep at arm's length. It's not about shutting people out; it's about letting the right ones in.

Life post-divorce is about recalibrating. And sometimes, recalibration means reassessing family dynamics. So, ask yourself: Who's the rock? Who's the anchor? Make choices, not sacrifices. Your well-being and peace of mind? They're worth it. Remember, at the end of the day, you're the captain of your ship. Steer it right.

Daily Challenge: Today, assess the role your family members are playing in your post-divorce journey, and take a proactive step to set healthy boundaries with those who may be anchoring you down, ensuring you prioritize your own well-being and peace of mind.

Daily Reflection:

What resonated with you from today's lesson? How can you apply this truth in your life?

_____

_____

_____

_____

Day 158: Reconnect or Disconnect- Old Acquaintances

L ife after a split isn't a time to tiptoe; it's a time to make choices. Choices that impact the very core of who you are and who you're about to become. So, let's get real about those old acquaintances.

Remember that guy you used to hang out with who always seemed to pull you into his drama? Or that couple you and your ex would double date with? It's decision time, man. Are these connections still serving you, or are they remnants of a past you're trying to move beyond?

You're evolving, growing, reshaping yourself. And just like a snake shedding its skin, not everything from your past life is gonna fit into this new one. Some folks will align with this journey, while others? They might be anchors. Now, don't get it twisted. This isn't about blaming or seeing them as bad; it's about recognizing what works for YOU.

Every person you keep in your life is an investment – of time, of energy, of emotional bandwidth. Post-divorce, your bandwidth is precious. Guard it. Ask yourself: Do these old acquaintances lift you up? Inspire you? Support the new you? Or do they drag you back into old patterns, old dramas, and old mindsets?

Now, here's the punchline. YOU and only you get to decide who gets a seat at the table of your life. Choose wisely. You don't need a crowd; you need a crew. A crew that vibes with where you're headed. So, whether it's reconnect or disconnect, make the call. And remember, this is about shaping YOUR world, no apologies, no looking back. Forward is the only direction we're going, my man.

Daily Challenge: Take a moment today to evaluate the people in your life and ask yourself if they align with your journey of self-improvement and growth post-divorce, and don't hesitate to make the necessary choices to surround yourself with those who support your new path.

Daily Reflection:

What resonated with you from today's lesson? How can you apply this truth in your life?

_____

_____

_____

_____

Day 159: Social Media Cleanse- Time for a Reset

Listen, man. Social media is a double-edged sword. On one side, it's the highlight reel of people's best moments, tailored and filtered to perfection. On the other? It's the comparison trap, the ex's new life broadcasted, and the temptation to stalk and sulk. Let's be clear: after a divorce, it's neither your friend nor therapist.

Stop scrolling, hoping to catch a glimpse of her new life. And for God's sake, don't let yourself get baited into posting passive-aggressive crap hoping she sees it. What's that gonna achieve? A few fleeting moments of satisfaction? Nah, that's not the game we're playing. We're playing the long game. And in the long game, you've got to look out for number one: YOU.

Hit that reset button. Cleanse that feed. Unfollow. Mute. Whatever it takes. This is the time for you to recalibrate, refocus, and reclaim. Every second you waste thinking about her post-divorce life is a second you're stealing from your future.

Now, I'm not saying go dark and delete everything. But curate, man. Curate! Follow pages that motivate, inspire, and educate. Replace her photos with quotes that fuel your fire, or better yet, your achievements. And if anyone, ANYONE, brings negativity or reminds you of the past? Cut them off. No questions, no remorse. This is your space, your mental real estate. Only premium content allowed.

So, get your digital act together. Reframe, redefine, and reignite. The virtual world should be a tool, not a trap. Use it to build the life you want, not mourn the one you lost. Start fresh. It's time for your reset.

Daily Challenge: Today, take control of your digital world by curating your social media feed to be a source of motivation, inspiration, and positivity, unfollowing and muting anything that doesn't serve your well-being and focusing on building the future you deserve.

Daily Reflection:

What resonated with you from today's lesson? How can you apply this truth in your life?

_____

_____

_____

_____

Day 160: Networking- It's Not Just for Business

Life's changed; the ring's off, and you might think the world's caved in. But here's a reality check for you - it hasn't. You've just been given an all-access pass to the biggest networking event of your life, and I ain't talking business cards and LinkedIn profiles. I'm talking real, raw, human connection.

Get it out of your head that networking is just about climbing the corporate ladder or making that next big sale. It's about building your life from the ground up, especially now. That guy at the gym you see every morning? He's not just a spotter; he's a potential wingman, a confidant, someone who might have walked the very path you're on. And the neighbor you nod to but never really talked to? Maybe he's got insights on single parenting or knows where the best singles spots in town are.

You're in a phase of rediscovery, man. Every person you meet, every interaction, it's an opportunity. Not just to network in the traditional sense, but to rebuild, reforge, and redefine who you are and what you stand for.

But here's the catch - you've got to be genuine. None of that fake "Hey, how's the weather?" crap. Dive deep. Ask the hard questions. Be vulnerable. Share your story and listen to theirs. This is your time. Not just to network, but to interconnect with the world around you in ways you never imagined.

So don't waste another second. Life's out there, waiting. Go network the heck out of it. And remember, it's not about business cards; it's about life cards. Collect 'em, cherish 'em, and play 'em right.

Daily Challenge: Reach out to someone new today, strike up a genuine conversation, and discover the untapped connections that can enrich your life during this phase of rediscovery.

Daily Reflection:

What resonated with you from today's lesson? How can you apply this truth in your life?

_____

_____

_____

_____

Day 161: Gossip- How to Deal with the Rumor Mill

Gossip? Man, it's the currency of the weak, the echo in empty rooms where real stories don't exist. After a split, everyone's got something to say, right? Like they were in your living room when things went down, or like they paid your bills. But here's the kicker: they weren't. They didn't. So, their two cents? It's worth even less.

Let them talk. If you weren't interesting, they wouldn't be wasting their breath. But while they're talking about yesterday, you're already on tomorrow. Remember, when they whisper behind your back, it only means you're ahead of them. Rumors are a sign that you're doing something right, or at the very least, doing something worth noticing. But it doesn't define you.

Now, here's where it gets real. Don't fuel the fire. Keep your head high, hustle hard, and let your actions speak. People expect you to snap, to be bitter, to vent. But every time you don't, every time you rise above, you gain power. Gossip might be a temporary high for them, but your success? That's a legacy. And legacies outlast rumors every time.

Engaging with gossip is like wrestling with a pig; you both get dirty, but only the pig enjoys it. Don't be the guy wallowing in the mud. Aim higher. Let the rumor mill churn. They'll get tired, move onto the next story, and you? You'll still be standing, stronger, wiser, and ready for whatever life throws at you next.

Daily Challenge: Rise above the gossip and focus on building your legacy through actions that speak louder than any rumor.

Daily Reflection:

What resonated with you from today's lesson? How can you apply this truth in your life?

_____

_____

_____

Day 162: Single Life in Social Circles

Here's the thing, fellas. Post-divorce life? It's not the time to sit in a dim room reminiscing about the good old coupled-up days. No. This is the era of the solo warrior, the lone wolf, the solo shot caller. But let's keep it real, being single in your social circles, especially if they're filled with couples, can feel like you're wearing neon at a black-tie event.

Remember the days you could go anywhere, do anything, without a second thought or a lengthy discussion? Those days are back. But here's where guys trip up: they see this newfound freedom as a loss. Loss of companionship, loss of couple privileges. Flip the narrative. See it for what it is: raw, unadulterated freedom.

Social gatherings? Yeah, you might get the pity eyes or the "how you holding up?" twenty times in one evening. But don't get lost in their narrative. While they're sipping their wine, recounting couple's vacations, or lamenting about date nights, remember you're in control. You're the master of your fate, the captain of your evening, and the solo artist of your life's track.

Social media? It's a double-edged sword. On one hand, you've got your ex's life on parade, and on the other, a window to a world of opportunities. Filter out the noise, the unnecessary drama, the constant couple posts. Curate your feed, your circle, your life. And those single pals who've been waiting in the wings? They aren't a reminder of your 'downgraded' status. They're the gatekeepers to adventures you've forgotten existed. Dive into those waters, rekindle those friendships. You're not half of a whole anymore; you're a complete unit.

Daily Challenge: Today, embrace your status as a solo warrior, and at a social gathering, initiate a meaningful conversation with someone new, reminding yourself that you are the master of your own destiny and capable of building new connections and experiences.

Daily Reflection:

What resonated with you from today's lesson? How can you apply this truth in your life?

_____

_____

_____

_____

Day 163: Children's Friends' Parents

Children's friends' parents - let's cut the crap and dive straight into this. Divorce isn't just about you and your ex; it's a ripple effect. The wave hits everyone, especially the circles your kids move in. You remember those BBQs, soccer games, and school events? The camaraderie with other parents? Yeah, that's shifted now.

You might think that everyone's whispering about the split when you drop your kid off at school. And maybe some are, but here's the raw truth: most people are too caught up in their own lives to give yours more than a passing thought. And those who gossip? They're just distracting themselves from their own problems.

Now, when you face these parents, you've got choices. You can slink around, avoiding eye contact, feeling awkward. Or you can stride in, head held high, and own your narrative. The divorce doesn't define you, your character does.

It's not about being best buddies with everyone. Let's face it, post-divorce, some parents will side with your ex, and that's okay. You don't need fair-weather friends. But remember, it's your kids who are the main players in this game. Don't let your discomfort rob them of their friendships.

Connect with those who matter. A nod, a handshake, or just a simple "Hey, how've you been?" It's about acknowledging the situation without being consumed by it. And those awkward moments when you have to converse about carpools or birthday parties? Tackle them with grace. Let your kids see that strength.

Daily Challenge: Today, when you drop your kid off at school, choose to stride in with confidence, head held high, and engage with other parents, owning your narrative and showing your character, because your worth isn't defined by whispers, but by your strength and authenticity in navigating this journey.

Daily Reflection:

What resonated with you from today's lesson? How can you apply this truth in your life?

_____

_____

_____

_____

Day 164: The Neighborhood- Friend or Foe?

Look, when life's train wrecks like a divorce happen, you start seeing the world differently. You start realizing not everything around you is as it seemed, especially the people. The neighborhood? It's not just about the houses and streets. It's about those faces, those supposed 'friends' that you wave to every morning.

Here's the real deal: Not everyone's going to have your back. Some might choose sides. Others might pretend like they're Switzerland – neutral – but behind closed doors, they're picking teams. It stings, doesn't it? The guy you had beers with last Friday, now suddenly too busy to hang? The neighbor you helped move their couch, now whispering behind your back?

Here's a thought – maybe it's not about them being foes. Maybe it's about you figuring out who the real friends are. Divorce has a crazy way of showing you who's real and who's just there for the show. Your journey right now? It's not about pleasing the neighborhood or fitting into some mold. Screw that! It's about cutting out the dead weight, trimming the fat, and surrounding yourself with those who lift you up, not drag you down.

You don't need the whole neighborhood on your side. What you need is a tribe – even if it's a tribe of one or two – who'll have your back, who'll listen without judgment, who'll stand by you when the chips are down. So, take a good look around. Your neighborhood might be filled with foes masquerading as friends. Or maybe, just maybe, there are a few diamonds in the rough. Cherish them. As for the rest? Wave, smile, and keep walking. You've got bigger things ahead.

Daily Challenge: Today, make a list of those who have shown genuine support and friendship during this challenging time, and take a moment to express your gratitude to them for being the diamonds in your life.

Daily Reflection:

What resonated with you from today's lesson? How can you apply this truth in your life?

_____

_____

_____

_____

Day 165: Social Events- Flying Solo

Look, walking into a social event post-divorce, solo? Yeah, it can feel like you're that kid again, first day at a new school. But remember, the anxiety you feel? It's just noise. External chatter. What they think, the side glances, the whispered conversations - all noise. Here's the raw truth: your journey, your growth, isn't for public consumption.

You're not half a person because you're now single. You might even be more of a person now. More raw, more real, more YOU. Flying solo at events is not a mark of loneliness; it's a badge of honor. It screams, "I've been through the wringer and here I stand, stronger than ever."

There will be moments, sure. You'll see couples laughing, and that pang of 'what once was' might hit. But then you gotta ask, was it ever really like that for you? Or is nostalgia painting over the cracks? Instead of wishing for a past that probably wasn't as rosy as your memory suggests, revel in the NOW.

Bask in the freedom of choosing where you sit, who you talk to, when you leave. No compromises. You dictate your vibe. And here's another secret: people are drawn to authenticity. To raw, unbridled truth. So when you walk in, shoulders squared, acknowledging your solo status without a shred of shame, you're a beacon. You're not the guy who got divorced. You're the guy who had the balls to redefine his life.

And as for the ones who can't handle your newfound solo energy? Cut them off. Your growth isn't for everyone, and that's okay. Your journey? It's not about them. It's all about you. Own it.

Daily Challenge: Embrace the solo spotlight today, knowing that your journey is about your growth, not their judgment, and shine as the authentic, redefined version of yourself.

Daily Reflection:

What resonated with you from today's lesson? How can you apply this truth in your life?

_____

_____

_____

_____

Day 166: The "Divorced Guy" Label

Listen, guys, there's a label that might get slapped on you the moment those papers are signed: "Divorced Guy." Yeah, it's a thing. But here's the deal: labels are for jars, not for humans. If anyone tries to box you in with that label, remember, they're showing their limited mindset, not defining your potential.

Divorce isn't a tattoo on your forehead. It's an experience, a part of your journey. And you know what? Everyone has their stuff. That coworker who whispers behind your back? He might be battling an addiction. That gym buddy who seems to have it all together? Maybe he's facing bankruptcy. But do we go around calling them "Addicted Guy" or "Bankrupt Guy"? No.

So, why let anyone reduce you to your relationship status? Don't own that label. Don't wear it. Don't let it define your next steps or how you see yourself. Your worth isn't tied to a marital status, a bank account, or any thing that can be labeled.

It's easy to get caught in the pity party or the fear of judgment. But let's be real. Every one of us is evolving. You might've been a husband yesterday, today you're a divorced guy, but what about tomorrow? Entrepreneur? Adventurer? World traveler? Best-selling author? It's all on the table.

Shake off the label. Don't let it confine you. People will talk, they always do. But while they're talking, be too busy building, growing, and evolving. Let them catch up to the narrative you're creating, not the other way around. Remember: You're not just a "Divorced Guy." You're a guy with ambition, dreams, and a future that's still being written. Own that.

Daily Challenge: Today, challenge yourself to break free from the "Divorced Guy" label by taking one concrete step towards pursuing your ambitions and dreams, reminding yourself that your worth goes far beyond your past relationship status.

Daily Reflection:

What resonated with you from today's lesson? How can you apply this truth in your life?

_____

_____

_____

Day 167: Peer Pressure- Stand Your Ground

After a divorce, everyone's got an opinion, right? Your friends, family, and that dude from the gym you hardly talk to. They think they know how you should handle your business, how to move on, who to date next. Suddenly, everyone's got a Ph.D. in "Your Life." Let me tell you something: You've got to stand your ground. Peer pressure after a divorce isn't just about resisting bad habits; it's about staying true to your journey.

You see, everyone's path is different. What worked for Joe might not work for you. And that's okay. But the moment you start caving to what everyone else thinks is best for you, you lose your footing. You lose that internal compass that's trying to guide you through the mess. Sure, listen to advice. But at the end of the day, the decisions? They're yours. Own them.

Let's be real here. Some friends, as much as they mean well, they'll steer you wrong. They'll want you to dive into the dating pool before you're ready, drown your sorrows in booze, or even bad-mouth your ex at every chance. They're reacting, not reflecting. You've got to be bigger than that.

When you feel that pressure, that urge to fit into the post-divorce mold others have crafted for you, I want you to remember one thing: You're the author of your story. Not them. You. Stay grounded. Stay true. Navigate this new world with your head held high, understanding that not every voice has earned a say in your narrative. Stand your ground. Own your journey. And let the rest be just noise.

Daily Challenge: Today, resist the urge to conform to others' expectations and remember that you are the author of your own post-divorce story – stay true to your unique journey and let your decisions reflect your authentic self.

Daily Reflection:

What resonated with you from today's lesson? How can you apply this truth in your life?

_____

_____

_____

_____

Day 168: Team Building- Forge New Alliances

After a divorce, it's not just about picking up the pieces; it's about building a fortress with them. Listen, there's a moment in every man's life where he realizes the world isn't going to just hand him a golden ticket. Divorce? That might be your moment. Sure, it's rough, but it's also a chance to assess your team, your circle.

Who's still standing beside you? Who bailed at the first sign of trouble? Those fair-weather friends? Those aren't allies; they're background noise. Time to crank up the volume on the real players in your life, and mute the rest. Cut off the dead weight, but also recognize that now's the time to forge new alliances.

It's not about replacing old friends with new ones. It's about surrounding yourself with people who genuinely get it, who uplift, challenge, and push you. Life's short. Do you want to spend it with people who have your back only during the highs? No! You want warriors by your side, through thick and thin.

Jump into new hobbies, new ventures, new environments. Find those people who are grinding, evolving, pushing boundaries. Not just the ones who "kinda get you", but those who live and breathe the same passion and drive. Forge alliances with people who have been through the wringer and come out stronger, because they'll show you how it's done. They'll pull you up when you're down and cheer the loudest when you're winning.

So, look around. If your team isn't solid, if you're surrounded by naysayers or those stuck in the past, it's time for a change. Forge new alliances, build a stronger, tighter circle. You've got this next chapter to conquer; make sure you've got the right team with you.

Daily Challenge: Take a close look at your circle today and evaluate who truly supports your journey forward after divorce, then actively seek out and build alliances with those who share your passion and determination for the next chapter in your life.

Daily Reflection:

What resonated with you from today's lesson? How can you apply this truth in your life?

_____

_____

_____

_____

Day 169: Social Skills- Time for a Tune-Up

Life after a split isn't just about mending a broken heart; it's about recalibrating your social compass. Listen, you've been part of a duo for so long, you might've forgotten what it feels like to fly solo in the social scene. Let me tell it to you straight: You're not the same guy you were when you entered that relationship. You're stronger, wiser, maybe a bit rough around the edges, but you've evolved.

The way people look at you, the whispers behind your back, the hesitant approaches from mutual friends – let 'em talk. Because while they're busy talking, you're gonna be busy redefining. But here's the thing: social skills are like muscles; if you don't use them, they atrophy. You've been in couple-mode for so long that you might've lost touch with how to interact as a single man in the world.

Remember this: It's not about fitting back into old molds or trying to be the guy you were before. Screw that. It's about tuning up those social skills for the man you are now. Maybe you're out of practice. So what? Dive in. Go to events. Engage with colleagues. Reconnect with old buddies. Meet new ones. Feel awkward? Embrace it. That discomfort? It's growth happening in real-time.

Social media? A double-edged sword. Be genuine. Don't use it as a platform for pity or passive aggression. And those mutual connections? If they're not lifting you up, cut 'em loose. You don't need the dead weight. Bottom line: Your social life isn't about quantity, it's about quality. Surround yourself with people who reflect the man you want to be, not the one you were. Time for a tune-up, champ. Not because the world expects it, but because you deserve it.

Daily Challenge: Embrace the discomfort of recalibrating your social life and take deliberate steps to build a quality circle of friends who reflect the evolved, stronger, and wiser man you've become post-divorce.

Daily Reflection:

What resonated with you from today's lesson? How can you apply this truth in your life?

_____

_____

_____

_____

Day 170: Be the Organizer- Take Control

Y ou're the master of your ship, the captain of your destiny. Stop waiting for someone else to make the first move, or dictate how your post-divorce narrative should go. You think those old friends are going to automatically gravitate towards you or away from your ex? Think again. It's not about loyalty; it's about inertia. People are creatures of habit. If you wait for them to act, you'll be waiting a long time.

You've got to be the magnet. The center. The guy who's throwing the barbecue on the weekend, organizing the poker nights, setting up the camping trips. You don't have to wait for an invite, be the one sending them out. In the process, you're not only building a community but also showcasing your strength, resilience, and leadership.

Your life's been shaken up, but that doesn't mean you let the pieces fall wherever they may. Pick them up. Arrange them. Create a mosaic. And if there are pieces – or people – that no longer fit, it's okay to leave them out. Your life, your rules.

In this chaos, there's a hidden gift: the chance to rebuild. And not just rebuild, but to design. Think about it. You've got the tools, the drive, and the freedom. Dive into the discomfort of the unfamiliar. Don't sit in the bleachers; be the guy who's calling the shots, on the field, changing the game.

Your divorce isn't a handicap, it's a catalyst. The question is: Are you going to use it to fire up your engines or just sit in the aftermath of the explosion? Grab that steering wheel, set your course, and be the organizer of your life. Take control. No one else is going to do it for you.

Daily Challenge: Take the reins of your life and be the initiator – plan a social gathering or activity to reconnect with old friends and create new connections, showing the world that your divorce is a catalyst for positive change.

Daily Reflection:

What resonated with you from today's lesson? How can you apply this truth in your life?

_____

_____

_____

_____

Day 171: Professional Networks- Keep It Classy

Let's get one thing straight: the workplace isn't a therapy session, and your colleagues? They aren't your therapists. We all got emotional baggage, but guess what? At work, it's about the hustle, the grind, the passion for what you're doing. The divorce? It's a chapter in your life, not a blaring headline in your professional career.

I get it. The whispers, the side glances when you walk into the room, the unsolicited "you okay, man?" It's all annoying. But here's the red pill truth: how you handle this sets the tone for how others perceive you. Are you the victim? Or are you the guy who rises from the ashes, phoenix style?

Sure, it's tough. Your personal life's a mess, but this isn't the time to slack. You've got a reputation to maintain and, more importantly, a mission to pursue. Your work, your ambition, it's bigger than your marital status. Don't give people a reason to doubt your capabilities or professionalism because of your personal setbacks.

Now, when those rumors come creeping or a nosy colleague gets a bit too inquisitive, keep it classy. Be firm, be polite, and redirect to the work. It's none of their business. You're there to work, to bring value, to crush it. Not to gossip or divulge personal details.

And one more thing: find solace in your work. Dive in, get passionate, and use that energy. Take your personal setbacks and transform them into professional comebacks. Your divorce doesn't define you, your hustle does. So, suit up, chin up, and keep it classy. Let your work do the talking.

Daily Challenge: Today, focus on channeling your energy into your work, setting aside personal distractions and gossip, as you remind yourself that your professional achievements define your worth in the workplace, not your divorce.

Daily Reflection:

What resonated with you from today's lesson? How can you apply this truth in your life?

_____

_____

_____

_____

Day 172: Social Stamina- Build It Up

Look, life after a split isn't just an emotional roller coaster, it's a social marathon. And if you're going to navigate that, you need stamina. Social stamina. Think about it: suddenly every friend is asking questions, every gathering feels like a minefield, and don't even get me started on social media. It's exhausting, isn't it? But here's the thing—sitting in the corner and lamenting isn't an option. You've got to face the world, head held high, and that takes guts.

You know that friend who just wants the gossip? That coworker who looks at you with that mix of pity and curiosity? That family member who never liked her in the first place? They're all watching, all waiting. And you've got two choices: crumble or conquer.

Building up your social stamina isn't about pretending everything's okay. It's about recognizing that even if things aren't great right now, you've got this. It's about redefining who you are in the eyes of others. It's about reclaiming your narrative.

It's training, man. Just like hitting the gym, but for your social muscles. Go to that party. Have that awkward conversation. Post that picture of you having a great time. With every social challenge you face, you're pushing your limits, stretching your comfort zone.

There's no magic potion, no overnight fix. But with time and effort, you'll build resilience. You'll find yourself less affected by the whispers, less bothered by the glances. Because you'll know that you're more than the sum of your past relationships. You're a force to be reckoned with. In the end, your social stamina will be your shield, your strength. So, lace up, step out, and show the world what you're made of. It's time to run that marathon.

Daily Challenge: Today, embrace a social situation that makes you uncomfortable, whether it's attending a gathering, having a difficult conversation, or sharing a genuine moment on social media, and remember that every step forward is a stride toward building your social stamina and reclaiming your narrative.

Daily Reflection:

What resonated with you from today's lesson? How can you apply this truth in your life?

Day 173: Trust- A Scarce Commodity

Trust. It's the foundation, the bedrock of any relationship. But let's not kid ourselves; after a divorce, trust isn't just broken, it's shattered. Some pieces are so tiny, you wonder if they can ever be put back together. And hey, I get it. Trust has become a scarce commodity. You feel like you've just been handed a counterfeit bill and you're doubting every transaction you've ever made.

But here's the cold, hard truth: Just because one person broke your trust doesn't mean everyone will. You can't project the failings of one onto the many. It's not fair to them, and it's surely not fair to you. Locking yourself in a fortress, shields up, might seem like the answer, but all you're doing is boxing yourself into a prison of paranoia.

You think trust is about the other person? Wrong. It's about you. It's about having the guts to face vulnerability again. It's about accepting the possibility of pain, but not letting it deter you. Because here's another truth bomb: Without trust, you're in a perpetual state of limbo. Half-hearted relationships, jobs, friendships, always with one foot out the door.

Listen, no one's asking you to blindly trust again. That'd be stupid. But challenge yourself. Start small. Rebuild that trust muscle, just as you'd hit the gym for physical strength. Question, understand, validate. But give people a chance. The world isn't out to screw you over. There are genuine souls out there, just as hurt and skeptical, but trying nonetheless.

Trust might be scarce now, but it's not extinct. It's a choice, a deliberate step to say, "Yeah, I've been burnt, but I won't let that define my future interactions." So take the risk. Open up, bit by bit. Let trust be that rare commodity that, when you find it, it's worth its weight in gold.

Daily Challenge: Today, challenge yourself to take a small step towards rebuilding trust by opening up and being vulnerable in a new or existing relationship, recognizing that trust is not just about others but also about your own courage to trust again.

Daily Reflection:

What resonated with you from today's lesson? How can you apply this truth in your life?

_____

_____

_____

_____

Day 174: The Ex's Friends- A Diplomatic Zone

Alright, listen up. The ex's friends? They're a diplomatic minefield, a tightrope you've got to navigate with the precision of a surgeon and the grace of a ballet dancer. But you know what? They're not your problem anymore. Don't let loyalty politics mess with your head.

Here's a reality check: Not all of them were ever genuinely your friends. For some, you were just an add-on, an accessory to her life. And that's okay. That's the nature of relationships. You don't need validation from them. If they ghost you or take sides, let them. It's a reflection of their character, not yours.

But there are going to be some in that group who matter. Those who've had your back, laughed with you, shared moments. Those, my friend, are the golden ones. And it's not about "choosing sides" with them. It's about mutual respect, trust, and genuine connection. Be straight with them. No drama, no gossip. Just real talk.

Post-divorce social dynamics? They're messy. But they also offer clarity, a lens to see who's real and who's just fluff. The ones who stick by you, respect your boundaries, and understand the depth of your journey, they're keepers. The rest? Just noise. Background static.

Don't get sucked into the social media vortex of stalking, blocking, or petty games. Rise above it. Your energy's too valuable for that circus. Engage with those who add value to your life, cut ties with the drain, and don't think twice. Your peace, your growth, your next chapter, that's the priority. Stay focused and keep moving. Don't get dragged into the murky waters of her social circle's drama. Stay on your path. Period.

Daily Challenge: Today, focus on nurturing the genuine connections in your life, and don't let the drama of your ex's social circle distract you from your path to peace and growth.

Daily Reflection:

What resonated with you from today's lesson? How can you apply this truth in your life?

_____

_____

_____

_____

Day 175: The Holiday Conundrum- Where to Go?

Navigating the first holiday season post-divorce? That's a mind game. Suddenly, that comfortable, familiar spot at the family table feels like it's on another planet. And the jingles, the laughter, the traditions? They can feel like daggers if you let them.

But here's the deal: This isn't about where your body sits during the holidays. It's about where your head's at. Dwelling on the past? It's a trap. Mourning the old traditions? A sinking ship. Now's the time to rewrite the narrative. You've got a blank canvas, and you're the artist.

You worried about showing up solo to that family dinner or office party? Don't be. People will talk; they always do. But what they say, it's noise. It's all background chatter. Your value isn't determined by whispers or sideways glances.

Ask yourself, where do YOU want to be? Who lifts you up? Who's got your back? That's your North Star. Maybe it's a solo trip to somewhere you've never been. Maybe it's volunteering, giving back, and finding purpose outside the old grind. Or maybe it's just hanging with a few genuine pals, laughing, and making new stories.

The point is, you define your holidays now. You're not bound by old expectations or obligations. You're free. And sure, freedom can be a little intimidating, but it's also exhilarating. So embrace the uncertainty, the novelty. Dive into the unknown with both feet. This holiday, carve out your own space, on your terms. After all, it's your world now. Everyone else? They're just living in it.

Daily Challenge: Embrace the holiday season as an opportunity for self-discovery and redefining your traditions, focusing on what truly brings you joy and fulfillment, regardless of others' perceptions or expectations.

Daily Reflection:

What resonated with you from today's lesson? How can you apply this truth in your life?

_____

_____

_____

_____

Day 176: Small Talk- Master the Art

Life after a split can feel like you've just been kicked out of a plane without a parachute. Suddenly, every coffee break, every family gathering, every random chat with a neighbor feels like you're tiptoeing through a minefield. Because small talk? It's everywhere. And now, with the weight of a divorce in the backdrop, even the most mundane chat can feel loaded.

Here's the truth: no one cares about the weather, bro. Small talk isn't about the words; it's about the connection. It's about signaling, "Hey, I see you." It's a handshake for the soul. But post-divorce? It can be an emotional rollercoaster. The innocent, "How's the family?" or "Doing anything fun with your partner this weekend?" can sting. Hard.

But here's the red pill you've got to swallow: hiding ain't gonna make it easier. Dodging social events or biting back sarcastic remarks? That's the easy way out. The coward's route. Instead, master the art of small talk. Reframe it. See it as a skill, a weapon even.

Be upfront. Keep it light. Redirect when you need to. Someone asks about the ex? "Ah, we're taking things day by day. But tell me about that new project you're working on." Take control of the narrative. Decide what you're willing to share, and what's off-limits. And remember, it's okay to set boundaries.

Don't let the weight of your past control your present. Small talk doesn't have to be small. With the right mindset, it can be a gateway – a bridge to new connections, opportunities, and a fresh start. So, step up, and own the conversation. Every single one.

Daily Challenge: Embrace the power of small talk by proactively steering conversations in a positive direction and setting boundaries to ensure that your past doesn't overshadow your present interactions.

Daily Reflection:

What resonated with you from today's lesson? How can you apply this truth in your life?

_____

_____

_____

Day 177: Vulnerability- Show It Sparingly

You've heard it all before, right? "Be vulnerable. Show your feelings." But let's get one thing straight: there's a difference between being genuine and wearing your heart on your sleeve for every Tom, Dick, and Harry. Not everyone deserves to see your raw, unfiltered soul.

See, vulnerability isn't about bleeding out for the world. It's about knowing who's worth the bleed. In the aftermath of a divorce, it's easy to mistake sympathy for empathy. That dude at the bar? He might nod along, but does he really get it? Does he deserve to hear your story?

It's like this: imagine your vulnerability as currency. And, like any currency, you don't go throwing it around aimlessly. You invest where it matters. Post-divorce, there's gonna be chatter — the whispers, the side glances. Do you really want to add fuel to that fire by oversharing? By giving away pieces of yourself to people who don't value it? No way!

Here's the deal. You should be vulnerable with those who've earned it. The ones who've been in the trenches with you. The ones who understand the weight of the ring that once sat on your finger. This isn't about hiding or pretending. It's about wisdom. It's about knowing that vulnerability is power, but only when it's shared in the right spaces.

Remember this: showing vulnerability is strength, no doubt. But doing it sparingly? That's strategy. It's about discerning the difference between those who are just there for the show and those who'll stand by you when the curtains fall. Know the difference. Show your scars but do it wisely. Be real, be raw, but remember — vulnerability is gold. Don't squander it.

Daily Challenge: Today, practice discernment in sharing your vulnerability by choosing wisely who deserves to see your raw, authentic self, and invest your emotional currency where it truly matters.

Daily Reflection:

What resonated with you from today's lesson? How can you apply this truth in your life?

_____

_____

_____

_____

Day 178: Loyalties- Know Where They Lie

Loyalty. We throw that word around like it's a participation trophy. But post-divorce, in the aftermath of the storm? That's when you see who's truly loyal and who's just been riding the wave for their own benefit.

You'll find friends who'll stick by your side, even when the waters get murky. Those are the gold. But you'll also find some who drift, whose loyalty was more to the couple-version of you, or maybe even just to her. And here's the hard truth: That's okay. It stings, no doubt, but it's also a blessing in disguise. Because loyalty shouldn't be conditional. It shouldn't waver based on your relationship status or the narrative floating around.

Post-divorce, the social landscape shifts. You'll see friends picking sides. And as much as you'd like to think otherwise, you're not immune to the whispers, the subtle side glances, the dinner parties you're no longer invited to. But dude, do you really want to be in places where you're not genuinely wanted? Screw that.

Your energy is precious. And in this phase, every ounce of it needs to be directed toward rebuilding, redefining, and rediscovering yourself. So, cut off the dead weight. Let go of the fair-weather friends. Keep your circle tight. Lean into the friends who have your back, who check in on you, who pull you up when you're spiraling down.

And when it comes to work or those unavoidable family functions? Be professional, be cordial, but know where your real loyalties lie. You owe no explanations, no justifications. Be loyal to yourself, your growth, your peace. Everyone else? They can either join the ride or watch from the sidelines. Your choice, your terms. Period.

Daily Challenge: Today, evaluate your circle of friends and acquaintances and prioritize those who have shown unwavering loyalty and support during your divorce journey, as you continue to build a life filled with genuine connections and personal growth.

Daily Reflection:

What resonated with you from today's lesson? How can you apply this truth in your life?

_____

_____

_____

Day 179: Social Balance-The Mix That Works

Life after divorce isn't just about picking up the pieces; it's about reshuffling the deck. You've got friends, family, coworkers, all weighing in on your life post-breakup. Here's the truth, brother: not everyone in your current circle fits into your next chapter.

Listen, you don't need that buddy from college who keeps telling you there are "plenty of fish in the sea" while pouring another shot. Nor do you need that aunt who's already planning to set you up with her yoga instructor. And the workplace? Keep it professional. Don't let Jim from accounting become your unsolicited relationship counselor.

But cutting off the dead weight doesn't mean isolating yourself. No! It means finding a balance. Surround yourself with people who fuel your soul, not just feed your ego. That buddy who hits the gym with you at 5 AM? Keep him close. Your cousin who checks in just to chat about the game? That's real. They're in it for YOU, not for the drama.

Social media? A double-edged sword. While it's tempting to lurk or flaunt your newfound freedom, don't get sucked into the digital void. Your worth isn't determined by likes, comments, or whoever she's now "Facebook official" with.

Here's the mix that works: Quality over quantity. Real connections over fair-weather friends. Growth over stagnation. Seek out those who uplift, challenge, and resonate with the man you're becoming. And the ones who don't? Thank them for their time, wish them well, and keep moving forward. Your journey's just getting started, and you decide who gets a seat on this ride.

Daily Challenge: Evaluate your circle of influence today and make a conscious effort to nurture relationships that uplift and support your journey post-divorce while gracefully letting go of those that no longer align with your growth.

Daily Reflection:

What resonated with you from today's lesson? How can you apply this truth in your life?

_____

_____

_____

Day 180: Social Milestone- Take Stock, Make Changes

Your divorce wasn't just a split from your partner, it was a tectonic shift in your entire social world. It's a whirlwind of emotions, judgments, and unsolicited advice. You've got mates siding with you, some ghosting you, and some caught in between, not sure which way to lean. The workplace is buzzing, whispers in corridors and the hush-hush chatter at the water cooler. Add family gatherings and social media to the mix, and it feels like you're in a pressure cooker.

Here's the thing, man: it's your life, and you've got a right to choose who gets the VIP pass. Cut out the toxicity. Anyone who drags you down, doubts your narrative, or can't respect your journey doesn't deserve your time. Period. This isn't high school drama; this is your life's reboot.

It's about quality, not quantity. That coworker spreading rumors? They're background noise. The aunt pitying you at family dinners? Send her love and move on. And those mutual friends forcing you to choose sides? They don't get it. It's not about sides; it's about healing and growth.

Go on a social media detox. That Facebook timeline and those Instagram stories aren't going anywhere. But every second you spend scrolling is another moment lost from rebuilding your life. Now's the time to surround yourself with those who uplift you, who get the grind, the pain, the rebirth.

Your new chapter isn't about being bitter. It's about being better. So, take stock. Reevaluate. Make the changes. Let go of the weight, stand tall, and sprint into this next phase with the right crowd cheering you on. Because, mate, this comeback? It's going to be legendary.

Daily Challenge: Today, make a list of the people in your life who genuinely support your journey post-divorce, and take a moment to express gratitude for their presence and encouragement.

Daily Reflection:

What resonated with you from today's lesson? How can you apply this truth in your life?

_____

_____

_____

_____

Identity Reboot

Embark on a transformative journey, confronting the man in the mirror. Revamp your bucket list with new goals, redefining yourself. Explore the name game, reevaluating self-identity. Assess your personality traits—keep, tweak, or delete? Core values are ripe for an update, while hobbies reveal what truly inspires you. Establish a personal brand and ignite passion projects. Write your narrative and refine your fashion sense. Adopt the power pose, envision your five-year future, and expand your skill set. Are you ready to gamble on your reinvention? Rediscover romance, embrace your social persona, and craft your life philosophy. Reflect, assess, and build a legacy.

Day 181: The Man in the Mirror- Face Yourself

Listen, fellas. Divorce? It's rough, no doubt. But while you're out there battling legal documents, splitting assets, and figuring out your new normal, there's one fight you can't ignore: the one with the man staring back at you from the mirror.

You've been through the wringer, and it's easy to lose yourself in the chaos. But now's the time, more than ever, to face yourself head-on. You might not like what you see. Maybe you see regrets, mistakes, or just raw pain. But guess what? That reflection? It's the starting point, not the endpoint.

The truth is, no amount of external validation, no rebound relationships, no nights out with the guys, will fill the void if you don't square up with yourself first. You've got to confront those demons, the insecurities, the fears, and the doubts. Dive deep, understand what went wrong, and more importantly, what you want for your future.

Rediscover passions you forgot you had. Remember that hobby you gave up because you "didn't have the time"? Dive back in. It's about getting back to the core of who you are. It's about rebuilding, not just from the outside but deep within.

Sure, the gym's great, and a new wardrobe can give you a fresh feel. But true transformation? That happens when you have the guts to look yourself in the eyes and decide who you want to be moving forward. Every scar, every wrinkle, every tear - they've made you who you are. Own it.

So, next time you face that man in the mirror, challenge him. Demand more from him. Push him. Because on the other side of this pain, there's a version of you that's stronger, wiser, and ready to conquer whatever life throws next.

Daily Challenge: Today, look yourself in the mirror and have an honest conversation with the man staring back at you; ask yourself what steps you can take to rediscover and embrace your true passions and strengths.

Daily Reflection:

What resonated with you from today's lesson? How can you apply this truth in your life?

_____

_____

_____

_____

Day 182: The Bucket List Revamp

Divorce isn't just an end; it's a new beginning. And what better way to mark a fresh start than revisiting that old bucket list? Yeah, I'm talking about that list you tucked away, thinking someday you'd get around to it. Well, guess what? Someday is today.

You've changed. Your life has changed. So why should your dreams stay the same? Tear up that old list and start from scratch. Those things you thought were off-limits, too crazy, or just not your style? It's time to give them a second thought. Maybe you've held back because of someone else's expectations, fears, or judgments. Not anymore. This is your life, your goals, your dreams. Own them.

And hey, while you're at it, think bigger. Always wanted to skydive? Book it. Dreamed of backpacking through Europe? Start planning. That cooking class you've been putting off because it wasn't "manly" enough? Who cares! Do it. This isn't about proving something to the world or your ex; it's about proving something to yourself.

This is your chance to rewrite your narrative. To challenge yourself. To discover passions you never knew you had. To meet new people, learn new things, and experience life from a completely different perspective. So, pick up a pen, grab a piece of paper, and start dreaming again.

In the wake of a divorce, it's easy to get lost in the pain, the what-ifs, and the could-have-beens. But redirect that energy. Use it as fuel. Let it drive you towards the things you've always wanted to do but never had the guts or the time or the freedom. Remember, life's too short for regrets. Make this revamp count.

Daily Challenge: Embrace your new beginning by revisiting your old bucket list, tearing it up, and daring to dream bigger, pursuing the passions and adventures you've always desired but held back from, proving to yourself that this is your chance to rewrite your narrative.

Daily Reflection:

What resonated with you from today's lesson? How can you apply this truth in your life?

_____

_____

_____

_____

Day 183: What Do You Want to Be Called?

Divorce isn't just a legal process or an emotional trainwreck. It's a chance to redefine who you are. So, ask yourself: What do you want to be called? Not just by your kids, family, or friends, but by your most important critic: the man in the mirror.

Before the divorce, you might've been "husband," "provider," or "the rock." Now, some of you might be feeling more like "the guy who failed" or "the one left behind." But here's the hard truth: You decide the label. Not society, not your ex, not anyone else. You.

Use this time for some serious introspection. Because self-care isn't just about hitting the gym or finding new hobbies. It's about deciding the narrative for the next chapter of your life. Do you want to be the victim? Or the guy who took a hit and came out stronger, wiser, and more in tune with himself?

Your journey doesn't end with the ink drying on the divorce papers. In many ways, it's just beginning. This is your rebirth. A chance to reevaluate, reset, and reinvent. Take control of your narrative. Define yourself not by your past mistakes or by what happened to you, but by your aspirations, your values, and how you show up for yourself and those you care about.

So, take a long look in the mirror and ask again: What do you want to be called? Whatever it is, own it, embrace it, and live up to it. Because the only one who's really labeling you is you. Make it count.

Daily Challenge: Look in the mirror today and affirm the label you choose for yourself, then take a step towards embodying that identity with purpose and determination.

Daily Reflection:

What resonated with you from today's lesson? How can you apply this truth in your life?

_____

_____

_____

_____

Day 184: Personality Traits- Keep, Tweak, or Delete?

So, you've been through the wringer, and here you stand. Divorce isn't just about splitting assets; it's about dissecting who you are. It's a mirror held up to your face, and man, sometimes the reflection isn't pretty. But here's the deal: it's time to dissect those personality traits of yours. Some you'll keep, some need a tweak, and others? Toss 'em out.

First up, those golden traits. Maybe you're loyal, hardworking, or the funniest guy in the room. Keep those. They're your essence, your foundation. Don't let the bitterness or hurt change that core. Embrace it, strengthen it.

But here's the hard part: the traits that need some fine-tuning. Maybe you've been too passive, or your patience has been thinner than paper. It's not about reinventing yourself completely but refining. Put in that emotional elbow grease. Adjust, learn, grow. You're not set in stone; you're clay. Mold yourself.

And then, there's the delete pile. We've all got those traits we're not proud of. Stubbornness that doesn't serve you? Jealousy that gnaws at you? Ditch them. They've held you back long enough. They might've contributed to where you are now, but they don't dictate where you're headed.

Listen, this is your chance. A reset button on how you act, react, and interact. It's like spring cleaning for your personality. Brutal? Absolutely. Necessary? More than you know. By the end of this, you'll be a version of yourself you respect more, and others will too. Dive deep, be honest, and get to work. The best version of yourself is waiting. Don't keep him waiting too long.

Daily Challenge: Today, take a moment to reflect on one trait that needs fine-tuning and make a conscious effort to adjust and improve it, bringing you one step closer to becoming the best version of yourself.

Daily Reflection:

What resonated with you from today's lesson? How can you apply this truth in your life?

_____

_____

_____

_____

Day 185: Core Values- Time for an Update

Look, life threw you a curveball, and while you're patching up the wounds, there's something deep down that needs attention: your core values. See, life events like this don't just test your resilience; they put a magnifying glass on what you truly stand for. And let's be real, maybe those values need a refresh.

You've evolved, grown, and faced some harsh realities. It's not the same ball game anymore. The values that got you into a marriage might not be the ones to get you through a divorce or into the next chapter of your life. Don't cling to them out of habit or comfort.

It's time to sit down, dig deep, and ask yourself the tough questions. What truly matters to you now? Is it honesty, because maybe there wasn't enough of that before? Is it self-respect, because perhaps you lost a bit of that along the way? Or is it growth, because you've realized you're not the same man you were and you're hell-bent on becoming better?

Listen, core values aren't just words on a paper or motivational quotes on a wall. They're the foundation, the bedrock. They dictate your decisions, shape your relationships, and set the trajectory for where you're headed. If they're outdated, you're navigating with a broken compass.

So, while you're rebuilding, give yourself the gift of clarity. Reframe those values. Let them reflect the man you are now and the one you're striving to become. It's not just about recovery; it's about rediscovery. Dive in, do the work, and come out with a core that's not just healed, but stronger and more defined than ever.

Daily Challenge: Take a moment today to reflect on your core values, and if necessary, redefine them to align with the resilient and evolved man you are becoming in this new chapter of your life.

Daily Reflection:

What resonated with you from today's lesson? How can you apply this truth in your life?

_____

_____

_____

_____

Day 186: Hobbies Revisited- What Makes You Tick?

Dive deep, man. That divorce? It's a chapter, not the whole book. But now, more than ever, you've got to ask yourself: what makes you tick? You've been so wrapped up in the 'us' that you might've forgotten the 'you'. Remember those hobbies you shelved when life got in the way? It's time to dust them off.

You used to love jamming on that guitar or hitting the open road on your bike. Maybe it was painting, writing, or hiking up those trails. Whatever set your heart on fire, it's time to reignite that passion. Not for anyone else, not to show off on social media, but for YOU. Because when the nights get lonely and the silence deafening, it's those passions that'll pull you through.

You see, hobbies aren't just time-fillers. They're soul-fillers. They're the things that remind you of who you are at your core, what drives you, what gives your life color and zest. They reconnect you with a version of yourself that's raw, real, and unapologetically passionate. They're a bridge to a time when things were simpler, and joy came easy.

And guess what? Now's the perfect opportunity to dive back in. So, pick up that old guitar, strap on those hiking boots, or grab that paintbrush. Rediscover the thrill, the challenge, the peace, or whatever it was that drew you in. Let it consume you, let it challenge you, let it heal you.

Because at the end of the day, life's too short to forget what makes you tick. Dive in, lose yourself, find yourself. It's your journey, and your passions are the compass. Don't lose sight of them. Not now, not ever.

Daily Challenge: Today, dust off that forgotten hobby, and spend at least 30 minutes immersing yourself in it, reigniting your passion and rediscovering the joy it brings to your soul.

Daily Reflection:

What resonated with you from today's lesson? How can you apply this truth in your life?

_____

_____

_____

_____

Day 187: Your Personal Brand- Make It Stick

Your personal brand isn't just your online presence or your job title. It's the energy you bring into a room, the reputation you've built over years, and the way people perceive you. And guess what? It's one of the most powerful tools you've got in your arsenal.

You might be thinking, "Why does it matter?" Here's the deal: Your personal brand is the story you tell the world, and it directly impacts your relationships, opportunities, and overall well-being. As you navigate this challenging phase, you need to ensure that your brand isn't tainted by the emotions and narratives of the past.

Start with self-awareness. Take a hard look in the mirror. Who are you? What do you stand for? What do you want people to say about you when you're not in the room? Now, align your actions, decisions, and interactions with that vision. Rebuild, if you have to. If there are aspects of your brand that have taken a hit during the divorce, now's the time to reset and make amends. Apologize where necessary, rebuild trust, and most importantly, stay consistent.

Engage with authenticity. Whether it's on social media, at work, or in personal interactions, be genuine. People can spot a fake from a mile away, and nothing damages a brand more than inauthenticity. Lastly, invest in yourself. Learn new skills, read books, hit the gym, or take up a hobby. Growth isn't just personal; it adds layers to your brand.

Remember, you're not defined by your past or your present circumstances. Your personal brand is a culmination of your actions, choices, and values. Own it, protect it, and make it stick. Your future self will thank you for it.

Daily Challenge: Take a moment to reflect on the image and reputation you want to project to the world, and actively align your actions and interactions with that vision, ensuring your personal brand reflects your true, authentic self amidst the challenges of divorce.

Daily Reflection:

What resonated with you from today's lesson? How can you apply this truth in your life?

_____

_____

_____

_____

Day 188: Passion Projects- Ignite the Fire

When the world feels like it's crumbled, when the pieces of your identity seem scattered, guess what you have? Yourself. And within you lies a fire, a passion, a drive that maybe you've forgotten about or put on the back burner. Now, more than ever, is the time to reignite that flame. Dive deep into those passion projects.

You know that thing you always said you'd do? That hobby you pushed aside because life got in the way? That dream you shelved thinking it wasn't the right time? Guess what? The universe just handed you a reset button. The canvas is blank, and you're holding the brush. Paint the masterpiece you always wanted.

Remember, passion projects aren't just about distraction; they're about rediscovery. They connect you to a part of yourself that's authentic, that's untouched by any relationship or external circumstance. They remind you of your capabilities, talents, and dreams. They are the fuel when everything else feels empty.

Diving into what you love does more than just keep you busy. It rebuilds you. It brings clarity. It's the reminder you need that life isn't just about surviving; it's about thriving. So, whether it's that book you wanted to write, that guitar collecting dust in the corner, or that startup idea you scribbled on a napkin – now is the time. Dive in headfirst.

The world might've thrown a curveball, but you? You hit back by living with purpose, with passion, with fire. Don't just rebuild your life; make it legendary. Your passion projects are more than just hobbies; they're the heartbeat of your new beginning. Embrace them.

Daily Challenge: Today, take a step towards reigniting your passion by setting aside at least 30 minutes to work on that project or dream you've been putting off, and let it remind you of your limitless potential.

Daily Reflection:

What resonated with you from today's lesson? How can you apply this truth in your life?

_____

_____

_____

_____

Day 189: Your New Narrative- Write Your Story

You've been handed a script you never asked for, and suddenly, you're cast in a role you never auditioned for. Divorce. The title no one wants. But here's the twist: you're not just the lead actor; you're the director. You see, life's thrown you a curveball, but that doesn't mean you stand there and take the hit. It means you grab the bat, adjust your stance, and swing back with all you've got. Your story isn't written by your past or by societal expectations. It's penned by your actions, your mindset, and most crucially, your resilience.

Dwelling on what was? That's not for you. Regret and resentment? They're chains, and you're not here to be bound. You're here to break free, to redefine, to rise. This is the chapter where you take the narrative back, where you say, "This is my story, and here's how it's going to go."

Self-care isn't just about bubble baths and meditation sessions. It's about the mental game. It's about having the audacity to look in the mirror and say, "I decide who I am. I decide where I go from here."

So, what's your new narrative? Is it the guy who got knocked down and stayed there? Or is it the one who used the fall as a stepping stone, who learned, evolved, and thrived? Remember, every setback, every tear, every challenge is just a plot twist. And the best stories? They're the ones with the epic comebacks.

Your divorce isn't your final chapter; it's the plot twist. And now? Now's the time you pick up the pen and write a story that's worthy of you. No one else. Just you. Because at the end of the day, this is your narrative. Own it.

Daily Challenge: Today, take a step towards rewriting your narrative by choosing one positive action that reflects the resilient and empowered person you want to become in this new chapter of your life.

Daily Reflection:

What resonated with you from today's lesson? How can you apply this truth in your life?

_____

_____

_____

_____

Day 190: Fashion Sense- Dress the New You

You've been through the wringer, man. Divorce? It's a beast. But here's the thing: it's also a rebirth. A chance to reinvent, to rediscover, and yeah, to re-dress. Let's talk fashion.

Your wardrobe isn't just about clothes; it's a statement. It says who you are, where you've been, and most importantly, where you're headed. You're not the same guy you were. Don't dress like him. It's time to redefine. It's not about impressing anyone else; it's about feeling good, confident, and owning your new identity.

Start with the basics. Clean out that closet. Those shirts from college? Gone. That tie you wore on your first date? It's not serving you anymore. Create space for the new. Don't cling to the past; it won't fit the future you.

Next, invest in yourself. And I'm not talking about breaking the bank. I'm talking about buying smart, quality over quantity. Get a few classic pieces that fit well. Trust me, a well-fitted suit or a sharp casual look can change the game. Not sure where to start? Get advice. There are tons of resources out there, from online style guides to personal shoppers.

But remember, it's not just about looking good on the outside. It's about feeling empowered from within. Every time you dress the new you, you're telling the world – and yourself – that you're evolving, growing, and moving forward.

Fashion is more than fabric. It's an attitude, a mindset. It's the armor you wear as you tackle this new chapter. So, gear up, redefine your style, and let the world see the new, unstoppable you. Remember, this isn't just about changing clothes; it's about embracing change itself. Own it.

Daily Challenge: Embrace the opportunity for reinvention and self-expression through your wardrobe today, selecting clothing that reflects the confident, evolving, and unstoppable man you're becoming after divorce.

Daily Reflection:

What resonated with you from today's lesson? How can you apply this truth in your life?

_____

_____

_____

Day 191: The Power Pose- Stand Tall

Listen, gentlemen, let's cut straight to the chase. The world doesn't give two cents about your feelings, but you should. Divorce has a way of knocking even the strongest man off his feet, but guess what? It's time to get back up, and not just stand, but stand tall. Enter the Power Pose.

You've probably heard of it. Maybe you've even scoffed at it. But here's the real deal: body language isn't just about showing the world who's boss; it's about reminding yourself of your own power. When life throws you curveballs like divorce, you don't slump. You expand. You take up space. You OWN that space.

Think about it. When you're feeling down and out, your body naturally wants to curl up, make itself smaller, hide. It's a natural response to stress and defeat. But you're not about that life. You're about facing challenges head-on. So why let your body say otherwise?

The Power Pose is more than just standing tall. It's a mental shift. It's about asserting your dominance, not over others, but over your own doubts and fears. Two minutes. That's all it takes. Stand in front of a mirror, legs apart, hands on hips, chin up, chest out. Feel the energy surge. Feel the confidence build. It's not magic; it's science.

Self-care isn't just about spa days and meditation. It's about reclaiming your space, your power, and your confidence. So, the next time you're feeling the weight of the world on your shoulders, remember to stand tall. Embrace the Power Pose. Let every cell of your body scream, "I've got this." Because guess what? You absolutely do.

Daily Challenge: Today, embrace the Power Pose for just two minutes, reminding yourself of your inner strength and resilience in the face of divorce's challenges, because you've got this.

Daily Reflection:

What resonated with you from today's lesson? How can you apply this truth in your life?

_____

_____

_____

_____

Day 192: Mastering Your Life

You're at a crossroads, shaped by the decisions you've made. If you're discontented, remember it's within your power to pivot. Mediocrity shouldn't be your standard. Aim for experiences and achievements that make life memorable. Unraveling the complications in your life is squarely on you. Begin by facing yourself, accepting your flaws, and committing to transformative choices.

Recognize your shortcomings and don't scapegoat others. The key to improvement is self-awareness and responsibility. Engage with those who challenge and uplift you. Detach from those who pull you into mediocrity. Seek relationships that nurture growth.

Don't get trapped living someone else's aspirations. Listen to your heart; it's your life, your journey. Letting others map out your path will only lead to dissatisfaction. Your well-being is fundamental. Adopt a healthy diet, avoid substance abuse, and commit to regular exercise. Without health, everything else falters.

People judge you based on appearances. Ensure your physical presentation aligns with the impression you want to convey. A good skincare routine can be a solid starting point. Ditch activities that drain you. Instead, engage in ones that boost your confidence. Replace screen time with real-life experiences that enrich your well-being.

To be free from monetary worries, budget wisely. Reduce debts, especially those with high interests. Smart choices about your dwelling and vehicle can free up funds for investment or debt clearance. If your job doesn't ignite passion or isn't paying enough, it's time for change. Harness platforms online to upgrade your skills. Having multiple income sources can be both a safety net and an inspiration. Remember, a life that's merely 'functional' can become monotonous.

Daily Challenge: Reflect on your current direction and commit to making at least one transformative choice today that aligns with your vision for a better future.

Daily Reflection:

What resonated with you from today's lesson? How can you apply this truth in your life?

_____

_____

_____

Day 193: Skill Set- What's in Your Arsenal?

You think divorce is just about heartbreak and legal battles? Think again. It's a whole new game, and to thrive, not just survive, you've got to level up. Dive deep into self-improvement, and I'm not just talking about hitting the gym or finding a new hobby. Let's get real about the skills you've got and the ones you need.

What's in your arsenal? If the answer is "not much," then it's time for a wake-up call. You've been handed a golden opportunity to reinvent yourself. Gone are the days when you can coast by. The world is changing fast, and if you don't adapt, you'll be left behind.

Think about the skills that got you where you are today. Are they enough for where you want to go tomorrow? If your answer isn't a resounding "yes," then it's time to get to work. Whether it's leveling up your tech know-how, diving into personal finance, or mastering the art of communication, there's a world of knowledge out there waiting for you. And guess what? It's all accessible.

But here's the thing: acquiring new skills isn't just about personal growth. It's about empowerment. When you're equipped with the right tools, you become unstoppable. You're in control of your destiny. You're not just reacting to the world around you; you're shaping it.

So, take a hard look in the mirror. Are you the best version of yourself? If not, what's holding you back? Drop the excuses. The world doesn't owe you anything. But you owe it to yourself to be the best version of you. Dive into learning. Expand your horizons. And most importantly, never stop growing. Because in this game of life, especially post-divorce, your skill set isn't just an asset; it's your lifeline. Grab it.

Daily Challenge: Today, identify one skill or area of knowledge you've been neglecting or want to improve, and take a concrete step towards mastering it, because your growth is your empowerment.

Daily Reflection:

What resonated with you from today's lesson? How can you apply this truth in your life?

_____

_____

_____

_____

Day 194: Risk Tolerance- Ready to Gamble?

Listen up, guys. Life after divorce is a lot like stepping into the stock market. You've got assets, you've got liabilities, and let's be real – you've got some emotional debts. But the most crucial thing you've got? Your risk tolerance. Are you ready to gamble?

Let's break this down. Risk tolerance isn't about being reckless. It's about understanding what you're willing to lose and what you're striving to gain. Whether it's diving into a new relationship, starting a fresh business venture, or even just changing up your daily routine, every move you make post-divorce is an investment in your future.

You've been burnt, and that sting? It's real. But let me tell you something: playing it too safe, staying in that comfort bubble, isn't going to get you anywhere. Growth, real growth, happens when you push boundaries. But here's the catch: you need to be smart about it. Like any savvy investor, you've got to do your homework. Weigh the pros and cons. Understand the stakes. And only then, make your move.

Remember those sleepless nights, wondering if you made the right choice? Now's not the time to second-guess. Now's the time to double down on yourself. Because if you're not willing to bet on yourself, who will?

Self-care isn't just about bubble baths and meditation. It's about making choices that reflect the life you want to lead. So, ask yourself: are you ready to take that risk? Are you ready to back yourself? Because the biggest gains come from the boldest moves. Don't let fear dictate your portfolio. Dive in, play smart, and watch your stock rise. Because man, you're worth investing in.

Daily Challenge: Today, identify one area of your life where you've been playing it safe since your divorce, and take a calculated risk to move closer to your goals and dreams.

Daily Reflection:

What resonated with you from today's lesson? How can you apply this truth in your life?

_____

_____

_____

Day 195: Rediscovering Romance

Listen up, guys. Divorce is a game-changer, no doubt about it. But here's the thing: just because one chapter closed doesn't mean the entire book is done. You've got a ton of pages left, and it's high time to dive into the world of rediscovering romance.

I get it; the dating scene might seem like a minefield now. But remember, romance isn't just about candlelit dinners and weekend getaways. It's about connection, vulnerability, and understanding your worth. Yes, you've been through the wringer, but that's given you depth, resilience, and a clearer understanding of what you want and, just as importantly, what you don't.

You might be tempted to jump into the dating pool, guns blazing, to prove something. But slow down. This isn't about proving anything to anyone. It's about understanding yourself, your needs, and your boundaries. Don't just date for the sake of dating or to fill a void. Dive in when you feel ready, not when society says you should.

Remember, the romance game has changed. The landscape might look different with apps, online dating, and new norms. But the core of it, the real essence of romance, hasn't. It's still about two people connecting on a deeper level. So, when you step back into it, bring your authentic self. Not the wounded version or the rebound guy, but the genuine, self-aware, and emotionally available you.

In the world of romance, vulnerability is the real MVP. It's not about playing games or wearing masks. It's about showing up, scars and all, and finding someone who appreciates the journey you've been on and is excited about where you're heading. So gear up, take a deep breath, and remember: your romantic story is far from over. It might just be getting to the best part.

Daily Challenge: Embrace the journey of rediscovering romance with authenticity, patience, and a focus on connecting on a deeper level, rather than rushing into it for validation or to fill a void.

Daily Reflection:

What resonated with you from today's lesson? How can you apply this truth in your life?

_____

_____

_____

_____

Day 196: Your Social Persona

Hey there, fellas, let's dive into something often overlooked: your social persona. In the midst of divorce chaos, remember, how you project yourself matters more than you think. You're the author of your story, make it epic. Don't let divorce define you; instead, let it refine you. Negativity drags you down. Surround yourself with positivity and watch how it elevates your life.

Hit the gym, eat well, and get enough sleep. A healthy you radiates confidence. Upgrade your wardrobe. When you look good, you feel good.

Don't retreat into solitude. Connect with friends, family, and new acquaintances. Human connection is your lifeline. In conversations, listen more than you speak. It shows respect and deepens your connections.

Be intentional about how you use social media, and curate a positive digital space. Therapy isn't weakness; it's strength. A therapist can help you navigate the emotional battlefield. Define your purpose and set clear goals. Having a vision will drive your actions and reshape your future. Life's about growth. Embrace change, adapt, and watch your social persona evolve.

Opening up about your struggles takes courage. It also invites others to support and connect with you. Remind yourself daily that you're worthy of love, success, and happiness. It rewires your mindset. Your social persona isn't a mask; it's the reflection of your inner strength and growth. Take control, craft it with intention, and watch how it transforms your life. Self-care isn't selfish; it's self-empowerment. Own it.

Daily Challenge: Today, strive to be the author of your own story by projecting positivity and confidence in your social interactions, and remember that self-care and self-empowerment are essential components of your journey through divorce survival.

Daily Reflection:

What resonated with you from today's lesson? How can you apply this truth in your life?

_____

_____

_____

_____

Day 197: Life Philosophy- Create Your Manifesto

Alright, gentlemen, let's cut through the noise and get real. You're facing one of life's toughest battles – divorce. But guess what? This is your opportunity to redefine your life, and it starts with crafting your own manifesto.

Life's a rollercoaster, and there are no guarantees. It's about time you took control. No more pointing fingers or dwelling on what went wrong. You're the captain of your ship, and it's time to steer it in the right direction.

Embrace the pain; it's your greatest teacher. This divorce, as brutal as it is, can be your catalyst for personal growth. You're not a victim; you're a warrior. In this chaos, seek clarity and rediscover your purpose.

Your manifesto should be straightforward: grind relentlessly, learn from every setback, and savor every win, no matter how small. Life's not a sprint; it's a marathon, and the pain you're feeling is just part of your training.

As you emerge from this wreckage, rebuild yourself stronger than before. Cultivate meaningful relationships, prioritize your physical and mental health, and master your finances. Never stop evolving; your journey has just begun.

A real man doesn't crumble in the face of adversity; he rises. Your divorce isn't the end; it's your rebirth. Manifest your destiny, and never settle for less than you deserve. Remember, life owes you nothing – it's what you make of it that counts. So, craft your manifesto and let it guide you toward a brighter future.

Daily Challenge: Today, craft your personal manifesto, outlining your commitment to embracing the pain, seeking clarity, and redefining your purpose in the face of divorce, as you steer your life in a new and empowering direction.

Daily Reflection:

What resonated with you from today's lesson? How can you apply this truth in your life?

_____

_____

_____

Day 198: Communication Style- Speak Your Truth

In the battlefield of divorce, men, it's crucial to wield the sharpest sword in your arsenal: your communication style. Forget the sugar-coated lies society feeds you.

Your voice matters, and silence is not your ally. In this brutal dance of separation, you must be assertive, unwavering, and honest. No more playing the victim; you're the author of your narrative now.

Your truth might sting, but it's your sword of liberation. Express your desires, your concerns, and your boundaries. Don't tiptoe around the flames; walk through them, and let your voice roar like thunder.

But beware, gentlemen; this isn't a free pass for aggression. Maintain your dignity; don't resort to insults or blame. Communicate with respect, even when they don't. Realize that she may not understand or agree with your truth, but that's not your problem. You're not here to win debates; you're here to protect your interests and your sanity.

Listen too, because communication is a two-way street. Understand her perspective, not to appease but to navigate this storm. Be a rock, unshaken by emotional manipulation. Remember, speaking your truth is your weapon against gaslighting and manipulation. Document conversations, emails, texts; have proof of your journey.

Lastly, gents, don't let guilt or shame silence your truth. Divorce is not a confession booth; it's a battlefield. Speak boldly, stand tall, and carve your path through the chaos. In the divorce survival guide for men, your truth is your sword, your shield, and your salvation. Use it wisely.

Daily Challenge: Today, embrace the power of your truth as your sword of liberation – speak honestly, assertively, and respectfully in your interactions, letting your voice be a beacon of strength on your journey through divorce.

Daily Reflection:

What resonated with you from today's lesson? How can you apply this truth in your life?

_____

_____

_____

_____

Day 199: Look Inward to Move Forward

In the brutal arena of divorce, there's no room for weakness. If you're a man facing this storm, here's the raw, unfiltered truth: Look inward to move forward. Your gut-wrenching journey starts with a gut check. No, it's not about blame or finger-pointing. It's about YOU. Your choices, your growth, your path ahead.

Divorce is your crucible. It's a relentless mirror that reflects your strengths and exposes your flaws. It's easy to play the victim, to wallow in self-pity, or to drown in anger. But that's not how warriors are forged.

Dig deep. Embrace the pain. Face your demons. This is your opportunity for rebirth. The scars you carry now will either define you or refine you. It's your call. Will you let this chapter break you, or will you rise like a phoenix from the ashes?

Rediscover your identity. Reconnect with your passions. Remember who you were before the chaos. Divorce is a battle, but it's also a classroom. Learn from it. Let it fuel your hunger for self-improvement. Channel that energy into becoming the best version of yourself.

Lean into your support system. Your friends, family, or therapist – they're your allies. Vulnerability is not weakness; it's strength. There's no magic formula, no shortcut. It's going to hurt, and it's going to take time. But remember, pain is the price of transformation.

Inward reflection is your compass. It will guide you through the wreckage, help you find your footing, and lead you toward the life you deserve. So, toughen up, brother. Look inward, own your story, and rebuild your life from the inside out. It's your journey, your destiny. Seize it.

Daily Challenge: Today, commit to a moment of deep self-reflection, confronting one aspect of your journey that needs growth and transformation, and take a tangible step towards making that change.

Daily Reflection:

What resonated with you from today's lesson? How can you apply this truth in your life?

_____

_____

_____

_____

Day 200: Milestone Day- Assess Your Progress

Listen up, fellas. Today is your Day 200, and it's a milestone that demands your attention. You've weathered the storm of divorce, and you've got the scars to prove it. But guess what? Scars make you stronger. Take a long, hard look in the mirror today. See that guy staring back at you? He's not the same man who started this journey. He's battle-tested, battle-hardened, and ready for whatever life throws his way.

On this day, do a gut check. Ask yourself the tough questions. Are you still mired in bitterness and resentment, or have you found the power to let go? Have you allowed this experience to define you, or are you shaping your own destiny?

You've learned some brutal truths about life, love, and yourself. it's raw, unfiltered reality. You can't change the past, but you can decide your future. Assess your progress. Have you rebuilt your identity? Are you back on your feet financially? Are you learning to trust and love again? Are you building a life that makes you proud?

Remember, it's okay to stumble. It's okay to have setbacks. But it's not okay to stay down. Use this milestone as fuel. You've got another 165 days to make this year count.

Your future is a blank canvas, and you hold the brush. Paint it with the vibrant colors of self-discovery, growth, and resilience. Take no prisoners, and let no one define your worth but yourself.

Today, on Day 200, you're not just surviving; you're thriving. Keep grinding, keep evolving, and keep showing the world that divorce couldn't break you. You're a force to be reckoned with, and you've only just begun.

Daily Challenge: Embrace your scars as a symbol of your strength, reflect on how far you've come, and reaffirm your commitment to shaping your own destiny with resilience and self-discovery as your guiding principles.

Daily Reflection:

What resonated with you from today's lesson? How can you apply this truth in your life?

_____

_____

_____

Day 201: Legacy Building

When the dust settles and you've gone through the emotional wringer of divorce, it's time to focus on something powerful: building your legacy. Forget the self-pity and victim mindset. Instead, harness that pain and turn it into fuel for something bigger.

Legacy building isn't just about wealth or status; it's about leaving an indelible mark on this world. Start by reinventing yourself. That means taking your pain and transforming it into purpose. Channel that energy into becoming the best version of yourself. Your legacy begins with self-improvement.

Next, think about your impact on those around you. Are you being the father you want to be? Are you supporting your loved ones in their journeys? A legacy is about the positive influence you have on others, especially your kids.

Financial stability is crucial, but it's not just about money; it's about financial wisdom. Learn from your mistakes, make smart choices, and secure your future.

In this new chapter, forge meaningful connections. Surround yourself with people who uplift and inspire you. Collaborate, build businesses, and create something bigger than yourself. Lastly, remember, life isn't just about you. It's about contributing to society. Make the world a better place, whether through charitable work, mentoring, or any other means that align with your values.

Your divorce doesn't define you. Your legacy does. It's time to step up, be a man, and leave a mark that the world will remember. Start today; the world is waiting for your greatness.

Daily Challenge: Transform your pain into purpose by taking a tangible step towards self-improvement, whether it's learning a new skill, pursuing a hobby, or setting a goal for personal growth.

Daily Reflection:

What resonated with you from today's lesson? How can you apply this truth in your life?

_____

_____

_____

_____

Day 202: Financial Identity

In the gritty aftermath of divorce, your financial identity becomes the anchor of your rebirth. It's time to strip away the illusions and face the cold, hard truth. Your wallet isn't just a leather-bound accessory; it's your lifeline.

No more joint accounts. No more shared debts. It's your time to seize control. Reclaim your financial autonomy, and build your empire from the ashes. Embrace your budget, sweat those savings, and invest in your future like a relentless entrepreneur.

You're not just a man. You're a financial warrior, battling for your dreams. Your income is your artillery; your investments are your army. Forge ahead with calculated risks, and watch your wealth grow like a raging wildfire.

But beware the seductive traps of post-divorce indulgence. Your newfound freedom can turn into a reckless binge if you're not careful. Keep your eyes on the prize, and remember, your financial identity isn't just about dollars—it's about securing your legacy.

Celebrate every milestone, no matter how small. Pay off debts, watch your credit score soar, and accumulate assets. It's not about revenge; it's about rising higher, stronger, and wealthier than ever before.

In the chaos of divorce, let your financial identity be your guiding star. Make it unbreakable, unstoppable, and undeniably yours. Because, in the end, you'll emerge not just as a survivor, but as a thriving titan of your own destiny.

Daily Challenge: Today, take a fearless step towards financial independence by creating a comprehensive budget that empowers you to take control of your financial destiny.

Daily Reflection:

What resonated with you from today's lesson? How can you apply this truth in your life?

_____

_____

_____

_____

Day 203: Your Space, Your Rules

In the world of divorce, gentlemen, you've got to remember one thing: Your Space, Your Rules. This is your battleground for self-discovery and rebirth. Don't let anyone define it but you. Your home is your sanctuary. Reclaim it. Redesign it. Make it a reflection of your new life. Toss out the relics of the past, those remnants of a failed partnership that no longer serve you. Fill the void with things that ignite your passion and purpose.

Your time is precious. Guard it fiercely. Embrace the freedom to pursue your interests, ambitions, and hobbies. Don't let guilt or pressure dictate your schedule. Set your priorities and stick to them. Your time is a non-negotiable asset. Your boundaries are your armor. Learn to say no when necessary. Protect your emotional and mental well-being. Surround yourself with people who uplift you and distance yourself from those who drain your energy. You owe no one an explanation for choosing your own path.

Your goals are your north star. Rediscover your ambitions, your dreams, and the things that make your heart race. Forge a path forward that excites you, not one dictated by expectations or obligations.

Your self-worth is non-negotiable. Your value as a man transcends any relationship status. Own your strengths, acknowledge your flaws, and embrace personal growth. Remember, you're the author of your narrative.

In this journey, it's not about revenge or bitterness. It's about empowerment. It's about creating a life on your terms, unapologetically. It's about taking back control and thriving in your space, on your rules. Rise, gentlemen, for your best days lie ahead.

Daily Challenge: Today, take a bold step to reclaim and redesign your physical space, whether it's rearranging furniture, redecorating, or adding something new that reflects your new life and aspirations.

Daily Reflection:

What resonated with you from today's lesson? How can you apply this truth in your life?

_____

_____

_____

_____

Day 204: Emotional Intelligence

Emotional Intelligence is not some soft, touchy-feely concept. It's the backbone of your survival in the storm of divorce. It's not about denying your emotions; it's about mastering them. Real men don't hide behind a wall of anger. They confront their emotions head-on. In divorce, anger, sadness, and anxiety will hit you like a freight train. You can either let them derail you, or you can harness them as fuel for growth.

Your EQ (Emotional Quotient) will determine your trajectory. It's the ability to understand, manage, and use your emotions to your advantage. In the darkest moments, it's your EQ that'll keep you sane.

Don't bottle it up; don't lash out recklessly. Channel your emotions into productivity. Seek therapy if needed; it's not weakness, it's strength in recognizing your limitations.

Your kids are watching. They're learning how to handle life's curveballs by observing you. Be their role model in emotional resilience.

Navigating the post-divorce world requires emotional finesse. It's about co-parenting, dealing with your ex, and rebuilding yourself. Your EQ is your GPS in this uncharted territory.

In the dating game, EQ is your secret weapon. Women are drawn to men who can communicate, empathize, and connect on an emotional level.

Remember, real strength is not just physical; it's mental and emotional too. Your EQ is your armor, your sword, and your shield. Embrace it, and you'll not just survive; you'll thrive after divorce.

Daily Challenge: Today, embrace the power of emotional intelligence by acknowledging and harnessing your emotions, using them as fuel for personal growth, and setting an example of emotional resilience for your children.

Daily Reflection:

What resonated with you from today's lesson? How can you apply this truth in your life?

_____

_____

_____

Day 205: Body Language

In this chaotic whirlwind of separation, where emotions swing like a pendulum, there's one tool you possess but might be overlooking: your body language.

Look, divorce isn't just a mental game. It's a physical one. Every smirk, shoulder shrug, or hunched posture sends a message, not just to others, but to your own psyche. Your mind is closely watching, always on the lookout, trying to figure out if you're crumbling or conquering.

Your stance in a room can dictate your mental state. Stand tall, even when the weight of the world tries to bring you down. Use your posture as a rebellion against defeat. When you communicate with your lawyer, your ex, or even your kids, let your presence be known. Plant those feet, look straight, and exude a confidence, even if you're quaking inside.

Eyes. They reveal so much. While words can deceive, eyes hardly ever do. In meetings, negotiations, or confrontations, your gaze can be your armor or your weakness. Locking eyes isn't about intimidation; it's about respect—respect for yourself, showing you're here, present, and undeterred.

Your arms, your hands—they talk. A firm handshake, not a vice grip, states your intent. Crossed arms? Maybe it's comfort, but it often screams defense. Be aware, but don't overthink. Just let your body sync with your mindset.

Look, divorce is messy. No one said it'd be a walk in the park. But amidst the mess, remember this: your body speaks volumes. Let it speak strength, resilience, and progress. Even when words fail, let your silent warrior guide you. Don't just survive, man; thrive.

Daily Challenge: Today, consciously pay attention to your body language in every interaction, stand tall, maintain eye contact, and use your physical presence to communicate strength and resilience in the face of divorce challenges.

Daily Reflection:

What resonated with you from today's lesson? How can you apply this truth in your life?

_____

_____

_____

_____

Day 206: Digital Identity

Hey man, let's talk about something raw, real, and incredibly relevant today: your digital identity. That online persona, those social media profiles, and the online breadcrumbs of your past, present, and future. Post-divorce, it's even more critical than you think.

Think of your digital identity as your online handshake. In an age where a Google search tells more about you than a two-hour conversation, you've got to be proactive about what you're projecting. Maybe in the past, your profiles were all about couple photos, anniversaries, and shared experiences. Now? You're redefining. You're reshaping. But here's the kicker: this isn't about erasing your past. No. It's about taking charge of your narrative moving forward. Your story isn't done; it's just turning a page. You're evolving, not erasing.

Don't shy away from the difficult process of updating your digital identity. Yeah, it's gonna sting when you change that relationship status or archive those memories, but trust this - authenticity wins. If you're faking happiness or curating a facade, people see through it. Own your journey, scars, highs, and lows.

Let's be real. It's not just about scrubbing the ex from your Instagram. It's about asking, "Who am I in this digital age? What values, passions, and dreams do I want to share?" Understand this: your online identity isn't just about what's happening in the digital world. It's a reflection of your internal world, your mindset, your growth.

So, redefine and own your digital space. Be raw. Be authentic. But most importantly, be unapologetically you. You've survived one of life's toughest punches – now show the world who you've become.

Daily Challenge: Take a step towards redefining your digital identity today by making an intentional update or post that reflects your authentic self and the journey you're on after divorce.

Daily Reflection:

What resonated with you from today's lesson? How can you apply this truth in your life?

_____

_____

_____

_____

Day 207: Leadership Style

You're going through one of the toughest times in your life, but guess what? It's also one of the most transformative. It's in this crucible that real leadership is born. You know who you are deep down? You're a leader, and not the kind that needs a title or an office. You lead by example, with grit, integrity, and authenticity.

Your divorce doesn't define you. Your reaction to it does. It's time to step up. While everyone's looking for pity parties, you're hunting for opportunities. Not just for yourself, but for those around you.

If you have kids, they're watching. And they'll remember the man who didn't crumble under pressure but instead turned adversity into a masterclass of resilience.

But hey, don't mistake leadership for bravado. It's not about fronting a tough image. It's about being real, being vulnerable, admitting when you're wrong, and making amends. A leader knows when to push forward and when to step back and listen. It's about understanding that strength isn't just muscle and testosterone; it's wisdom, patience, and self-awareness.

And if anyone tells you to "man up" in the traditional sense, remind them that a real man knows his worth, values emotional intelligence, and isn't afraid of evolving. Divorce isn't an end. It's a new chapter. Lead the narrative of your story.

Command the helm of your ship. No matter the storm, you've got the mettle to navigate through. Now go out there and show the world the leader you've always been.

Daily Challenge: Embrace your role as a leader in your own life today, demonstrating resilience, vulnerability, and wisdom as you navigate the challenges of divorce and set a positive example for those around you.

Daily Reflection:

What resonated with you from today's lesson? How can you apply this truth in your life?

_____

_____

_____

_____

Day 208: Social Impact

Listen up, gentlemen. You think divorce is just a personal battle? Think again. You're now on the frontlines of the societal boxing ring where everyone's got an opinion about your life. Friends, family, the random dude at the bar. Even your mailman probably has a take.

You gonna let them dictate your worth? No. The chatter? It's just noise. Background static. Tune it out. The real game is played inside, in the heart, where resilience meets grit. The "he said, she said"? Doesn't matter. What matters is the man you see in the mirror. That's your competition, your harshest critic, and your biggest fan.

Look, society's got a script. A formula. "Poor guy, he's divorced." Screw that. You're not a sob story or a cautionary tale. You're a warrior sculpted by the fires of hardship, emerging stronger, wiser, and unfazed.

So, here's the deal: Every time someone tries to put you in a box because of your divorce, break that box. Build your own narrative. Own your journey, your mistakes, your growth. Dive into your passions, surround yourself with positive vibes, and drown out the BS.

Remember, the world's gonna try and tell you who you are. It's up to you to show them. And trust me, once you embrace your story and your truth, that social impact? It'll be about how you turned adversity into your superpower. That's the real win.

Daily Challenge: Today, silence the external voices and judgments, and focus on being the author of your own narrative, taking one step closer to embracing your story and truth as a powerful survivor of divorce.

Daily Reflection:

What resonated with you from today's lesson? How can you apply this truth in your life?

_____

_____

_____

_____

Day 209: Break Your Chains

Listen up! Here's the deal: We're all slaves to our own narratives. Have you ever said, "I can't do this," or "That's just how I am"? When you say these things, you're literally building an invisible box around yourself. And guess what? You're the architect of that box. The bricks? They're every self-deprecating thought you've ever had, and the mortar? That's the emotional weight you attach to those thoughts. Over time, those thoughts become your reality, your identity.

But here's the real game-changer: What if you could retrain your brain? What if instead of saying, "I can't," you start your day with, "I can learn"? It's a choice, a shift in mindset. And if you make that choice every day, you build a new identity. Instead of locking yourself in that box, you're breaking free, brick by brick. Imagine, just for a moment, replacing those doubts with confidence, that fear with anticipation. It's simple math: New Thought + New Action = New Reality. Don't let a label define you. Rewire your brain with positive, empowering affirmations.

Maybe you've been in that job for a decade because it's familiar. Maybe you avoid certain activities because they challenge your self-imposed label. "I'm not a public speaker," "I can't write," "I'm bad with technology." Familiar, right? But here's the catch: Every time you avoid something based on these self-beliefs, you're passing up on opportunities. Opportunities to grow, to impress, to experience, and to evolve. Imagine the doors you could open, the people you could meet, and the experiences you could have if you only took the leap.

Every time you find yourself saying "I am…," "I have…," or "I can't," take a breath. Think. Do you want to keep that thought, or are you ready for an upgrade? Remember, you've got the power to redefine your narrative. Break those chains and embrace the potential inside you. The choice is yours: stay in that box or shatter it. Choose wisely.

Daily Challenge: Today, challenge yourself to catch and replace any self-limiting beliefs with empowering affirmations, taking a step closer to breaking free from the narrative that no longer serves you.

Daily Reflection:

What resonated with you from today's lesson? How can you apply this truth in your life?

_____

_____

_____

_____

Day 210: Identity Milestone

Divorce isn't just about splitting assets or a last name; it's a deep dive into the chaos of identity. Here you are, 210 days in, and it's time to get real about who you are and who you're becoming.

Remember the guy before marriage? The one with raw passion and fire in his belly? Don't lose him because of someone else's inability to see his value. Your identity was never just about being someone's husband. It's the essence of you – your experiences, dreams, and grit.

Sure, you could look back and wonder, "What if?" But, why? That's a road to nowhere. The chapter's done. What you do now, how you move forward – that's on you. Who do you want to be?

Here's the raw truth: No one's going to hand you a fresh identity. You've got to carve it out. Use the pain and scars as your foundation, not as chains holding you down.

People will talk. Some will say you've changed or lost your way. So what? They're not walking your path. Rediscovering yourself is a journey most won't understand, but it's yours to own.

Your worth? It isn't measured by a relationship that didn't last. It's about what you learn and how you grow from it. You're more than a label. You're a fighter with a destiny in your hands.

Look forward, man. The best version of you is yet to come. Forge your identity and own your future. Get after it.

Daily Challenge: Embrace the journey of self-discovery today by reflecting on your true essence, dreams, and passions, and take one concrete step towards becoming the best version of yourself.

Daily Reflection:

What resonated with you from today's lesson? How can you apply this truth in your life?

_____

_____

_____

_____

Money Talks

Face yourself in the mirror, revamp your bucket list with new goals, and ponder the power of your name. Evaluate your personality traits—keep, tweak, or delete? It's time to update your core values and revisit hobbies that make your heart sing. Establish a personal brand, ignite passion projects, and write your life's narrative. Elevate your fashion sense, embrace the power pose, and envision your five-year future. Expand your skill set, embrace risk, and rediscover romance. Define your social persona, create your life philosophy, and reflect on your legacy.

Day 211: Financial Audit- The Cold, Hard Numbers

Gentlemen, let's cut the crap and dive straight into this: your financial life after a divorce isn't going to fix itself. It's a brutal wake-up call, but one you need right now. Every dime, every transaction, every investment - it's all up for scrutiny. This isn't the time to sugarcoat or hide behind comforting lies; it's about facing the cold, hard numbers.

Divorce? Yeah, it's tough. But using it as an excuse to remain in financial limbo? That's a choice. Don't be that guy who lets his wallet bleed because he's too proud, or too scared, to take a good, hard look at his finances. And trust me, ignorance in this game? It's not bliss. It's bankruptcy.

Remember when you used to save for those sneakers or that dream vacation with your partner? Now it's about saving yourself. If there's debt, don't pretend it's not there. If there are assets, know their worth. Not tomorrow, not in a week. Now. This isn't just about survival; it's about thriving in a new reality. Everyone's talking about "self-care" these days, right? Well, let me break it down for you: self-care is also about ensuring your finances aren't in the gutter. Because when you're awake at 3 AM, stressing about bills, that's not self-care, that's self-destruction.

Get out a spreadsheet, or even a piece of paper, and start listing. Incomes, expenses, debts, assets. Know where every cent is going because every cent counts. Consult professionals if you need to. Financial planners, advisors, accountants - they're all there to help you navigate the mess, and trust me, their advice is worth its weight in gold.

Your financial health post-divorce is a direct reflection of how seriously you take yourself. You wouldn't neglect a gaping wound, so why let your finances bleed out? Get real, get gritty, and get it together. The future you will thank you for it.

Daily Challenge: Take a fearless look at your financial situation, create a comprehensive list of your income, expenses, debts, and assets, and commit to taking concrete steps today to secure your financial future post-divorce.

Daily Reflection:

What resonated with you from today's lesson? How can you apply this truth in your life?

_____

_____

_____

_____

Day 212: Budget Reboot- The New Normal

Hey there, champion. So, life's thrown you a curveball named 'divorce'. Tough, ain't it? But guess what? That's just a chapter, not the whole book. Let's get something straight: life post-divorce? It's not a downgrade, it's a reset. And just like you'd reboot a laggy computer, it's time for a budget reboot.

Your financial situation's probably looking different now, and that's okay. It's expected! But this isn't the time to wallow in what you've lost. It's time to get strategic with what you've got. No more autopilot spending. Every dollar you earn and spend? It's a tool, a weapon. Use it wisely.

Reality check: you're the captain of your own ship now, more than ever. No one's going to sail it for you. Those fancy dinners or that flashy car you were financing to impress? Reconsider. Not for anyone else, but for you. Prioritize. Streamline. Think needs, not just wants. This is your game, and only you decide the moves.

Here's some hard truth: Post-divorce, your financial stability isn't just about money. It's about self-worth. It's about self-respect. It's a reflection of how you value yourself. Every financial decision is now a step towards rebuilding, towards claiming the life you deserve.

You might be tempted to go on a spending spree, a sort of 'freedom celebration'. Resist that urge. Think long game. Instant gratifications are fleeting; your financial health and peace of mind? That lasts. Don't trade long-term prosperity for short-lived pleasure.

Bottom line? The old playbook? Toss it. This is the era of the new normal. Get lean, get mean, and get clear on what matters. In this reboot, every cent counts, every decision matters. Your future self will thank you. So gear up, take charge, and dominate this new chapter. You've got this.

Daily Challenge: Today, take a hard look at your finances and identify one unnecessary expense you can eliminate or reduce to start building a stronger financial foundation for your future.

Daily Reflection:

What resonated with you from today's lesson? How can you apply this truth in your life?

_____

_____

_____

_____

Day 213: Credit Report- Know Your Score

Gentlemen, let's get one thing straight: just as you should know the weight you're lifting at the gym or the balance in your bank account, you need to know your credit score. Why? Because in the real world, this number is one of the rawest reflections of your financial health. It's more than just digits on a screen. It represents your reliability, your word, your promise.

Here's the hard truth: Life doesn't care if you've gone through a divorce. It doesn't give you a pass on your responsibilities. Your bills will keep coming, those payments aren't going to pause out of sympathy. And if you think your ex or the world owes you some financial slack, you're living in a dream. Wake up.

Post-divorce, everything changes. Assets get split, responsibilities shift, and guess what? If your name's on a debt, that debt's coming for you, regardless of the sob stories. Don't hide from it; confront it. You don't want to be the guy blindsided when he's trying to buy a new car or get a new apartment because of a tarnished credit score.

You see, credit is trust. It's a handshake agreement that you're good for your word. It tells lenders, landlords, and sometimes even employers that you've got your act together. It's a reflection of your discipline, your integrity, and your capacity to handle adult life. A low score? It's shouting that you're a risk. It might not be fair, but it's the reality.

Now, you might feel sucker-punched by the divorce, but the truth is that no one else cares about your personal drama. Your credit score doesn't care about your heartbreak. Get ahead of the curve. Check your credit report. Know where you stand. Find out if there's any misinformation dragging you down. Dispute it. Make plans to repair what's broken, and protect what's still intact.

Daily Challenge: Today, take the first step towards financial empowerment post-divorce by checking your credit score and reviewing your credit report to ensure it accurately reflects your financial standing and integrity.

Daily Reflection:

What resonated with you from today's lesson? How can you apply this truth in your life?

_____

_____

_____

_____

Day 214: Debt Demolition- Start Chipping Away

Man, let's talk straight. You're going through the wringer of divorce, and it's crushing from all angles. But amidst the emotional chaos, there's another demon lurking – debt. That towering mountain of money owed can feel as suffocating as the legal papers piling up. But here's the truth: debt is just a number. And like any number, it can be reduced, tackled, and ultimately erased.

Don't wait for a better day or a sign. Start today. Right now. In the face of adversity, we've got two options – crumble or conquer. Be the man who chooses to conquer. Rip that band-aid off and face your finances head-on. Don't run, don't hide. It's time to chip away at the debt, even if it's a dollar at a time. Think of every cent you knock off that debt as a piece of your freedom. It's tangible. It's real. And it's yours to claim.

Stop with the excuses. "It's too much," "Where do I start?" "I can't." Toss that garbage mindset out the window. You've faced heartbreak, you've faced setbacks, and you've faced legalities that can choke the spirit out of anyone. And yet, here you are. Standing. Breathing. Ready to take on another battle. Debt? It's just another adversary.

The real question is, are you going to let numbers on a paper define you? No. You're bigger than that. You're tougher than that. Approach your debt with the same ferocity and determination that you've approached every other challenge in your life. No half measures, no waiting for tomorrow.

Remember this – every empire, every success story, every comeback started with a single step. Your financial freedom, your ticket out of the debt dungeon, it starts with acknowledging the beast and then swinging at it, day after day. The world respects a fighter, and right now, it's time to put on those gloves and get in the ring. Let's demolish that debt. You've got this.

Daily Challenge: Today, take the first step in conquering your debt by creating a budget and identifying one expense you can cut or reduce, no matter how small it may seem.

Daily Reflection:

What resonated with you from today's lesson? How can you apply this truth in your life?

_____

_____

_____

Day 215: Asset Allocation

Divorce can throw you off your game, especially when it comes to assets. Look, nobody marries with the intention of splitting up later, but life throws curveballs. So, if you're in the midst of this storm, you need to be sharp, and you need to be strategic. Asset allocation during divorce isn't about being greedy or vindictive. It's about ensuring that you don't come out of this life-altering event broke and directionless. You've worked hard for what you have. This isn't the time to let emotions dictate your decisions. Leave the emotions for the therapy sessions and focus on the numbers, facts, and figures here.

Know your assets inside and out. I'm talking about everything: the family home, investments, retirement funds, and even those baseball cards collecting dust in the attic. And while we're on this topic, remember debts are also part of the equation. Be proactive. If you wait for things to come to you, they never will. Get a good lawyer and financial adviser. Surround yourself with people who won't sugarcoat things, who'll tell it to you straight. You need a team that's going to fight for your best interest, not just someone going through the motions.

Avoid the blame game. It doesn't matter whose fault it was or who did what. Pointing fingers won't add zeroes to your bank account. Prioritize clarity over being right. Think about the long game, not just the immediate satisfaction.

Your future self will thank you for making calculated moves now. This phase of life is temporary, but the financial decisions you make can have long-lasting repercussions. You owe it to yourself to be pragmatic, forward-thinking, and assertive. Stay sharp. Stay strategic. And above all, stay true to yourself.

Daily Challenge: Today, challenge yourself to create a detailed inventory of your assets, including all financial holdings and possessions, and take the first step towards securing your financial future by seeking professional legal and financial advice.

Daily Reflection:

What resonated with you from today's lesson? How can you apply this truth in your life?

_____

_____

_____

_____

Day 216: Emergency Fund- The Safety Net

You think going through a divorce is just about heartbreak and tears? Nah, man. It's about grit, hustle, and financial resilience. And guess what? Your finances don't care about your feelings. Your bank account doesn't care if you're sad, angry, or trying to find yourself. It just sits there waiting for the next bill, the next unexpected expense, the next life curveball. So what's your move?

Emergency fund. Boom. That's it. You want a safety net? This is your parachute when life pushes you off the plane without a warning. And trust me, it WILL push you. It's not about "if" but "when". But here's the kicker: YOU have the power to cushion that fall.

Here's your reality check: stop blowing cash on the latest gadgets, those nights out, the things that make you feel "better" for a moment. Instead, hustle for that emergency stash. It's your armor.

Your shield against the unexpected storms. Because guess what? Rainy days don't announce themselves. They just pour. And when they do, will you be the guy who's scrambling, or the guy who's prepared?

The emergency fund isn't a "nice-to-have". It's a "I'm-glad-I-had-that". A buffer between you and the chaos. So get serious. Get strategic. And build that fund. Because in the raw, real game of life, money is more than just green paper; it's freedom, stability, and the power to rebound.

So, ask yourself: Are you going to be a victim of circumstance or the master of your own fate? The choice is yours. Hustle for it.

Daily Challenge: Take a hard look at your financial habits and commit to building that emergency fund, because financial resilience is not just about surviving; it's about thriving in the face of life's unexpected challenges.

Daily Reflection:

What resonated with you from today's lesson? How can you apply this truth in your life?

_____

_____

_____

_____

Day 217: Tax Implications- Don't Get Blindsided

L et's get real for a second. Divorce isn't just an emotional punch in the gut. It's a financial whirlwind, and you're standing right at the center of it. You think you've got it all figured out, right? You're haggling over the house, the car, the dog, but what about taxes? Don't be that guy who walks away from the negotiation table only to get slapped with unexpected tax implications.

Let's talk about tax, man. The money you've worked your butt off for? The government wants a piece of that pie, especially when your marital status shifts. This ain't about being bitter or playing the blame game. It's about being SMART. It's about not letting your hard-earned money slip through your fingers because you weren't informed. Think about alimony. Think about asset division. They don't just affect your pocket; they influence your tax bracket.

You need to get ahead of this. Dive into the nitty-gritty. Understand the difference between filing jointly and separately. Get to know how selling the marital home can hit you with capital gains. If you're paying alimony, know the implications. If you're receiving it, be ready for the flip side.

Divorce isn't just a mental game; it's a numbers game. And like any game, the player with the most information and the best strategy wins. Nobody's saying you have to become a tax guru overnight. But what you can't do is bury your head in the sand and pretend like this storm is going to pass without touching you.

So, step up. Get a good accountant, do your research, and have those tough conversations. Make sure that when the dust settles, you're standing on solid financial ground, not sinking in tax quicksand.

Daily Challenge: Take charge of your financial future today by seeking expert advice, understanding tax implications, and actively managing your finances during this divorce journey.

Daily Reflection:

What resonated with you from today's lesson? How can you apply this truth in your life?

_____

_____

_____

_____

Day 218: Retirement Planning- The Long Game

Facing divorce, brother? Think your financial world's imploding? Hold on, take a deep breath, and look beyond today. The narrative? Retirement planning. It's the long game you can't afford to sleep on, especially when life's chaos throws you curveballs.

Listen up: everyone's got a story, and right now, your plot's taking a twist. But remember, life isn't about the chapter you're in, but the whole book. Divorce might feel like a setback, but let it be a set up for a smarter financial future. That retirement nest egg? It's not just about kicking back on a beach sipping cocktails.

Now, I get it. It's hard. Money's tight, and the emotional riptide's making it hard to think straight. But you've got to zoom out. What you do now, in this emotional maelstrom, can set the trajectory for the rest of your life. Compounding interest isn't just a finance term; it's the principle that small, consistent efforts now can lead to significant payoffs later.

Divorce might force you to split assets, but it also presents an opportunity. Reset. Reevaluate. Rethink how you approach your finances. The reality? Time's your most significant asset, not money. But if you play your cards right, time can be converted into money. Every penny, every investment decision, needs to be made with an eye on that distant horizon. Sure, treat yourself occasionally, but don't lose sight of the big picture.

The market will fluctuate, life will throw lemons, but your resilience, foresight, and a relentless focus on that retirement goal will be your North Star. So, gear up, recalibrate, and make those informed choices. No sugarcoating here: it's a grind. But man, when you're older, looking back at this time, you'll be proud you played the long game. It's not just about surviving; it's about thriving.

Daily Challenge: Amidst the emotional turmoil of divorce, take a step towards your long-term financial stability by setting a specific retirement savings goal and researching investment options to secure your future.

Daily Reflection:

What resonated with you from today's lesson? How can you apply this truth in your life?

_____

_____

_____

_____

Day 219: Investment Strategy- Time to Diversify

Life has a funny way of throwing you curveballs, doesn't it? Just when you think you've got everything sorted, BAM! Divorce hits, and suddenly, everything you had invested emotionally, physically, and even financially seems like it's going down the drain. But hold on a minute, this isn't the end; it's just a new beginning.

Think about it in terms of your investment portfolio. You wouldn't put all your money in one stock, would you? Why? Because it's risky! If that stock tanks, so does your entire financial future. Diversification is the name of the game in the world of finance, and it should be the same in life. Too many of us make the mistake of investing everything - our identity, our emotions, our future - into one relationship. And when that relationship sours? We're left scrambling, feeling like we've lost everything.

Now's the time to diversify. If you've been banking solely on your partner for happiness, it's time to spread those investments. Dive deep into passions you've shelved. Reconnect with friends you've sidelined. Take that pottery class you always joked about. You're not just one role, one relationship, or one failure. You're a complex individual with so much to offer, and it's time you spread your investments.

You want returns on your emotional investments? Diversify. Don't let the heartbreak of one relationship determine your entire emotional stock market. Your self-worth isn't tied to one person, one relationship, or one failure. It's tied to you, your resilience, your passions, your drive, and your ability to adapt and diversify. Divorce isn't the end. It's a financial call to diversify your life's investments. Don't put all your stock in one person. Spread it out. Live large. Invest in YOU. And watch the returns flood in.

Daily Challenge: Identify one aspect of your life where you've been too focused on a single source of happiness or fulfillment and take a step towards diversifying your interests and investments in yourself.

Daily Reflection:

What resonated with you from today's lesson? How can you apply this truth in your life?

_____

_____

_____

Day 220: Income Streams- Don't Rely on One

L ife's unpredictable. That's a fact. If you've been through the wringer of a divorce, you get it. You once relied on the idea of forever with one person, but look where that got you. It's a tough pill to swallow, but a crucial lesson: don't put all your chips on one square. Same goes for your finances. You might have a cushy job right now, raking in a solid paycheck every month. But what happens when that comfort zone shatters? Think it can't? Divorce probably felt that way once too.

Don't be the guy that leans heavily on a single income stream. It's like betting your entire life on black, spinning the wheel, and hoping for the best. But life doesn't play by Vegas rules.

Consider this: If you had multiple small streams of cash flow coming in from various investments, you wouldn't be as crushed if one went south. That's diversification. It's not about spreading yourself thin; it's about building a safety net. It's about ensuring that when one rope snaps, you've got ten more holding you up.

Get curious. Dive into real estate, stocks, bonds, peer-to-peer lending, starting a side hustle, or even flipping garage sale finds. Heck, buy a vending machine if that's your jam. The point is to be proactive. Look for opportunities, learn, and jump in. Fear is what stops most folks from even starting, but you've already faced one of life's toughest battles. So, what's a little market fluctuation to you?

In the end, it's simple math: the more you diversify, the less risk you carry. So, gear up. The same grit and resilience you're applying to rebuild post-divorce? Channel that energy into building diverse income streams. Because when life throws a curveball, you'll be ready with a full arsenal. And trust me, that's power.

Daily Challenge: Embrace the lesson of diversification in life, just as you've learned from divorce, by taking one step today to explore and invest in a new income stream or financial opportunity.

Daily Reflection:

What resonated with you from today's lesson? How can you apply this truth in your life?

_____

_____

_____

_____

Day 221: Real Estate- Keep, Sell, or Buy?

Hey, you're here, in the thick of the storm, making those hard choices after the fallout of a divorce. Suddenly, those bricks and mortar? They're not just assets, they're pivotal decisions you need to make. Let's talk straight about that real estate of yours. Listen, the game's changed, but the rules remain. Real estate's always about timing, value, and strategic foresight. But now, it's not just about ROI in monetary terms—it's about the ROI in your life. What does this asset mean to you emotionally, financially, and in the long-term vision of your life post-divorce?

If that house or property is suffocating you with memories, then maybe it's time to cash out. You can't put a price on mental clarity. On the other hand, if that property is your ticket to financial freedom, if it's going to be the passive income you've been dreaming of, then buckle up and keep it. Your future self might just thank you for it.

Maybe you're tempted to buy. It might seem counterintuitive when the chips are down, but if you've got the capital and see an opportunity? Go for it. Fresh starts aren't just about emotional detox; they're about laying down new foundations, both metaphorically and literally. Now, let's not kid ourselves. This isn't just about market value. It's deeply personal. But in the throes of a major life change, never let emotion be your only compass. Mix it with logic, foresight, and a dose of guts. There's no one-size-fits-all answer here.

Real talk? Whatever you decide with that property, make sure it aligns with the man you're becoming, not the man you were. That's the only way to truly win, in real estate and in life. Remember, buildings are just buildings, but you, my friend, are a powerhouse of resilience and reinvention. Make the decision that fuels that. No compromises.

Daily Challenge: Take a hard look at your real estate holdings, assessing their emotional and financial significance in your post-divorce life, and make a decision that aligns with the man you're becoming, not the man you were.

Daily Reflection:

What resonated with you from today's lesson? How can you apply this truth in your life?

_____

_____

_____

_____

Day 222: Financial Advisors- Friend or Foe?

Listen, gentlemen, I get it. Divorce shatters your world. You're emotionally wrecked, and your finances? It's like walking through a minefield blindfolded. This is the time you're thinking about those investment financial advisors, right? But are they your knights in shining armor or just wolves in sheep's clothing?

Let's keep it 100. Not every financial advisor out there has your best interests at heart. Some are just looking to pad their own pockets. They see your vulnerability – a man fresh out of a life-altering event like divorce – and they think, "Easy prey." You've got to watch out for these sharks.

But, and it's a big BUT, there are those genuine advisors out there, who genuinely care. They're not just looking at you as another paycheck. They're looking at your financial health, helping you rebuild, ensuring your future looks a lot sunnier than your past.

Divorce already took a lot out of you; you don't need someone else draining your pockets. So, do your homework. Dive deep. Read reviews, ask for referrals, meet them face to face, ask the hard questions. Look into their eyes. Can you trust them?

Money's a tool. In the right hands, it builds empires. In the wrong ones? It's gone before you know it. Know your financial DNA. Know what you need, and more importantly, what you don't.

Divorce? It's a setback, not the end. But you've got to be smart, especially about where your money's going. Your financial future isn't just about you; it's about your kids, your next chapter, your legacy. So, financial advisors? Friend or foe? That's on you to decide. But remember, knowledge is power, and your gut? Trust it.

Daily Challenge: Today, take the time to research and evaluate potential financial advisors with the same dedication and scrutiny you'd apply to any life-changing decision, ensuring they align with your financial goals and values as you navigate the post-divorce landscape.

Daily Reflection:

What resonated with you from today's lesson? How can you apply this truth in your life?

_____

_____

_____

_____

Day 223: Insurance Needs- Update Your Policies

In the throes of a divorce, the last thing on your mind might be insurance. But hear me out. It's time to get real about the nitty-gritty. Because believe it or not, updating your policies can mean the difference between sailing through your next chapter or hitting financial rocks hard.

First things first. Life isn't a fairy tale, and neither is insurance. Your ex probably isn't going to swoop in and make sure you're taken care of if something goes sideways. Remember, insurance isn't just for you. It's for those you leave behind, your legacy.

Ever thought about your life insurance policy? Post-divorce, that bad boy might still have your ex as the primary beneficiary. While you might've had lovey-dovey feelings for them once upon a time, things have changed. And your hard-earned money should reflect that. Adjust it. Redirect it. Make sure it aligns with your current situation, not a chapter you've closed.

Same goes for health, auto, and property insurance. Who's covered? Who benefits? Don't let old emotions dictate where your dollars go today. Emotionally, you're moving on, so make sure everything else is moving along with you. And health insurance? Brother, if you were on your spouse's plan, you've got to reassess that quick. The last thing you need is a health crisis on top of everything else. Be proactive. It's no longer their responsibility; it's squarely on your shoulders.

Stop making excuses. "It's complicated" or "I don't have time" doesn't fly here. This isn't just some trivial task to be brushed off. This is about taking control, being the captain of your ship. The seas might be rough now, but steering with clarity will get you to calmer waters. Face it head-on. Don't let past decisions linger like ghosts, haunting your present. Tackle this insurance mess. No procrastinating. No evasion. Your future self will thank you.

Daily Challenge: Take charge of your financial future by reviewing and updating your insurance policies to ensure they align with your current circumstances, because your legacy and well-being depend on it.

Daily Reflection:

What resonated with you from today's lesson? How can you apply this truth in your life?

_____

_____

_____

_____

Day 224: Child Support and Alimony- The Facts

Child support and alimony. Let's cut through the noise and get real. There's a ton of stigma around these terms, especially for men. Society often paints a picture that if you're paying, you've lost. It's not about winning or losing; it's about responsibility.

You had a life with someone. Whether it was love, convenience, or a whirlwind of both, commitments were made. Kids may have come into the picture, lifestyles were adopted. Now, things have changed, and you're on the other side. So, what now? Do you complain about every dollar that leaves your account? Or do you step up and understand that, for a time, this is your role? Child support isn't a punishment. It's for the kids. It's to ensure that even if mom and dad aren't under the same roof, the kids don't suffer. They didn't ask for the split. They didn't ask for the change. But they sure deserve stability.

Alimony, on the other hand, can be a bitter pill. Maybe you think, "Why should I support an adult who can work?" But remember, alimony isn't forever. It's transitional. There were agreements, spoken or unspoken, in your relationship. Maybe one of you sacrificed career for family. Maybe one of you supported the other's dreams at the expense of your own. This is the fallout.

Stop seeing child support and alimony as chains. They're not. They're commitments that come from choices you made. Handle them like a man, with dignity. If you think the amounts are unfair, fight legally, not emotionally. Advocate for yourself without tearing down your ex. And most importantly, keep the kids out of it. Life's tough. Divorce is tougher. But it's in these gritty moments that true character is shown. How you handle this says more about you than any paycheck ever will. Stand tall, face the facts, and move forward. Because this is just a chapter, not the entire book.

Daily Challenge: Embrace your responsibility with grace, understanding that child support and alimony are not about winning or losing but ensuring stability for your children and honoring commitments made during your relationship.

Daily Reflection:

What resonated with you from today's lesson? How can you apply this truth in your life?

_____

_____

_____

Day 225: Frugality vs. Quality- Find the Balance

Hey, listen up! I get it – post-divorce, money becomes a different beast. Suddenly you're wondering if you need to pinch pennies, cut corners, and opt for the cheaper route every time. But let me throw some straight talk your way: while frugality is crucial, never compromise on quality where it counts.

Life's thrown you a curveball, and now more than ever, you've got to be strategic. Being frugal isn't about buying the cheapest thing on the shelf; it's about maximizing value. It's understanding that sometimes you spend a little more upfront to save a lot in the long run. Got that? If you're buying a tool or appliance, don't just go for the cheapest one. Consider its durability, reviews, and warranty. A pricier item might last three times longer than the cheap version. Do the math.

But here's the flip side: not every expense needs the 'best of the best'. Brand-name cereal? Seriously, dude? That generic brand probably tastes the same, if not better. New car straight out of the dealership? A slightly used one can be just as good without the instant depreciation.

And let's talk experiences. Those moments you share with your kids or the times you invest in yourself for personal growth? Quality over everything. Some experiences are priceless and worth every dime. Don't let frugality rob you of beautiful memories or genuine growth.

Look, post-divorce, it's easy to fall into extremes. Some of you might want to drown the sorrows in extravagant purchases. Others might lock up every penny. Find the balance. Every dollar you spend is a vote for the kind of life you want to lead. You've been through enough; don't add regrettable financial decisions to the mix. Invest smartly, spend wisely, and always, always prioritize value. You've got this.

Daily Challenge: Today, commit to making a list of your essential expenses and evaluate where you can prioritize quality over cost, ensuring that your financial decisions align with your long-term goals and values.

Daily Reflection:

What resonated with you from today's lesson? How can you apply this truth in your life?

_____

_____

_____

Day 226: Financial Milestone- Where Are You Now?

Listen, divorce is a tornado that rips through your finances. One day you're splitting bills and planning vacations together, and the next, you're trying to figure out how to budget on a single income. Maybe you're shelling out on lawyer fees, or figuring out how alimony and child support play into your monthly expenses. But here's the raw truth: lamenting the past won't rebuild your bank account. You've got to stare your finances in the face, however grim they might look, and take the reins. No one's coming to save you; you have to save yourself.

Where are you now? Are you drowning in debt? Struggling to keep up with expenses? Or are you on the other side, with a stable footing, trying to figure out what's next? Pinpoint your exact financial position. It's time to get real. Money is about mindset as much as it's about the dollars and cents. You can't undo the financial hit of a divorce, but you can change your attitude towards your current situation. Stop seeing yourself as a victim. Yes, it's tough. Yes, it's not fair. But guess what? Life isn't about fairness. It's about resilience, adaptability, and action.

Maybe you need to downsize, maybe you need to hustle more, or maybe it's time to explore that business idea you've always put off. Your financial situation post-divorce is a starting point, not an end. It's a call to pivot, to reassess, to hustle.

Don't let money, or the lack thereof, define you. Let your response to the situation do that. You're not the first guy to face financial challenges after a divorce, and you won't be the last. But if you face it head-on, with determination and a no-BS attitude, you might just be one of the few who come out stronger, wiser, and even wealthier on the other side. Remember, you're the master of your destiny, not your past. Own your future, starting with your finances. Now

Daily Challenge: Embrace your financial reality, assess your current situation, and commit to taking control of your finances with determination and resilience, knowing that your response defines your future, not your past..

Daily Reflection:

What resonated with you from today's lesson? How can you apply this truth in your life?

_____

_____

_____

_____

Day 227: Financial Education- Never Stop Learning

Listen up, gentlemen. Divorce? It's not just about heartbreak or courtroom drama. It's about getting your finances straight, and I don't just mean figuring out alimony. Money talks, and post-divorce, it might be screaming. You got hit hard? Join the club. But let's not play a sad violin. Instead, let's hustle. Because guess what? Divorce can be your wake-up call.

Money's not just paper; it's power. Don't know the difference between stocks and bonds? Time to learn. Cryptocurrency sounds like alien talk? Get on that spaceship. Waiting for someone else to manage your money? Dude, it's your wallet, your future. Financial literacy isn't a school subject; it's real-world survival. The world's moving fast, and if you're still thinking a savings account is where it's at, you're trailing behind. Dive deep, get your hands dirty. Read. Listen. Engage. There are podcasts, courses, seminars out there. Get on YouTube – it's free!

When was the last time you took a risk? Not a gamble, an educated risk. Investments, stocks, real estate - scared? Don't be. Fear is the killer of dreams, and last I checked, you still have a lot of dreaming left. The road might be rough, but what's new? You've tackled bigger monsters. Let's make this clear: It's not about becoming the next Wolf of Wall Street. It's about understanding your money. It's about growth, resilience, and getting back on that horse. Life threw a curveball? Swing harder. Every setback is a setup for a comeback. Don't just survive; thrive.

In your journey, you're gonna meet naysayers. They might be in the mirror. Tell them to shut up. You're in the driver's seat now. And if there's one thing you're going to invest in, it's yourself. Let's get to work.

Daily Challenge: Embrace financial empowerment and commit to learning one new thing about managing your money today, whether it's exploring an investment option, reading a finance article, or watching a financial education video.

Daily Reflection:

What resonated with you from today's lesson? How can you apply this truth in your life?

_____

_____

_____

_____

Day 228: Side Hustles- Extra Cash, Extra Freedom

Listen, man, I get it. Divorce is like having the rug pulled out from under you. Everything's messy, and the financial hit? It's no joke. But here's where you pivot. Instead of wallowing, look at this as the push you never knew you needed.

You've been given a raw deal? Time to double down and hustle like never before. I'm talking side hustles. Not just for the extra cash (though, let's be honest, that's a bonus) but for the freedom. The freedom to take control when everything else seems out of control.

You remember those ideas you shelved, thinking, "One day, maybe"? Guess what? TODAY is that day. That idea for a podcast, the knack you have for woodworking, that online course you could teach – the world is waiting. Not tomorrow, not in a year, NOW.

And you might be thinking, "I don't have the time or energy." But here's a hard truth: Time and energy aren't things you find; they're things you MAKE.

Imagine the thrill of that first sale, that first client. The taste of success when you're rebuilding? Nothing's sweeter. It's more than just money in the bank; it's a reminder that you're still in the game, and you're playing on your terms.

You're not just earning extra, you're learning extra. Every challenge, every obstacle is teaching you resilience, adaptability, and grit. Skills that no cushy job can teach you.

Now, don't get me wrong. This isn't about escaping reality. It's about facing it head-on, with an army of side hustles behind you. It's about showing yourself, your ex, and the world that you're not just surviving; you're THRIVING. So, dust off that idea, invest in yourself, and make it happen.

Daily Challenge: Embrace the opportunity in adversity by taking one concrete step today toward launching or expanding a side hustle that aligns with your passion and potential.

Daily Reflection:

What resonated with you from today's lesson? How can you apply this truth in your life?

_____

_____

_____

_____

Day 229: Business Ventures- Time to Take the Plunge?

Divorce? It shatters you. But it also rebuilds you. And here's the real-talk: Your personal life may have crumbled, but that rubble? It's the foundation of your next empire. You've been through the ringer, faced your demons, and now you're standing here, wiser, stronger. Why are you still on the sidelines?

Every adversity has a silver lining. Maybe you've been harboring that business idea, that entrepreneurial itch. But something held you back.

The fear of failing, the fear of judgment, or just the weight of responsibilities. Now? You've got a different perspective. You've faced one of life's toughest battles; what's a little business risk compared to that?

Don't wait for a "better time." There's never going to be a perfect moment. The stars won't align and hand you success on a silver platter. But that fire in your belly, that's real. It's your asset, your competitive edge.

Now is when you channel all that pain, all that emotion into something tangible, something that has potential. Dive deep into research, network like you never have before, and execute relentlessly. Remember, failing in business is not about falling down; it's about staying down.

Divorce taught you resilience. Use it. Every 'no' you hear, every door that gets slammed in your face, is just a detour, not a dead end. So, ask yourself: are you going to let divorce define you, or are you going to use it to redefine your destiny? Time's ticking. Take the plunge.

Daily Challenge: Embrace the strength and wisdom you've gained through divorce, and take the leap to pursue your entrepreneurial dreams without waiting for the perfect moment, knowing that resilience will guide you through any setbacks on your path to redefining your destiny.

Daily Reflection:

What resonated with you from today's lesson? How can you apply this truth in your life?

_____

_____

_____

_____

Day 230: Savings Goals- Short Term vs. Long Term

Listen up, fellas. Going through a divorce? That's tough. Real tough. But let's talk about where your head needs to be, financially. Yeah, I know it's hard to think about money when you're going through emotional hell, but you can't afford to let it slide.

In the immediate, you've got some financial fires to put out. Lawyers, settlements, possibly alimony. That's your short-term: immediate, pressing, and cannot be ignored. But don't get so lost in the short-term that you neglect the long run.

Look, you're building a new life. That life is gonna need some capital. Whether it's a new place to live, investments for your future, or maybe even funding your passions or side hustles, you need to be planning. That's your long-term. It's not just about the here and now, but where you want to be 10, 20, 30 years from now. And I get it, short-term financial struggles can feel suffocating. But you can't let them choke out your future. You've got to be ruthless about setting aside something for the long haul, even if it's a small amount at first.

Divorce can rip away your past, but don't let it rob your future. Be smart. Be proactive. Whether it's a dollar or a hundred dollars, start setting aside money for your future. Make sacrifices. Prioritize. Think about where you want to be, who you want to be, and start planting the seeds now.

This isn't just about financial freedom; it's about reclaiming your life. So get clear on your savings goals. Balance the immediate with the eventual. And remember, every single decision you make today will either set you up for success or failure tomorrow. Choose wisely.

Daily Challenge: Take a hard look at your finances and make a commitment to allocate even a small portion of your income toward a long-term savings goal, ensuring that your divorce doesn't compromise your financial future.

Daily Reflection:

What resonated with you from today's lesson? How can you apply this truth in your life?

_____

_____

_____

_____

Day 231: Big Purchases- Plan Wisely

Big purchases after a divorce? Listen, I get it. The impulse to buy something new, flashy, to show the world – and maybe yourself – that you're still "the man". That fresh start feeling mixed with a dose of ego can be intoxicating. But pump the brakes. Do you really need that sports car, or is it a Band-Aid for a bruised ego? Is that luxury apartment a solid investment or a dive into financial instability?

Divorce is a seismic shift, a life quake. And yeah, sometimes it feels like your very core is shaken. But those tremors? They can make your judgment shaky, too. Now's not the time to make hasty financial moves. Not when you're trying to navigate the stormy seas of emotional recovery, legal battles, and rebuilding your life from the ground up.

Don't mistake me – investing in yourself post-divorce is crucial. But think experiences over things. Skills over shiny objects. Take that money and put it into something lasting: maybe a course to boost your professional life, a trip that genuinely expands your horizons, or even therapy to navigate the emotional labyrinth you find yourself in.

Because here's the truth – the satisfaction from that new purchase? It's fleeting. The deep-rooted, soul-nourishing satisfaction from investing in your growth, in understanding yourself better, in setting the stage for a future built on wisdom? That's forever.

Remember, healing and growth after a divorce isn't about how much you can show off to the world. It's about the inner work, the personal journey, and making decisions that set you up for genuine happiness and success. So, before you swipe that card, ask yourself: Is this purchase for the man I was, the man I am, or the man I aspire to be? Adjust your compass accordingly.

Daily Challenge: Before making a big purchase today, ask yourself if it aligns with your long-term growth and happiness, and if it's an investment in the man you aspire to become post-divorce.

Daily Reflection:

What resonated with you from today's lesson? How can you apply this truth in your life?

_____

_____

_____

_____

Day 232: Wills and Trusts- Secure Your Legacy

Divorce isn't just about the here and now; it's about the legacy you'll leave behind. Yeah, I get it, the emotional quagmire can suck you in, but we're going to zoom out a bit. Let's talk Wills and Trusts. Brother, when the game of life smacks you in the face, you've got two choices. You can either let it keep you down, or you can step up and own your future.

That future isn't just for you—it's for your kids, your family, whoever you deem deserving. Your legacy is at stake. You think those papers you drafted when love was still in the air still hold water? Think again. Post-divorce, everything has changed. And if you haven't updated your will or trust, you're playing a risky game.

It's more than just possessions; it's about ensuring that your assets, your sweat, tears, and lifelong grind, end up where you want them to. It's about control.

Now, if the idea of leaving a legacy hasn't hit you yet, let it sink in. We're talking about what's left when you're gone. Whether it's your kids' education, a cause you're passionate about, or just ensuring your hard-earned money goes to the right hands—it's your call to make. Not making that call? That's leaving it to chance, and believe me, chance is not your pal here.

Remember, legacy isn't just about wealth; it's about intention, purpose, and heart. It's about carving your name into the future.

So, grab that pen, find a sharp legal mind, and get your affairs in order. Because, trust me, nobody else will do it for you. Secure your legacy. Own your tomorrow. Today.

Daily Challenge: Take a concrete step towards securing your legacy by setting up a meeting with a trusted legal advisor to review and update your will and trust documents, ensuring your intentions for the future are crystal clear.

Daily Reflection:

What resonated with you from today's lesson? How can you apply this truth in your life?

_____

_____

_____

_____

Day 233: Financial Scams- Stay Alert

In a world where trust is as fragile as a thin sheet of ice on a sunny day, getting through a divorce isn't just an emotional minefield; it's also a crash course in financial vigilance. Listen up, fellas. As you unravel the threads of a shared life, predators lurk in the shadows, ready to exploit your emotional vulnerability.

Know this: emotional turbulence is the con artist's best friend. They can smell desperation a mile away, and when they do, they strike.

They'll promise you fast solutions to your financial problems, assurances to reclaim what you feel the divorce stole from you. Tempting? Yes. But remember, when it sounds too good to be true, it probably is.

Take those rose-colored glasses off. This isn't about cynicism, it's about clarity. We live in a world filled with Ponzi schemes, fake investment opportunities, and 'friends' who suddenly have the "perfect" business proposal just when you're at your lowest.

Don't bite. Sure, there's a part of you that wants to recoup, maybe even come out ahead, but don't let that desire blind you to reality.Keep your wits about you. Consult with genuine financial advisors, ones with solid reputations and proven track records. Double, no, triple-check every opportunity.

Your wallet, post-divorce, isn't just about the bills in it; it represents your hard work, your future, and your renewed independence. Guard it with your life. Don't let the snakes slither in when the walls are down. Stay alert, stay informed, and most importantly, stay in control.

Daily Challenge: Today, take the first step towards securing your legacy by making a commitment to update your will and trust to reflect your new post-divorce reality and ensure your intentions for the future are crystal clear.

Daily Reflection:

What resonated with you from today's lesson? How can you apply this truth in your life?

_____

_____

_____

_____

Day 234: Crypto and Stocks- Risk and Reward

Divorce can feel like the worst market crash you never saw coming. But here's the kicker: Just as with stocks and crypto, life has its own risk-reward balance. You've heard the tales of the brave who rode the volatile waves of Bitcoin or Ethereum, who saw potential where others saw chaos. They knew the drill - no risk, no reward.

The same guys who, during a stock market dip, double down on their beliefs, buy the dip, because they've done their research, they know their value, and they're playing the long game.

Now, let's bring it home. Your marriage didn't pan out, but that doesn't make you a failing stock. Think of yourself as a cryptocurrency in its early stages. Yeah, there's a dip right now, but where's the trajectory headed? Up. That's where.

Maybe your marriage was a blue-chip stock, stable for years but suddenly nosedived. Or perhaps it was a high-risk crypto, all-consuming passion and heart-pounding highs, but with gut-wrenching lows. Whatever it was, now's the time to reassess. Do your 'emotional research'. Recognize your value. Then, make strategic moves for your future.

You're the CEO of your life. Some trades work out, others don't. But the market keeps moving, and so should you. Every risk in life, like in stocks or crypto, carries potential reward. It's hard to see now, but trust the process.

The next big rally might just be around the corner. Stay invested in yourself. Keep holding onto hope. And always remember - dips are just opportunities in disguise. Don't sell yourself short.

Daily Challenge: Embrace the mindset of a savvy investor in your own life today; assess your emotional portfolio, recognize your worth, and make strategic moves towards a brighter future after divorce.

Daily Reflection:

What resonated with you from today's lesson? How can you apply this truth in your life?

_____

_____

_____

_____

Day 235: Financial Negotiations- Make the Right Deal

Look, man, let's cut to the chase. Divorce isn't a game, but if it were, the financial negotiations would be the final boss battle. Too many guys get screwed over because they approach this process emotionally charged, wanting to get it over with or, worse, letting guilt decide their fate.

Snap out of it. Your future depends on this. This isn't about winning or losing; it's about setting yourself up for the next phase of your life. Think strategy, not revenge. The more you let emotions dictate your moves, the more vulnerable you are to making poor decisions. And trust me, bad financial choices now will haunt you for years.

Get educated. Know your assets, know your liabilities, and for God's sake, understand your rights. Your hard-earned money, properties, and investments are on the line. Don't get blindsided by not doing your homework. You might be thinking, "Hey, I can be generous. I just want peace." Peace is great, but being overly generous out of guilt or a misguided sense of nobility? That's a fast track to regret. Get yourself a good lawyer who isn't afraid to get their hands dirty. This is about securing your future, not appeasing your past.

This isn't about screwing over your ex. It's about ensuring you walk away with what's fair. Because once those papers are signed and that deal is inked, there's no CTRL+Z in real life.

Navigate this wisely, strategically, and with the raw, unabashed intent to thrive in your post-divorce life. You owe that to yourself. Don't be the guy that looks back with regrets. Be the guy who made the right deal.

Daily Challenge: Today, focus on the financial negotiations of your divorce with a clear and strategic mindset, remembering that it's about securing your future, not seeking revenge or appeasing the past.

Daily Reflection:

What resonated with you from today's lesson? How can you apply this truth in your life?

_____

_____

_____

_____

Day 236: Legal Financial Matters- Cover Your Bases

L egal financial matters during a divorce? Here's the brutal truth: if you don't protect your assets, no one else will. Not your lawyer, not your soon-to-be-ex, and certainly not the court system. It's a battlefield out there, and if you're not prepared, you'll be outmaneuvered and outplayed.

I've seen men reduced to tears, not from the heartbreak of a failed marriage, but from realizing they've been stripped of their hard-earned financial assets. Divorce is a game where stakes are high and the rules are murky. But here's your advantage: knowledge. Understand the laws, know your rights, and be proactive.

Stop waiting for things to sort themselves out. The world won't hand you fairness. Dive deep into your finances. Get every single document, every statement, every shred of evidence of your assets. It's not about hiding wealth; it's about protecting what's rightfully yours. And get a good lawyer, not just any lawyer. This isn't a time to be frugal or trust that 'gentleman's handshake' nonsense.

Do you have joint accounts? Time to reconsider their structure. Alimony? Understand its ins and outs. Debts? Know whose name they're under. Ignorance is a luxury you can't afford right now. And remember, while you're navigating this treacherous path, maintain your integrity. This isn't about screwing over your ex. It's about ensuring that you're not the one left out in the cold.

And one last thing: even when it feels like the world is against you, don't play the victim. Own your situation. The road ahead might be tough, but armed with knowledge and determination, you'll come out the other side stronger. Protect your assets, protect your future. Because, ultimately, you're the CEO of your life, and the buck stops with you.

Daily Challenge: Take control of your financial destiny today by gathering all relevant documents, understanding your rights, and securing the best legal counsel to protect your assets during this divorce battle.

Daily Reflection:

What resonated with you from today's lesson? How can you apply this truth in your life?

_____

_____

_____

_____

Day 237: Lifestyle Choices- Can You Afford Them?

Divorce isn't just a slap in the face emotionally; it's a sucker punch to your finances. Suddenly, that twice-a-week steakhouse dinner? Maybe it's time to rethink it.

The lease on the sports car? You might want to consider something more economical. Those high-end whiskey tastings? Could be time to shift to a more modest beverage.

Listen, guys, this isn't about dwelling on what you're losing. It's about understanding what you can GAIN by making smarter choices. The world doesn't owe you anything, and neither does your ex. It's easy to fall into a trap, thinking that keeping up with the Joneses or holding onto your old lifestyle proves something. But who are you proving it to? Your ex? Your buddies? Yourself?

The reality is simple: every dollar you burn on things that don't bring genuine value to your life is a dollar you're robbing from your future. Those are resources you could be investing in personal growth, in rebuilding, in creating a life that's about substance over show.

Be brutally honest with yourself. If your lifestyle choices are more about ego than genuine enjoyment, it's time to reevaluate. Life post-divorce is an opportunity—a clean slate. It's your shot to cut the fat, to strip away the pretense, and to get real with who you are and what you want.

Dive deep, redefine your priorities, and start making choices that serve YOU. Not the you that's trying to impress, but the you that's building a meaningful, authentic life from the ground up. Don't waste it trying to maintain an image. Instead, invest in creating a life you don't need to escape from.

Daily Challenge: Take a hard look at your expenses today and identify one non-essential item or luxury you can cut back on to invest in your future self, aligning your financial choices with your true priorities and values.

Daily Reflection:

What resonated with you from today's lesson? How can you apply this truth in your life?

_____

_____

_____

_____

Day 238: Holidays and Gifts- Budget Smartly

Listen up, guys. Life after a divorce isn't just some sob story where you play the victim. No. It's your movie, and you're the leading man. So, let's talk holidays and gifts. You know, those things that have probably been costing you an arm and a leg every year?

Let's get real for a moment. Did you overspend last Christmas, trying to mask the pain with price tags? Were you that guy flashing your card, thinking, "If I just buy her that expensive necklace, maybe she'll see how much I care?" Yeah, I get it. We've all been there. But post-divorce? That mindset needs to get dumped faster than last week's leftovers.

Here's your new mantra: *Value over Price*. It's not about how much you spend, but the thought you put into it. Your kids don't need the latest tech gadget; they need quality time with their dad. Your family and friends? They don't want your pity purchases. They want YOU. Present, authentic, and undistracted.

And as for dating again? Let's cut the crap. If you think your way into someone's heart is by flashing your wallet, then buddy, you're missing the point. No authentic connection is built on materialism. Show them who you are, not what's in your bank account.

Be smart. Make a budget. Stick to it. Your bank account and your sanity will thank you. Holidays aren't about the price tag; they're about the moments. And trust me, those moments? Priceless. Get out there and live them. Fully.

Daily Challenge: Embrace the mantra 'Value over Price' in every aspect of your life – whether it's gift-giving, spending time with loved ones, or building new relationships; focus on genuine connections and meaningful moments, not the price tags.

Daily Reflection:

What resonated with you from today's lesson? How can you apply this truth in your life?

_____

_____

_____

_____

Day 239: Financial Freedom- What Does It Mean to You?

Financial freedom after a divorce isn't just about crunching numbers or rejigging your savings account. No, it's about reclaiming control and harnessing power over your own life.

It's that liberating feeling of striding confidently into a future you've crafted with your own two hands, where no ex-spouse can dictate your expenses, or tie you down with lingering debts.

Brother, this is your moment to redefine the essence of freedom. Is it owning a sleek condo downtown? Or maybe it's that ability to pick up and travel without looking at price tags. Or perhaps it's just the simple peace of mind knowing you're not shackled by monthly alimony payments or old debts.

What society, your ex, or even your own past self might've told you about money doesn't hold weight anymore. This is your narrative now. Tear down those old, restrictive financial beliefs. They're worth nothing if they're built on guilt or the need to "keep up" with someone else's life.

No one's going to hand you a cheat sheet to financial autonomy. You've got to hustle, grind, make smart choices, and sometimes, get a little bruised to understand your worth. But that grit? It's going to set you up for a future where your money, time, and life are truly yours. No compromises. No settling.

So ask yourself, man to man: What does financial freedom mean to you? Once you've got that answer, chase it with everything you've got. Because at the end of that pursuit? That's where real empowerment lies.

Daily Challenge: Today, take a bold step towards your vision of financial freedom by identifying one concrete action you can take to regain control over your finances and start building the future you desire.

Daily Reflection:

What resonated with you from today's lesson? How can you apply this truth in your life?

_____

_____

_____

_____

Day 240: Financial Milestone- Ready for the Next Step

Listen, guys, let's get one thing straight: Divorce? It sucks. It's emotionally draining and can feel like your whole world is falling apart. But here's the thing: while you're licking your wounds and feeling sorry for yourself, your finances are taking a hit. You can either cry about it, or you can get your act together and make moves.

Money. It's not just about dollar signs. It's freedom. It's choices. It's the scoreboard of life sometimes. But guess what? No one cares about your backstory. The world isn't going to wait for you to feel ready. The bills won't stop. So, what's it gonna be?

Here's your wake-up call: Your financial reality just changed. Accept it. Whether you're paying alimony or splitting assets, it's a new ball game. And honestly? This could be the best thing that ever happened to you. Why? Because you're at rock bottom, and the only direction is UP.

Every adversity, every setback, is an opportunity in disguise. Time to double down. Start a side hustle, renegotiate your debts, invest wisely, and most importantly, educate yourself. You think this is the end? No. It's the beginning of your financial rebirth.

Stop letting the past dictate your future. The old you? He's gone. The new you? He's financially savvy, determined, and hungry for success. Your ex got the house? Fine. Go build an empire. You're on child support? Cool. Make sure your kids see a role model who faced adversity and came out swinging.

You've got this. But it starts with a decision. A commitment. Stop playing the victim card. Dive deep into your finances. Learn. Hustle. Grow. In a year? You won't even recognize the guy in the mirror. Why? Because he's a winner. And winners? They don't whine. They work. Period.

Daily Challenge: Embrace your financial reality, take control, and make a commitment to work on your finances today, because your future success starts with the decisions you make now.

Daily Reflection:

What resonated with you from today's lesson? How can you apply this truth in your life?

_____

_____

_____

_____

The Dating Game

Prepare for the world of new relationships with 30 days of dating wisdom. Are you ready to date again? Swipe through online dating, master the art of the approach, and keep your text game sharp. Make your first date count and discern between chemistry and compatibility. Play it safe with sexual health, read signals accurately, and navigate the friend zone. Learn from rejection, handle the ex-factor, and conquer the crucial third date. Juggle multiple people with care, spot red flags early, and adapt old dating etiquette to the modern world. Explore emotional availability, assess long-term potential, and pass the litmus test of meeting friends. Reflect on your dating journey.

Day 241: Dating Readiness- Are You There Yet?

You think you're ready to jump back into the dating game, huh? Listen, I get it. The ink's barely dry on those divorce papers, and you're itching to feel desirable again. But hold on a minute. Let's cut through the crap—because now's the time to be brutally honest with yourself.

The question isn't just about when you should start dating again; it's also about how prepared you are for what's ahead. Dating isn't what it used to be, and neither are you. You've been through the wringer, man. Emotions are still raw, experiences still fresh. Ask yourself—can you bring something good to the table? Not just for her, but for you. Do you even know what you want anymore?

Look, you're not just picking up a new hobby here. Relationships can be life-changing. They can elevate you or drag you right back into the mud. You owe it to yourself to be in a stable place, emotionally and mentally, before inviting someone else into your life.

Here's the kicker: A new relationship won't fix you. Don't use someone else as a band-aid for your issues. It's not fair to her, and it's a disservice to yourself. You might think you're over your past, but wounds have a way of reopening when you least expect it.

Face yourself, your flaws, your strengths, before diving into something new. Work on who you are, alone, because that's the guy you'll bring into any relationship. Get right with yourself first, and then—only then—you're ready to date.

Daily Challenge: Take an honest look in the mirror today, reflecting on whether you're truly prepared for a new relationship, and if not, commit to investing in self-improvement and self-discovery before seeking companionship.

Daily Reflection:

What resonated with you from today's lesson? How can you apply this truth in your life?

_____

_____

_____

_____

Day 242: Online Dating- Swipe Right or Left?

Alright, listen up. Online dating post-divorce, especially when you're just getting back out there, isn't for the faint of heart. Let's cut the crap — everyone shows their best self, but the pics are filtered and the bios are as polished as a politician's speech. You swipe right, they swipe left; you swipe left, they swipe right. It's a messy roulette.

You've got two options: Dive in headfirst or stay clear. If you're gonna dive in, do it with both eyes open. Don't kid yourself that Ms. Right Now might morph into Ms. Right. It rarely works that way. More often, you'll face a sea of misaligned expectations and disappointments. But hey, it's also a numbers game, a battlefield where each swipe gives you another bullet in the chamber.

Remember, you've got more to offer than a profile pic. Don't let the rejections eat you up. Not everyone's gonna see your worth, and that's their loss, not yours. And for heaven's sake, don't let this digital mirage mess with your self-esteem. You're more than a collection of pixels on a screen. You're a living, breathing human who's survived the trenches of a marriage and come out the other side. Don't forget that.

But don't think online dating's your only option. The best connections often come when you're not even looking. The coffee shop you frequent, the buddies you hang out with, even a random grocery store encounter—life's full of opportunities if you're open to them. So, if you're gonna swipe, swipe. But don't let it define you. Keep your head up, your eyes sharp, and your heart open. Just don't forget to guard that heart with a bulletproof vest. Got it? Good.

Daily Challenge: Embrace the world of online dating with resilience, knowing that rejections don't define your worth, but also remain open to unexpected offline opportunities for connection.

Daily Reflection:

What resonated with you from today's lesson? How can you apply this truth in your life?

_____

_____

_____

_____

Day 243: First Moves in the Real World

Alright, listen up. Divorce isn't the end; it's the start of something new, whether you see it or not. I get it, man, your world's collapsing. You're thrown into this storm, and the emotions hit you like a freight train. But guess what? Life doesn't pause; it doesn't give you a breather. So, you can't either.

Your first move? Get a grip. Stop the emotional bleeding because nobody's coming to save you but you. Wake up and smell the harsh reality. You need a lawyer, and not just any lawyer, but a pitbull who's gonna fight for you, understand your rights, and not let you get screwed over. Don't know the first thing about legalities? Time to learn, buddy. Ignorance ain't bliss; it's a one-way ticket to getting played.

Next, face your feelings. Don't shove 'em down or pretend you're good. Anger, sadness, anxiety—feel them, but don't let them control you. This isn't the time for self-pity; it's the time for self-preservation.

Look, you've got responsibilities: kids, property, a life built together. Time to untangle that web, and it ain't gonna be pretty. But you gotta show up. For your kids, for your financial future, for your own sanity. This is your life, and if you don't take the reins, someone else will.

Finally, self-care isn't just spa days and yoga; it's setting boundaries, standing up for yourself, rediscovering what makes you tick. Your identity's been through the wringer, sure, but now's your chance to redefine it. You're not just "her husband" or "their dad," you're you—take that back.

This is the real world, and it waits for no one. Take your life back, one day at a time.

Daily Challenge: Today, face your feelings head-on, acknowledge them, and remember that allowing yourself to feel doesn't make you weak; it makes you resilient on the path to rebuilding your life.

Daily Reflection:

What resonated with you from today's lesson? How can you apply this truth in your life?

_____

_____

_____

Day 244: Text Game- Keep It Sharp

Look, you've gone through a lot—divorce ain't for the faint of heart. You're reentering the world, and maybe you're even thinking about dating again. Listen up; the game's changed. Technology? It's the field now. Texting ain't what it used to be; it's not about "hey, what's up?" It's a strategy, man, a real playbook.

First off, stay authentic. Yeah, you can find a thousand pick-up lines on the internet, but you aren't a clone; you're a unique guy with his own flavor. Make sure that comes across. A sense of humor? Great, flash it. Intellectual? Drop a few smart lines. Just don't pretend you're something you're not. Trust me; authenticity breeds confidence, and confidence is the real game-changer here.

Grammar and spelling—don't slack. You're an adult. Nothing screams "I don't care" more than sloppy texts. You're taking the time to engage, so take the time to spellcheck. Respect for her translates to respect for yourself.

Timing, dude, is everything. Don't play those childish games—waiting two days to text back. But don't pounce the second she texts, either. Find the sweet spot. Keep her engaged but don't come off as needy. You have a life; make sure she knows it.

And for the love of God, don't overdo emojis. You're not a teenager. Words have power; use them. Want to be flirtatious? Lean into the language. You've got this whole rich vocabulary to draw from; make her smile with your words, not some yellow cartoon face.

In the end, man, it's about quality, not quantity. You're rebuilding yourself; take this chance to rebuild how you communicate too. Keep it sharp. Keep it real. Keep it you.

Daily Challenge: Embrace the art of authentic and well-timed communication in your post-divorce dating journey, letting your unique personality shine through in your messages, respecting both her and yourself, and using words to connect rather than relying on emojis or playing games

Daily Reflection:

What resonated with you from today's lesson? How can you apply this truth in your life?

_____

_____

_____

Day 245: The First Date- Make It Count

Look, man, here's the deal—dating post-divorce ain't a joke. You've been out of the game for how long? The world's shifted, you've shifted, and let's not even talk about dating apps, alright? So, that first date? Gotta make it count. Don't come at it like you're negotiating a business deal, but don't walk in without a plan, either.

First off, it's not about impressing her with your car, your watch, or your paycheck. Cut that crap out. You're not the same guy who got married all those years ago; you've weathered storms, come out the other side. Show that depth, not your surface bling.

Now, about the conversation. Engage, don't dominate. She's got stories too, let her tell 'em. Don't be that guy monopolizing the conversation talking about his ex. You're not there for therapy; you're there to connect.

Listen, if you're thinking of turning this into something long-term, stop. Pump the brakes. You're not shopping for spouse 2.0 here. You're searching for connection, companionship, maybe a bit of fun, who knows? Your mindset needs a reset if you're slipping into old habits, measuring her up against life goals and retirement plans. Remember, you've grown, evolved, but guess what? So has she. She's not a stand-in for someone else; she's a whole other equation. Solve for X by being present, being authentic.

At the end of the night, if sparks fly, great. If not, who cares? You've still got yourself, your interests, your life. You're a whole person on your own, and that's your trump card in this whole dating game. So make that first date count, but know that it's just a date. Not your past, not your future. Just a moment in the now. Enjoy it.

Daily Challenge: Approach your first post-divorce date with authenticity, leaving behind the old comparisons and expectations, and focus on genuinely connecting with the person in front of you, knowing that your worth is not defined by this date's outcome.

Daily Reflection:

What resonated with you from today's lesson? How can you apply this truth in your life?

_____

_____

_____

_____

Day 246: Chemistry vs. Compatibility

Y ou think chemistry's the answer, right? Fireworks, electric jolts, that "we just get each other" feeling? Guess what, my man, chemistry's the easy part. It's the spark, but not the fuel. So you had great chemistry but still ended up divorced? Yeah, you need to hear this: Chemistry ain't compatibility.

Compatibility's the nuts and bolts, the daily grind, the "can we stand each other when the lovey-dovey stuff's gone?" That's the question, brother. Chemistry will have you riding high, making you think you can conquer the world. But it fades, it always does.

Compatibility's what's left staring back at you when that magic's spent. Can you work as a team, handle conflicts, and keep the respect alive? Or are you left with a shell of a relationship, built on nothing more than some butterflies in the stomach?

You gotta wake up. The romantic Hollywood crap, where love conquers all? Not real. The love that lasts, the love that survives life's storms—that's built on compatibility. The silent language of knowing what the other needs without a word, of being there when life gets messy, of enduring not just the highs but the lows, too. Stop blaming your divorce on a loss of "chemistry." Look deeper. Was the compatibility ever there? If it wasn't, man, that's your lesson learned.

And hey, don't beat yourself up. Divorce is not failure; it's a masterclass in self-discovery. As you untangle yourself from this chapter, focus on what really matters. Find someone whose pieces fit with yours in the boring, everyday sense, not just when the sun sets and the mood's right. Trust me, in the long run, compatibility trumps chemistry. Every time.

Daily Challenge: Reflect on your past relationships and consider whether you've prioritized chemistry over compatibility and commit today to seek a deeper connection built on shared values and everyday compatibility in your future relationships.

Daily Reflection:

What resonated with you from today's lesson? How can you apply this truth in your life?

_____

_____

_____

_____

Day 247: Sexual Health- Play It Safe

Man, let's get real. We're talking sexual health here, and this isn't some high school health class you can doze through. You're navigating a divorce, a life upheaval, but that doesn't mean you toss common sense out the window. Your body isn't separate from this equation, okay? You're not invincible.

Hooking up post-divorce? It's not just a game. You might feel like you've got something to prove, but this ain't the place for reckless behavior. Sleeping around unsafely isn't freedom; it's playing Russian roulette with your health. Forget that macho nonsense that tells you protection is optional. Nah, man, it's mandatory.

Listen, a condom isn't your enemy; think of it as your wingman, having your back when things get hot. Don't believe the lie that it 'kills the vibe.' Know what really kills the vibe? STIs. Unplanned pregnancy with a fling. Waking up with more regret than you already might have. You think a divorce is complicated? Try adding a herpes diagnosis on top of that.

Sexual health isn't a 'her' responsibility; it's a 'you' responsibility. If you're not mature enough to have that conversation with a partner, you're not mature enough to be in that bed. Point blank.

So, own your life, your choices, your body. Sexual health is an ongoing dialogue, not a one-time chat. Make the doctor's appointments, get tested. It's not just for you, it's respect for her too, even if she's not in your life for the long haul. This is the real world, man, no do-overs. Play it smart. Play it safe.

Daily Challenge: Prioritize Your Sexual Health - Remember, your journey through divorce doesn't mean compromising your well-being; today, commit to making responsible choices and protecting your sexual health for a brighter future

Daily Reflection:

What resonated with you from today's lesson? How can you apply this truth in your life?

_____

_____

_____

Day 248: Reading Signals

Reading signals on dates is like navigating a minefield blindfolded—you think you're doing it right until you're not. Fellas, let's cut the crap. You're out there, newly divorced or separated, trying to make sense of the dating scene again. And it's different, isn't it? Yeah, because you're different.

But here's the deal: It's not just about understanding if she's into you. It's about understanding you. Are you listening to her words, her tone, her body language? You're not a kid anymore; you can't afford to be sloppy. You have to read between the lines, not to manipulate but to genuinely understand the person sitting across from you.

This isn't just dating; this is life skills 101. You ignore these signals; you end up in bad relationships, lousy deals, crummy friendships. Pick your poison. Don't tell me you didn't see it coming. Most times, you did, but you ignored it because it wasn't convenient. Listen, comfort zones are graveyards for growth. And if you've been through a divorce, staying stagnant is the last thing you need.

Let's get one thing straight—your intuition isn't broken, but it might be rusty. Start using it. Notice the little inconsistencies, the subtle shifts. If something feels off, it probably is. Don't let your hunger for companionship cloud your judgment. You've already navigated the messy corridors of a divorce; you've got a PhD in life's hard knocks.

Get back out there but do it smarter, wiser, better. And for God's sake, if the signals say run, then lace up those Nikes and sprint.

Daily Challenge: Today, as you step back into the dating world, focus on sharpening your intuition by paying close attention to the signals and subtleties in your interactions, ensuring you're making choices that align with your growth and well-being.

Daily Reflection:

What resonated with you from today's lesson? How can you apply this truth in your life?

_____

_____

_____

_____

Day 249: The Friend Zone- Navigate or Evacuate

You think you're stuck in the friend zone? Man, let's get real. This is a self-imposed prison, and guess what? You've got the key. Now, I get it. You're heartbroken, your marriage fell apart, and you're clinging to any emotional connection you can find. But listen, do you really want to be that guy who hangs around, pining over someone who only sees you as a buddy?

This isn't a rom-com, my man; life's not scripted. You don't get the girl just by being the persistent nice guy. If she's not into you, that's it. Full stop. Move on.

You're draining your emotional battery for someone who's not gonna recharge you back. Not fair to you, not fair to her. Consider this, too. You're fresh off a divorce. Your emotions are a mess. Are you sure you're not just projecting your need for validation onto this woman?

Take some time for self-assessment. Divorce screws with your head; it distorts your self-image. Before getting tangled in any sort of emotional web, figure out who you are now, outside the realm of marital bliss or whatever that was.

Look, if you genuinely value the friendship, no harm in keeping that connection alive. But if it's eating you from the inside, it's time to hit the eject button. It's not just about escaping the 'friend zone.' It's about reclaiming your emotional space, your sense of self, your life.

Don't negotiate your self-worth. Friend zone or not, know what you bring to the table. If she's not buying, don't slash your prices; find another customer. Navigate or evacuate, the choice is yours. But make that choice for you, no one else. Got it? Good. Now act on it.

Daily Challenge: Today, challenge yourself to let go of the emotional attachment that's holding you back and take a step toward reclaiming your sense of self and your life outside of this self-imposed friend zone.

Daily Reflection:

What resonated with you from today's lesson? How can you apply this truth in your life?

_____

_____

_____

_____

Day 250: Rejection- Don't Fear It, Learn From It

Look, rejection stings. I get it. Nobody likes the swipe-lefts, unread messages, or those dreaded texts that say, "Hey, let's just be friends." But here's the deal—you can't let rejection turn into this soul-crushing thing. You need to pull the value from it, learn the lesson, and keep going.

You're gonna get ghosted; it's inevitable. But every ignored message is data, man. It's telling you what's not working so you can pivot. This is an experiment, not a life sentence. If you treat each interaction as an opportunity for growth, that nasty feeling of being dismissed starts to lose its edge. You gotta develop a thick skin and not take things too personally.

Let me break it to you straight: Online dating is a battlefield, but it's also a numbers game. You can't win if you're not in the game. So what if you get rejected ten times? On the eleventh try, you might find someone who genuinely makes your heart race. Every "no" gets you closer to that coveted "yes."

If you're sitting there, wallowing in self-pity, thinking the world's out to get you, snap out of it. Life's too short. Be audacious. Throw yourself out there, but do it strategically. Fix your profile, pick better pictures, and for God's sake, don't open with "Hey, what's up?" Make yourself memorable.

And remember, everyone's feeling the same way. Even that woman who ghosted you is dealing with her own rejections and insecurities. It's a brutal cycle, but you've got the power to break it. Instead of fearing rejection, embrace it as a chance to improve. Show up, learn, pivot, and you'll find what you're looking for.

Daily Challenge: Embrace rejection as a stepping stone, not a stumbling block, and use it to refine your approach, knowing that each "no" brings you one step closer to your ultimate "yes" in the dating world.

Daily Reflection:

What resonated with you from today's lesson? How can you apply this truth in your life?

_____

_____

_____

Day 251: The Ex-Factor- When She Comes Back

You get that text, right? "Hey, how've you been? It's been a while." It's her. Your ex. She's back on your phone, your screen, your life. You feel your pulse quicken. Man, don't let that emotional whirlpool suck you in. She's not reappearing 'cause she's seen the light; she's testing the waters to see if you're still her safety net.

It's a game. Pure ego. A kid touching the stove to see if it's still hot. You were hot once, but let me tell you, you're not an emotional plaything. She walked out, remember? Don't serve yourself up on a platter. What are you, leftovers? Nah, man, you're a whole feast, and don't let anyone treat you less than that.

This isn't about hating her. It's about respecting you. That's your currency now. Self-respect is the foundation you rebuild on. If she could bail once, she can bail again. Maybe next time it's when you need her most. Emotional yo-yos? Forget it.

Look, when you're out there making yourself into the man you want to be, the man you're proud to be, you won't have time for this. You'll be busy building your life, brick by solid brick. You'll meet women who don't want to play games.

They'll see your worth and match it with their own. Those are the relationships that won't just float your boat, they'll power your ship.

So next time she texts, do me a favor: Read it, let your heart wobble for just a second, and then remember who you are. Swipe delete. Archive that chapter; don't reread it. Your future doesn't have room for reruns.

Daily Challenge: When that text from your ex appears, remember your worth, stand firm in self-respect, and choose to focus on building your future, not revisiting the past.

Daily Reflection:

What resonated with you from today's lesson? How can you apply this truth in your life?

_____

_____

_____

_____

Day 252: The Third Date- The Make or Break

Look, you've made it to the third date. High fives and fist bumps, right? But listen up; this isn't a victory lap. It's the moment of truth, my man. This date sets the tone, shows if there's real substance behind the smiles and flirty texts. Are you aligned in your goals, values, and visions for the future? Are you even headed in the same direction?

Cut the crap, drop the show. You're not auditioning for some Hollywood rom-com; you're seeing if you can build a life with this person. The third date's your chance to get raw and real. No games. No facades.

You've been burned before, and you know the cost of diving in without checking the water's depth. No one's got time for another emotional wreck; you've been through the wringer enough to know that. It's easy to get swept up, to start envisioning a future filled with sunshine and rainbows. Easy, but reckless. You need to ask the hard questions now—about kids, money, career ambitions, lifestyle. Even about the touchy subjects like past relationships.

It's not prying; it's necessary due diligence. Because trust me, you don't want to discover six months down the line that she hates the career path you're passionate about, or that she's got zero interest in the family life you've been dreaming of.

So take the third date seriously. Look her in the eyes, ask the questions that make your stomach churn, that make you vulnerable. Yes, you're taking a risk, but that's what life is, isn't it? A series of gambles, big and small. The key is to go in with both eyes wide open. Assess the risks, then decide if it's a gamble worth taking.

Daily Challenge: Muster the courage to ask the tough questions and have an honest conversation about your goals, values, and visions for the future, ensuring you're both heading in the same direction before getting too deeply invested.

Daily Reflection:

What resonated with you from today's lesson? How can you apply this truth in your life?

_____

_____

_____

_____

Day 253: Dating Multiple People- Juggle with Care

Look, dating multiple people after a divorce isn't a crime, but it's not a game either. You're not some character in a rom-com, juggling dates like they're bowling pins. These are human beings with feelings, and guess what? So are you. Emotional stakes are high; handle with care, man.

Here's the deal: You're newly single, and there's a whole dating landscape out there waiting for you to explore. It's tempting, it's invigorating, it feels like a shot of adrenaline straight to your veins. But hold up. Are you even ready? Do you even know what you want? If you're dating multiple people just to fill the void, you're doing it wrong.

No one's saying don't date. Go ahead, meet people. Life's too short to sit around moping. But do it with integrity. Be upfront. If you're seeing more than one person, let them know. It's not just about being honest with them; it's about being honest with yourself.

What are you getting out of this? Is it a self-esteem boost? Is it to forget the hurt? Understand your motives, because if you don't, you risk becoming the very thing you probably criticized in your past relationship—someone who takes more than they give.

And look, if you find someone who makes your heart skip a beat, who changes the way you think about love, don't screw it up by keeping one foot out the door. No one ever achieved greatness by playing it safe. So, stop juggling, stop calculating, and start living. You've been through hell; you deserve heaven. Don't settle for purgatory.

Daily Challenge: Today, commit to dating with integrity and clarity, understanding your own motives and being honest with both yourself and the people you're dating, because your heart deserves authenticity, not a game.

Daily Reflection:

What resonated with you from today's lesson? How can you apply this truth in your life?

_____

_____

_____

_____

Day 254: Red Flags- Spot Them Early

You walk into love thinking it's forever, right? Look, I get it. Romance sweeps you off your feet. It's all roses and candlelit dinners. But what happens when those roses start to wilt?

When the flicker of the candle is no longer charming but a warning sign, a blinking red alert? That's when you've got to stop, take a step back, and open your eyes, man. Reality check.

Some of you are ignoring red flags like they're traffic suggestions. Why? Are you afraid of being alone? Do you think you won't find anyone better? Listen, you've got one life, one shot at this.

You can't afford to ignore red flags like infidelity, manipulation, or disrespect. Don't romanticize them as quirks or challenges to overcome. If she's giving you hell now, what makes you think it'll turn into heaven later?

Know your worth. You're not someone's emotional punching bag or second option. Stop selling yourself short by ignoring the signs. Wake up! If she's hiding her phone or constantly undermining you, there's a problem. If your gut is screaming at you, listen to it. That's your primal self looking out for you.

Divorce sucks but living a lie sucks even more. You think being alone is scary? Try being in a relationship where you're emotionally isolated. Yeah, think about that.

Act before you have to react. If you spot red flags early, you're not jumping ship; you're steering away from an iceberg. You're a captain, not a casualty. Keep it real, keep it honest, and above all, keep yourself in mind. No one else will.

Daily Challenge: Today, vow to trust your instincts and commit to recognizing and addressing any red flags in your relationship with courage and honesty, because your happiness and well-being are worth protecting.

Daily Reflection:

What resonated with you from today's lesson? How can you apply this truth in your life?

_____

_____

_____

Day 255: Dating Etiquette- Old Rules, New Twists

Listen up, gents. Dating after divorce isn't what it used to be, and you can't approach it like you're 20 with zero baggage. You're a different person now, molded by the good, the bad, and the downright ugly from your past relationship. Embrace it. You've got lessons in your back pocket that can make you a catch in this wild dating world, but only if you play your cards right.

First off, let's trash this notion that you've got to act like a desperate salesman on a first date. You're not selling anything. You're evaluating compatibility as much as she is. So, ditch the scripted lines. Be authentic, be you. She smells insincerity miles away, trust me.

Now let's talk about your ex. A date's not a therapy session. Unloading your emotional cargo about your ex-wife doesn't make for flirty banter. That stuff's for your boys or your therapist, not the woman sitting across the table sipping a Cosmo. She wants to know you're into her, not hung up on someone else. You dig?

And this one's crucial—don't let bitterness seep in. You're out there again because you're ready for something different, something better. So don't sabotage your chances by taking jabs at women or relationships. Yeah, you've been burned, but so what? You think she hasn't? We're all carrying scars, man. But it's the guy who wears them with grace who scores the second date.

Last thing: chivalry. In this swipe-right era, the old-school moves still matter. Hold doors, offer your coat, pick up the check. These acts show you're a grown man, not a boy playing at love. So go ahead, step back into the dating ring. You're not the same man you were, and that's your secret weapon. You've got this.

Daily Challenge: Today, embrace your unique journey and bring authenticity to your date by being genuinely yourself, leaving behind scripted lines and any lingering bitterness, and remember that chivalry never goes out of style – let your evolved self shine brightly in the dating world.

Daily Reflection:

What resonated with you from today's lesson? How can you apply this truth in your life?

_____

_____

_____

_____

Day 256: Emotional Availability- Yours and Theirs

You want to talk emotional availability? Man, let's get into it. Listen, divorce turns everything upside down, and suddenly you're expected to navigate a hurricane of feelings. Emotional availability? You wonder if you've got any of that left.

Here's the cold truth: You can't control your ex's emotional state, but you sure can control yours. You think by bottling it all up, you're doing everyone a favor? Nah, you're digging a deeper hole.

It's like locking your emotions in a box and then wondering why life feels so hollow. Break the lock, let them out, and make room for growth.

Your kids are watching. Your friends, your family—they see how you handle this. You think you can hide behind the mask of the stoic guy who's got it all under control? Ditch the act. It's time to own your emotions, not bury them.

You're not a robot; you're a man who's gone through hell and is still standing. If you've got anger, recognize it. Got sorrow? Feel it. It's when you engage with your emotional state that you can truly start to heal. Don't let your divorce rob you of your ability to connect emotionally—with yourself and others.

And for those who find their ex emotionally unavailable, don't sweat it. Don't let their icy walls make you build your own. That's on them, not you. Make the decision to be better, not bitter. Remember, you're setting the stage for your next chapter. Make sure it's one where you're emotionally equipped to take on the world.

Daily Challenge: Embrace your emotions today, whether it's anger, sorrow, or joy, and recognize that owning your feelings is a crucial step towards healing and building meaningful connections in your life post-divorce.

Daily Reflection:

What resonated with you from today's lesson? How can you apply this truth in your life?

_____

_____

_____

_____

Day 257: Long-Term Potential

Alright, listen up, man. You're wondering if she's the one, or maybe you're even questioning whether you've still got what it takes for a long-term relationship. Stop overthinking it. You're the captain of your ship; your life is what you make it. Get real with yourself first. Know what you bring to the table and be proud of it. Confidence isn't just sexy; it's the backbone of any enduring relationship.

If you're unsure about yourself, how can she be sure about you? But hold on, it's not just about you; it's about what she's bringing to the table, too. Does she elevate you? Does she add to your life in ways that make you want to be a better man? That's what you need to be asking.

Now, let's cut through the crap. If you're holding on because you're afraid to be alone, you're doing both of you a disservice. Scarcity mindset has no place in a meaningful relationship. You've got to believe you're worthy of someone who's as invested in the future as you are. Stop settling for complacency; go after that intense, equal partnership you deserve.

And hey, relationships aren't a fairy tale. You're gonna argue, get annoyed, and sometimes wonder why you're even together. But if you're committed to growth, both as a couple and as individuals, you're on the right track.

The best relationships aren't just about moonlit walks and romantic dinners. They're about mundane Tuesdays, when you're both exhausted but still make time for each other. It's about getting into the nitty-gritty of life, getting your hands dirty, and building something together. Don't waste your time on something that doesn't make you strive to be better. Life's too short for mediocre love. Get in it for the real deal or get out.

Daily Challenge: Take a deep dive into self-reflection, embrace your confidence, and ask yourself if your current relationship elevates both you and your partner to be the best versions of yourselves, because mediocrity has no place in your pursuit of genuine love and growth.

Daily Reflection:

What resonated with you from today's lesson? How can you apply this truth in your life?

_____

_____

_____

_____

Day 258: Meeting the Friends

All right, listen up, fellas. Meeting the friends of someone you're dating is a big moment. It's like stepping into the locker room of their life. Forget the dinner dates, the movies, and all the Instagram posts. When you meet their crew, you're diving into the deep end. This isn't a sandbox game; you're not an NPC they can ignore. You're front and center, in the spotlight.

Let me hit you with the truth — if you don't vibe with their friends, you're fighting an uphill battle. Friends have been through breakups, birthdays, and late-night talks. They hold clout. You think you're just meeting some random people? Nah, you're meeting the board of advisors of your relationship.

So, what's the game plan? Be you. Authenticity isn't negotiable; it's the ticket to the game. Fake it and you won't just lose the room, you'll lose her too, sooner or later. Don't roll in there like a used car salesman with a quota. Friends can smell desperation a mile away.

Here's the emotional meat you've got to get: you're auditioning for a part in a well-established series, not a pilot episode. Don't be the guy who tries too hard and turns it into the "All About Me" show. Listen. Engage. Respond. They're taking your measure just like you're sizing them up. Mutual respect, not one-upmanship.

All said, meeting the friends isn't just about ticking a box. It's a temperature check on the vibe, the energy, and even the longevity of what you've got going. Navigate it like a pro, and you're not just winning the room; you're locking in a foothold in her world. Mess it up, and you've got yourself a first-class ticket to Singleville. So, ready to step up or step out?

Daily Challenge: Today's challenge is to be your authentic self and engage with your date's friends genuinely when you meet them, showing respect and building connections, because this moment is more than just a social gathering; it's a key factor in the success of your relationship.

Daily Reflection:

What resonated with you from today's lesson? How can you apply this truth in your life?

_____

_____

_____

_____

Day 259: Dating Milestone

Look, man, let's cut the crap. You're divorced or getting there, right? Your heart's a mess, but listen, life hasn't stopped, and neither should you. You're gonna think about dating again. Maybe you're already swiping on Tinder as you read this. But listen up, because diving back into the dating pool isn't about plugging a gap in your life. Nah, it's about leveling up.

You're gonna meet someone, and it might be fire right off the bat, but slow down, buddy. First milestone, ask yourself: "Am I even ready?" If the thought of your ex still churns your gut, maybe pump the brakes.

Be honest, don't kid yourself. You're not in this to create more drama, you're in this to find someone who complements the awesome guy you're becoming. Second milestone, let's call it the "Reality Check." Yeah, you meet up, sparks fly, but are you both after the same thing? Casual? Serious? Make sure you're on the same page; don't assume anything.

Third milestone, it's the "Peel Back the Layers." At this point, you've been out a few times, you dig each other. Now what? You start digging deeper. Share your ambitions, your fears, your favorite songs. If you can't be vulnerable, what's the point?

Final milestone, man, this is it: "Long-Haul or Pit Stop?" You're past the honeymoon phase. The butterflies are gone, but in their place, maybe there's something real. Maybe not. This is when you find out. And you gotta make that call. So, where are you on this journey? Gauge it, don't rush it. Make every milestone count. You're not filling a void; you're building a new chapter. Act like it.

Daily Challenge: Today, as you navigate the dating world post-divorce, focus on the "Reality Check" milestone – ensure that you and your potential partner are on the same page about your relationship goals, and don't assume anything.

Daily Reflection:

What resonated with you from today's lesson? How can you apply this truth in your life?

_____

_____

_____

_____

Day 260: Cohabitation

Look, cohabitation might've felt like the dream setup, right? You're sharing space, bills, maybe even a pet. But let's not romanticize it. You thought you were getting a sneak peek into marital bliss? Nah, man, you're stepping into a legal and emotional minefield, especially when the relationship goes belly-up.

See, the law doesn't care if you've been playing house for years. No ring, no commitment, at least in the eyes of the law. You're not entitled to half the assets; you don't get spousal rights. You'll find yourself neck-deep in legal loopholes you didn't even know existed. And don't even get me started on the emotional entanglements. Trying to disentangle your life from someone else's without the compass of legal protocols? That's its own kind of hell.

Now, I'm not saying cohabitation is the devil. But understand what you're getting into. You're not just sharing a Netflix account; you're merging lives, my man. And unmerging? That's not as simple as hitting "unsubscribe." Your feelings, your shared memories, they don't vanish. You need to strategize, you need to hustle just as hard getting out as you did getting in.

It's easy to slide into living together. It's convenient, it's economical, it's fun. But listen, if you're not prepared to untangle that intricate web, don't step into it. Cohabitation is a pseudo-commitment, full of real-life consequences. Make sure you're up for that. Because when things go south, it's not just a matter of packing your bags and deleting some photos. You're dismantling a life. Are you ready for that?

Daily Challenge: Today, reflect on the importance of being prepared for the complexities of cohabitation and the potential challenges of untangling your life from someone else's, and commit to approaching it with intention and a clear plan.

Daily Reflection:

What resonated with you from today's lesson? How can you apply this truth in your life?

_____

_____

_____

_____

Day 261: The Relationship Status Dilemma

Look, man, if you're staring at that "it's complicated" relationship status on Facebook and you're not sure whether to switch it to "single," we need to talk. The first question is: What are you waiting for? Your life's not some rom-com where a grand gesture turns everything around.

The relationship status dilemma is real; I get it. You're wrestling with commitment, you're not ready to toss the past in the trash. But let me break it to you, straight up: The dilemma exists because you allow it to. You're hanging on to what-ifs, clinging to a version of life that ain't reality.

Here's the cold truth: you're at a crossroads. You can choose the easy way, stagnate in indecision, let life keep punching you. Or you can take control. Yeah, divorce sucks, man. No one wants to be that guy who failed at love. But guess what? Holding onto something that's already sunk is a different kind of failure. It's like refusing to abandon a sinking ship. Makes you think, doesn't it?

Who are you loyal to? A failed relationship, or yourself? Real change starts when you own your situation. Don't be the guy frozen by the relationship status dilemma.

Be the guy who takes life by the reins, who knows his worth, who moves forward no matter how heavy the baggage. And about that baggage—drop it. You don't need it where you're going.

So switch that status, man. But more importantly, switch your mindset. Your life starts the moment you stop hesitating. And trust me, the best version of your life doesn't include a "it's complicated" label.

Daily Challenge: Today, take a bold step towards clarity and self-empowerment by making a decision that aligns with your well-being, even if it means changing your relationship status – because your life deserves simplicity, not complications.

Daily Reflection:

What resonated with you from today's lesson? How can you apply this truth in your life?

_____

_____

_____

_____

Day 262: Dating Expenses- Who Pays?

Listen, I get it. You're back in the dating scene, and you want to pull out all the stops—impress, make a statement. But slow down, cowboy. Don't drop stacks of cash on someone you've just met. Ever heard of a concept called "sunk cost"? It's the time and money you invest that you never get back. If you go big from the get-go, not only are you setting an unsustainable precedent, but you're also tossing your resources into a black hole.

Here's what you do instead: keep it simple. Fire up a video chat; gauge the vibe. Take her out for coffee or something equally casual. Because chances are, you're gonna go on a plethora of first dates. Some will click; most won't. You're gonna get ghosted, blocked—deal with the whole spectrum of flakiness.

You want to find someone who's into you, not your wallet. Start slow, build up. If there's chemistry, the quality of your dates should escalate naturally. Don't play yourself by going all-in on the first hand. Keep your chips, play them wisely, and know when to fold. Dating's not about the flash; it's about the substance. Get that right, and you won't just save money; you'll invest in something far more valuable: a genuine connection.

There's no harm in being a gentleman. Open the door, be courteous, show respect; these are basics that never go out of style. But get this straight: being a gentleman doesn't mean being a meal ticket. There's a line between showing interest and becoming someone's free dining experience. Don't cross it. Reserve those four-course meals and Broadway tickets for someone who's sticking around, someone who's invested in you as much as you're invested in her. Until then, play it smart. Being a gentleman doesn't mean you can't also be savvy.

Daily Challenge: Today, challenge yourself to embrace the art of simplicity in your dating life. Focus on building genuine connections rather than impressing with extravagant gestures, and remember that being a gentleman doesn't equate to being a financial provider; invest wisely in those who invest in you.

Daily Reflection:

What resonated with you from today's lesson? How can you apply this truth in your life?

_____

_____

_____

Day 263: Vulnerability- When to Open Up

Alright, let's dive into this. Look, vulnerability's not your enemy; it's a freaking tool, man. You've got this macho image in your head, thinking showing any sort of weakness is gonna crumble your world. Spoiler: it won't. But bottling everything up? That's the real ticking time bomb.

Now, don't get me wrong. I'm not saying spill your guts to the next guy who sits next to you at the bar. Vulnerability comes with discernment. Choose wisely who gets a backstage pass to your inner world. It's a sacred space; don't let just anyone trample through it.

Remember, you're going through a divorce, not a personality transplant. If you're a private guy, you don't need to morph into Mr. Share-It-All.

What I am saying is that when you do decide to talk, really talk. Don't scratch the surface. Get into the meat of what's bugging you—the fears, the uncertainties, the anger. Man, you've got to let it breathe.

And yeah, vulnerability is a two-way street. It builds trust, creates connections. What's life without a connection, right? Isolating yourself, putting up these walls, it's like being a lone wolf without a pack. How long can you really survive like that?

So put your ego on the shelf. Real strength? That comes when you recognize that you're human, that you've got your own brand of messed-up, and you share it. Not with everyone, but with someone, man. Share it where it counts. Because here's the kicker: if you can't be real with anyone else, how the hell can you be real with yourself?

Daily Challenge: Embrace vulnerability as a powerful tool for healing and growth by sharing your true thoughts and feelings with someone you trust, allowing meaningful connections to flourish in your life.

Daily Reflection:

What resonated with you from today's lesson? How can you apply this truth in your life?

_____

_____

_____

Day 264: Romance vs. Reality

Look, man, you've been sold this idea of romance like it's a fairytale. You watch the movies, read the books, and think love conquers all. But wake up! Life's not a Nicholas Sparks novel. You don't just ride off into the sunset with your soulmate, no problems, no issues, just everlasting love. Get real.

Love takes work. Relationships take work. And sometimes, no matter how much sweat and tears you pour into it, things crumble. Maybe it's you, maybe it's them, maybe it's just the universe playing tricks. But it happens, and it's gut-wrenching.

You can't clutch onto this storybook idea when you're staring down the barrel of divorce papers. Idealizing romance won't help you sort out alimony, or who gets the house, or how to explain this mess to your kids. Romance won't keep your social life from imploding or magically pay your bills.

So cut the crap. Stop blaming yourself for not living up to some Disneyfied version of love. Because real love? It's not always fireworks and Champagne.

Sometimes it's compromise, silent dinners, heated arguments, and yes, signing some godforsaken legal documents that make you question everything.

Understand this: Love is part of life, not your entire existence. Don't let the fallacy of cinematic romance keep you from the hard truths you need to face now. Adapt, learn, grow. There's no room for make-believe when you're redefining your life. It's time to separate the movie script from your actual script. Get your head in the game; you've got a new chapter to write.

Daily Challenge: Today, challenge yourself to let go of the unrealistic expectations you may have about love and relationships, and instead, focus on embracing the reality that love takes effort, resilience, and a willingness to adapt to life's unexpected twists and turns

Daily Reflection:

What resonated with you from today's lesson? How can you apply this truth in your life?

_____

_____

_____

Day 265: The Love Languages

Alright, let's get real here. You've heard of love languages, right? You think it's just some soft, sentimental crap? Think again. This is hardcore emotional intelligence. Knowing your love language and your ex's? It's like knowing the cheat codes to a video game. You wouldn't play a game without understanding the rules, so why play the most complex game of all—love—without a rulebook?

Listen, we've got five of these languages: Words of Affirmation, Acts of Service, Gifts, Quality Time, Physical Touch. Understand them; it's crucial. Maybe your love tank fills up when someone tells you, "You're incredible." That's Words of Affirmation. Maybe your ex needed to spend quality time with you to feel loved, and you missed that because you were too busy scoring with Acts of Service. You were fixing the sink but not the relationship. See the disconnect?

This isn't some new-age mumbo jumbo. This is strategy, man. If you know what makes you tick, you communicate better. If you know what makes her tick, you avoid misunderstandings that blow up into full-blown fights. Knowledge is power. Emotional intelligence? That's like lifting weights for your brain and your heart.

But I get it, you're getting divorced or you're already there. You're thinking, "Why does this even matter now?" It matters because you've got a life after her. Maybe you'll date again; maybe you'll make better friendships. Hell, this stuff is useful even at work. You need to understand human behavior, including your own.

And let's not forget, if you've got kids, they've got love languages too. You want to raise emotionally intelligent human beings? Start speaking their emotional language

Daily Challenge: Today, take some time to reflect on your own love language and try to identify the love language of someone close to you, whether it's your ex-spouse, a friend, or a family member, and find a way to connect with them using their love language.

Daily Reflection:

What resonated with you from today's lesson? How can you apply this truth in your life?

_____

_____

_____

_____

Day 266: Ghosting

Ghosting. It's that dark pit in today's dating and relationship scene. One moment you're sharing laughs, dreams, and heartbeats; next thing you know, silence. Absolute zero. Radio-freakin'-silence. It feels like you've been punched in the gut, doesn't it?

You might be asking, "What did I do wrong?" or "Why the cold shoulder?" The truth? It's not always about you. Maybe they've got baggage, maybe they're scared, or maybe they're just not mature enough to confront their own feelings.

But here's what you need to hear: Their actions define them, not you. Ghosting speaks volumes about their character and where they're at in life. So, do you want to stake your happiness on someone who can't even afford you a simple conversation? No!.

It stings, I get it. But every time someone ghosts you, think of it as them doing you a favor. They're trimming the fat from your life, making room for those who truly value you. Those who have the guts to be upfront, to communicate, to be real.

If you've ghosted someone before? Own it. Learn from it. Be better. Communication is a mark of maturity, and it's time to step up. Every person you connect with deserves respect, and if things aren't working, say it.

In the vast arena of relationships, ghosting is the coward's exit. Don't be that guy. And don't let being ghosted break you. Rise, rebuild, and reenter the fray, wiser and stronger than before. Your worth isn't based on someone's inability to see it. Remember that.

Daily Challenge: Embrace open and honest communication in your relationships, refusing to let the actions of others define your worth and committing to treat others with the respect and honesty you deserve.

Daily Reflection:

What resonated with you from today's lesson? How can you apply this truth in your life?

_____

_____

_____

_____

Day 267: Dating Apps- The Pros and Cons

You think swiping right's gonna solve your problems? Ha, not so fast, man. Look, dating apps can be a playground, sure, but they're also like a casino—you might strike gold or leave feeling wrecked. It's easy to get sucked in, scrolling for hours, ego soaring with every match. But remember, you're more than a profile picture and a two-line bio.

First off, don't underestimate the convenience. You've got access to a world of potential dates, right in your pocket. But here's the kicker: it's easy to become a swipe zombie. Auto-pilot mode. Swiping away without genuinely connecting. You think you're casting a wide net, but really, you're spreading yourself thin.

Ah, the paradox of choice. More doesn't always mean better. In fact, it can paralyze you. Too many options, and you find yourself in a loop of never actually choosing, always hunting for the next big thing.

And let's talk about that dopamine hit. Every 'ding' is a jolt to your self-esteem. Feels good, doesn't it? But beware, it's like a sugar rush—short-lived and ultimately empty. Don't rely on external validation to feel worthy. That's gotta come from inside, man.

But here's a pro that's hard to ignore: exposure. Maybe your social circle's smaller post-divorce. Dating apps expand that. They put you back in the game, give you a chance to meet people you'd never bump into otherwise.

Listen, if you're gonna dive into the dating app scene, be intentional. Know what you're looking for, but more importantly, know yourself. Don't let swipes define you. If you're straight with yourself, dating apps can be a tool, not a trap. And who knows, amidst all the noise, you might just find someone who resonates with your vibe. But you gotta play smart. Got it?

Daily Reflection:

What resonated with you from today's lesson? How can you apply this truth in your life?

_____

_____

_____

_____

Day 268: When It Doesn't Work Out

Alright, listen up. You've been through the wringer, got your battle scars from a divorce that left you reeling. But here you are, considering stepping back into the dating game. Good on you, man. First, get this through your head: You're not the same guy you were. You've got a PhD in Life's Hard Knocks now, so act like it.

People will tell you to be careful, to not rush into things. Nah, man, you gotta dive in but with your eyes wide open. And let's be real, it's not always gonna work out. So what? You're not looking for another soulmate straight out the gate, are you? I hope not. You're looking to find out what life offers a man who's already been through hell and back. Maybe you'll get burned again, but maybe you'll find something that lights you up, something worth the risk.

Not every woman you meet is gonna understand what you've been through, and they don't have to. Your past is your backstory, not your current episode. Still carrying that emotional baggage? Drop it. Your next relationship isn't a do-over; it's a whole new game, buddy.

And yeah, maybe she looks great and things start heating up. But if she's throwing up red flags like a matador in a bullfight, don't ignore 'em. You've already seen what ignoring your gut can cost you. You've got instincts; use 'em. And if it doesn't work out, don't crawl back into your cave and swear off love forever. Lick your wounds, sure, but then get back out there.

Embrace the failures and the stumbles; they're proof you're trying. In the end, the person you need to have the best relationship with isn't some new woman; it's you. Get that part right, and the rest? Man, it's just gravy.

Daily Challenge: Today, as you navigate the world of dating apps, challenge yourself to be intentional and authentic in your interactions, seeking meaningful connections over mindless swipes and external validation.

Daily Reflection:

What resonated with you from today's lesson? How can you apply this truth in your life?

_____

_____

_____

_____

Day 269: Don't Lose It in the Dating Game

In the dating world after divorce, listen, it's tempting to go all-in. You're back in the game, right? You might think it's time to make up for lost years, jump from one date to the next, maybe even try to find a rebound to fill that void. Stop. You're missing the point.

This isn't about patching up the past. It's not about someone else defining your worth. You're not some incomplete puzzle looking for a missing piece. You're a whole masterpiece, but you need to realize that for yourself. Emotional stability? That's on you. Happiness? Same thing. Don't pass the buck to someone you just met over drinks.

So, before swiping right on Tinder or hitting the bars, get your house in order. Know who you are and what you bring to the table. And I'm not talking about the cash in your wallet or the car you drive. Those things are superficial band-aids. They don't fix what's inside. What's inside needs a foundation, and that foundation starts with self-respect.

The most attractive trait isn't a six-pack or a fat bank account; it's confidence rooted in self-worth. When you navigate the dating landscape with this mindset, you won't just find a partner; you'll find the right partner. Yeah, you might face rejection, but who cares? A 'no' isn't a verdict on your character; it's a sign that you're still searching for someone who recognizes your value.

Own your journey. This isn't a sprint to the next person willing to share a bed with you. It's a marathon toward someone who'll complement your life, not complicate it. Keep the wisdom with you: Maintain your frame, your integrity. Your worth isn't up for negotiation, man. Don't lose yourself in the dating game. Because the moment you do, you've already lost.

Daily Challenge: Before diving back into the dating world after divorce, take a moment to reflect on your self-worth and build a foundation of self-respect, recognizing that your true value lies within, not in someone else's validation.

Daily Reflection:

What resonated with you from today's lesson? How can you apply this truth in your life?

_____

_____

_____

_____

Day 270: Dating Milestone

Ah, so you've been hitting the dating scene already, have you? You've clocked some miles on this new terrain. You're not a rookie, but let's gut-check your approach, shall we? Let's cut through the BS. Are you dating as a distraction, or are you actually open to finding a connection? Don't kid yourself; be brutally honest. Because if you're just using dates to wallpaper over the holes in your life, stop wasting everyone's time, including your own.

Now, let's talk intentionality. If you're genuinely open to something meaningful, how much of 'you' are you really showing? Or are you tossing around a facade like a poker player bluffing his way through a high-stakes game? Look, a bluff might win a hand, but it won't win you the game. If you want real connection, you've got to show your cards.

How do you handle your ex-talk? Are you presenting it as a baggage claim, or as a chapter in the book of you? Big difference. No one wants to hear how your ex "did you wrong" over cocktails. Be upfront about your past, but don't let it overshadow the person you've become. Keep the focus on the now, the man standing in front of her.

Let's be straight—dating after divorce can feel like navigating a minefield in a blindfold. But the fact you're back in the game tells me you're resilient, you adapt, you rise. Take a moment to acknowledge that. You've gone from sharing a life to starting anew. That's no small feat.

Ready for a curveball? Emotional intimacy. Yeah, it's the toughest nut to crack. Don't shy away from it; dive in. Be vulnerable, be present, and above all, be genuine. Because real recognizes real, and when you get down to it, isn't that what you're searching for?

Daily Challenge: Reflect on your dating intentions and be brutally honest with yourself about whether you're seeking a distraction or a genuine connection, then commit to showing your true self and embracing emotional intimacy in your dating journey after divorce.

Daily Reflection:

What resonated with you from today's lesson? How can you apply this truth in your life?

_____

_____

_____

_____

Forgive to Live Free

Delve deep into the weight of resentment and ask yourself why carry it any longer? Learn the art of self-forgiveness and take inventory of grudges that hold you back. It's time to drop the blame game and embark on an emotional detox through the forgiveness ritual. Embrace compassion as the antidote to anger and harness the power of open dialogue. Explore the nuances of apologies—when to give them and how to accept them graciously. Discover the liberation in letting go of control and the profound impact forgiveness has on your life. Finally, celebrate your forgiveness milestone and savor the freedom of letting go.

Day 271: The Weight of Resentment- Why Carry It?

You're walking around with this weight on your shoulders, this resentment. But let me ask you, what's the point? You're mad, you're furious, maybe even boiling over, and I get it, I really do.

Divorce is a battlefield and sometimes you're left carrying wounds. But resentment? It's like adding fuel to a fire that's already scorching you. Look, resentment doesn't damage anyone but you. It's not a weapon against your ex; it's a self-inflicted wound. You hold onto this bitterness and what happens?

You can't sleep, can't think straight, can't even enjoy a simple meal or a night out with the guys. Worst of all, you're giving away your power, handing the keys to your emotional well-being to someone else. Why would you do that?

Here's the kicker. The only one stopping you from dropping this emotional baggage is you. Nobody else. You control your feelings, your reactions, your life. Don't let resentment set the agenda. It's a trash emotion, one that breeds more darkness and hate, sucking the joy out of your life.

So what do you do? You acknowledge it, you feel it, and then you let it go. You've got to excavate that bitterness, take a hard look at it, and then chuck it aside. Your future doesn't have room for the weight of past mistakes or disappointments.

You're forging a new path, remember? And on this path, resentment has no place. Ditch it, reclaim your power, and focus on what you can control. Trust me, you'll feel lighter for it.

Daily Challenge: Today, make a conscious effort to identify any lingering resentment and take a step towards letting it go, knowing that by releasing it, you're taking back control of your emotional well-being and paving the way for a brighter future.

Daily Reflection:

What resonated with you from today's lesson? How can you apply this truth in your life?

_____

_____

_____

_____

Day 272: Self-Forgiveness- Step One

You're beating yourself up, huh? Sitting there, replaying every mistake, every word you shouldn't have said, every action you regret. Stop it. Listen, divorce sucks, we get that. But life's not a courtroom where you're always on trial. Self-forgiveness, my man, that's the juice you need. Stop crafting your narrative like you're the villain of your own life. Sure, you made mistakes. Who hasn't? No one gets a playbook for marriage, let alone divorce.

You did what you thought was right in the moments you had. Maybe it turned out wrong, but that's how we learn. No wisdom comes gift-wrapped in success; it's born from the crapstorms we survive.

But here's the kicker: If you don't forgive yourself, you'll be dragging that iron ball of guilt everywhere, and guess what? No one wants to be around that guy. It's like you're walking into every room with this giant, invisible "I'm a screw-up" sign hanging over your head.

It affects how you talk to your kids, your friends, your coworkers—hell, even the barista who's just trying to sling you a cup of joe in the morning.

Why are you taking yourself out of the game before it's even started? Forgive yourself so you can give yourself the chance you deserve. You can't change the past, but every moment, every interaction— it's a building block for a better future.

You're the architect of what comes next, but first, you've got to clear the debris. Tear down that wall of regret and start laying a foundation in self-forgiveness. Then, my friend, you're not just surviving; you're thriving.

Daily Challenge: Today, practice self-forgiveness by identifying one specific mistake from your past, acknowledging it as a lesson learned, and letting go of the guilt that's been holding you back.

Daily Reflection:

What resonated with you from today's lesson? How can you apply this truth in your life?

_____

_____

_____

_____

Day 273: Identifying Grudges- Take Inventory

Alright, let's get straight into it. You're going through a divorce, right? Man, I get it, your emotions are all over the place. But listen, you've got grudges piling up like unpaid bills. Those grudges? They're weights around your ankle, man. You think they're harming your ex or whoever else you're mad at? Nah, they're eating you up, stealing your focus, and sapping your energy.

The first thing you need to do is own it. Recognize that you're holding onto resentment and grudges. You think keeping score is gonna bring you peace? Trust me, it won't. Accept that some things just didn't go your way. And that's okay. Life isn't fair; no one promised you it would be.

Next, take inventory. Write down the names and the reasons. See them for what they are: roadblocks to your progress. Understand this: forgiveness isn't about them, it's about you.

It's about reclaiming your mental real estate and evicting those grudges. Give yourself permission to move on. If you don't, you're gonna stay stuck in this emotional quagmire, and who wants that?

And once you've taken stock, make a game plan. Confront the issue head-on or let it go; the choice is yours. But make it a conscious choice, alright? Don't let it fester like an open wound. That's a one-way ticket to misery, my man.

Time's ticking. Your life's not on pause. You got dreams to chase, goals to conquer. But first, you need to clear the emotional cache. Wipe the slate clean. It's liberating, man. You'll feel lighter, more focused, and ready to tackle what's ahead. So stop giving a VIP seat to your grudges. Take inventory, then kick 'em to the curb. You've got a life to live.

Daily Challenge: Today, make a list of the grudges and resentments you're holding onto, and take the first step towards emotional liberation by consciously deciding whether to confront them or let them go.

Daily Reflection:

What resonated with you from today's lesson? How can you apply this truth in your life?

_____

_____

_____

Day 274: The Blame Game- Drop Out

The Blame Game? Man, listen. You're sitting there, pointing fingers, stewing in resentment, right? It's her fault, society's fault, maybe even your in-laws? Stop. Just stop. Blame's like a drug; gives you a high, a rush of righteous indignation. Makes you feel good, right? But it's a mask, my man—a mask for your insecurity, your fear, your regret.

You've got to pull yourself out of that mire. You think it's helping you? Nah. The world keeps spinning, life keeps moving, but you? You're stuck, spinning your wheels in the mud of blame. Get unstuck.

Here's the raw truth. Divorce sucks. It tears you down, messes with your identity, even messes with your sanity. But guess what? You have the choice, every day, to rise above it.

You can either wallow in self-pity, let the anger boil in your veins—or you can take a good hard look in the mirror and say, "Today, I choose to own my life."

Forget fault. Fault's in the past. You're living in the now, and if you're always looking back, you're going to slam into a wall going forward. So focus.

What do you control? Your actions, your responses, your frame of mind. The rest is static, noise in the background of a life that's waiting for you to reclaim it.

Wipe your slate clean. Own your actions, own your reactions, own every single day from here on out. Break free from the blame game, and start playing the one game that matters: your life, your rules.

Daily Challenge: Today, choose to let go of blame and take ownership of your life by focusing on what you can control—your actions, your responses, and your mindset.

Daily Reflection:

What resonated with you from today's lesson? How can you apply this truth in your life?

_____

_____

_____

_____

Day 275: Emotional Detox- The Forgiveness Ritual

You walk into a room, the air heavy with a mix of regret and bitterness. You're not the first guy to be here, but today, it's your stage. You've been through the legal mess, wrestled with your feelings, tackled the social dynamics, and here you are, standing at the precipice of a life free from the weight of past grudges. But you can't move forward if you're clinging to resentment like it's a lifeline.

Forgiveness, man, it's not for them; it's for you. When you're shackled by anger, you're just handing over your power, letting someone else dictate the tempo of your emotions.

Don't mistake this; forgiveness doesn't mean rolling over. It's not about saying what happened was okay. It's about saying you're okay, regardless of what went down.

Imagine all that emotional junk as a boulder you've been dragging around. Now picture yourself chipping away at it, bit by bit, until you've got nothing but dust. That dust? Scatter it to the winds. That's emotional detox. The forgiveness ritual is your chisel, and every swing frees you a little more.

Quit living your life as a reaction to someone else's actions. Grab hold of the narrative, take control, and rewrite your story. You're not a supporting character in anyone else's drama; you're the protagonist in your epic.

You want to talk about strength? Real strength isn't holding onto grudges like they're trophies. No, real strength comes from the capacity to let go, to reset, and to move forward, unburdened. Don't just survive; own your life, start to finish. Now go out there and swing that chisel.

Daily Challenge: Today, commit to chipping away at the boulder of resentment by taking a step towards forgiving someone from your past, understanding that it's a powerful act of self-liberation, not an endorsement of their actions.

Daily Reflection:

What resonated with you from today's lesson? How can you apply this truth in your life?

_____

_____

_____

_____

Day 276: Compassion- The Antidote to Anger

Compassion? You might be wondering, "What's that got to do with me right now? I'm pissed off, hurt, disappointed. Why should I care about compassion?" But listen up. Compassion isn't just about being a good guy or trying to win karma points. It's your weapon, your shield against a world that's always ready to throw punches at you, especially when you're down.

You're angry, I get it. You want to snap back, give the world a piece of your mind. But hear me out—anger's a fire that consumes you before it ever touches anyone else. It feeds off your energy, your focus, your well-being. You're the one losing sleep, grinding your teeth, while the source of your anger probably doesn't even know or care.

Flip the script. Compassion's that tool in your belt most people don't even know they have. It cools down that boiling point. You think compassion makes you weak? Nah, it makes you strategic. While anger clouds your judgment, compassion clears up the fog. It allows you to see the situation for what it is, not what your heightened emotions want it to be. Compassion lets you navigate the maze of post-divorce life with clarity.

Think of compassion as emotional intelligence. You're sizing up your opponent—not to land a punch, but to understand them. Maybe your ex messed up; maybe you did. But by understanding where they're coming from, you're gaining insights into your own missteps, your own blind spots. That's how you grow. That's how you move on.

In the end, compassion's not just for them; it's for you. Because, guess what, you can't control how others act, but you better control how you react. So, stop surrendering your peace of mind to the power of your anger. Reclaim it. Own it. Compassion's your path to do just that.

Daily Challenge: Today, practice compassion by taking a step back when you feel anger rising, and try to understand the perspective of someone who may have hurt you, recognizing that it's a powerful tool for your own emotional well-being and growth.

Daily Reflection:

What resonated with you from today's lesson? How can you apply this truth in your life?

_____

_____

_____

Day 277: Open Dialogue- The Power of Conversation

Look, let's cut to the chase. You're going through a divorce; it's raw, it's painful, and it messes with your head. But here's the kicker: Your lifeline is open dialogue. Yeah, you heard me. I'm talking about real, raw, unfiltered conversation, not just with your lawyer, your therapist, or your buddies who are all too eager to slam your ex. I mean dialogue with yourself, too.

Man up and stop dodging your emotions. Face them. Acknowledge them. Then you're ready to engage with others. That doesn't mean you spill your guts to everyone you meet. Be selective.

Find people you can talk to without judgment. Sometimes you'll need a swift kick in the ass, other times a bit of wisdom. Your boys got your back, but don't overlook the women in your life; they offer perspectives you need to hear.

Dialogue isn't a one-and-done deal. It's a process. One that requires you to be honest, not just with others but with yourself. It's that straightforward conversation that'll give you insights you've been too afraid to admit. Ever wonder why your marriage failed? That answer ain't gonna magically pop up unless you're willing to delve deep.

Look, I get it. You think you're an island, emotionally self-sufficient. News flash: You're not. You're a human being, and we, my man, are wired for connection.

Own your failures, confront your fears, and for God's sake, stop hiding behind a facade. Get real, and get talking. That's how you move from surviving to thriving. That's how you reclaim your life.

Daily Challenge: Today, challenge yourself to have an honest and open conversation with at least one person, whether it's a friend, family member, or therapist, about your feelings and experiences during this divorce journey.

Daily Reflection:

What resonated with you from today's lesson? How can you apply this truth in your life?

_____

_____

_____

Day 278: The Apology- When and How to Give It

You messed up. Yeah, it happens. We're all human. But listen, an apology isn't just saying "sorry" and moving on. That's weak sauce. An apology is your chance to own your actions, your failures. It's more than just lip service; it's a commitment to change.

Don't apologize because you got caught, or because you want to smooth things over. Apologize because you recognize your mistake, and you're man enough to admit it. But before those words leave your mouth, take a hard look at yourself. Are you willing to do the work to make sure you don't screw up again? If not, keep your apology to yourself; it's worthless.

Now, timing is crucial. Choose a moment when both of you can focus on the conversation, not in the middle of an argument or when you're rushing off to work. An apology needs room to breathe.

And the words you choose? They matter. Skip the "if I've offended you" garbage. You did offend; that's why you're apologizing. Get to the point. "I messed up. I hurt you. I'm sorry."

Lastly, an apology has two parts: saying sorry and making amends. What are you gonna do differently next time? Show through your actions that you're committed to change. That's how you build trust, man. That's how you show you're different from all the other guys who just say sorry and go back to their old ways.

Remember, an apology isn't for you. It's for the person you hurt. Make it count.

Daily Challenge: Today, take a hard look at your past mistakes, and choose one specific action you can commit to changing to demonstrate your growth and commitment to those you've hurt.

Daily Reflection:

What resonated with you from today's lesson? How can you apply this truth in your life?

_____

_____

_____

_____

Day 279: Accepting Apologies- Grace in Action

Accepting apologies demands incredible strength. It's not about being weak or gullible; it's about embracing grace—a grace that flows from your core, unshaken by life's storms. In the tumultuous terrain of divorce, pain can cut deep, leaving wounds that ache long after the separation papers are signed.

Apologies, when they come, may seem scarce, and their sincerity, questionable. But here's the red-pill truth: Accepting an apology doesn't equate to forgetting or condoning their actions. It's a bold declaration that you refuse to let their negativity dictate your future.

By granting forgiveness, you seize the reins of your life's narrative. You choose to unshackle yourself from the chains of anger and resentment, setting your spirit free. It's not about absolving them; it's about liberating yourself.

In the world of post-divorce survival, grace becomes your superpower—a force that propels you forward. It's the audacity to say, "I won't let your mistakes define my happiness." It's the unwavering commitment to emerge from the crucible of pain stronger, wiser, and more resilient.

So, when you accept apologies, you're not displaying weakness; you're demonstrating your incredible inner strength. It's the power to rise above bitterness and craft a life filled with positivity and personal growth.

Remember, forgiveness isn't a gift to them; it's a gift to yourself. In those moments of grace, you become the hero of your own story, rewriting your destiny with resilience, dignity, and an unwavering commitment to thrive.

Daily Challenge: Embrace the power of forgiveness today, not as a gift to them, but as a gift to yourself, allowing your spirit to soar unburdened by the weight of the past and shaping your destiny with resilience and dignity.

Daily Reflection:

What resonated with you from today's lesson? How can you apply this truth in your life?

_____

_____

_____

Day 280: The Closure Myth- Is It Real?

The closure myth, fellas. Let's break it down. In the stormy aftermath of divorce, we often chase an elusive beast called closure. We believe it'll magically heal our wounds and provide a neat ending to the chaos. But here's the harsh truth: closure, as we imagine it, might be a myth.

Life rarely hands us tidy conclusions. Sometimes, you won't get that heartfelt apology, that clear explanation, or that sense of "everything's okay now." And that's okay. Closure doesn't always come wrapped in a bow.

Realize this: closure is an inside job. It's not about the other person; it's about you. It's about accepting that some things will remain unresolved, and that's alright. Closure is finding peace within yourself, regardless of external factors.

So, stop waiting for that perfect moment when all loose ends tie up neatly. Instead, focus on your own growth and healing. Embrace the fact that you can move forward, even without every question answered.

It's not a weakness to let go of the closure myth; it's a strength. It's saying, "I won't let the past dictate my future." You have the power to write your own ending, one filled with resilience and self-discovery.

In the world of divorce survival, closure might be elusive, but inner peace and strength are attainable. Don't let the myth hold you back. It's time to redefine closure on your terms.

Daily Challenge: Today, let go of the idea that closure depends on external factors, and focus on finding inner peace and strength to move forward, even without all the answers.

Daily Reflection:

What resonated with you from today's lesson? How can you apply this truth in your life?

_____

_____

_____

_____

Day 281: Forgiveness and Reconnection

Forgiveness is the ultimate act of self-love. It's not about them; it's about you. When you carry the weight of anger and resentment, you're dragging your past into your future.

In the chaos of divorce, it's easy to hold onto grudges, to blame, to resent. But understand this: Forgiveness doesn't excuse their actions; it frees you from their grip. It's a declaration that your peace of mind matters more than their wrongdoings.

Reconnection, on the other hand, is a bridge to your future. Reconnect with yourself first. Reconnect with the passions and dreams you shelved during the storm. Rediscover the essence of who you are.

Then, consider reconnecting with those who matter most – your children, your family, your true friends. Divorce might have strained these bonds, but it doesn't have to sever them. Show up with authenticity and vulnerability.

And yes, maybe even consider reconnecting with love. It's a risk, but life is too short to shut the door on happiness. But, tread carefully, ensuring you've healed scars before diving in again.

Forgiveness and reconnection are your compass on this journey. They guide you toward a future where you're unburdened by the past. They're not easy, but they're essential.

Remember, you're not weak for forgiving, and you're not naive for reconnecting. You're powerful for choosing a path that leads to growth, love, and a life you deserve. So, let forgiveness be your armor, and reconnection be your roadmap to a brighter tomorrow.

Daily Challenge: Today, make a conscious effort to release one specific grudge or piece of resentment that's been weighing you down, and choose forgiveness as the first step towards freeing yourself from the past.

Daily Reflection:

What resonated with you from today's lesson? How can you apply this truth in your life?

_____

_____

_____

Day 282: Setting Boundaries

Setting boundaries is your battle armor in the divorce arena. It's not about building walls; it's about protecting your peace and sanity.

Listen up, gentlemen. Divorce can be a war zone, and without clear boundaries, you'll be collateral damage. Your ex might test your limits, push your buttons, but remember this: boundaries aren't a sign of weakness; they're a demonstration to your self-respect.

Picture this: You're in the ring, gloves on, facing emotional punches. Your boundary is that line in the sand, saying, "No, you can't cross." It's not a suggestion; it's a rule, a non-negotiable.

Your time, your space, your peace—these are sacred. Don't let anyone trample them. When you set boundaries, you protect your mental and emotional well-being. You show that you won't tolerate disrespect.

Now, some might call it selfish, but it's self-preservation. You're not shutting people out; you're letting them in on your terms. It's about balance, not isolation.

So, gentlemen, embrace boundaries with pride. Say no when it's necessary. Don't be afraid to put yourself first. In the tough journey of divorce survival, boundaries are your shield.

They keep you strong, focused, and ready for whatever comes your way. Stand tall, and don't apologize for safeguarding your sanity. That's the real wisdom, and it's vital for your post-divorce journey to thrive.

Daily Challenge: Today, practice setting a clear and non-negotiable boundary in your interactions, reaffirming your self-respect and commitment to protecting your peace and sanity during the divorce process.

Daily Reflection:

What resonated with you from today's lesson? How can you apply this truth in your life?

_____

_____

_____

_____

Day 283: Emotional Scars

Emotional scars from divorce run deep. They're the battle wounds of a war you never signed up for. But here's the raw truth: those scars don't define you; they refine you. In the crucible of heartbreak, you discover strength you never knew you had. Every tear, every sleepless night, every moment of despair becomes a chisel, shaping you into a more resilient version of yourself.

These scars are your badges of honor. They testify to the love you gave, the fights you endured, and the pain you overcame. They're proof that you dared to love, even when it cost you dearly.

Don't hide your emotional scars; wear them proudly. They're a sign of your survival and your capacity to love again. They're not blemishes; they're the roadmap of your journey.

Embrace your emotional scars as a part of your story, not as a sentence of despair. They're not signs of weakness but symbols of your courage. Through them, you learn to empathize, to heal, and to cherish the beauty of life.

Remember, the most beautiful people are those who have known suffering, who've faced the darkness and emerged as beacons of light. Your emotional scars are your transformation, your rebirth, your red-pill awakening.

Let them be a reminder that you are not broken; you are forged in fire. And from those ashes, you rise, stronger, wiser, and more capable of embracing life's twists and turns.

Daily Challenge: Today, take a moment to reflect on your emotional scars and see them not as wounds, but as badges of resilience, proof of your capacity to love, and a roadmap of your journey toward a stronger and wiser self.

Daily Reflection:

What resonated with you from today's lesson? How can you apply this truth in your life?

_____

_____

_____

Day 284: Retrain Your Brain

Reprogramming your mind post-divorce? That's the ultimate power move, my friend. It's all about taking the wheel of your life and steering it towards a future that screams success. Let's break it down.

First, you've got to understand this: your thoughts matter – big time. The ideas you entertain, they're like architects drawing up your life's blueprint. Negative thoughts? They're the wrecking ball. Positive thoughts? They're the foundation. And guess what? It's not some mystical mumbo-jumbo; it's backed by solid science.

But here's the kicker - you've got to break free from your past. Those old patterns, they're like rusty chains holding you back. You need to cut loose, my friend. Create a vision of your future so vivid it feels like déjà vu. See it, touch it, taste it. This isn't just daydreaming; it's hacking into your own brain's operating system.

Now, let's talk meditation. It's not some woo-woo practice; it's your secret weapon. When you meditate, you tap into the quantum field, where the possibilities are endless. It's like hitting Ctrl+Alt+Delete on your mind and starting fresh.

But here's the real deal: it takes discipline and consistency. No half-baked attempts here. You've got to commit to this journey of self-mastery.

So, what are you waiting for? It's time to take control, rewire your mind for success, and create that future you've been craving. It's not easy, but it's within your reach if you're ready to put in the work. So, let's get after it and start reprogramming your mind today. Your destiny is waiting.

Daily Challenge: Today, commit to actively replacing one negative thought with a positive one, and take a step towards creating a vivid vision of your future post-divorce.

Daily Reflection:

What resonated with you from today's lesson? How can you apply this truth in your life?

_____

_____

_____

_____

Day 285: Family Ties- The Complicated Web

Divorce rips through the fabric of family life, tearing apart bonds you once thought unbreakable. It's a brutal awakening to the reality that blood doesn't guarantee loyalty, and that sometimes, the ones closest to you can hurt you the most. In this chaos, you must confront a painful truth - forgiveness isn't about absolving them; it's about freeing yourself. Holding onto anger and resentment is like gripping hot coals; it burns you, not them.

Family ties, once strong, now resemble a complex web of emotions. But remember this, my friend: you're the spider at the center, and you decide whether to trap yourself or weave a new path.

Forgiving doesn't mean forgetting or condoning their actions; it's a radical act of self-preservation. Release the burden of bitterness. Cut the threads that tie you to their negativity, for they are the chains that hold you back.

As you navigate this treacherous terrain, embrace the power of forgiveness. It's not a sign of weakness but a evidence to your strength. Reclaim control over your life and build healthier connections.

In this journey, recognize that not everyone deserves a seat at your table. Prioritize those who uplift and support you, even if they aren't bound by blood. Forge a new family of your choosing, one that nurtures your growth and heals your wounded spirit.

Family ties may be complicated, but your path to forgiveness is clear. Be ruthless in cutting toxic threads, resilient in rebuilding bonds, and unwavering in your pursuit of a better life. You've got this.

Daily Challenge: Today, take a step towards forgiveness by writing down one thing you're willing to let go of and release from your heart, freeing yourself from the weight of resentment and anger.

Daily Reflection:

What resonated with you from today's lesson? How can you apply this truth in your life?

_____

_____

_____

_____

Day 286: Workplace Resentment

In the brutal arena of post-divorce survival, workplace resentment can become a venomous snake, coiled and ready to strike. But remember this, my fellow warrior: You're a battle-hardened gladiator, and resentment has no place in your arena. In the corporate battleground, politics, jealousy, and backstabbing are as common as the morning coffee. But here's your secret weapon: forgiveness. It's not about absolving their sins; it's about unshackling your soul.

When you forgive, you break free from the chains of bitterness. You become a force of nature, unstoppable and unbreakable. Your colleagues may try to undermine you, but they can't touch a man who's forged in the fires of resilience.

Your success will be your ultimate revenge. Not to prove them wrong, but to prove yourself right. Rise above the noise, focus on your mission, and let your achievements speak louder than any grudge ever could.

In the concrete jungle, your resilience is your greatest weapon. Instead of dwelling on workplace politics, channel your energy into ambition. Every day is a new chance to build, to grow, to conquer.

So, my fellow survivor, shed the weight of resentment. Embrace forgiveness. It's not a sign of weakness; it's a declaration of strength. By forgiving, you release yourself from the past and pave the way for a triumphant future.

Forge your new identity as a relentless, resilient warrior. Let the echoes of your success drown out the whispers of workplace resentment. In this battle, you're not just a survivor; you're a conqueror, redefining success on your own terms.

Daily Challenge: Today, make a conscious choice to let go of one grudge or resentment at work, and channel that energy into pursuing your goals and achieving success on your own terms.

Daily Reflection:

What resonated with you from today's lesson? How can you apply this truth in your life?

_____

_____

_____

_____

Day 287: Forgiving the Unforgivable- Is It Possible?

In the brutal aftermath of divorce, you might find yourself grappling with a question that cuts deep: Can you truly forgive the unforgivable?

Let's be brutally honest here. It won't be easy. You've been hurt, betrayed, and scarred. The wounds are fresh, and the pain is real. Forgiveness? That sounds like a tall order.

But here's the truth: Forgiveness isn't about letting someone off the hook. It's not about saying what they did was okay. It's about freeing yourself from the chains of anger and resentment.

You see, holding onto that bitterness is like drinking poison and expecting your ex to drop dead. It's a lose-lose game. The more you cling to that grudge, the more power you hand over to the very person who hurt you.

Forgiveness isn't about them; it's about you. It's about reclaiming your power, your peace, and your future. It's about acknowledging that your happiness matters more than their wrongdoings.

Does it mean you forget or condone what happened? No. It means you refuse to let it define you. You choose to rise above the wreckage of your past.

Forgiving the unforgivable is a radical act of self-love. It's your declaration that your healing matters, and your happiness is non-negotiable.

So, is it possible? Absolutely. But it won't happen overnight. It's a journey, a battle, and a triumph. And when you finally do it, you'll find strength, resilience, and a life worth living. You've got this.

Daily Challenge: Today, take a small step towards forgiveness by writing down one thing you're willing to let go of and release from the weight of your past, knowing that it's the first step towards your own healing and freedom.

Daily Reflection:

What resonated with you from today's lesson? How can you apply this truth in your life?

_____

_____

_____

Day 288: Reconciliation- When Is It Worth It?

In the turbulent aftermath of divorce, the question of reconciliation looms like a shadow in the corners of your mind. Is it worth it? Should you give it a shot? The answer isn't a one-size-fits-all solution. It's about knowing when to hold on and when to let go.

You see, forgiveness isn't a weakness; it's a superpower. It takes strength to consider mending what's broken, but it also takes wisdom to recognize when it's time to walk away.

Ask yourself: Has the foundation cracked beyond repair? Are the walls built on trust irreparably shattered? Or is there a glimmer of hope, a flicker of love, worth rekindling?

Reconciliation demands brutal honesty. It means facing the demons of your past, the pain, the betrayal, and the scars. It's not a convenient escape from loneliness or a desperate attempt to salvage comfort.

When you contemplate reconciliation, remember this: It's not about going back to who you were; it's about evolving into who you can be together. It's a journey that requires both parties to change, grow, and heal.

But beware the trap of toxic nostalgia. Don't let the fear of being alone or societal pressures blind you to the harsh truth. Sometimes, the healthiest choice is to move forward independently.

Reconciliation should never be driven by fear or loneliness; it should be fueled by love, respect, and a shared vision for a better future. It's about rebuilding trust and rewriting the story with wiser, stronger characters.

Daily Challenge: Today, take a moment to reflect on your feelings and motivations regarding reconciliation, and ask yourself if your desire to reconcile is grounded in love, respect, and a genuine shared vision for a better future, rather than fear or loneliness.

Daily Reflection:

What resonated with you from today's lesson? How can you apply this truth in your life?

_____

_____

_____

_____

Day 289: Letting Go of Control- It's Liberating

Letting go of control? Man, that's a tough pill to swallow. But you know what's harder? Clinging onto something that's already out of your grip, letting it shred your heart and sanity apart. Listen, life after divorce can feel like a car skidding on black ice, and your instinct is to slam hard on the brakes, right? But what does that get you? More chaos. More spinning out.

Think of control as that brake. The harder you press, the more uncontrollable things get. You think holding onto resentment, constantly checking on her social media, or rehashing those past arguments gives you power? Nah, bro, it's the exact opposite. It's like building your own prison and throwing away the key.

You want to thrive after this heartbreak? Start by letting go. Letting go doesn't mean you don't care. It means you care enough about yourself to not let the past dictate your future. Forgive not because she deserves it, but because YOU deserve peace. It's self-respect. It's reclaiming your life.

It's about recognizing that true strength isn't in holding onto pain but in releasing it. So what if you can't control the situation? You can always control your response.

Don't get stuck in the narrative that you need to have a grip on everything. Because here's the raw truth: control is an illusion. The real magic? It's in surrendering, adapting, and moving forward with a liberated spirit.

Drop the reins. Unclench that fist. Breathe. Let that go. Liberation awaits, and man, it's a hell of a ride.

Daily Challenge: Today, practice letting go of one thing that's been weighing on your mind or heart, and remind yourself that true strength lies in releasing, not in holding onto pain.

Daily Reflection:

What resonated with you from today's lesson? How can you apply this truth in your life?

_____

_____

_____

_____

Day 290: How Forgiveness Impacts Your Life

Forgiveness. Let's cut the fluff and get right to it. This isn't about holding hands, singing Kumbaya, or lighting candles. It's raw, real, and powerful. When someone wrongs you – be it your ex-spouse, a friend, or even yourself – that resentment you hold? It's a chain. A weight. An anchor. Think of it as carrying a boulder on your back every day. Tiresome, right?

Now, ask yourself: who's really suffering from holding onto that anger? Spoiler: it's you. Every moment you invest in resentment, you're stealing from your future.

While you're seething in the past, life's moving on without you. Opportunities missed. Relationships strained. Joy drained.

Forgiving doesn't mean condoning or forgetting. No. It means understanding that the power to free yourself from the shackles of the past lies within. It's a choice. Your choice.

Are you going to let past pain dictate your future? Or are you going to take control, acknowledge it, let it go, and say, "I choose to move on"?

There's power in forgiveness, man. It doesn't make you weak. It's the ultimate act of strength. It's taking control of your narrative. It's saying, "I won't let this define me." It's about investing in your mental and emotional well-being.

Letting go is the best thing you can do for yourself. So, drop the weight. Embrace the present. And let forgiveness be the fuel to a brighter, bolder, better you. Don't just survive. Thrive.

Daily Challenge: Today, make a conscious choice to forgive someone who has wronged you, and in doing so, release the heavy burden of resentment that's been holding you back from living your best life.

Daily Reflection:

What resonated with you from today's lesson? How can you apply this truth in your life?

_____

_____

_____

_____

Day 291: Time Heals- But You've Got to Help It Along

Forgiveness is often portrayed as this magical pill you take, and voila, everything's better. But let's cut the crap. It doesn't work like that, especially when betrayal, disappointment, and hurt are involved. People tell you time heals all wounds. Sure, it does, but not without your active participation.

You think those emotions are just going to pack up and leave on their own? Think again. Time's like a doctor. It sets the bone, but you have to do the physiotherapy. You can't just wallow in self-pity and expect time to do all the work.

If you're waiting for a day when you wake up completely free of pain without doing anything about it, brace yourself for disappointment.

Real forgiveness? It's an active process. It's a daily, sometimes hourly, choice to release the hurt. It's acknowledging the pain, the betrayal, but choosing to not let it define or control you.

Not for their sake but for yours. Because holding onto resentment is like drinking poison and expecting the other person to drop dead. Spoiler: it's you who's getting harmed.

So, what's the play? Every time you feel that bitterness bubbling up, take a step back. Analyze it. Understand it. Then, consciously choose to let it go. Remember, forgiving doesn't mean you have to forget or reconcile. It means deciding that you won't let the past hold you hostage.

You're bigger than your past, and you have a future waiting that won't care about it. Get out of your own way. Forgive, not because they deserve it, but because you deserve peace.

Daily Challenge: Today, make a list of the people or situations you need to forgive, and start the process of letting go, freeing yourself from the chains of resentment and reclaiming your power to shape your future.

Daily Reflection:

What resonated with you from today's lesson? How can you apply this truth in your life?

_____

_____

_____

Day 292: Forgiveness Journal- Track Your Progress

Divorce can tear you apart, make you question every choice, every moment, and every whispered promise. And here's the hardest pill to swallow: Holding onto that resentment, that anger?

It's like gulping poison and expecting the other person to die. Your fury isn't doing any damage to them, but it's corroding your spirit, your essence, your daily life.

Start a forgiveness journal. Not for them. Do it for you. Every time you jot down a thought, an anger, a slight, you're acknowledging it. You're saying, "I see you. I recognize the pain." And by recognizing it, you can start the process of letting it go.

It's not about erasing the past or pretending that wrongs didn't happen. It's about giving yourself permission to heal. It's about saying, "This happened, but I won't let it define me. I won't let it chain me down."

Your journal isn't a place for you to wax poetic about them, or an altar to past wrongs. It's a record of your journey. Each entry is a step away from the poison of resentment and a step towards reclaiming your life.

In the raw, unfiltered way that is life, some days will be tougher. You might feel the heat of anger more fiercely. On those days, write more.

Pour it all out. And then, when you're ready, let it go. That journal? It's the roadmap to a future where you're free from the chains of past pain. Embrace it.

Daily Challenge: Begin your forgiveness journal today, taking the first step towards releasing the poison of resentment and healing your spirit.

Daily Reflection:

What resonated with you from today's lesson? How can you apply this truth in your life?

_____

_____

_____

_____

Day 293: The Final Conversation- Seal the Deal

You wanna talk forgiveness post-divorce? Let's cut the crap. Holding onto resentment after a breakup? That's not "being a man." It's letting someone live rent-free in your head. What's that doing? Keeping you stuck, mate.

Listen, I get it. She hurt you. Maybe she messed up big time. But every second you're stewing in that anger, that bitterness? You're handing over control. Why the hell would you do that? You think holding a grudge is power? Nah, real power is saying, "I'm bigger than this." It's letting go for YOU, not for her.

That last conversation, sealing the deal with forgiveness? It's not waving a white flag. It's saying, "I've got better things to do than be pissed off." It's acknowledging the pain, sure, but not letting it define you.

She made a mistake? Cool. Thank her. Thank her for showing you who you DON'T want to be. And then? Move. On.

The world's full of opportunity, of next chapters, of new stories to write. Stop rereading the last one. Start penning a new narrative.

It's time. Have that final internal convo. Give yourself permission to drop the weight, step into the light, and hustle forward.

Because guess what? There's a world waiting for the best version of you. Don't rob yourself, or the world, of that guy. Go on, seal that deal. For you.

Daily Challenge: Take a step towards forgiveness by writing down one thing you're grateful for in your life today, and let it remind you that your future is brighter without the burden of resentment.

Daily Reflection:

What resonated with you from today's lesson? How can you apply this truth in your life?

_____

_____

_____

Day 294: Social Dynamics- Forgiveness in Groups

Social dynamics after a divorce isn't just about how you and your ex navigate the waters; it's also about understanding and forging your place among friends, family, and colleagues in this new chapter. You'll find quickly that people, even those who claimed neutrality, can become unintentional carriers of resentment, feeding your rage and stoking fires you're trying hard to put out.

Let's cut to the chase: harboring resentment is like chugging poison and waiting for the other person to die. It won't happen. The toxicity you hold only corrodes your spirit, not theirs. It's not machismo to hold onto grudges; it's idiocy. It's a waste of energy, time, and life.

Here's the reality: in group settings, your rage becomes intense, almost a tangible cloud that hangs over everyone. It might feel good to have others walk on eggshells around you, mistaking your bitterness for power. But understand this—it's not respect you're earning; it's pity.

You want power? Real power? It comes from a place of forgiveness. It doesn't mean you need to forget, or let people walk all over you. But letting go of that venom gives you the clarity to operate from a place of strength, not emotion. It grants you the ability to navigate social scenarios with grace, authority, and command.

Ask yourself: Do you want to be the guy who drags his past into every group meeting, every family dinner, every guys' night out? Or do you want to be the man who has the strength to acknowledge the past, leave it there, and move with purpose and poise into the future? Choose the latter. Remember, forgiveness isn't about them—it's about you, your peace, and your place in the social hierarchy. Don't let divorce define you; let your capacity to rise above it do that.

Daily Challenge: Today, make a conscious choice to let go of a grudge or resentment that's been weighing you down, and embrace forgiveness as a source of personal strength and growth in your social interactions.

Daily Reflection:

What resonated with you from today's lesson? How can you apply this truth in your life?

_____

_____

_____

Day 295: Emotional Growth

Listen up, fellas. Life doesn't come with a manual. And guess what? Neither does forgiveness. No one's out there handing you a script telling you, "It's Day 295, time to forgive and move on." But here's the raw truth: forgiveness isn't about the person who hurt you; it's about freeing yourself. It's about emotional growth.

You see, harboring resentment and anger is like drinking poison and expecting the other person to die. Sounds ridiculous, right? That's because it is. Every time you cling to that bitterness, you're tying a chain around your soul, anchoring yourself to a past you can't change. But here's the deal: forgiveness is your way of cutting that chain.

Think of the energy you waste on resentment, the sleepless nights, the stress, the heart palpitations. For what? To prove a point? Who are you trying to prove it to? The ex? The world? Or is it your ego? Being angry is easy. Staying bitter is comfortable because it's familiar. But you know what's tough? Embracing the pain, acknowledging it, and deciding that it won't define you. Because, at the end of the day, holding onto grudges won't change the past, but it can definitely ruin your future.

Real growth comes from making choices that are HARD. Choices that elevate your mindset and spirit. Choosing forgiveness is choosing yourself, your peace, and your future.

Your story isn't about the pain; it's about how you rise from it. So, are you going to let a chapter from the past hold you hostage? Or are you going to pen a future filled with promise, lessons, and triumphs? Remember, champions aren't defined by the fights they lost, but by how they recover and push forward. Choose to grow. Choose to forgive. You owe it to yourself.

Daily Challenge: Today, take a step towards forgiveness by writing down one thing you can let go of and release the burden of resentment from your heart, knowing that it's a crucial step towards your emotional growth and future happiness.

Daily Reflection:

What resonated with you from today's lesson? How can you apply this truth in your life?

_____

_____

_____

_____

Day 296: Revenge vs. Forgiveness- Choose Wisely

Revenge. It's that seductive whisper that creeps into your ear in the darkest hours, tempting you to even the score. It promises satisfaction, closure. But here's the hard truth: revenge is a hollow victory. It's that extra drink that seems like a good idea but only deepens the hangover. You pour your energy, your rage, and your focus into causing someone else pain, only to realize it doesn't lessen your own.

Now, forgiveness? That's the real power move. It's not about saying what happened was okay or forgetting the pain. It's about reclaiming control. Control over your emotions, your future, your sanity. While revenge keeps you tethered to the past, forgiveness sets you free. When you forgive, you're not doing it for the other person; you're doing it for yourself. You're choosing to move forward with your life, unburdened.

Some of you might think, "I can't just forget!" And I get it. But forgiveness isn't about forgetting, it's about releasing. It's about understanding that holding onto grudges is like gripping a burning coal, expecting the other person to get burned. Guess what? They won't. You will.

Life's too short to waste on vendettas and paybacks. While you're stewing in anger, plotting, the world is moving on. Opportunities pass, relationships fade, moments are lost. Don't miss out on the beauty of now because you're obsessed with the pain of then.

Take that energy, that passion, and channel it into building, not destroying. Pour it into your passions, your purpose, and most importantly, into healing. At the end of the day, revenge will always be a game where the score never settles. Forgiveness, on the other hand, is the ultimate win. Choose wisely, my friends. Don't drink the poison and wait for the other person to die.

Daily Challenge: Today, resist the allure of revenge and choose forgiveness as your ultimate act of self-liberation, allowing yourself to move forward unburdened by the weight of anger and resentment.

Daily Reflection:

What resonated with you from today's lesson? How can you apply this truth in your life?

_____

_____

_____

_____

Day 297: The Power of Now- Live in the Moment

L isten up, guys. We've all been there. Hurt, pain, betrayal. The echoes of what was done to us – or what we did to others – can hang heavy. But if there's one thing life and business have taught me, it's that dwelling on the past is a guaranteed path to nowhere. And revenge? It's just a fancy word for clinging to pain and letting someone else dictate your emotions. Ain't nobody got time for that!

Forgiveness? It's not about them. It's about you. It's about freeing yourself from the chains of yesterday and grabbing hold of today. Every moment you spend plotting, planning, and steeping in resentment is a moment you've handed over. That's a moment you're not building your empire, a moment you're not setting up your comeback, a moment you're not living YOUR life.

Understand this: life doesn't give you a rewind button. Yesterday is gone. Those mistakes, the hurts, the regrets? Can't change 'em. But you have NOW. And "now" is your most powerful asset. So, you're holding onto grudges? You're chaining yourself to the past? Ask yourself why. Why are you giving power to something that's over and done with?

The magic happens when you harness the energy you've been pouring into past pain and redirect it. Look at what's right in front of you. This moment. This opportunity. This life that's waiting to be seized.

When you embrace the power of now, you transform. You're no longer the guy bogged down by old stories; you're the guy writing a new one. And guess what? That new story? It's one hell of a tale of resilience, strength, and unstoppable ambition.

Daily Challenge: Today, choose to break free from the chains of the past by forgiving, not for their sake but for your own, and seize the power of the present moment to create your story of resilience, strength, and unstoppable ambition.

Daily Reflection:

What resonated with you from today's lesson? How can you apply this truth in your life?

_____

_____

_____

_____

Day 298: Gratitude- The Path to Forgiveness

Listen up. After a divorce, life isn't about carrying the burdens of the past; it's about crafting the masterpiece of your future. But here's the kicker: you've got some dead weight, and it's holding you back.

You think everyone's watching, judging? Maybe they are. But who cares? Your worth isn't defined by whispers in the break room or sideways glances at family dinners. Yeah, it stings. But it's momentary. Your life? That's the long game.

Mutual friends? Some are real; others are just there for the drama. Filter them. You don't need a crowd; you need a tribe. Quality over quantity, every single time. If they're gossiping more than they're supporting, cut them out. No second thoughts.

And social media? It's a double-edged sword. It connects, but it also reminds. Unfriend, unfollow, do whatever it takes to give yourself peace. If you're stalking your ex at 3 AM, you're not winning. Redirect that energy. Build yourself, not the narrative of a past that doesn't define you.

Facing single friends again? Embrace it. They're not pitying you; they're rooting for you. And if they're not, then again, snip snip. Cut that weight.

You'll face rumors at work, awkward family gatherings, and shifts in social dynamics. It's inevitable. But remember, you're in control. You dictate your life story, not them. Rebuild trust, redefine your social circle, and step into the new you. It's about growth, not baggage. And sometimes, the best way to grow? Cut off the dead weight and soar.

Daily Challenge: Embrace your power to shape your own narrative and cut off any dead weight – be it toxic friends, social media distractions, or negative thoughts – that's holding you back from crafting the masterpiece of your future after divorce.

Daily Reflection:

What resonated with you from today's lesson? How can you apply this truth in your life?

_____

_____

_____

_____

Day 299: The Freedom of Letting Go

The reality is, post-divorce, not everyone in your circle has your back. The brutal truth? Some people are like old band-aids, sticky and uncomfortable. The more you hang onto them, the more they hinder your healing. Listen, man, it's not about being cold-hearted, but it's about getting real with what and who serves your growth.

Think about it. You've been through the wringer, right? You've faced the emotional and legal battles, and now you've got this post-divorce baggage that everyone seems to have an opinion about. Everyone's got something to say, from those workplace whispers to the not-so-subtle side-eyes at family gatherings. And let's not even start on the social media vultures, waiting to pick apart every status and photo.

But here's the game changer: you don't owe anyone a thing. Your life. Your rules. It's time to let go of the dead weight. That 'friend' who's suddenly too busy? The family member who constantly brings up your ex? That coworker who thrives on gossip? Cut them off. And feel no guilt about it.

Your post-divorce life isn't about fitting into old molds or sticking to the script. It's about redefining your narrative. It's about understanding that sometimes, to move forward, you've got to leave some folks behind.

Look, growth isn't comfortable. But neither is clinging onto people and situations that drag you back into the mud. Freedom isn't just about the legal papers saying you're divorced. It's about mentally and emotionally freeing yourself from toxic connections. Dive deep, embrace the freedom of letting go, and watch yourself rise. You've got this. No apologies. No looking back. Just pure, unadulterated forward motion. Go get it, champ.

Daily Challenge: Today, take a bold step towards your own healing and growth by identifying and distancing yourself from at least one toxic person or situation that's been holding you back since your divorce.

Daily Reflection:

What resonated with you from today's lesson? How can you apply this truth in your life?

_____

_____

_____

_____

Day 300: Forgiveness Milestone

Alright, let's get real. It's been 300 days. Three. Hundred. Days. How many of those days have you let the weight of the past drag you down? But today, let's shift that narrative. Today is about acknowledging your journey, a freaking milestone. It's time to realize that forgiveness isn't about saying what happened was okay; it's about saying you're not going to let it control you anymore.

Let me lay it out straight: forgiveness is your freedom. You've carried the baggage, the resentment, the anger. Maybe even rage. But who's it burning? Not her. Not the guy she might be seeing. It's burning you. Your energy, your spirit, your potential.

You might think holding onto that anger gives you power. Nah, man. It's a chain. But today, 300 days in, you're faced with a choice. A choice to snap that chain. Look back. See the hurt, the pain, the betrayal. Recognize it. But don't let it be your anchor. Because, dude, you're built for more than that.

You've grown, whether you see it or not. You've faced the darkest nights and still woke up the next day. That's strength. That's resilience. So today, make the choice. Choose to forgive. Not for her, not for them, but for you. To reclaim your narrative. To write a story where you're not the victim, but the hero. The hero who faces his demons and says, "Not today."

Celebrate this milestone. Day 300. And remember, every step forward is a step away from what held you back. Today, take that step. It's time.

Daily Challenge: On this 300th day of your journey, choose forgiveness as your path to freedom, recognizing that it's not about condoning the past but about releasing the chains that have held you back, and take a step forward towards reclaiming your narrative and becoming the hero of your own story.

Daily Reflection:

What resonated with you from today's lesson? How can you apply this truth in your life?

_____

_____

_____

_____

New Normal

Days 301 to 330 mark the start of your new life post-divorce. It's a phase of transformation, where you'll reboot routines, form new habits, and find balance in work and life. Navigating social reentry with care, you'll rediscover hobbies and passions.

Financial planning takes the stage, while health becomes a priority. Your living space gets a makeover, and your social circle expands. These days are about crafting an empowered and fulfilling new life, one step at a time.

Day 301: The Reset Button- Your New Life Begins

Life's thrown you a curveball, hasn't it? Bet you didn't see that one coming. But here's the thing, brother: every moment of pain, every sleepless night, every ounce of confusion? It's leading you somewhere. And let me tell you, it's somewhere good. Think of it as hitting the reset button on a game console, only the game is your life.

You've got a chance now. A real, raw, and rare opportunity. An opportunity to rebuild, rebrand, and relaunch yourself. Forget the naysayers and those pitying glances. Let them talk.

While they're busy with their gossip, you'll be busy shaping the life you truly want, the life you deserve. This isn't about starting from scratch; it's about refining, refocusing, and redirecting.

Are you tired? Good. Are you hurt? Even better. You know why? Because that pain, that fatigue, it's fuel. It's the raw energy you need to light up your new path. Forget who you were, and focus on who you're becoming.

The guy who faced the storm head-on. The guy who turned adversity into an advantage. The one who took life's hardest punch and used it to propel himself forward.

This is your comeback story. No fairy tales, no sugarcoating. Real, gritty, full of ups and downs, but at its core, it's authentic. Your authentic story. And guess what? It's just getting started. Hit that reset button with everything you've got. Your new life? It starts now. Dive in, man. Dive in deep. Because the world hasn't seen anything yet.

Daily Challenge: Embrace the opportunity before you and use the pain and fatigue as fuel to shape the life you truly want, starting today.

Daily Reflection:

What resonated with you from today's lesson? How can you apply this truth in your life?

_____

_____

_____

_____

Day 302: Routine Reboot- Structure Your Day

Routine is more than just a timetable of to-dos. It's your compass in the storm, your anchor when you're adrift. Post-divorce, everything's in chaos. Your bed feels too big, your home too quiet. The coffee machine brews two cups out of habit. But here's the kicker - you've got a golden ticket here, an opportunity that few get. It's called a reboot.

Who made the rules that said your day starts with that blaring alarm and ends with late-night regrets? Screw that. This is your narrative now, man. You get to redefine every moment. Start with your morning. Instead of reliving memories with that coffee mug, why not switch to tea? Or have a smoothie. Get to the gym when the roosters are up. Let them wonder how you've got that new fire in your eyes.

Your 9-to-5 doesn't have to be a grind. If you're working remote, change the scenery. Work from a cafe, a library, a co-working space. Surround yourself with go-getters, with those hustling just as hard. Their energy is infectious, trust me.

And evenings? They're yours. Join that hobby class you've been putting off, write, paint, dance, sing, do whatever makes your soul light up. Don't drown in TV reruns or booze. Create, don't stagnate.

Your routines are more than just patterns, they're affirmations. Each choice, each act, screams to the world – and to yourself – who you are. So, who are you now? A victim, wallowing in what was? Or the protagonist, hungry for what's next? It's time to hit that routine reboot. Let the world catch up with you.

Daily Challenge: Embrace the power of routine as your compass for post-divorce life – redefine your mornings, revamp your work environment, and invest your evenings in activities that ignite your passion and purpose.

Daily Reflection:

What resonated with you from today's lesson? How can you apply this truth in your life?

_____

_____

_____

_____

Day 303: Stop the Self-Sabotage Now!

Listen up! This is you we're talking about. Don't throw your life away on choices that aren't truly yours. Your Dream, Not Theirs: You've been listening to everyone but yourself? Wake up! Don't be that guy having a midlife meltdown because you're living someone else's dream. And, hey, think twice before marrying or having a baby just because someone else says it's time. Your life, your rules.

Life's Not Fair. Deal With It: Stop waiting on life to hand you a golden ticket. It ain't coming. Jealous of others? Why? They're just trying to figure their stuff out too. Stop making life about you, and grab the wheel.

Address Your Demons: Got issues? Cool, who doesn't? But ignoring them isn't the answer. Therapy helped me. Check out BetterHelp – it's online, easy, and they're offering 10% off your first month. Go on, give happiness a chance. Losers Aren't Ladders: Those "fun" friends holding you back? Time for new company. Don't let guilt trap you in mediocrity.

Respect Your Body: Drink? Fine. Drink and drive? Are you nuts? Don't abuse your only temple. Drugs, excess alcohol, and laziness are the expressway to regrets. Take control. Your body's worth it. Materialism? Nah: Obsessed with the next shiny thing? Temporary happiness won't fill that void. Focus on experiences, mental health, and real joy. Stuff fades, memories don't. Credit Crunch: Your credit score is more than a number – it's power. Control your spending, ditch those cards if you can't handle them, and remember – failing is learning.

Just Say 'No': Being a people-pleaser? That's a one-way ticket to nowhere. Set boundaries. Prioritize YOU. Now, go out and OWN your life! Don't blame the world for your choices; take charge and thrive.

Daily Challenge: Reevaluate your life choices and commitments, ensuring that you're living authentically according to your dreams and values, not someone else's expectations or pressures.

Daily Reflection:

What resonated with you from today's lesson? How can you apply this truth in your life?

_____

_____

_____

_____

Day 304: Work-Life Balance- Find Your Equilibrium

Finding equilibrium post-divorce isn't just about work-life balance. It's deeper than that. It's about soul balance. Life's thrown you a curveball, and it's up to you to adjust your swing. But here's the thing: balance isn't about a 50-50 split between work and personal life. It's about giving 100% to wherever you are, in whatever moment you're in.

When you're grinding at work, be there. Be present. Let that hustle be your therapy, your outlet. Dive deep into projects, collaborate, innovate. Let the world see your fire and determination, that relentless drive that's been forged from your trials. But when the workday ends, truly end it. Shut that laptop. Silence that phone.

Now, your personal life. Dive into it just as hard. Connect with your kids, your friends. Pick up a new hobby, or get back to an old one you've neglected.

Dance in the living room, cook a meal from scratch, hit the gym, read a book, take a walk. Whatever it is, do it with all of you.

Remember, balance isn't static. It's not a perfectly still teeter-totter. It's dynamic. Some days work might pull harder, and some days your personal life might demand more. The key? Flexibility. Adaptability. And a relentless commitment to living with purpose, regardless of where you are.

That equilibrium you're chasing? It's not external. It's internal. It's in the choices you make every single day. Choose to show up. Choose to be present. Choose to live with intention. That's how you find your equilibrium. That's how you reclaim your life.

Daily Challenge: Today, commit to giving 100% of your focus and energy to the present moment, whether you're at work or in your personal life, and remember that true equilibrium is found within your choices and commitment to living with intention.

Daily Reflection:

What resonated with you from today's lesson? How can you apply this truth in your life?

Day 305: Social Reentry- Navigate with Care

Stepping back into the social arena post-divorce? It's not just about reentry; it's about redesigning how you show up. You're not the same dude you were before, and guess what? That's your advantage. The world might be looking at you with a mix of pity, curiosity, or even indifference. But here's the thing: your narrative isn't written by the crowd's whispers; it's authored by your actions and decisions. Do you want to be the guy who's constantly defined by his past, or the one who's crafting his present?

You might be tempted to fall back into old routines, old hangouts, and maybe even reconnect with toxic relationships. Easy? Sure. Beneficial? No! This is the time to be picky about who you spend your energy on. Who's adding value to your life? Who's just there for the drama?

Reentering the social scene isn't just about filling up your calendar. It's about aligning with people and places that resonate with the man you're becoming. And, it's okay to be cautious. Dive into situations where you feel growth, not where you're simply trying to mask the pain.

Remember, every interaction is a reflection of your journey. You've been through a war, but it's not about the battle scars; it's about the wisdom you've gathered. So, hold your head high. Own your story, but don't let it be the only thing you talk about. Listen more, speak less. Learn. Grow. And while you're at it, remember to laugh a little.

Social reentry? Sure, navigate with care. But more importantly, navigate with purpose. And always, always respect the man in the mirror. He's been through hell, but he's still standing. And that's worth everything.

Daily Challenge: Today, take a conscious step to redefine your social interactions, seeking out those that align with your personal growth and values, and remember to laugh and respect the man you've become on this journey.

Daily Reflection:

What resonated with you from today's lesson? How can you apply this truth in your life?

_____

_____

_____

_____

Day 306: Hobbies and Passions- Rekindle or Discover

Hobbies and passions. They aren't just pastimes; they're lifelines. In the chaos of splitting lives, assets, and emotions, it's easy to forget who you were before all of this. Who you *are*. That guy who had fire in his belly, a zest for life, a curiosity that was insatiable? He's still there. And now? Now's the time to either rekindle those flames or light some new ones.

When was the last time you did something just for the pure joy of it? Not because it was expected or needed, but just because it made your heart race a bit faster? Maybe it was picking up that guitar, painting, hiking, or diving deep into a book on ancient civilizations. Whatever it was, it was your escape, your therapy.

In the midst of recalibrating your life, you might think: "I don't have time for that." Wrong mindset. You don't have time *not* to. These aren't frivolous pursuits; they're vital to your well-being, your mental health, your very essence.

Here's the truth: A hobby isn't an indulgence; it's a necessity. It's the thing that keeps your brain from spiraling, that gives you a break from the relentless thoughts of what went wrong. It's what helps you rebuild your identity, separate from any relationship or societal expectation.

Maybe it's time to revisit an old passion. Or, maybe it's time to discover something completely new. Dive in deep. Get lost in it. Let it consume you. Because in those moments, when you're fully engaged and alive, you remember: This is who I am. Not defined by a relationship gone sour, but by the fire that burns within. Rekindle it or discover it. Just make sure it's burning bright.

Daily Challenge: Today, reconnect with a hobby or passion that once set your soul on fire, or embark on a new adventure that ignites your curiosity and reminds you of the vibrant person you've always been.

Daily Reflection:

What resonated with you from today's lesson? How can you apply this truth in your life?

_____

_____

_____

_____

Day 307: Financial Planning – Are You Sticking To The New Budget

Financial planning after a divorce isn't just about dollars and cents, it's about reclaiming control. It's a straight-up reminder that you've got this, that you can rewrite the narrative of your life, starting with your wallet.

You set a budget earlier, remember? That wasn't just an exercise in mathematics; it was a pledge to yourself. A commitment to the man you are becoming, to the future you are carving out. Every time you stick to that budget, you're not just saving pennies; you're building discipline. Every time you stray, you're not just splurging; you're chipping away at your promise to yourself.

Think about that next impulse buy, that fancy gadget, or that pricey night out. Is it worth more than your peace of mind, your next step forward, your vision for the future? Get real with yourself. It's not about deprivation; it's about prioritization.

Your financial choices now lay the groundwork for your new normal. Do you want that to be a shaky foundation built on whims and impulses, or do you want it solid, grounded in purpose and intent? The flashy car or the startup capital for your dream venture? The lavish trips or the investments that'll secure your future?

Here's a reality check: Post-divorce life isn't a sprint; it's a marathon. Every decision you make, especially the financial ones, aren't just about the now. They're about the long game. The legacy you're building, not just for you but maybe for your kids, for the next chapter, for the mark you want to leave on this world. So, ask yourself this: are you sticking to the new budget you set? Not for the sake of being frugal, but for the future you've envisioned? It's more than money; it's your life's blueprint.

Daily Challenge: Today, reaffirm your commitment to financial discipline by reviewing your budget and making choices that align with your vision for the future, reminding yourself that every decision is a step toward reclaiming control and rewriting the narrative of your life.

Daily Reflection:

What resonated with you from today's lesson? How can you apply this truth in your life?

_____

_____

_____

_____

Day 308: Health Check- Physical and Mental

Post-divorce, everything might seem upside down. The heart, the mind, the body. But here's the raw truth: this is your wake-up call. Yeah, life threw a curveball. But are you going to sit there, letting it define you? Or are you going to get up and take control?

Your health – both mental and physical – isn't a luxury, it's a necessity. That body of yours? It's the only one you've got. And that mind? It's your most potent asset. So, stop neglecting them. Every pain, every sleepless night, every stressful thought chips away at your well-being. But you've got the power to change the narrative.

Hit the gym. Not for her, not for anyone else, but for you. Feel every rep, every drop of sweat. It's not just about looking good; it's about feeling alive, reclaiming your strength. And that mind? Feed it. Books, meditation, therapy. Dive deep into self-reflection. Understand your past but don't be a prisoner to it.

Sure, you can binge-watch shows and down a six-pack, seeking temporary relief. But where's that going to get you long-term? Nowhere. The battle isn't against her, or the world. It's within you. The resilience, the drive, the unyielding spirit – they're all there, waiting to be ignited.

People will talk. They'll have opinions, judgments. Let them. At the end of the day, when you look in the mirror, it's your reflection, your journey. Rise above the chatter. Commit to your health. It's not just about survival; it's about thriving. So, are you in? Because this new chapter is yours to write. No excuses, no looking back. Health is wealth, and it's time to get rich.

Daily Challenge: Today, take the first step towards reclaiming your physical and mental well-being – whether it's a workout, a moment of meditation, or seeking professional help – because your health is the foundation upon which your new life is built.

Daily Reflection:

What resonated with you from today's lesson? How can you apply this truth in your life?

_____

_____

_____

Day 309: Home Makeover- Space Reflects Mindset

Your living space isn't just about four walls and a roof; it's a direct reflection of your mindset, your energy, your journey. When you walk through that door, what greets you? Is it chaos, remnants of a past life, or memories that don't serve your growth? Or is it clarity, inspiration, and a launchpad for the next chapter?

Look, post-divorce, it's easy to let things go — to let that old couch gather dust or to let those walls stay painted in colors chosen by another person for another time. But here's the straight talk: if your space isn't evolving with you, it's holding you back. Every single time you walk in and get that uneasy feeling or that pang of a memory you'd rather forget, it's chipping away at your progress.

You've been through the wringer, and you've come out stronger on the other side. Your space needs to scream that story to anyone who walks in, especially to yourself. It's time to declutter, to repurpose, and to reimagine.

Ditch what doesn't serve you. Maybe it's time to bring in fresh colors, swap out old furniture, or even just rearrange what you've got.

This isn't just about aesthetics. It's about purpose. So, every morning when you wake up and every evening when you come back, you're reminded of who you are now and where you're headed. Reinvent your space, and you reinvent a part of yourself. Dive in, and let your home be the sanctuary of your new normal. Remember: as you change, let your space evolve with you.

Daily Challenge: Today, take one small step to transform your living space into a reflection of your new, empowered self—whether it's decluttering a corner, rearranging furniture, or adding a touch of positivity through decor.

Daily Reflection:

What resonated with you from today's lesson? How can you apply this truth in your life?

_____

_____

_____

_____

Day 310: New Connections- Expand Your Circle

Finding new connections post-divorce isn't just about being social or avoiding loneliness. It's about rediscovery. It's about understanding that life has chapters, and sometimes, the people that fit into one chapter might not fit into the next. And that's okay. Life isn't a static picture; it's a movie, always in motion, always evolving.

Dive into new communities. Not for the sake of replacing what was lost but to discover what else is out there. Think of it as an upgrade, not a reset. There are individuals out there who resonate with the person you are now, the battles you've faced, the wisdom you've gained.

You see, post-divorce, you're not the same guy. You're wiser, stronger, more attuned to your own needs and boundaries. So why should your social circle remain the same? Step out. Attend that workshop. Join that club. Take that salsa class if it piques your interest. The point isn't to fill a void but to expand. To grow. To evolve.

Remember, every individual you meet is a universe in themselves, with stories, experiences, and perspectives you haven't explored. Some will challenge you, some will vibe with you, and some, well, they'll teach you more about yourself than about them. And that's the magic of it. The world is massive, diverse, and waiting for you. Expand that circle, not because you have to, but because you owe it to yourself to see just how vast and rich life can be. Step out. Dive deep. Grow big.

Daily Challenge: Embrace the opportunity for personal growth and self-discovery by actively seeking out new connections and communities that align with your evolving self, reminding yourself that life is a dynamic journey, and expanding your social circle can be a transformative experience.

Daily Reflection:

What resonated with you from today's lesson? How can you apply this truth in your life?

_____

_____

_____

_____

Day 311: Time Management- Prioritize What Matters

Time management isn't just about squeezing more hours out of the day; it's about clarity on what truly matters. Listen up: after a split, your world's turned upside down, and it's easy to get lost in the chaos, to let days blend together, reacting instead of acting. Don't let that be you.

Here's the cold truth: your time is finite. Every second you spend brooding, regretting, or wallowing? That's time you'll never get back. Instead, focus on what's ahead. What's the one thing that, if done today, would make the biggest difference in your life? Do that. Not tomorrow. Today.

Delete distractions. Those friends who are just there for the gossip, the apps on your phone that keep you mindlessly scrolling, the endless replaying of 'what ifs' in your mind – ditch them. Because you don't have time for what doesn't serve your goals.

Now more than ever, you need to be ruthlessly selective. What do you really want for yourself? Reconnect with passions, dreams that got sidelined, and set boundaries. This is the era of YOU. A restart. But it doesn't just happen; you have to be intentional about it.

It's not about being busy; it's about being productive. It's about realizing that time is the most valuable currency you have. So invest it wisely. Prioritize yourself, your growth, and your future. The clock's ticking. Let's get after it.

Daily Challenge: Today, identify the one action that will move you closer to your post-divorce goals and make it your top priority, eliminating distractions and reclaiming your precious time to focus on your personal growth and future.

Daily Reflection:

What resonated with you from today's lesson? How can you apply this truth in your life?

_____

_____

_____

Day 312: Boundaries 2.0- Set and Respect

Reinventing yourself post-divorce isn't just about rediscovering passions or resetting finances. It's about boundaries. Yeah, those invisible lines we often blur in relationships. Boundaries 2.0 - it's the upgrade you didn't know you needed. And trust me, it's game-changing. In the hustle of marriage, you might've let things slide. Maybe you stopped standing up for what you truly believed in, or perhaps you gave more than you should have, thinking compromise was the answer to everything. But let's get one thing straight: compromise and self-sacrifice aren't the same thing.

You see, boundaries aren't just about saying no; they're about saying yes to yourself. Yes to respect. Yes to self-worth. Yes to growth. Those moments when you felt unheard, undervalued, or overshadowed? That's when boundaries were missing or overlooked. But that was then. This is now. It's time to set those boundaries and respect them. Not just for yourself, but for others too. If you don't value your own limits, why should anyone else? Whether it's how you want to be treated, how you allocate your time, or how you handle finances, you define the rules now. Not society, not your ex, not anyone.

Boundaries 2.0 is about clarity. It's about understanding your value, reinforcing it, and not settling for anything less. It's about moving from the passenger seat to the driver's seat of your life. Let others know where the line is drawn. Not with arrogance, but with self-assurance. Remember, life post-divorce isn't about retracing old steps; it's about carving out new paths. Redefine your boundaries, respect them, and watch as the world begins to respect you back. It's a journey of empowerment. Let's get it.

Daily Challenge: Today, commit to identifying one area in your life where boundaries have been blurred or neglected, and take the first step towards setting clear and empowering boundaries in that area, affirming your self-worth and growth.

Daily Reflection:

What resonated with you from today's lesson? How can you apply this truth in your life?

_____

_____

_____

_____

Day 313: Parenting Dynamics- Adapt and Update

Parenting after divorce? It's a whole new ballgame, but guess what? It's not about you anymore. It's about them - your kids. They didn't ask for this change, but they're counting on you to step up. And you will. Why? Because that's what we do. We adapt. We pivot. We overcome.

You're not just "Dad on weekends" or "every other holiday" father. You're a full-time, 24/7 Dad. Divorce papers can't redefine that. The court's schedule? It's just a piece of paper. Your heart, your commitment, your love for your kids? That's etched in stone.

Changes are inevitable. Your ex might have new rules, there might be a new adult in the picture, but you can't let that shake your core. Be consistent. Be present. Show up for soccer games, piano recitals, and even the mundane moments. Those bedtime stories? They matter. That random call just to check in on them? It counts.

No more "old ways" of doing things. Embrace the update. Because the game has changed, but the players are still the same. And your role? It's as vital as ever. You're shaping lives, molding futures, and ensuring your kids grow up knowing that change doesn't equal absence. That love isn't conditional.

The parenting dynamics might shift, but your dedication doesn't waver. You adapt, you update, and you make sure your kids never doubt where you stand. In their corner. Always. Ready to give it all for their well-being. This is your new playbook. Run with it.

Daily Challenge: Today, make a conscious effort to adapt and embrace the changes in your parenting dynamics, ensuring your kids feel your unwavering presence and love throughout the day, no matter what challenges arise.

Daily Reflection:

What resonated with you from today's lesson? How can you apply this truth in your life?

_____

_____

_____

Day 314: Dating Revisited- The New Landscape

Embracing the dating scene again post-divorce isn't just about swiping right or left, trying to land a date, or filling a void. It's about recalibrating your understanding of the game, your role in it, and what you genuinely want from it.

Look, the landscape's changed. Not just because of technology or new dating norms, but because YOU have changed. The man diving back into the dating pool now is not the same guy who left it. You're wiser, scarred, but more authentic. Embrace that. Wear your experiences, not as baggage, but as badges of resilience.

You'll face rejection. Heck, you might even be the one dishing it out sometimes. But remember, it's not about tallying up matches or dates. It's about finding quality, connection, and genuine vibes. The world's full of surface-level interactions. You've been through the ringer; you don't have time for fluff.

And as you navigate this new terrain, maintain your self-worth. Your value isn't determined by a text back, a second date, or someone's fleeting validation. It's grounded in the self-awareness you've cultivated and the growth journey you've embarked upon.

Lastly, be honest. With yourself and others. If you're looking for something casual, own it. If you're searching for something deeper, don't settle for less. The dating world is vast, and there's room for every kind of connection. But the most crucial connection? The one you have with yourself. That's the compass guiding you through the wild world of modern romance. Dive in, but never lose sight of who you've become.

Daily Challenge: Embrace the post-divorce dating scene with authenticity, resilience, and a commitment to genuine connections, remembering that your self-worth is not defined by external validation, and stay true to your own desires and intentions.

Daily Reflection:

What resonated with you from today's lesson? How can you apply this truth in your life?

_____

_____

_____

_____

Day 315: Emotional Stability- Maintain Your Ground

Navigating post-divorce life? It's not just about rebuilding the tangible stuff, but it's that internal game. Emotional stability? That's your foundation, man. We're not talking about suppressing emotions or pretending everything's cool when it's not. Nah, this is about understanding your emotions, harnessing them, and not letting them control the game.

You see, life's gonna throw punches. Some days, memories will hit you like a freight train. Some days, loneliness will try to take the driver's seat. But here's the deal: you can't let these emotions dictate your every move. Recognize them, yes. Respect them, sure. But don't let them own you.

Your emotions? They're signals, not dictators. They tell you where you're at, where you've been, but they don't have to chart out where you're going. That's your job. If you let every emotional wave dictate your actions, you're setting yourself up for a rollercoaster you didn't sign up for.

It's time to build that emotional muscle. Like hitting the gym for your mind. It's about knowing that the heartbreak, the anger, the regret—they're all part of the journey, not the destination. You might've lost a partner, but you've gained a clearer path to self-awareness.

In this post-divorce phase, it's about grounding yourself. It's about understanding that while the ground might've shaken, it hasn't swallowed you whole. You're still here, still breathing, still capable of growth. Embrace the emotions, learn from them, but don't let them steer the ship. Your future isn't written by your past, it's crafted by your present. Maintain your ground, and let that emotional stability be the compass to your new normal. Stand firm, and let the world see the storm doesn't shake you.

Daily Challenge: Today, when faced with a surge of emotions, take a moment to acknowledge them, breathe, and remind yourself that you are in control of your actions and decisions, steering your own ship towards a brighter future.

Daily Reflection:

What resonated with you from today's lesson? How can you apply this truth in your life?

_____

_____

_____

_____

Day 316: Career Goals- Refocus and Aim High

When life pulls the rug out from under you, when the marriage ends and the papers are signed, there's a vacuum. An empty space that can either suck you into an abyss of despair or become a launch pad. Here's the thing: a lot of guys get trapped in that void, but not you. Why? Because this is your moment to pivot, to refocus, and aim way, way higher in your career.

You've faced personal setbacks. So what? That's life. Now, what are you going to do with the lessons you've learned? See, adversity breeds resilience. You've got a kind of armor now that most men don't. Your battles have given you an edge. Use that. Channel that energy, that determination into your career.

Maybe you've been coasting in your job. Maybe you've been stuck, scared to take that leap, to pitch that idea, to launch that startup, to ask for that raise. But here's your wake-up call: there's no better time than now. Think bigger. Aim higher. Stop playing small. The world doesn't need another guy just going through the motions. It needs leaders, innovators, men with grit, with vision. Men like you.

Reframe your narrative. You're not the guy who lost in love; you're the guy who won in life, who used pain as a catapult. Your career isn't just about making money anymore; it's about making a statement. So recalibrate, set those sights sky-high, and don't let anything or anyone, especially your past, tell you where your limits lie. Go own that boardroom, run that project, start that business. And always, always aim higher. Your next chapter? It's gonna be epic. Let's go.

Daily Challenge: Embrace your past adversities as the source of your resilience and motivation; today, take a bold step in your career, whether it's pitching that idea, pursuing a new opportunity, or launching your own venture, and remember, your past doesn't define your limits—aim higher!

Daily Reflection:

What resonated with you from today's lesson? How can you apply this truth in your life?

_____

_____

_____

_____

Day 317: Personal Branding- Who Are You Now?

Your identity took a hit, didn't it? Divorce can feel like being thrown into the roughest seas, and now you're asking yourself, "Who am I now?" Personal branding isn't just for celebrities or entrepreneurs. It's for you, especially right now. It's your narrative, your vibe, your essence. It's how you show up in this world. Post-divorce, this is your chance to redefine and repurpose yourself. No more labels. Not "her ex-husband," not "that guy who got dumped." Who are you really, at your core?

Find that. Believe in that. What do you stand for? What fires you up in the morning? What values are non-negotiable? Understand these and wear them with pride. Build your brand around authenticity. No more facades, no more putting on a brave face for society. This is about your raw, unfiltered essence.

You've been through the wringer. That gives you depth, perspective, a story. Use it. Your struggles, your lessons, your victories – these aren't just anecdotes. They're your brand's foundation.

And here's a pro tip: your personal brand isn't static. As you grow, evolve, and learn, so does it. So, don't box yourself in. You might've been the silent, brooding type, but now maybe you're feeling more vocal, more present. Embrace it.

Be ruthless about self-awareness. Dive deep into self-reflection. When you emerge, you'll have a clearer vision of who you are and what you stand for. That's your brand, your unique stamp on this world. Own it, rock it, live it. Remember, it's not about starting over; it's about starting better.

Daily Challenge: Embrace the opportunity to redefine and repurpose yourself by identifying your core values, passions, and unique story, and start living your authentic brand with pride and authenticity.

Daily Reflection:

What resonated with you from today's lesson? How can you apply this truth in your life?

_____

_____

_____

_____

Day 318: Local Community- Get Involved

Getting involved in your local community post-divorce isn't just about keeping busy or filling a void; it's about rediscovery. It's diving headfirst into a sea of new experiences, new relationships, and most importantly, a deeper understanding of who YOU are.

Remember, divorce isn't the endgame; it's a chapter in your story. Think of it this way: you've got this incredible opportunity in front of you. A blank slate. And it's time to pick up the brush. Your local community? That's your palette. Dive into that local theater group, that neighborhood cleanup drive, the weekend soccer league. Be the guy who steps up, not the one who steps back.

Here's the thing – involvement isn't just altruism; it's self-growth. Every event you attend, every hand you shake, every project you spearhead – you're redefining yourself. Stripped of labels – no longer just the 'ex-husband' or 'the divorced guy' – you become the doer, the dreamer, the go-getter.

What community involvement does is provide perspective. While you're out there helping others, sharing stories, laughing over coffee or sweating through a community workout, you realize the world is bigger than your pain. And guess what? It needs you. Not the you from yesterday, dwelling on what was lost, but the you of today, ready to create, connect, and conquer.

The process of rebuilding isn't solo work. Your community is there, waiting with open arms, ready to show you sides of yourself you've never met. So, don't just get involved. Immerse. Dive in. Because your post-divorce life isn't just about healing; it's about thriving. The community is your stage, man. Time to step up and shine.

Daily Challenge: Today, take the first step towards rediscovery by actively seeking out a local community event or group to join, and be the guy who steps up to embrace new experiences and relationships.

Daily Reflection:

What resonated with you from today's lesson? How can you apply this truth in your life?

_____

_____

_____

_____

Day 319: Long-Term Planning- Vision Board

Let me drop some truth on you: I've taken more knocks in life than most. The school of hard knocks? Yeah, I graduated summa cum laude. I'm pulling back the curtain on my experiences, hoping you won't have to learn the hard way.

Firstly, understand that health isn't just wealth – it's everything. All the riches and accolades in the world mean nothing if you're not around to enjoy them. And time? It's the silent dealer, doling out moments that you get to fill. You decide whether it's with purpose or procrastination. Don't waste it scrolling mindlessly or binging shows.

And when it comes to expressing love, do it now, do it often. I learned the bitter truth when I lost someone without warning. Words left unsaid haunt longer than any ghost.

Life will also teach you about people. Your family? They're a crazy, irreplaceable bunch. Friends, on the other hand, can be chosen. And believe me when I say, quality beats quantity. But be cautious; not everyone's as golden-hearted as you might think. I've been burned, scammed, and learned the hard way. Protect yourself, and value genuine connections over superficial ones.

Speaking of genuine, let's talk success. Money's a tool, not the end game. You can't buy contentment or real joy. And sometimes, success might look different from your dreams. That's okay. Adapt, grow, and remember: a closed door often leads to an open window.

In this chaotic dance called life, the best moves are made with passion, purpose, and persistence. So, lace up, dive in, and make every step count. The world's waiting for your next move.

Daily Challenge: Today, focus on your health by committing to a 30-minute exercise routine or a mindful moment of self-care, because taking care of yourself is the foundation for rebuilding your life after divorce.

Daily Reflection:

What resonated with you from today's lesson? How can you apply this truth in your life?

_____

_____

_____

_____

Day 320: Cultural Reset- Movies, Music, Books

Listen, here's the deal: post-divorce, your world's been flipped upside down, but it's not the end of your movie, music, or literature game. In fact, it's the very beginning. The culture? It's vast. And here's your opportunity to hit the reset button. You've been consuming the same stuff, the same storylines, the same tracks over and over, and why? Comfort? Time for change.

Remember when you were the guy who had the scoop on the latest indie band before they blew up? Or when you'd talk hours about that foreign film no one else watched? Get back to that guy. Dive deep into the stuff you've never heard of. Become the guy who's always one step ahead in the culture game.

You used to bond over a shared Spotify playlist? Cool, but now's your time. Make a new one. Fill it with tracks that pump you up, make you feel something raw and real. Every beat, every lyric? That's your new anthem.

Those movies she never wanted to watch with you? Watch 'em. Dive into a new series, a new genre. Watch a documentary on something you know nothing about. Expand your mind. And books? Don't even get me started. There's wisdom, stories, lives lived and lessons learned in those pages. Soak it up.

Culture isn't just about killing time. It's about understanding yourself, growing, and connecting with the world around you. It's about moving forward. So, stop scrolling the same feeds, listening to the same tracks. Break the loop. Go discover, go learn, and most importantly, go live. Your new narrative starts now. Embrace it.

Daily Challenge: Embrace the opportunity to hit the reset button on your cultural consumption today – explore new music, movies, literature, and art that challenge and inspire you, rediscovering the guy who's always one step ahead in the culture game.

Daily Reflection:

What resonated with you from today's lesson? How can you apply this truth in your life?

_____

_____

_____

_____

Day 321: Networking- Build Your New Tribe

Stepping into your new normal means understanding one crucial thing: you're not alone on this journey. You've weathered the storm, and now, it's time to build. Build your tribe. Build your network. Your connections, the people you surround yourself with, will be the scaffolding for the new heights you're aiming for.

You see, networking isn't just about business cards or LinkedIn endorsements. Nah, it's deeper than that. It's about surrounding yourself with people who get it, who get *you*. It's about connecting with those who'll push you, challenge you, and support you. It's about being vulnerable enough to say, "I need help," and wise enough to recognize when someone else does. It's about mutual growth.

Some of the friends from your old life might stick around, and that's golden. But some won't, and that's okay too. This is the moment to actively choose your tribe. The kind of people who will celebrate your wins and have your back on the down days. The ones who'll call you out when you're slacking and push you beyond your perceived limits.

Embrace the new. Attend gatherings, join clubs, initiate conversations. Step out of that comfort zone. Why? Because that's where magic happens. That's where you find the tribe that resonates with your energy, your aspirations, your dreams.

The people you surround yourself with right now will lay the foundation for the life you're rebuilding. So, think about it. Who's in your corner? If you don't like the answer, change it. Build your new tribe, and let them elevate you to the version of yourself you've always wanted to be. Your future self will thank you.

Daily Challenge: Today, reach out to at least one person who inspires and motivates you, and take a step towards building a meaningful connection with them, whether through a message, a call, or an invitation to meet in person.

Daily Reflection:

What resonated with you from today's lesson? How can you apply this truth in your life?

_____

_____

_____

Day 322: Weekend Vibes- New Ways to Unwind

Finding that new rhythm after the storm isn't just about the daily grind, it's about those weekend vibes too. Gone are the days of the old routines, the things you did as a duo. Now? It's time to carve out a new groove, find fresh ways to unwind and recharge.

Think about it: weekends are your canvas. Blank, open, waiting. Will you fill them with remnants of the past, or seize them as opportunities to craft new experiences? Don't get bogged down by nostalgia. That's a quicksand that'll pull you in if you let it. Stay moving, stay hungry for the new.

Was there something you always wanted to try but kept on the back burner? A hobby, a sport, a new spot in town? This is your moment. Dive in. Maybe it's hitting up that local hiking trail you heard about or experimenting with culinary skills. Embrace the discomfort of the new because it's in that space that you grow.

Connections matter too. You've got friends, old and new, who've got your back. Lean into those relationships. Make plans, keep busy, create memories. And if solitude calls, answer it. There's a difference between being alone and feeling lonely. Own your solitude. Discover its power. Let it recharge you.

Weekends post-divorce can feel daunting, but it's all about perspective. You're not losing out; you're gaining. Gaining new experiences, new memories, a new understanding of yourself. Shift your mindset from what's gone to what's coming. Remember, every weekend is a fresh shot to do something epic, something meaningful. Make it count.

Daily Challenge: Embrace the weekends as a blank canvas for creating new experiences, whether it's trying something you've always wanted, connecting with friends, or enjoying your solitude, and remember that every weekend is an opportunity for growth and meaning.

Daily Reflection:

What resonated with you from today's lesson? How can you apply this truth in your life?

_____

_____

_____

_____

Day 323: Travel Plans- Expand Your Horizons

It's time for a reset, a literal and figurative journey out of your comfort zone. Travel. And I'm not talking about the five-star, luxury resort kind. I'm talking about the kind where you grab a backpack, step into a place where nobody knows your name, and expand your horizons. Because there's a massive world out there waiting for you to experience, to challenge every preconceived notion you've held onto.

Remember when you were a kid and everything was an adventure? Before the days of routine and predictability bogged you down? It's time to bring back that spirit. Maybe it's the streets of a bustling city you've never been to, or the serenity of a mountaintop. Whatever it is, it's a journey to discover not just new places, but new parts of yourself.

Every interaction, every unfamiliar road, every language barrier, every new food — it's a lesson. It's about resilience, about learning to navigate challenges and coming out on the other side stronger, wiser. It's a mirror reflecting back to you who you really are when stripped away from the life you once knew.

So, lace up those shoes, book that ticket. Don't let the fear of the unknown hold you back. Use this time to truly find yourself, to expand your world view, and realize that every sunset and sunrise in a different land is a step towards healing and rediscovery. The world is a book, and staying put is reading just one page. Turn the page, man. Your story is waiting.

Daily Challenge: Embrace the spirit of adventure and embark on a journey to an unfamiliar place, whether near or far, to challenge your comfort zone and discover new aspects of yourself in the process.

Daily Reflection:

What resonated with you from today's lesson? How can you apply this truth in your life?

_____

_____

_____

_____

Day 324: Reflections- Acknowledge Your Journey

You've been running, and whether you realize it or not, you've covered some serious ground. Reflect back on Day 1. Remember that raw, visceral pain? That feeling of being lost in a thick fog of emotion? Compare that to now. You're not the same man. You've weathered storms, navigated complex emotions, rebuilt shattered foundations. That's growth. Real, tangible growth.

Many guys in your shoes would've been paralyzed by their circumstances. They'd have let the pain define them. But not you. You hustled, you learned, you adapted. Every single day, in small ways and big, you moved forward. Even on days when it felt like you were sinking, you were learning how to swim.

It's easy to forget our progress, especially when daily life keeps hitting us with fresh challenges. But take a moment, dude. Breathe it in. Acknowledge the journey you've been on, the battles you've faced, the mountains you've climbed.

Now, don't dwell. This isn't about patting yourself on the back and getting complacent. No way. This is fuel. Because if you've come this far from where you began, just think about where you can be a year from now, two years, a decade!

This is just a chapter in your book, and there's so much story left to write. Don't just acknowledge your journey, own it. Because from where I'm standing, it looks like the making of a legend.

Daily Challenge: Embrace the growth you've achieved on this journey and use it as fuel to propel yourself forward, knowing that you have the power to shape the legendary chapters of your future.

Daily Reflection:

What resonated with you from today's lesson? How can you apply this truth in your life?

_____

_____

_____

Day 325: Skill Building- Never Stop Learning

The moment you think you've got it all figured out, that's the exact moment you're losing the game. Life after divorce? It's uncharted waters, brother. And if you're not evolving, adapting, and picking up new skills, you're stagnant. And nobody, I mean nobody, has time for that.

There's a world out there bursting with opportunities to learn, to adapt, to grow. Picking up new skills? It's not just about distraction from the pain, though it does help. It's about empowerment. It's about proving to yourself that no matter what curveballs life throws, you can step up to the plate.

See, the game has changed. You're not just navigating single life; you're navigating the challenge of becoming the best version of yourself. Want to be better? Good. Now work for it. Dive deep. Learn a new language, pick up a guitar, hit a boxing class, or dive into the world of coding. Whatever ignites that fire, whatever makes you feel alive and hungry again, chase that.

Every new skill is another tool in your arsenal, another way to show the world, but more importantly, show yourself that you're not done. Far from it. Life might have given you a setback, but every day is a new opportunity. Every skill, every lesson, every mistake, and every win is a brick in the fortress you're building.

You've got two choices: sit back and let life happen, or grab it by the horns and steer. Dive into the unknown. Embrace the discomfort of learning. Because on the other side of that discomfort? That's where the real magic happens. That's where you find the version of yourself that can handle anything. So go, chase it. Never stop learning.

Daily Challenge: Embrace the discomfort of learning something new today, whether it's a skill, a hobby, or a passion project, and take one step closer to becoming the best version of yourself.

Daily Reflection:

What resonated with you from today's lesson? How can you apply this truth in your life?

_____

_____

_____

_____

Day 326: Confidence Boosters- Empower Yourself

You've heard it before, but let's get it straight: confidence isn't something you're just born with. It's crafted, chiseled, built brick by brick. Every setback, every "no", every doubt-filled night? That's just another brick. But you're the architect here. Lay it down, build it up. Diving deep into the world post-divorce isn't for the faint of heart.

It's raw, it's real, and it's relentless. But guess what? So are you. That pain you're feeling? It's the old you shedding away, making room for the unstoppable force you're about to become.

Too often, we let the narrative of our past dictate the story of our future. Flip that. Your past? That's just the prequel. The real story starts now, with a blank page and a world full of possibilities. And if you're looking for a sign? This is it.

Get back to basics. Remember what lights you up, what gets that fire in your belly raging. Dive into that passion project, hit the gym, read that book. Fill your life with the stuff that reminds you of who you really are, and who you're becoming.

It's not about faking it till you make it. It's about recognizing your worth, your value, and going out there and owning it. Nobody's going to hand it to you on a silver platter. Confidence is claimed, not given. So what are you waiting for? You've got the tools, the drive, the fire.

Now, go out there and build that empire of confidence. Remember, it's not about proving them wrong; it's about proving yourself right. Empower yourself. Own your narrative. Change the game.

Daily Challenge: Embrace the challenge of building your confidence brick by brick, knowing that every setback and doubt-filled moment is an opportunity for growth and self-empowerment on your journey of post-divorce reinvention.

Daily Reflection:

What resonated with you from today's lesson? How can you apply this truth in your life?

_____

_____

_____

_____

Day 327: Giving Back- New Ways to Contribute

Giving back isn't just about charity. It's about integrity. It's about understanding that even though you've been through hell, there's a world out there that needs you. Think about it. Your experiences, your pain, your growth—they've all built you up. They've forged a version of you that can understand, empathize, and uplift. So, what's stopping you from stepping up?

Life has kicked you, sure. But life has also taught you. The very same fire that brought you down has the power to light up someone else's world. Maybe it's mentoring a kid who's going through his parents' divorce. Maybe it's volunteering at a shelter, giving hope to those whose hope meter is running on empty. Or maybe it's just being that ear for a friend who needs it, because now, you get it.

This isn't about brownie points or karma. This is about understanding that every challenge we face shapes us into someone who can make a difference. It's about refusing to let your experiences be just about you. It's about turning pain into purpose. You have a unique perspective, a blend of toughness and compassion that only life's hardest lessons can instill.

You've been given a second shot at defining who you are. Make it count. There's a bigger play here than just recovering from your divorce. It's about rising above it, transforming from it, and using that wisdom to ignite a spark in others. So, while you're building this new normal, remember: your legacy isn't just about what you take from the world, but what you give back. Dive deep into that, and watch how the act of giving transforms not just those around you, but yourself.

Daily Challenge: Today, challenge yourself to identify one small way in which you can give back to others, whether it's offering a listening ear, volunteering your time, or sharing your experiences to uplift someone who needs it, and take a step towards turning your pain into purpose.

Daily Reflection:

What resonated with you from today's lesson? How can you apply this truth in your life?

_____

_____

_____

_____

Day 328: Resilience- Embrace Your Strength

Diving headfirst into resilience? Let's tackle it. Look, life's thrown you a curveball. Divorce? It's more like a punch in the gut when you least expect it. But here's the thing, brother, that pain, that uncertainty? It's not your weakness. It's your bloody proving ground. Every challenge, every hurtful word, every cold, sleepless night – they're not there to break you; they're there to mold you, to test the mettle you're made of.

Resilience isn't about pretending the hurt doesn't exist. It's about feeling that sting and choosing to move forward anyway. It's about looking adversity square in the eyes and saying, "Is that all you got?" You're more than this moment. More than this hurt. You're a sum of experiences, lessons, triumphs, and yes, failures. But those failures? They're just stepping stones, not gravestones.

Stop seeking validation. Your strength isn't defined by other people's opinions. Hell, it's not even defined by your past. It's sculpted right here, right now, in how you choose to react, adapt, and overcome. Remember, trees that face the strongest winds often have the deepest roots.

So, when the world's trying to label you, box you in, or keep you down, embrace that inner grit. Find solace in the fact that you're not the same guy you were yesterday, and tomorrow, you'll be even stronger.

Lean into the struggle, wear your scars with pride, and know that resilience is the fire that forges legends. Don't just survive this; own it. Stand tall, embrace your strength, and let the world see what you're made of.

Daily Challenge: Embrace the pain and uncertainty as opportunities to forge your resilience; in the face of adversity, choose to move forward with unwavering determination and the knowledge that you are becoming stronger with each challenge.

Daily Reflection:

What resonated with you from today's lesson? How can you apply this truth in your life?

_____

_____

_____

_____

Day 329: Your New Life- Revel in It

Your new life? It's a blank canvas, man. A chance to redefine who you are and what you stand for. Yeah, the past might've sucked, but guess what? The future is up to you.

You've got this incredible opportunity to rebuild, not just your routines, but your entire mindset. It's time to hustle harder for your own happiness. Start by injecting passion back into your veins. Remember those hobbies you pushed aside? Dive back in. Paint, write, surf, whatever makes your heart race.

And your health? It's non-negotiable. Hit the gym, nourish your body, and fuel your mind. You're a machine, and it's time to fine-tune it.

Financially? Take charge. Reevaluate your goals, create a game plan, and chase those dreams like a beast. Your bank account should never dictate your worth.

Your living space? Make it your sanctuary. It should scream "YOU." Rearrange, redecorate, or move if you want. This is your castle; design it like a king.

Social circles? Expand 'em. Surround yourself with people who lift you up, who believe in your potential. Cut loose the dead weight; they're just anchors.

This new life? It's about seizing control, unapologetically. There's no time for pity parties. Grind, grow, and get what's yours. It's time to rise, brother. Are you ready to conquer your new life? Yes, you are.

Daily Challenge: Embrace the opportunity to redefine yourself and your life, starting by reigniting your passions, prioritizing your health, taking charge of your finances, transforming your living space, and expanding your supportive social circles to create the life you truly desire.

Daily Reflection:

What resonated with you from today's lesson? How can you apply this truth in your life?

_____

_____

_____

_____

Day 330: New Normal Milestone- What's Next?

Here's the unvarnished truth, my friend: You've journeyed through the darkest storms of divorce, and now, it's time to embrace your new normal. No more dwelling in the wreckage. This is your moment of rebirth.

Your routines, once shattered, are now yours to reconstruct. Remember, it's not about merely surviving; it's about thriving. Forge new habits that uplift you. That means hustling at work while making space for the passions and hobbies you had set aside. It's about becoming a force of nature.

Finances? Take control. Craft a financial plan that secures your future. You're not relying on anyone else anymore. It's your path to financial freedom. Your health? Non-negotiable. Prioritize it like never before. Hit the gym, run that extra mile, fuel your body with what it deserves. Your health is your wealth.

Your living space? Make it yours. Redecorate, reimagine, create a sanctuary where you thrive. This is your sanctuary of self-discovery. Expand your social circle. Reconnect with old friends and welcome new faces. Surround yourself with those who uplift you, who reflect your journey towards a brighter future.

This is your chance to craft an empowered, fulfilling life. There's no script, no preordained path. It's you, carving your destiny with the chisel of resilience. So, what's next? Whatever the hell you want it to be. This is your story, your narrative. Embrace it with the ferocity of a warrior and the wisdom of a sage. It's time to rise and conquer, my friend. Your new normal is a canvas; now, paint your masterpiece.

Daily Challenge: Today, take the first step towards rebuilding your routines and embracing your new normal by setting aside dedicated time for one of your long-forgotten passions or hobbies, and let it remind you of the strength within you.

Daily Reflection:

What resonated with you from today's lesson? How can you apply this truth in your life?

_____

_____

_____

_____

You Survived, Now Thrive

As you journey through Days 331 to 365, it's time to reflect on the past year of your life post-divorce. These days mark a profound period of self-assessment and growth.

You'll review your milestones and emotional inventory, embracing the lessons learned along the way. It's a time to express gratitude for your support network and celebrate your resilience and transformation.

Financially, you'll recap gains and losses, while in relationships, you'll navigate a new landscape. You'll also plan for the future, set intentions, and bid a fond farewell to Year One, ushering in the dawn of your next chapter with hope and optimism.

Day 331: Redefining Your Success

Hey, you! Ever feel like you're playing catch-up in life? Like you're running someone else's race and can't keep up? Don't sweat it. Too many of us fall into the trap of age-based benchmarks. You're 30 and haven't launched a business? Chill. Life isn't a fixed timeline. Your purpose and passion don't come with an expiration date.

Success? It's personal. Maybe you're all about that jet-setting life or, heck, living off the grid in a tent. Maybe it's about the luxury cars for you. That's cool. Define YOUR success. And be open to it changing. Me? 15 years ago, success was owning gyms. Today? It's sharing insights on YouTube. Life's unexpected, so roll with it.

Been there, done that, and let me tell ya – your definition of success can flip. I remember when my world came crashing down. Best thing ever.

Don't strive for perfection. Aim for progress. It's okay to stumble and mess up. The real win? Learning from it and pushing forward. You're progressing? Congrats, you're succeeding. Cut out those toxic habits, like drowning your fears in a bottle. Challenge yourself – no booze for 30 days. See the change. And hey, that shady crew holding you back? Ditch 'em. Your crew should be leveling you up, not pulling you down. Remember, your vibe attracts your tribe.

Started from the bottom? Good. That grind gives you a unique edge. Less resources? No problem. Stay driven, stay curious, and success will taste so much sweeter. Remember: be optimistic, stay humble, and always be hungry.

Daily Challenge: Today, take a moment to reflect on your own definition of success, write it down, and embrace the idea that it can evolve over time – then share your evolving vision with a supportive friend or family member to reinforce your commitment to personal growth.

Daily Reflection:

What resonated with you from today's lesson? How can you apply this truth in your life?

_____

_____

_____

_____

Day 332: Unlocking Your Unique Greatness in an Average World

Hey, you! Let's get real for a moment. Ever dive into your social media feed and feel like you're just not living up to the hype? Those glitzy posts of everyone "killing it" got you questioning your worth? Let me break it down for you.

See, the game isn't about reaching that shiny 1%. It's about embracing who YOU are and maximizing what YOU can bring to the table. We all have our super strengths and our, well, not-so-super ones. And that's okay. The hustle is about improving from where YOU stand, not where you think the world wants you to stand.

I get it. Growing up, my pockets were empty, and my confidence? Even emptier. But I turned my focus to what I could control. My style. My physique. They became my arenas of self-improvement. Maybe you're not gonna be the next Elon Musk or LeBron James, but what if you could be the best YOU?

Too many of us get caught up in this race to be what social media glorifies. That's a trap! Stop setting unattainable benchmarks based on other people's highlight reels. It's like trying to drink from a firehose—exhausting and pointless. Your real growth? It's measured by YOUR progress, not theirs. Worked harder today than you did yesterday? That's a win! Improved in ways that matter to YOU? That's the real deal.

Bottom line: Stop aiming for universal perfection—it's a mirage. Choose your battles, dominate in those, and celebrate your unique greatness in this average world. You've got this! Don't measure against everyone else; just outdo YOUR yesterday. And remember, starting from average doesn't mean staying average.

Daily Challenge: Instead of comparing yourself to others on social media, focus on one area of self-improvement that matters to you and take a concrete step towards becoming the best version of yourself.

Daily Reflection:

What resonated with you from today's lesson? How can you apply this truth in your life?

_____

_____

_____

_____

Day 333: Lessons Learned- Wisdom Gained

Lessons learned, my friend, they're your battle scars, not your baggage. Every shattered dream, every betrayal, they're your university of hard knocks, and the tuition fee is high. But guess what? You've earned that degree in resilience.

See, life's punches, they don't define you; they refine you. You've been through the emotional wringer, tasted the bitterness of heartbreak, but you didn't crumble. You stood tall when your world crumbled.

That wisdom you've gained, it's worth more than gold. You know now that love isn't just a fairy tale; it's a choice, a commitment. You understand the importance of boundaries and self-respect. You've learned that happiness, real happiness, starts within.

You've discovered the power of reinvention. You're not who you were, and you wouldn't want to be. You've upgraded, my man. You've unearthed passions you'd long buried. You've embraced change with open arms.

Those sleepless nights, they've gifted you clarity. You've uncovered your strengths and confronted your weaknesses. You've learned the art of forgiveness, not for them, but for your peace of mind.

So, don't carry your past like a burden; carry it like a badge of honor. Embrace those lessons, my friend, because they've molded you into the remarkable man you are today. Your journey is far from over; your best days are still ahead. Keep moving forward, armed with the wisdom you've earned.

Daily Challenge: Today, let go of the weight of your past and wear your battle scars as a badge of honor, for they have forged the resilient and remarkable man you are becoming.

Daily Reflection:

What resonated with you from today's lesson? How can you apply this truth in your life?

_____

_____

_____

_____

Day 334: Your Support Network- Give Thanks

Listen up, brother. In the storm of divorce, your support network becomes your lifeline. Those friends who stood by your side, the family that lent an ear when you needed it most, they're your unsung heroes.

It's easy to get lost in the anger and resentment, but don't forget to look around and appreciate the soldiers who've been fighting in your corner. They're the ones who offered a shoulder when your world crumbled, who reminded you of your worth when you doubted it the most.

Your support network, they're your compass pointing you toward the new you. They're the reason you're still standing, still fighting. So give thanks. Not just on Thanksgiving, but every day.

Tell your best friend you love 'em. Hug your mom. Send a text to your brother, even if it's just to say, "Hey, thanks for having my back." Because, my friend, gratitude is the glue that strengthens those connections.

And when the dust settles, and you've rebuilt your life, don't forget the ones who stood by you through the chaos. They're the real MVPs, and they deserve to know it. So give thanks, and watch how the bonds of brotherhood grow stronger, even in the midst of the toughest battles.

Daily Challenge: Today, reach out to at least one person in your support network and express your gratitude for their unwavering presence in your life during this challenging journey of divorce.

Daily Reflection:

What resonated with you from today's lesson? How can you apply this truth in your life?

_____

_____

_____

_____

Day 335: Rise Above Average

Hey you! Dive into this dose of cold, hard truth. You've been spoon-fed some sugary tales by social media, society, even by your folks. They've whispered sweet nothings, hinting that you're destined for greatness just because you breathe. But here's the real talk: the majority of us? We're average. It's a pill that's hard to swallow but essential for growth.

Yet, inside that word "average" is a hidden promise. It means there's a whole other world of potential. To tap into it, it's going to take more than just dreaming. It demands hustle, sweat, tears, and, most importantly, heart. The grind doesn't understand background, inheritance, or luck; it only respects dedication.

You see those glittering 1% on social media? The ones that make you feel like your achievements are but a speck of dust? Remember this: social media isn't a mirror. It's a highlight reel, selectively showing the spectacular while masking the struggles. Comparing your every day to their best day? It's a trap. Your value isn't determined by someone else's curated feeds or flamboyant stories.

Then there's appearance. Yup, it matters. Not because the world is shallow but because your appearance reflects how you feel about yourself. Those first impressions? They're lasting. Looking good isn't about vanity; it's about self-respect. Show up as the best version of yourself, and the world will respond in kind.

And the people around you? Cut out the toxicity. Anyone dimming your shine doesn't deserve a front-row seat in your life. At the end of the day, remember: it's less about the cards you're dealt and more about how you play them. So, play them right and rise above.

Daily Challenge: Embrace your average, acknowledge your hidden potential, and commit to the hustle, sweat, and heart it takes to tap into it, knowing that your worth isn't defined by others' curated images or opinions but by your dedication and self-respect.

Daily Reflection:

What resonated with you from today's lesson? How can you apply this truth in your life?

_____

_____

_____

Day 336: Be The Genuine You, Not The Social Media You

The future is not about being the loudest, the richest, or the flashiest. It's about genuine kindness. Ever wondered about the difference between a 'nice guy' and a genuinely nice person? The 'nice guy' has an agenda. He does things expecting something in return. But real, authentic people? They're just kind. They help others without expecting anything back. Why? Pure heart.

And let's chat about society for a second. This "you're with us or against us" mindset? It's toxic. We used to respect differing opinions. Now? Disagree, and suddenly you're an enemy. People want to put you in boxes: alpha, beta, this, that. But life isn't black and white. Most of us are in the gray. Seeing rich, flashy personalities on social media and thinking that's success? Stop it. Don't fall for the highlight reel. True success? It's about self-worth and being the best version of you.

Money? Been there, done that. I've been broke, and trust me, having money is better. But only to a point. When you don't constantly worry about the next bill, you free up mental space. But equating cash with success? Wrong move. Real talk: Buying flashy things gives a temporary high, but it fades. Chasing those highs? Dangerous game.

Here's the real tea. You might feel pressure to fit a mold society's crafted for 'successful men'. Forget that. Success isn't about being an alpha or beta. It's about intention and character. Throughout your journey, your idea of success will evolve. But remember this: giving without expecting? It's a gift to yourself. It feeds the soul. So go on, be the best you. Not for the likes or follows, but for yourself.

Daily Challenge: Today, practice an act of kindness without expecting anything in return, and remember that genuine kindness is a gift to yourself that feeds your soul.

Daily Reflection:

What resonated with you from today's lesson? How can you apply this truth in your life?

_____

_____

_____

Day 337: Your Children- Celebrate Their Resilience

In the vast playbook of life and business, there's a secret weapon often overlooked: likability. Think of it as your quiet superpower, an edge that can transform relationships, careers, and yep, even connections with those spicy senoritas. Start by infusing every interaction with genuine compliments. There's no sweeter music to the ears than honest praise. It's like a feel-good exchange; you light up giving it and they glow receiving it. But remember, the key is authenticity. In a world crowded with facades, being genuinely you is refreshing. Drop the act, be open, be vulnerable. It magnetically draws people in, creating a space where they too can shed their layers.

Ever notice how some people can light up a room just by walking in? They're often the ones who embrace light-hearted humor, occasionally poking fun at themselves, all in good spirit. They radiate stories and experiences, making them captivating narrators in life's grand theater. And you? You can be that too. Broaden your horizons, absorb new experiences, and share.

Here's another secret sauce: social intelligence. Mastering the unspoken, from a genuine smile to understanding body language, can elevate connections. Dive into resources, like online courses, and you'll soon navigate social terrains with finesse. In a world of give and take, stand out by simply giving. Whether it's your time, a listening ear, or gestures of kindness, do it without expecting a return ticket. When you actively listen, you validate others, making them feel valued.

To sum it up, being likable isn't about reinventing yourself. It's about enhancing what's already there. It's about inviting people into your world with authenticity and warmth. And as you do, you'll find doors opening, opportunities knocking, and connections deepening. So, unlock that superpower and let your likability shine.

Daily Challenge: Embrace your likability superpower by giving genuine compliments, being authentic, and sharing stories with a light-hearted spirit, while mastering social intelligence and giving selflessly, to deepen connections in your post-divorce journey.

Daily Reflection:

What resonated with you from today's lesson? How can you apply this truth in your life?

_____

_____

_____

Day 338: Love Rediscovered- The New Relationship Landscape

Congratulations, my friend, you've traversed the treacherous terrain of divorce and emerged scarred but stronger. Now, it's time to set sail on the uncharted waters of love once again. You see, the scars you bear aren't battle wounds; they're badges of resilience. You've learned the hard way that love isn't a fairytale, but it's still worth chasing.

The new relationship landscape? It's not the same as when you left it. It's a wild, unpredictable beast. But here's the truth - you're not the same either. You've evolved, grown wiser, and discovered your worth. In this new chapter, keep your eyes wide open. Gone are the days of naivety. Now, it's about authenticity, about being unapologetically you. Don't settle; demand reciprocity, respect, and real connection.

Remember, vulnerability is not a weakness; it's your superpower. Show up as your true self, flaws and all, because authenticity attracts authenticity. And patience? It's your greatest ally. Love may not strike like lightning this time, but when it does, it will be worth the wait.

This journey isn't about finding someone to complete you; it's about finding someone who complements you. It's about two whole people, walking side by side.

So, my fellow survivor, embrace this new love landscape with open arms. Take risks, learn, and love like you've never been hurt before. You've survived; now, it's time to thrive in love's wild, beautiful chaos.

Daily Challenge: Embrace the new love landscape with an open heart, and today, make a list of the qualities and values that truly matter to you in a partner, setting clear intentions for the kind of love you deserve and are willing to give.

Daily Reflection:

What resonated with you from today's lesson? How can you apply this truth in your life?

_____

_____

_____

_____

Day 339: Career and Ambitions- A Year's Progress

Y ou made it through the storm, brother. A year of heartache, self-discovery, and reinvention. But here's the kicker – surviving isn't enough; you're built for more. Your career? It's your playground, a place to unleash your untamed ambition. Remember those dreams you had, the ones she might've dimmed? It's time to dust 'em off, my friend. You've got an edge now, a battle-tested resilience that most can't even fathom. That's your secret weapon.

No, it won't be easy. The climb is steep, but remember, you're not alone. Lean on mentors, network like a beast, and keep hustling. Your dreams aren't some distant fantasy; they're your new reality. Balance? It's not a myth. In this new life, you've got the reins. So, set boundaries, prioritize self-care, and carve out space for what truly matters – your happiness, your goals, your legacy.

And health? It's non-negotiable. Hit that gym, eat right, and get enough sleep. You're not just surviving; you're thriving, and that means fueling your body and mind for peak performance.

Your living space? It's a reflection of your newfound freedom. Redecorate, create an environment that screams, "This is MY life now!" Let every corner resonate with your aspirations. Your social circle? Expand it. Forge new connections, rekindle old friendships, and surround yourself with people who lift you higher. Energy is contagious, so choose wisely.

This is your year of progress, man. A year that defines you not by what you've lost, but by what you've gained – resilience, wisdom, and the unwavering belief that you can turn any setback into a comeback. Now, go out there and conquer your dreams. Thrive. Because you've not just survived; you've become the embodiment of strength and possibility. The world ain't seen nothing yet.

Daily Challenge: Today, take a concrete step towards reviving one of your long-forgotten dreams or aspirations that were dimmed by the past, and let your battle-tested resilience propel you toward making it a reality.

Daily Reflection:

What resonated with you from today's lesson? How can you apply this truth in your life?

_____

_____

_____

_____

Day 340: The Power of Gratitude- Count Your Blessings

Divorce didn't break you; it forged you. Now, it's time to thrive, to harness the power of gratitude like a warrior. Look back at how far you've come. Remember those nights you thought you couldn't bear the pain? Yet, you did. Remember the uncertainty? Yet, you found your way. Every scar, every tear, they're not weaknesses; they're badges of honor.

Life post-divorce, it's your canvas. You're the artist, and gratitude? It's your palette. Count your blessings. Not because it erases the past, but because it shapes your future. In the quiet moments, appreciate the simple things. The warmth of your morning coffee, the laughter of a friend, the chance to chase your passions. These are the building blocks of your new life.

Take a deep breath, my man. Feel the power of this moment. You've shed the weight of a broken relationship, and now, your wings are yours to spread. You're no longer defined by your past; you're sculpting your own legacy. Gratitude isn't just about saying "thank you" for what you have. It's about recognizing that you have everything you need to create a life that's uniquely yours. The pain was real, but so is your strength.

So, step into the world with your head held high. Embrace your journey, scars and all. The power of gratitude will guide you, light your path, and remind you that every day is a new canvas, waiting for your masterpiece. Survived? Yes, and now, it's time to thrive.

Daily Challenge: Today, take a few moments to write down three things you're grateful for, no matter how small they may seem, and carry that positive energy with you throughout the day as a reminder of your strength and the potential for growth.

Daily Reflection:

What resonated with you from today's lesson? How can you apply this truth in your life?

_____

_____

_____

_____

Day 341: Revisit and Reflect

The storm of divorce tested you in ways you never imagined. But look at you now - still standing, stronger and wiser. It's time to revisit those earlier writings, the raw and honest pages where you poured out your heart. This workbook journal isn't just a collection of words; it's a reminder of your journey. Those early entries might be filled with pain, confusion, and anger. But they're also infused with your resilience and determination.

As you flip through those pages, don't cringe at the past. Embrace it. Every tear-stained sentence, every angry scrawl - they're proof that you faced your demons head-on. You didn't run, you didn't hide. You met your pain in the arena. Now, reflect on how far you've come. See the evolution. Notice the growth. There's a fire within you that couldn't be extinguished. You've learned the hard way that life isn't fair, but you're not defined by your scars; you're defined by how you wear them.

Use this journal as a mirror, not to dwell on the past, but to see the transformation in your reflection. It's not about being a victim; it's about being a warrior. The pain you felt, the battles you fought - they've forged a man of steel.

So, my friend, close this chapter with pride. You survived the storm. Now, it's time to thrive. This journal is your reminder - you're not just a survivor; you're a conqueror. Carry that truth into the next chapter of your life and let it shine brighter than any darkness you've faced.

Daily Challenge: Open your journal, reread those early, raw entries, and with each word you wrote in pain, find a nugget of resilience and strength, allowing your past to fuel your determination for a brighter future.

Daily Reflection:

What resonated with you from today's lesson? How can you apply this truth in your life?

_____

_____

_____

_____

Day 342: Your New Identity- Embrace and Own It

The storm of divorce has tested you in ways you never imagined. But here's the beauty of it: you've emerged stronger, wiser, and battle-hardened. Now, it's time to confront a fundamental truth: you are not defined by your past, your ex, or the pain you've endured. You are defined by the person you choose to be today. This is your new identity, and it's a clean slate, my friend.

Embrace it with open arms. Embrace the freedom to rediscover yourself. Remember those passions you put on hold? Dust them off. Those dreams you shelved? They're yours to chase now. Own it. You've been through hell and back; that's your badge of honor. Your scars tell a story of survival, strength, and growth.

Don't seek validation from anyone but yourself. You don't need anyone else to define your worth. You're a warrior, a survivor. You've conquered your inner demons and emerged victorious. In this new chapter, life is what you make it. So, set audacious goals, chase your dreams relentlessly, and never settle for mediocrity. Your past doesn't dictate your future. It's a canvas, and you're the artist.

Thriving after divorce isn't a luxury; it's your birthright. Lean into your newfound independence. Invest in your passions, your health, and your happiness. Build the life you deserve, on your terms. You've survived. Now, it's time to thrive. This is your moment, your rebirth. Own it, brother, and let your new identity shine as an indication of your unbreakable spirit.

Daily Challenge: Embrace your new identity and the clean slate of possibilities it offers, setting audacious goals and chasing your dreams relentlessly, for you are defined by the person you choose to be today.

Daily Reflection:

What resonated with you from today's lesson? How can you apply this truth in your life?

_____

_____

_____

_____

Day 343: The Things You've Let Go- A Farewell

My friend, you've come through the fire, walked through the storm, and faced the darkest demons of your soul. You've let go of the weight that was dragging you down—whether it was a toxic relationship, bitterness, or the ghosts of your past.

You've tasted the bitter pill of heartbreak, and yet you stand taller and stronger. You're not a victim anymore; you're a survivor. But here's the real kicker: surviving isn't the endgame; thriving is.

In letting go, you've made space for something incredible. You've unleashed the power to craft your own destiny. Those painful scars you bear? They're not weaknesses; they're badges of honor, symbols of your resilience.

Now, as you look ahead, remember this: your past does not define you. Your future does. The pain you've felt is real, but so is the potential within you. The world is waiting for the unleashed version of yourself—the one who's unafraid, unabashed, and unapologetically YOU.

What are you passionate about? What sets your soul on fire? What dreams have you been sidelining? It's time to dust them off. Time to chase them with a fervor you've never known. You've let go of the baggage; now fill that space with ambition, purpose, and unwavering determination.

You're no longer shackled by the past; you're empowered by your future. Embrace the uncertainty; it's where growth thrives. Life is too short to dwell on what's gone; it's time to celebrate what's coming. You've survived; now, my friend, it's your moment to thrive. Seize it with everything you've got.

Daily Challenge: Today, identify one passion or dream that sets your soul on fire and take a small, concrete step towards making it a reality, because your future is waiting for the unleashed version of yourself.

Daily Reflection:

What resonated with you from today's lesson? How can you apply this truth in your life?

_____

_____

_____

_____

Day 344: Your New Skill Set- Tools for Life

Divorce wasn't just an end; it was your rebirth. Look around; you're standing on the battlefield of life, scars as badges of honor. You survived. But this isn't just about surviving; it's about thriving. What did you gain? A set of skills sharper than a double-edged sword. Resilience, empathy, and self-reliance, honed in the crucible of heartbreak. You know how to navigate chaos, make tough decisions, and emerge stronger.

Now, let's put that toolbox to use. Channel that resilience into your career; you're a force to be reckoned with. Use your newfound empathy to connect with others on a deeper level. And as for self-reliance? It's your secret weapon. You've learned that the only person you can truly rely on is yourself. Remember those hobbies you rediscovered? Keep nurturing them; they're your outlets, your passions. Pour your heart into them; it's therapy for the soul.

Financial planning isn't just a chore; it's your roadmap to freedom. Invest wisely, save diligently, and build your future. Health isn't a luxury; it's your foundation. Eat well, train hard, and cherish the body that carries your dreams.

Your living space? It's not just four walls; it's your sanctuary. Make it yours, from the colors on the wall to the pictures on the shelf. Your social circle? It's a reflection of your growth. Surround yourself with those who lift you higher, who celebrate your victories.

You've survived the storm. Now thrive in the sunlight of your new life. Embrace your scars, wear them as badges of strength, and remember, the future is yours to shape.

Daily Challenge: Embrace your scars as badges of strength, and use the resilience, empathy, and self-reliance you've gained to forge a path to thriving in your career, deepening connections, nurturing your passions, securing your financial future, and creating a sanctuary of well-being in your life.

Daily Reflection:

What resonated with you from today's lesson? How can you apply this truth in your life?

_____

_____

_____

_____

Day 345: The Keepsakes- Mementos and Memories

Now, it's time to sift through the keepsakes of your past, those mementos and memories that once bound you to a different life. See, memories are like old photographs, capturing moments in time. Some are bittersweet, etching lessons into your soul. Others are pure gold, reminders of laughter, love, and joy. Hold on to those, my friend, for they're the treasures that sustain you.

As you unpack the boxes of your past, don't let bitterness cloud your vision. Yeah, you've been through hell, but look around—your life is full of blank canvases. It's time to paint new memories, craft fresh keepsakes. Feel the freedom coursing through your veins? It's electric. Use it to reinvent yourself, to rediscover passions you left behind. Those dusty hobbies, neglected talents—breathe life into them once more. Embrace the symphony of your interests.

And finances? Tighten that ship, build a future fortified by wisdom. Invest in your health because vitality is your currency. A strong body and mind are the greatest assets. As your living space undergoes a makeover, let it mirror your evolution. Surround yourself with what inspires and uplifts you. Your sanctuary should breathe peace and purpose.

Finally, your social circle will expand. New friends, new allies—embrace them with an open heart. Let their stories inspire you, and in turn, inspire them with your resilience. So, here's the deal: You've survived the storm, and now, it's time to thrive. Keep the lessons, let go of the baggage, and sculpt a life that's truly yours. The keepsakes are the guideposts of your journey, but the future, my friend, is the masterpiece you get to create. Now, go and paint it bold, vibrant, and unapologetically yours.

Daily Challenge: Today, take a step towards reinventing yourself by dusting off an old hobby or talent that once brought you joy, and embrace the symphony of your interests as you embark on this journey of self-discovery and transformation.

Daily Reflection:

What resonated with you from today's lesson? How can you apply this truth in your life?

_____

_____

_____

_____

Day 346: Breaking the Cycle and Embracing Positivity

Listen up! You've got this unique gift, my friend. It's called self-reflection and freewill. Yep, YOU have the power to look at your past, your present, and then decide what you want your future to look like. Now, here's the kicker: If you don't believe that tweaking your mindset and actions will bring change, guess what? You're stuck! That's the real-life hamster wheel. Trust me, if you're running that cycle of doubt, you're basically setting yourself up for the same old outcomes.

We all have moments when we lean into negativity, even when things are going great. But guess what? That's not you being a downer; it's just those old-school survival genes trying to prep you for the worst. They're keeping you on your toes. I see so many of you getting frustrated, comparing your progress to others, or doubting your journey. Listen, that's okay! Recognizing that side of yourself? That's step one. It means you're becoming conscious of what's holding you back.

But here's the thing: When you're trapped in those negative emotions, your perception gets cloudy. You almost start seeking reasons to stay frustrated or fearful. And the more you live in that zone, the harder things become. It's like you're stuck in this negative feedback loop.

So, what can you do about it? Recognize when you're in that negative loop. Hit the pause button. Reset and go again. It's honestly that straightforward. When you actively make choices that uplift you, you'll naturally lean into more of those positive decisions. Even if it means stepping out of a situation for a hot minute to recalibrate, those small moves can flip the script on your entire day, health, or life trajectory. So, go out there and choose your vibe!.

Daily Challenge: Embrace the power of self-reflection and freewill today; when you catch yourself in a negative loop, hit the pause button, reset your mindset, and actively choose positivity to shape your future.

Daily Reflection:

What resonated with you from today's lesson? How can you apply this truth in your life?

_____

_____

_____

_____

Day 347: The New You in Relationships- Friends and Family

As you rebuild your life, remember this: the new you is a force to be reckoned with. Your strength, resilience, and wisdom are your most potent weapons. In the realm of relationships, be deliberate. Those who stood by your side during the chaos, hold them close. They're your anchors. They've seen you at your worst and still believe in your best.

But here's the truth - not everyone in your old circle will belong in your new chapter. People change, and so do your needs. It's okay to distance yourself from toxic ties. Your mental health and happiness are non-negotiable. In the family arena, redefine your role. If you're a dad, your kids are watching. Show them what it means to bounce back stronger. Be present, not just physically, but emotionally too. Be the kind of role model you wish you had.

Now, friendships. Forge new connections. Seek out those who inspire you, who share your values, and challenge you to grow. Build a tribe of like-minded warriors who push you to be the best version of yourself. And in the midst of it all, never forget who you've become. You're battle-hardened, wiser, and ready to conquer the world. The scars you carry are badges of honor, not signs of weakness.

So, my friend, take a deep breath. You've survived. Now, thrive. The new you is a powerhouse, a beacon of resilience, and a testament to the indomitable human spirit. Embrace this new chapter with open arms and let your light shine brighter than ever before. Your future is limitless.

Daily Challenge: Today, reflect on your relationships and take a deliberate step to nurture the bonds with those who supported you through your challenges, while also having the courage to distance yourself from toxic connections that hinder your growth.

Daily Reflection:

What resonated with you from today's lesson? How can you apply this truth in your life?

_____

_____

_____

_____

Day 348: A Letter to Your Future Self

Listen up, man. Writing a letter to your future self is not just some sappy exercise. It's a power move, a statement of intent. You've come through the fire of divorce, battled your demons, and rebuilt your life. Now, it's time to declare to the universe what you're about.

In this letter, don't hold back. Lay it all out - your goals, your dreams, your vision for the future. Promise yourself that you won't settle for mediocrity or play it safe. You've faced the darkness; now chase the light.

Tell your future self that you'll keep pushing boundaries, that you'll never lose that hunger for growth and self-improvement. And remind yourself, always, that you're a survivor, a warrior who's been through hell and back.

This letter is your contract with destiny. It's your battle cry, your rally call. Read it when you need motivation, when doubt creeps in, when life throws curveballs.

So grab that pen and write like your life depends on it, because it does. This letter is your reminder that you're in control of your destiny, and you're ready to shape it. You're not just surviving; you're thriving. Your future self is waiting. Make sure you're worth the wait.

Daily Challenge: Today, take a moment to write a letter to your future self, reaffirming your commitment to pursue your dreams, push boundaries, and thrive as a survivor of life's challenges.

Daily Reflection:

What resonated with you from today's lesson? How can you apply this truth in your life?

_____

_____

_____

_____

Day 349: Your New Comfort Zones- What Scares You?

Your new comfort zones lie beyond the battlefield of divorce. They're where growth happens, where you shed the skin of your former self, and emerge as a battle-hardened warrior of life.

What scares you? Is it the thought of dating again? Of trusting someone new? Or maybe it's the idea of taking that job you've always dreamed of, the one that's far outside your old cubicle.

Guess what? Those fears are your compass. They point the way to your next level. Your old comfort zone was a cage, familiar but confining. Your new one? A vast, uncharted territory, teeming with opportunities.

Remember, courage isn't the absence of fear; it's action in spite of it. So, face your fears head-on. Swipe right on that dating app. Take that interview. Start that business. Dare to dream again.

Don't let the pain of your past define your future. Use it as fuel to ignite your passion, purpose, and ambition. Embrace your scars, for they are your badges of honor.

You've survived the storm, my friend. You're not the same man who began this journey. You're wiser, stronger, and more resilient. Now, go out there and conquer the world, because your new comfort zones are waiting for you to make them your own.

Daily Challenge: Embrace your fears as stepping stones to growth, and take one bold action today that pushes you outside your old comfort zone, propelling you toward the new, exciting territory of opportunities and personal transformation.

Daily Reflection:

What resonated with you from today's lesson? How can you apply this truth in your life?

_____

_____

_____

_____

Day 350: A Final Moment with Your Old Self

In this final moment with your old self, it's time to reflect on the man you've become. The battles you've faced, the scars you've earned—they're all part of your journey. You see, divorce isn't a defeat; it's a rebirth. It's shedding the skin of a life that no longer serves you. It's daring to redefine who you are and what you stand for. It's about rediscovering your passions, your purpose, and your power.

Don't carry the baggage of resentment or regret into this new chapter. Instead, let gratitude for the lessons learned be your guiding light. Every trial, every heartache—they've forged you into a stronger, wiser version of yourself.

Now, as you step into this fresh, untamed future, remember this: you are the author of your story. You have the pen, the ink, and the blank pages. The narrative is yours to craft, and the possibilities are endless.

Embrace your newfound freedom, seize every opportunity, and chase your dreams unapologetically. It's time to honor the man you've become by becoming the man you've always wanted to be. So, raise a glass to your growth and your unyielding spirit. Toast to the future, where you stand tall, wear your scars with pride, and live a life that's authentically yours.

This isn't an ending; it's a magnificent new beginning. Your journey continues, and the best is yet to come. Welcome to the next chapter of your extraordinary life.

Daily Challenge: Today, reflect on one specific lesson you've learned from your divorce journey and take a proactive step towards integrating it into your new beginning.

Daily Reflection:

What resonated with you from today's lesson? How can you apply this truth in your life?

_____

_____

_____

_____

Day 351: Your Life Philosophy- Articulate It

Your life philosophy, brother, it's your North Star, your guiding light. After the storm of divorce, it's time to define it with clarity. Life ain't about just reacting; it's about owning it, crafting it. Your philosophy should be your personal compass, unwavering in the face of adversity. It's about understanding what truly matters to you.

So, ask yourself: What fuels your soul? What are your non-negotiables? What legacy do you want to leave? Listen, there's no universal answer. It's YOUR philosophy. Maybe it's about relentless self-improvement, being the best dad, or chasing audacious dreams. Or perhaps it's about finding joy in the small things, embracing simplicity.

Your life philosophy isn't a poster on the wall; it's the fire in your belly, the voice that drowns out doubt and fear. Now, you've been through hell, but remember, fire tempers steel. Your scars aren't badges of defeat; they're badges of strength.

Own your story, brother. Let your philosophy reflect your journey—how you've grown, how you've learned, how you've evolved. It's about flipping the script from victim to victor. You're not defined by your past; you're defined by your choices, your actions, your vision.

So, articulate that philosophy, tattoo it on your soul, and live it every day. Your post-divorce life? It's a canvas, and you're the artist. Paint it bold, paint it bright. It's your masterpiece in the making, and it's time to shine.

Daily Challenge: Today, take a moment to write down three key principles that will shape your life philosophy after divorce, and commit to living by them, one step at a time.

Daily Reflection:

What resonated with you from today's lesson? How can you apply this truth in your life?

_____

_____

_____

Day 352: Instantly Elevate Your Game!

Picture yourself walking into a room, the air electric around you, confidence oozing from every stride. Sound like a dream? Let's make it a reality, and here's how. Start with the shock therapy of cold showers. Think it's crazy? Think again. Diving into that chilly embrace every morning isn't just about bracing yourself against the cold—it's a mental win. Each shiver, each goosebump is a testament to your resilience, proving to yourself that you can embrace and overcome discomfort.

But while you're working on the inner you, don't forget the external. Everyone has something that nags them, be it the beginnings of a dad bod, a receding hairline, or something else entirely. If it's the latter, for instance, Bosley might be your game-changer. The point is, address these issues head-on. Not for the world, but for your peace of mind.

On the topic of peace of mind, consider cutting out alcohol. You'd be amazed how crystal clear the world looks without the hangover haze. Your skin will radiate health, and mentally? You're unstoppable.

As you embark on this transformative journey, remember the power of kindness. Three compliments a day might sound over the top, but the act of uplifting others has a boomerang effect. You're not just making someone's day; you're boosting your own self-worth. Plus, in the process, you might just cross paths with some inspiring new souls, broadening your horizons and enriching your social tapestry.

Lastly, physical movement is the magic elixir. Whether it's intense push-ups or a serene evening jog, the goal is consistency. Transform your body, and watch your mindset follow. In the grand narrative of life, this is your chapter of change. Embrace it.

Daily Challenge: Embrace the cold shower, reminding yourself that every shiver is a testament to your resilience and your ability to overcome discomfort, both inside and out.

Daily Reflection:

What resonated with you from today's lesson? How can you apply this truth in your life?

_____

_____

_____

_____

Day 353: The Year's Highs and Lows- A Balanced View

In the trenches of divorce, you've weathered storms you never thought possible. There were moments you questioned your strength, doubted your choices, and wrestled with the pain.

But here you are, standing at the end of this tumultuous year. It's time to take stock, my friend. Look back, not with bitterness, but with wisdom. Yes, there were lows - those dark nights of the soul when despair felt suffocating. But there were highs too - glimpses of hope, strength you didn't know you possessed, and a sense of newfound independence.

You're not the same man who started this journey. You've evolved, scars and all. Embrace those highs and lows as the ink of your story. They're what make you uniquely you. Don't dismiss the pain, for it's in the darkness that you found the flicker of your own light.

You've learned that forgiveness isn't about her; it's about your freedom. Gratitude isn't about denying hurt; it's about acknowledging growth. And this chapter? It's about balance.

As you move forward, remember the lessons. Cherish the moments of triumph. But also, honor the moments of vulnerability and uncertainty. They're all part of your journey, a journey towards a better you.

So, raise a glass to the year's highs and lows, for they've sculpted you into a man of depth, compassion, and wisdom. You're not just surviving; you're thriving, my friend. Keep pushing forward, and let the story continue.

Daily Challenge: Reflect on one lesson you've learned from the highs and lows of this journey and find a way to apply it to your life today, taking a step towards becoming a better and wiser version of yourself.

Daily Reflection:

What resonated with you from today's lesson? How can you apply this truth in your life?

_____

_____

_____

_____

Day 354: Unfinished Business- Tying Up Loose Ends

Unfinished business is the anchor weighing you down. It's the conversations you avoided, the dreams you postponed, the apologies you never made. But guess what? It's time to face it head-on. You've come this far, my friend. You've endured the storm, and now you're in the clearing. But there's one last battle—closure. Those lingering thoughts, regrets, and doubts need to be laid to rest.

The conversations you've been avoiding? Have 'em. The dreams you put on hold? Chase 'em. Those apologies you never uttered? Speak 'em. Why? Because you're no longer the man you were when this journey began. You're wiser, stronger, and more resilient. This is your redemption arc, your chance to rewrite the final scene.

It's not about winning her back or seeking validation. It's about reclaiming your power. You're not defined by your past, but you sure as hell can shape your future. Don't carry that baggage into your new life. Your future is bright, my friend, and it's time to walk into it unburdened. Let go of the past, make amends where needed, and embrace the freedom that comes with closing those chapters.

Unfinished business? It's your last challenge. But remember, challenges are where you shine. So go ahead, tie up those loose ends, and step into your new life as the man you were always meant to be—strong, resilient, and free. You got this.

Daily Challenge: Embrace closure and tie up those loose ends – have the conversations you've been avoiding, chase the dreams you put on hold, and speak the apologies you never uttered to free yourself from the anchor of unfinished business and step into your new life with strength and freedom.

Daily Reflection:

What resonated with you from today's lesson? How can you apply this truth in your life?

_____

_____

_____

_____

Day 355: The New Bucket List- Future Adventures

As you stand on the precipice of your new life, it's time to scribble a fresh chapter in your book of existence. The New You, my friend, has different dreams and hungers for uncharted adventures. Reflect on it: What's your new bucket list? How have your desires transformed over the past year? You see, divorce doesn't define you. It refines you.

Maybe it's climbing that mountain you always feared, launching that business you've dreamed of, or traveling to places you've only seen in your mind's eye. Now is your time to embrace the audacious. Life's too short to dwell on what's gone. It's time to let the past fuel your future. Turn your pain into rocket fuel. Use every setback as a setup for a comeback.

This is your moment to rebuild, not just your life but your dreams. The New You doesn't settle; he soars. He takes risks, loves deeply, and chases the extraordinary. It's not about forgetting your past; it's about forging a future that's uniquely yours. Keep your eyes on the horizon, your heart open, and your spirit unbreakable.

The New Bucket List isn't just a list of destinations; it's a testament to your belief in the limitless potential of your own life. So, what's on your list? What will you conquer next? The New You is ready to redefine his legacy. The world is waiting for your story. It's time to write it in bold, unapologetic letters.

Daily Challenge: Take a moment to reflect on your new desires and dreams, then jot down three audacious items for your New Bucket List that inspire you to embrace the audacious and turn your pain into rocket fuel for your comeback journey.

Daily Reflection:

What resonated with you from today's lesson? How can you apply this truth in your life?

_____

_____

_____

_____

Day 356: Approaching The One-Year Mark- A Day of Reflection

Approaching the one-year mark after divorce, you've weathered the storm and walked through the fire. Reflect on your journey - it's been a rollercoaster. The lowest point? That moment you hit rock bottom, feeling lost, shattered, and unsure if you'd ever see the light again. It's crucial not to forget this darkness, for it's where your strength was forged.

Now, let's talk about the high point. It might not be one grand moment but a series of small victories. It's when you realized you're smiling genuinely, enjoying life, and finding purpose outside of the old relationship. The high point is when you recognized your newfound toughness.

The most significant change? It's YOU. You're not the same man who started this journey. You've grown, evolved, and learned. You're more self-aware, more compassionate, and more in control of your destiny. You've reclaimed your identity, unburdened by the weight of the past.

Remember, this journey isn't about forgetting or pretending it didn't hurt. It's about rising from the ashes, stronger and wiser. As you approach the one-year mark, pat yourself on the back. You've turned pain into power and scars into strength. Embrace the new you, for you've emerged from the crucible of divorce with a heart full of wisdom and a spirit unbroken.

Daily Challenge: Take a moment to reflect on the lowest point of your divorce journey, embrace the memories, and acknowledge the strength that was forged in your darkest hours, reminding yourself that you are resilient.

Daily Reflection:

What resonated with you from today's lesson? How can you apply this truth in your life?

_____

_____

_____

_____

Day 357: Life's Simple Pleasures- Don't Overlook Them

In the whirlwind of life's chaos, it's easy to get caught up in the big game. But here's a truth you can't ignore, my friend: happiness is often found in the smallest moments. We chase big dreams, big paychecks, and big victories, thinking they hold the secret to a fulfilling life. But while you're on this journey post-divorce, don't forget to savor the simplicity that surrounds you.

It's in that first sip of morning coffee, the laughter of your kids, or the warmth of a cozy blanket on a chilly night. It's the taste of your favorite meal, the feeling of a good book in your hands, or the joy of a long-forgotten hobby. These are life's simple pleasures, and they're often the ones that matter most.

As you rebuild, take time to relish these moments. Embrace the beauty of a quiet sunset, the solace of a peaceful morning, and the warmth of a genuine smile. They're the stitches that mend the wounds of your past and pave the way for a brighter future.

Remember, happiness isn't a distant trophy; it's woven into the fabric of your everyday life. Don't overlook these moments in pursuit of something bigger. Instead, cherish them as the building blocks of your new, remarkable chapter.

Life's simple pleasures aren't just a side dish; they're the main course. So, as you journey forward, make room for gratitude and appreciation. Because in the end, it's these little things that make life extraordinary.

Daily Challenge: Find and savor at least three simple pleasures in your day, whether it's a cup of coffee, a shared laugh, or a moment of tranquility, and take a moment to truly appreciate them.

Daily Reflection:

What resonated with you from today's lesson? How can you apply this truth in your life?

_____

_____

_____

Day 358: Rising Strong: The Path to Your New Beginning

Listen up, champ. It's time to drop the excuses and face some truths. You're in the game, whether you like it or not. And yeah, hypergamy is a real thing. Women want a man who's on his grind, who's reaching for the stars, and who's pushing the envelope of his own potential.

Stop whining about the rules and start mastering the game. It's not about blaming anyone; it's about leveling up. You want to attract the kind of woman you desire? You've got to become the kind of man she desires.

What's that mean? It means getting off the couch, putting down the video games, and turning off the Netflix binge. It means hitting the gym, educating yourself, and hustling like your life depends on it because, in a way, it does. Your value isn't just about your paycheck or your car. It's about your mindset, your ambition, your discipline. It's about being the guy who can lead, who can inspire, who can handle his business.

Complaining won't get you anywhere. Action will. So, study, grind, and elevate your game. The world doesn't owe you anything. It rewards those who earn it. So be relentless. Be better. Be the kind of man who doesn't just play the game but dominates it.

Hypergamy is just a reminder that women are drawn to success, ambition, and strength. So, become the best version of yourself. And remember, it's not about playing the game; it's about becoming a game-changer. Now, go out there and own it. Your destiny is in your hands.

Daily Challenge: Today, commit to taking a concrete step toward self-improvement, whether it's starting a new fitness routine, enrolling in a course, or setting a specific career goal – because becoming the man you aspire to be starts with action, not excuses.

Daily Reflection:

What resonated with you from today's lesson? How can you apply this truth in your life?

_____

_____

_____

_____

Day 359: The Final Week- A Time for Quiet

In the final week of your divorce survival journey, my friend, it's time to reflect, recharge, and revitalize. This ain't the end; it's your new beginning, the culmination of the battles you've fought, and the wisdom you've gained. You've weathered the storm, and now, it's time to bask in the calm.

It's a week for quiet, not silence. A moment to sit with yourself and soak up the lessons. You've faced the hardest truths, confronted your fears, and emerged stronger. Remember, pain is the greatest teacher, and you've aced that class.

Now, take those lessons and apply them. Channel that newfound strength into your daily life. Be relentless in your pursuit of self-improvement. Keep grinding, keep hustling. Life's a game, and you're getting good at it.

As you step into this final week, remember that the past doesn't define you. Your divorce is a chapter, not your entire story. Embrace your scars; they're proof of your battles. Keep setting goals, keep pushing boundaries, and keep reinventing yourself.

No more dwelling on what was lost; focus on what you've gained. Freedom. Self-awareness. Strength. These are your trophies. This is your legacy.

The final week is your chance to savor the victories and carry them into your future. It's a time to celebrate the new you, the one who's wiser, stronger, and unstoppable. Life's a journey, my friend, and you've just unlocked a whole new level. Go out there and conquer it with everything you've got. You've got this.

Daily Challenge: Reflect on the lessons learned from your divorce journey, and set one new self-improvement goal to channel your newfound strength and resilience into your daily life today.

Daily Reflection:

What resonated with you from today's lesson? How can you apply this truth in your life?

_____

_____

_____

Day 360: The Circle Completed- A Personal Ceremony

Look back, not with regret, but with reverence for the lessons you've learned. In the crucible of divorce, you've been forged into a stronger, wiser version of yourself. You've faced your demons, battled your doubts, and emerged victorious.

Now, it's your personal ceremony, a moment to acknowledge your growth. Light a symbolic candle, stand tall, and raise a glass to your spirit. The scars on your heart are badges of honor, reminders of your unyielding spirit.

The future beckons, a blank canvas awaiting your masterpiece. Your path is yours to choose, your dreams yours to pursue. With each step, remember the strength that got you here. Life is a relentless teacher, and it's not done with you yet. But you, my friend, are ready. You've walked through fire and emerged unscathed. You've faced the storm and found peace within.

Embrace this moment of completion. Cherish the journey, for it has sculpted you into the magnificent work of art that you are today. You're not just surviving; you're thriving. With your head held high and your heart wide open, step into the future. The circle is complete, and your story, well, it's just beginning. Cheers to the man you've become, and the incredible adventures that lie ahead.

As you stand there, amidst the echoes of your past, take a deep breath. Inhale the sweet scent of newfound freedom. Exhale the weight of old wounds and regrets. You are reborn, a phoenix rising from the ashes. This personal ceremony isn't just an ending; it's a prologue to a life yet unwritten. What will your next chapter hold? Adventures? Triumphs? New love? It's all within your grasp.

Daily Challenge: Light a symbolic candle, raise a glass, and celebrate the strength and growth you've gained through your divorce journey, embracing this moment of completion as you look forward to a future full of adventures, triumphs, and new beginnings.

Daily Reflection:

What resonated with you from today's lesson? How can you apply this truth in your life?

_____

_____

_____

_____

Day 361: Looking Forward- Set Your Intentions

Now, it's time to set your intentions. See, the past? It's a rearview mirror, and you've been glancing at it for far too long. But guess what? The road ahead is where the real adventure begins. You're not defined by your divorce; you're defined by your hardiness. Your strength is your secret weapon. But here's the catch: you've got to aim that strength, focus it like a laser beam.

What do you want from this new life? What kind of man do you want to be? Set your intentions like a concrete wall, unbreakable and unwavering. Maybe it's about becoming the best father for your kids, showing them the power of determination. Maybe it's about achieving a level of success you've always dreamed of, proving you can rise from the ashes.

It's not just about survival; it's about thriving. It's about turning pain into power, adversity into advantage. You've got this fire within you, let it burn brighter than ever. And hey, don't forget those lessons from the past. They're your battle scars, your wisdom. Use them to your advantage. Remember what went wrong, but don't dwell on it. Use it to steer your ship toward smoother waters.

Your journey is just beginning. It's a blank canvas, and you're the artist. Paint a masterpiece. Craft a future that'll make even your strongest doubters raise an eyebrow. Set your intentions with unshakable resolve. You're a force to be reckoned with, and this new chapter? It's yours for the taking. Go out there and conquer it like the champ you are.

Daily Challenge: Today, define your intentions with unwavering clarity and commitment, like carving your path on a stone tablet, and take one concrete step towards your vision for a thriving future after divorce.

Daily Reflection:

What resonated with you from today's lesson? How can you apply this truth in your life?

_____

_____

_____

_____

Day 362: The Year in Pictures- A Visual Recap

Take a moment, man. A deep breath. Look back at the canvas of the past year. What do you see? Yeah, there were tough times. Dark moments when you thought you might not make it. But here you are, standing tall. Flip through those mental snapshots. The first 30 days, raw and uncertain. Faces of lawyers, legal battles waged. The shadows of anger and despair. Then, the day 91 - the glimmer of hope when you started rebuilding, embracing self-care like a warrior.

Kids' smiles and shared memories from day 121-150, a reminder that life goes on. You, nurturing your body and soul. Friends who stood by you and the newfound strength in your identity.

Financial charts and spreadsheets from day 211-240, showcasing your determination to secure your future. The day you dared to dip your toes back into the dating pool, ready for new adventures.

And day 301-330, the turning point. A picture of your new life taking shape - fresh routines, healthier choices, and a vibrant social circle. Your place, now a sanctuary of your own design.

Zoom out, my friend. See the whole picture. Every image, a brushstroke of your journey, your evolution. The scars, they tell stories of battles won. As you step into the new year, don't forget the lessons. Keep that fire burning. Cherish those who stuck by you, and let go of what no longer serves you. Embrace the future with open arms, for you've become a survivor, a phoenix rising from the ashes. You did it. You thrived.

Daily Challenge: Take some time today to reflect on the past year, acknowledge your journey, and make a list of three things you're grateful for amidst the challenges, reminding yourself of your strength and resilience.

Daily Reflection:

What resonated with you from today's lesson? How can you apply this truth in your life?

_____

_____

_____

_____

Day 363: Unveiling Your True Potential

In a world obsessed with instant gratification and shortcuts, genuine personal growth often gets overshadowed. The pursuit of self-improvement, while commendable, can sometimes spiral into an unquenchable thirst for the next quick fix, the next seminar, or the next course promising miraculous transformation.

Our digital age bombards us with curated success stories on smartphones and social media, leaving us perpetually feeling less than enough. Your mental strength is the bedrock of your journey. It's about confronting your inner demons, addressing past traumas, and, if necessary, seeking therapy. Remember, seeking help is a proof to your strength, not a sign of weakness. Mental toughness is your superpower.

Physical health and mental well-being are inextricably linked. Regular exercise and a balanced diet are not optional; they're fundamental. Your body is your temple, and your health is priceless. Exercise not only shapes your physique but also sharpens your mind. Find your connection with a higher power, whatever that means to you. Seek inspiration that transcends materialism. At the heart of spirituality lies the nurturing of relationships with supportive individuals. These connections provide love and security that material possessions can never replicate.

These three pillars – mind, body, and spirit – liberate you from the relentless pressure of societal expectations and superficial desires. Embrace them, and you'll unearth a deeper, more meaningful life that transcends the allure of quick fixes and external validations. This journey sets you free, infusing your life with enduring purpose, passion, and fulfillment. Remember, personal growth is a lifelong journey, not a destination. It's about progress, not perfection.

Daily Challenge: Embrace the power of vulnerability by sharing your journey and seeking support from a trusted friend or therapist, recognizing that seeking help is a courageous step towards mental strength and personal growth.

Daily Reflection:

What resonated with you from today's lesson? How can you apply this truth in your life?

_____

_____

_____

_____

Day 364: Owning Your New Confidence Without the Ego Trip

Hey, you! Remember those days when support was just a word in the dictionary and insecurities were your shadow? You might have felt you were just a whisper in a world of shouts, trying to stamp your worth every step of the way.

Now, you're wiser, older. You've hit your stride, found your voice, and boy, does it roar with confidence! But, hold up. There's a thin line between confidence and ego, and crossing it can turn your vibe from inspiring to insufferable.

First, always keep an eye on your roots. Those struggles, the heartbreaks, the times you nearly buckled? They weren't just roadblocks; they were signposts, teaching you humility, resilience, and grit. They're reminders that two steps back can lead to a giant leap forward. Keeping your past close ensures your feet stay firmly on the ground, even when you're on top of the world.

And speaking of the world: the one you surround yourself with matters. If all you hear are praises, it's time for an entourage audit. Real growth comes from feedback, even if it stings. The people who challenge you, push you, and sometimes even oppose you? They're gold. They prevent you from buying into your own hype.

Being vulnerable is another strength in disguise. Owning your weaknesses is just as crucial as flaunting your strengths. Dive deep, confront your demons, and if you need it, get help. And remember, chasing cash over contentment is a game no one wins. Real value is in happiness and connections. So, while you bask in your newfound confidence, ensure it's laced with humility. Engage, listen, learn, and never forget that true confidence isn't about proving, but improving. Keep growing, and keep glowing.

Daily Challenge: Embrace vulnerability and confront a personal weakness, seeking growth and improvement as you continue your journey with humility and self-awareness.

Daily Reflection:

What resonated with you from today's lesson? How can you apply this truth in your life?

_____

_____

_____

_____

Day 365: The New Dawn- Welcome to Your Next Chapter

Welcome to your New Dawn, a realm where the past is history, and the future is a blank canvas. This is your time to sculpt a life free from the echoes of yesterday. Redefine your surroundings. Transform your living space into a haven that mirrors your renewed spirit. Every corner should exude your essence.

Your journey is a narrative, and you're the author. Write it with daring strokes, introducing plot twists that surprise even yourself. Build your tribe. Forge connections that resonate with your authentic self. Surround yourself with those who celebrate your growth.

The hobbies you once cherished? They're not just relics; they're the heartbeat of your vitality. Dive back into them, infusing your days with passion. This New Dawn is your adventure, your odyssey. Are you ready to step into it with conviction? It's a clean slate, a fresh start, and it's brimming with potential. Embrace this chapter with open arms, knowing that the past is but a prologue. The New Dawn is your stage, and the spotlight is yours to command.

Daily Challenge: Today, begin the transformation of your living space by redecorating or rearranging it to reflect the new you, a symbol of your fresh start and the beginning of your journey towards a brighter future after divorce.

Daily Reflection:

What resonated with you from today's lesson? How can you apply this truth in your life?

_____

_____

_____

_____